Scotland

A CONCISE HISTORY

FITZROY MACLEAN

Scotland

A CONCISE HISTORY

Fifth edition
with new chapters by Magnus Linklater

58 illustrations

Here's tae us –
Wha's like us?

SCOTTISH SAYING

 Thames & Hudson

For Veronica

AUTHOR'S ACKNOWLEDGMENTS

My thanks are due to Lady Hesketh, Lady Antonia Fraser, Miss Janet Glover and Sir Iain Moncreiffe of that Ilk for their invaluable comments and criticism; also to Mr John Colville, C.B., C.V.O., for the additional verse of the National Anthem quoted on page 111; and finally to Miss Priscilla Thorburn for her invaluable help in preparing the text for publication.

PUBLISHER'S NOTE

For this fifth edition, Sir Fitzroy Maclean's analysis of Scotland's place in the United Kingdom in the early 1990s has again been left unchanged. Magnus Linklater, who contributed chapters 8 and 9 for previous editions, has now written chapter 10, bringing the story up to date.

First published in the United Kingdom in 1970 as *A Concise History of Scotland* by Thames & Hudson Ltd, 181A High Holborn, London WC1V 7QX

This edition, revised and expanded, first published in 2019

Scotland: A Concise History © 1970, 1993, 2000, 2012 and 2019
Thames & Hudson Ltd, London

British Library Cataloguing-in/Publication Data
A catalogue record for this book is available from the British Library

ISBN 978-0-500-29472-7

Printed and bound in the UK by CPI (UK) Ltd

To find out about all our publications, please visit **www.thamesandhudson.com.** There you can subscribe to our e-newsletter, browse or download our current catalogue, and buy any titles that are in print

CONTENTS

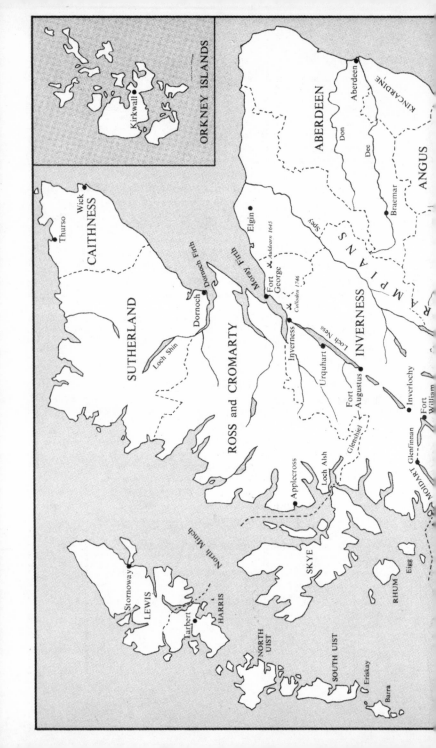

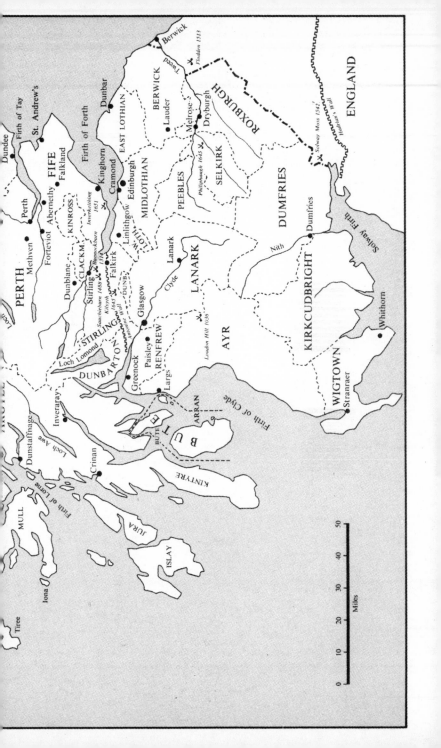

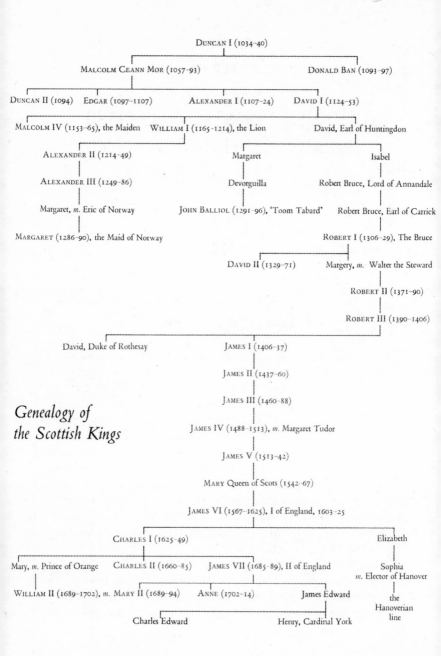

Genealogy of
the Scottish Kings

DUNCAN I (1034–40)

MALCOLM CEANN MOR (1057–93)   DONALD BAN (1093–97)

DUNCAN II (1094)   EDGAR (1097–1107)   ALEXANDER I (1107–24)   DAVID I (1124–53)

MALCOLM IV (1153–65), the Maiden   WILLIAM I (1165–1214), the Lion   David, Earl of Huntingdon

ALEXANDER II (1214–49)   Margaret   Isabel

ALEXANDER III (1249–86)   Devorguilla   Robert Bruce, Lord of Annandale

Margaret, m. Eric of Norway   JOHN BALLIOL (1291–96), 'Toom Tabard'   Robert Bruce, Earl of Carrick

MARGARET (1286–90), the Maid of Norway   ROBERT I (1306–29), The Bruce

DAVID II (1329–71)   Margery, m. Walter the Steward

ROBERT II (1371–90)

ROBERT III (1390–1406)

David, Duke of Rothesay   JAMES I (1406–37)

JAMES II (1437–60)

JAMES III (1460–88)

JAMES IV (1488–1513), m. Margaret Tudor

JAMES V (1513–42)

MARY Queen of Scots (1542–67)

JAMES VI (1567–1625), I of England, 1603–25

CHARLES I (1625–49)   Elizabeth

Mary, m. Prince of Orange   CHARLES II (1660–85)   JAMES VII (1685–89), II of England   Sophia
m. Elector of Hanover

WILLIAM II (1689–1702), m. MARY II (1689–94)   ANNE (1702–14)   James Edward   the
Hanoverian
line

Charles Edward   Henry, Cardinal York

CHAPTER ONE

'POLISHED FROM THE RUST OF SCOTTISH BARBARITY'

First Written Records

The early history of Scotland, like that of most countries, is largely veiled by what are known as the mists of antiquity, in this case a more than usually felicitous phrase. From piles of discarded sea-shells and implements of bone and stone, from monoliths and megaliths and mounds of grass-grown turf, from *crannogs* and *brochs* and vitrified forts, painstaking archaeologists have pieced together a handful of basic facts about the Stone and Bronze Age inhabitants of our country and about the first Celtic invaders who followed them in successive waves a good many centuries later. But it is not until the beginning of our own era that we come upon the first written records of Scottish history. These are to be found in the works of the Roman historian Tacitus, whose father-in-law, Cnaeus Julius Agricola, then Governor of the Roman Province of Britain, invaded what is now southern Scotland with the Ninth Legion in the year ad 81.

From Tacitus we learn that, having advanced from a base in northern England as far as the Forth-Clyde line, which it was his intention to hold by means of a chain of forts, Agricola established his headquarters at Stirling. Keeping in touch with his fleet as he pushed northwards, he encountered and heavily defeated the native Caledonians under their chieftain Calgacus in a pitched battle at Mons Graupius in eastern Scotland, which some identify as the Hill of Moncreiffe.

This was in the late summer of 83. After wintering on the banks of the Tay, Agricola was proposing to continue his advance northwards when early in 84 he suddenly received orders from Rome to withdraw. *'Perdomita Britannia et statim omissa'*, wrote Tacitus sourly, 'Britain conquered and then at once thrown away.' Subsequent Roman strategy towards Scotland seems to have been mainly defensive rather than offensive in intention. In 121 the Emperor Hadrian himself visited Britain and built his wall from Solway to Tyne. And twenty years after this we find the then Governor of Britain, Lollius Urbicus, building in his turn the Antonine Wall from Forth to Clyde.

Later again, in 208, the old Emperor Severus, no doubt encouraged by the series of spectacular victories he had won from Illyria to the Euphrates, tried a new approach to the problem, building himself a naval base at Cramond and then pushing northwards as far as the Moray Firth. But his Caledonian adversaries, wiser than their forefathers, avoided a pitched battle, and after three years of inconclusive skirmishing old Severus was back at Eboracum or York, dying from his exertions.

The tangled mountain mass of the Grampians and the dense forest which at that time covered much of central Scotland favoured guerrilla warfare and the Caledonians took full advantage of them. Not long after Severus' campaign the Romans abandoned the Antonine Wall and evacuated their northerly bases. For a hundred years or more Hadrian's Wall remained the Roman frontier and Britain to the south of it enjoyed a period of relative peace. Then, in the second half of the fourth century the tribes began to break through from the north in a series of ever bolder and more successful raids. At the same time Saxon pirates started to attack from across the North Sea. Had the Romans not had their hands full elsewhere, they might have returned to their original project of trying to conquer Scotland. As it was, trouble nearer home made it necessary for the Legions to be recalled and by the end of the fourth century the last remaining Roman outposts in Scotland had been abandoned. Thus Scotland only encountered the might of Rome spasmodically and never became a true part of the Roman Empire or enjoyed save at second hand the benefits or otherwise of Roman civilization.

By about 430 the Romans had also evacuated Britain south of Hadrian's Wall, leaving the inhabitants to their own devices and to the mercy of their more warlike and less civilized neighbours. Soon barbaric Teuton invaders from across the North Sea, the Angles and Saxons, had taken over most of what is now England, driving the native Britons westwards into Wales and Cornwall and northwards into Cumbria and Strathclyde.

Piets and Scots

Scotland was at this time divided between four different races. Of these the most powerful were the Picts, who were supreme from Caithness in the north to the Forth in the south. Of Celtic stock, they had, according to some authorities, originally arrived from the continent of Europe as part of the Celtic migrations which reached the British Isles at different times during the first millennium before Christ. Some said they were of Scythian origin.

The neighbouring Britons of Strathclyde, another Celtic race, speaking a kindred tongue, controlled the area stretching from the Clyde to the Solway and beyond into Cumbria. To the east, the country south of the Forth was now occupied by the Teutonic Anglo-Saxons who held sway over an area stretching southwards into Northumbria. Like their Anglo-Saxon kinsmen further south, they came from the lands lying between the mouth of the Rhine and the Baltic.

Finally, to the west, embracing what is now Argyll, Kintyre and the neighbouring islands, lay the Kingdom of Dalriada. This had been colonized in the third and fourth centuries of our era by the Scots, a warlike Celtic race from Northern Ireland, who, though at first overshadowed by the Picts, were eventually to give their name to all Scotland, which at this time was still known as Alba or Alban. Although Picts and Scots periodically combined to harass the Romans, the Scots, who spoke a different Celtic language and whose first loyalties were to their fellow Scots across the sea in Irish Dalriada, had from the start been in conflict with their Pictish neighbours. It was a conflict that was to take much bloodshed and several hundred years to resolve.

Christian Missionaries

In the course of the three centuries that followed the departure of the Romans, the Picts, the Scots, the Britons and finally even the Angles were all, nominally at any rate, converted to Christianity. The task that confronted the early Christian missionaries was not an easy one. Pagan prejudices and traditions were deeply rooted; the tribes they went among were warlike and at odds with each other; the country was mountainous and wild. But the age was one that threw up a whole sequence of men remarkable for their toughness, their strength of character and their devotion to their faith.

There are indications that already in Roman days little Christian communities existed north of Hadrian's Wall. There were no doubt Christians amongst the legionaries and from them the new faith spread to the native population. 'Places among the Britons unpenetrated by the Romans have come under the rule of Christ,' wrote Tertullian in 208, *'Britannorum inaccessa Romanis loca, Christo vero subdita.'* St Ninian, the first of the great Christian missionaries to Alban, was himself the son of Christian parents. After visiting Rome and being consecrated a bishop there, he returned in 397 or 398 to his native Strathclyde and there established a monastery, known as Candida Casa, at Whithorn near the Solway. This was soon to serve as a seminary and starting point for Christian missions, not only to the Britons, but also to the Picts. But, though St Ninian's missionaries pushed northwards up the Great Glen towards Caithness and Sutherland and, according to some accounts, even reached the Orkneys and Shetland, they seem, partly no doubt for linguistic reasons and partly for reasons of geography, to have had but little contact with Dalriada.

Through the centuries, the first Scottish settlers in Dalriada, while consolidating their hold on the territories they had conquered, had remained in close touch with their parent kingdom in Ireland. Then in about the year 500, Fergus MacErc and his two brothers, Angus and Lome, led a fresh Scottish invasion from Ireland and established a new dynasty with its stronghold at Dunadd near Crinan, which now became the capital of Scottish Dalriada. But Fergus and his successors continued to pay tribute to Ireland and to accept Irish suzerainty and it was from Ireland that towards the middle of the sixth century the first Christian missionaries reached Dalriada. The earliest of these was St Oran, who died of the plague in 548, after establishing Christian churches in Iona, Mull and Tiree, though not as yet on the mainland. Then in 563 St Columba arrived from Ireland and, having established himself on Iona, at once made it a base for his missions to the mainland and to the other islands.

Columba was by any standards a remarkable man. Of royal birth and powerful intellect and physique, he seems to have left Ireland under some kind of a cloud. In Scottish Dalriada his impact was to a high degree political as well as spiritual. Arriving on the scene at a moment when the Scots had suffered a crushing military defeat at the hands of the Picts, when their king had been killed, their morale was low and their very independence was threatened, he not only preached the Gospel, but at once took active measures to re-establish and consolidate the monarchy. Aidan the False, whom he now made king in place of the rightful heir to the throne, proved an astute and resourceful monarch. The good work which he began was carried on by his descendants, especially Eochaid the Venomous, who successfully infiltrated the enemy camp by marrying a Pictish princess. It was not long before the Scots were once again more than holding their own against the Picts.

From Dalriada, Columba penetrated far into northern Pictland, quelling a monster which he encountered in Loch Ness and easily getting the best of the pagan priests he found at the court of the local king. By his death in 579 Dunadd had become an established political capital, while Iona was the nucleus of a fast-expanding Church, organized, it may be observed, on lines that were not as yet episcopal.

From Ireland, too, came St Moluag, who founded a monastery in 562 on the Island of Lismore, and St Maelrubba, who established himself at Applecross a century later. From the west both travelled up and down Dalriada and far into Pictish territory, founding missions and monasteries as they went. Soon after St Columba's death St Aidan had gone out from Iona to convert the Angles of Northumbria, establishing himself on Holy Island near Bamburgh, while St Cuthbert, the apostle of the Anglo-Saxon Lothians, likewise drew his inspiration from the same source.

Though by the end of the seventh century all four of the kingdoms of Alban had been converted to Christianity, they were still far from being united among themselves politically. Nor were they in unison theologically with the rest of Christendom. Out of touch with Rome, the Celtic clergy had developed views on such subjects as the style of the tonsure and the date of Easter which struck the Vatican and their fellow Christians further south as deplorable. 'Wicked', 'lewd' and 'wrongful', were some of the phrases used in this connection by no less an authority than the Venerable Bede. In the end the Celts were to yield before superior wealth and organization. But they had made a notable contribution to the Christian heritage. 'The Celtic Church gave love', ran the saying, 'the Roman Church gave law.' It was the law that in the end prevailed.

Trouble, meanwhile, threatened from another quarter. From the end of the eighth century onwards the Norsemen began their attacks on Scotland, gradually gaining a foothold, and then more than a foothold, on the islands and coastal areas. By the end of the ninth century, they had conquered Orkney, Shetland and the Western Isles and these were followed by Caithness and Sutherland.

The divisions and disagreements of the four kingdoms weakened their resistance to the common enemy. Hostility still persisted between Picts and Scots, while the Britons of Strathclyde would have no truck with the Angles of Lothian and Northumbria. For a time it had seemed possible that the Angles would achieve ascendancy over their neighbours, but the decisive defeat of their King Ecgfrith by the Picts at the battle of Nectansmere in 685 effectively ruled this out.

Kenneth MacAlpin

It was not until the ninth century that some measure of unity was at last achieved. In the year 843 Kenneth MacAlpin, King of the Scots of Dalriada and at the same time a claimant to the Pictish throne, a man, we are told, 'of marvellous astuteness', fell upon the Picts, to whose ruling dynasty he was related, after they had been weakened by the raids of the Norsemen, and, having disposed of all rival claimants, made himself King of everything north of the Forth. From Dunadd he moved his capital to Forteviot in the heart of Pictish territory while the religious centre of his kingdom was shifted to Dunkeld. Thither he now transferred St Columba's remains from Iona. 'And so', says the Huntingdon Chronicle, 'he was the first of the Scots to obtain the monarchy of the whole of Albania, which is now called Scotia.'

Of the Picts, who had ruled over most of Scotland for more than a thousand years, little or nothing more was heard. They were, in the modern phrase, *gleichgeschaltet* and so have gone down to history as a shadowy, ill-documented race of people of uncertain antecedents, possibly tattooed or 'painted', for that, after all, is the Latin meaning of their name.*

Right up to his death in 858, Kenneth MacAlpin sought repeatedly to conquer the Angles of Lothian. But in this he was unsuccessful. His successors, involved as they were in continuous warfare with the Norsemen, fared no better, and it was not until more than a century and a half later, in 1018, that his descendant Malcolm II's victory over the Angles at Carham finally brought the Lothians under Scottish rule. In the same year the King of the Britons of Strathclyde died without issue and was succeeded by Malcolm's grandson and heir Duncan, who had managed to establish some kind of claim to the throne of Strathclyde through the female line. Sixteen years later, in 1034, Duncan succeeded his grandfather as King of Scotland. In this way the frontiers of the Scottish kingdom were still further extended, reaching far down into what is now English territory.

In 1040, after a short, rather unhappy reign, Duncan was killed in battle by Maelbeatha or Macbeth, the Mormaer of Moray, who claimed the throne both on his own behalf and on that of his wife, and now made himself king in Duncan's place. Macbeth appears, contrary to popular belief, to have been a wise monarch and to have ruled Scotland successfully and well for seventeen prosperous years. In 1050 we hear that he went on a pilgrimage to Rome and there 'scattered money among the poor like seed'. But seven years later he was defeated and killed by Duncan's elder son, Malcolm, who thus regained for his family his father's throne to which he had never abandoned his claim.

---

* With all due respect to W. C. Mackenzie, who dismisses it as 'an interpretation that leads nowhere'.

Malcolm and Margaret

Malcolm III, known to his contemporaries as Ceann Mor or Bighead, had been brought up in England from the age of nine. In 1069, twelve years after his return to Scotland, he married, as his second wife, the English Princess Margaret, who had taken refuge in Scotland with her brother Edgar the Atheling after the Norman Conquest of England in 1066.

The Norman Conquest was to prove almost as important for Scotland as it was for England. Henceforth England and her rulers were in one way or another to play an ever greater part in Scottish affairs. English and Norman influences were to make themselves increasingly felt in the Lowlands, while under Malcolm and his successors the foundations of feudalism were laid, at any rate in southern Scotland. Margaret, a saintly and determined young woman, set herself to introduce at her husband's Court English fashions and English customs. She also took the Scottish clergy in hand and, to their dismay, sought to impose on them the religious practices prevalent in England, celibacy, poverty, and so on. Soon, under her guidance, life at Court assumed a more civilized tinge, while in the Church a system of regular diocesan episcopacy gradually began to take shape. Malcolm, being himself English-educated, was inclined to share his wife's views and during his reign shifted the cultural centre of his kingdom southwards into Anglo-Saxon Lothian, thereby seriously offending the Celtic North.

But Malcolm's interest in his southern neighbour was strategic as well as cultural. The northern counties of England seemed to him to offer possibilities for expansion and in his brother-in-law Edgar the Atheling he had at his Court a ready-made claimant to the English throne. He accordingly launched a series of border-raids into Northumberland and Cumberland. These provoked retaliatory expeditions on the part of the Normans and in 1071 William the Conqueror finally invaded Scotland and forced Malcolm to pay homage to him at Abernethy. In the intervals of the fighting amicable relations were maintained between the two countries, for Malcolm had remained a popular figure at the English Court. In 1093, however, in the course of an attack on Alnwick in Northumberland (intended, it was said, to forestall a Norman invasion), he was killed in an ambush by one of his Norman friends named Morel. Queen Margaret, for her part, died three days later, piously uttering a prayer of thanks that such sadness should have been sent to purify her last moments. She was in due course canonized.

For thirty years after Malcolm's death, Scotland was in turmoil, ruled over by a succession of weak, insecure kings. The first of these was Malcolm's sixty-year-old brother, Donald Ban, who after his father's death, while Malcolm was in England, had been sent off to the Hebrides. He had thus fallen under Norse and Celtic rather than English or Norman influence and on his brother's death, having seized the throne, at once reversed Malcolm's Anglo-Norman attitudes and policies.

This did not endear the new king to William Rufus, who had succeeded to the English throne on the death of his father, William the Conqueror. In 1094 he sent Duncan, Malcolm's son by his first marriage, whom he had been holding in England as a hostage, to dethrone his uncle by force. Duncan succeeded in this. He was, however, almost immediately murdered and old Donald Ban restored to the throne. But not for long. In 1097 an Anglo-Norman force chased Donald out again and made Duncan's half-brother Edgar king in his place. Edgar believed in helping those who helped him, and during his reign more Normans than ever were settled in southern Scotland. He came to terms, too, with Magnus Barelegs, the King of Norway, formally ceding to him the Hebrides and Kintyre, of which the Norwegians had in fact long been in possession. Thus St Columba's sanctuary of Iona, for so long the burial-place of the Scottish kings, became Norse territory and old Donald Ban was the last of his dynasty to be buried there.

On Edgar's death in 1107 he was succeeded by yet another brother, Alexander, like him the son of Malcolm and Margaret. Alexander, however, only ruled over the land between Forth and Spey, leaving Argyll, Ross and even Moray to their own devices, while responsibility for Scotland south of the Forth was entrusted to his younger brother David. Alexander's sister Maud had become the wife of King Henry I of England, while he himself had married Henry's beautiful, luxury-loving natural daughter Sibylla. He was thus at one and the same time Henry's brother-in-law and son-in-law and in his reign the connection with England grew still closer and English and Norman influence greater than ever.

David I

In 1124 Alexander died and was succeeded by his brother David, the ninth son of Malcolm III and already the ruler of most of southern Scotland. David, by a long way the most remarkable of Malcolm and Margaret's children, was to rule Scotland for close on thirty years. They were to be eventful years for Scotland. Like his brothers, David had been brought up in England, where he had received a Norman education and made many Norman friends and where, we learn from the patronizing William of Malmesbury, his manners 'were polished from the rust of Scottish barbarity'. In addition to being King of Scotland, he was in his own right Prince of Cumbria, and, by his marriage to a rich Norman heiress, Earl of Northampton and Huntingdon. He was thus one of the most power-ful barons in England as well as being the English King's brother-in-law.

On returning to Scotland, he proceeded to distribute large estates there amongst his Anglo-Norman friends and associates, such as de Brus, Walter fitzAlan, a Breton who became his High Steward, de Bailleul, de Comines and many others, who thus became landowners on both sides of the Border. The Church, too, became the preserve of Norman prelates. Simultaneously David introduced into the Lowlands of Scotland some-thing more closely resembling a feudal system of ownership, founded on a new, French-speaking, Anglo-Norman aristocracy, who, although they intermarried and eventually merged with the old Celtic aristocracy, remained for a time separate and distinct from the native population, many of whom still spoke Gaelic, save in the south and east where they spoke a primitive form of English. In the Highlands, meanwhile, a dif-ferent, more patriarchal system prevailed and the King's writ counted for very little, while the Islands and parts of the mainland gave a loose allegiance to Norway.

In the course of his reign David sought, in so far as he could, to establish a national system of justice and administration under his own over-all control. Alexander had already appointed a number of Court officials, such as Chamberlain, Constable, Chancellor, Steward and Marshal. From these and from the bishops David selected a central governing body to advise him, to carry out his commands and to deal with major admin-istrative and judicial problems. He further appointed justiciars and sheriffs to administer justice. In the economic field he encouraged trade with foreign countries and established two royal mints and a standard system of weights and measures. He also granted the status of burgh to a number of towns, together with freedom from tolls, the right to hold markets and fairs and also monopolies in respect of certain products. In order to keep in touch with his subjects, though also on sanitary grounds, he and his advisers moved constantly about the country from one royal castle to another.

Being a devout man, David also turned his attention to ecclesiastical matters, founding more bishoprics (under Anglo-Norman bishops) at Glasgow, Brechin, Dunblane, Caithness, Ross and Aberdeen, establishing more parishes, building more churches and endowing more monasteries, among them Kelso, Dryburgh and Melrose. But, while he accepted in general the universal claims of Rome, David wished the Scottish Church to retain a certain autonomy. Though ordered by Pope Innocent III, under threat of excommunication, to acknowledge the supremacy of the Archbishop of York, the Scottish Bishops, with the King's encouragement, rejected this proposition out of hand and so started a dispute which was to drag on for the remainder of the century.

David's long reign was for the most part peaceful. In 1135, however, he chose to intervene in the dynastic disputes which developed in England, on the death of King Henry I, between his daughter Maud and her cousin Stephen. These he turned to his own advantage, successfully playing one side off against the other and, though defeated in 1138 at the Battle of the Standard near Northallerton, emerged, thanks to skilful negotiation, with precisely what he wanted, namely the greater part of Northumbria.

When David came to the throne in 1124, Scotland had, even by the standards of the day, been a primitive country with practically no towns and scarcely any industry or commerce. People lived in wooden houses and such trade as existed was conducted by barter. The different parts of the country were cut off from each other by barren stretches of uninhabited moorland and hill. It could hardly even be said that there was a common language. Latin, French, English and a number of Gaelic dialects were all spoken in different areas and by different classes of the population. In the absence of any established feudal system, local chieftains felt free to disregard the authority of the King and of the central government. The Church, with only three bishops and no properly organized system of parishes, had very little influence one way or the other. When David died in 1153 much had changed. In the Lowlands, at any rate, what remained of the old Celtic way of life had been swept away and a new, relatively efficient, Anglo-Norman order of things established in its place.

On David's death, the throne passed to his eldest grandson, Malcolm IV, a boy of eleven, known to history as the Maiden. At once, the King of Norway sacked Aberdeen; there was unrest in Moray, while Somerled, Lord of Argyll, sailed up the Clyde and sacked Glasgow. King Henry II Plantagenet, who had finally come to the English throne in 1154, seized the opportunity to send for little Malcolm and force him to return Northumbria to England.

The Auld Alliance

Malcolm did not live long. On his death in 1165 he was succeeded by his more enterprising brother William the Lion. Resenting the loss of Northumbria, William, after first concluding in 1165 a formal alliance with France, to be known to succeeding generations as the Auld Alliance, launched in 1174 a grand invasion of England at a moment when he had reason to hope that Henry II's attention was engaged elsewhere. But the enterprise misfired. Thanks to their own rashness and to an East Coast mist, attributed by both sides to divine intervention, the Scots were heavily defeated at Alnwick and William himself taken prisoner and sent by the English to Normandy. There he was forced to sign the Treaty of Falaise. By this humiliating document Scotland was placed under feudal subjection to England, the Scottish Church put under the jurisdiction of the English Primate, Northumbria confirmed as English territory and the main castles of southern Scotland garrisoned by English troops.

Fifteen years were to pass before William was able to redress the balance. In 1189 Richard Cœur de Lion of England, needing money for a crusade, agreed to hand back the castles occupied in 1174 and to renounce his feudal superiority over Scotland in return for 10,000 marks. Three years later, Pope Celestine III released the Scottish Church from English supremacy and decreed that thenceforth it should be under the direct jurisdiction of Rome. It was the beginning of more than a hundred years of peace between Scotland and England.

The King and the Chieftains

But the Scottish kings did not only have their English neighbours to contend with. The Celtic chieftains of the west, who still enjoyed a great measure of independence, were in a state of more or less permanent insurrection against the central monarchy. Fergus, Prince of Galloway, had rebelled no less than three times against Malcolm the Maiden before retiring to a monastery, and in the reign of William the Lion his sons rose again, massacring, with particular gusto, the Anglo-Norman garrisons which had been stationed in southern Scotland under the Treaty of Falaise. It was to be a long time before this last Celtic stronghold of the south-west was finally pacified.

Further north, in what is now Argyllshire, were the dominions of the Lords of Lorne and the Lords of the Isles. These regarded themselves with reason as independent rulers with no particular loyalty or obligations to the royal house of Scotland, their allegiance being rather to the kings of Norway. Already in the reign of Malcolm the Maiden, as we have seen, the part-Norse Somerled, King of Morvern, Lochaber, Argyll and the southern Hebrides and uncle by marriage to the Norwegian King of the Isles, had, as we have seen, shown his contempt for the Scottish kings by sailing up the Clyde and sacking Glasgow. An unlucky spear-thrust had laid him low and his followers had been beaten off by Malcolm's High Steward, Walter fitzAlan, Lord of Renfrew. But Somerled's descendants, the Macdougall Lords of Lorne and the Macdonald Lords of the Isles, were, in their turn, to carry on the tradition of independence.

When William the Lion died in 1214, he was succeeded by his son Alexander II, a capable ruler who put to good use the administrative machine created by David I. Alexander seems in his turn to have hankered after Northumbria, but in the end abandoned his claims and accepted a number of estates in northern England in settlement of the dispute. He was now free to turn to his own domestic problems. In his reign, as in those of his predecessors, there were insurrections in Galloway, Argyll, Moray and Caithness, and when he died in 1249, he was on his way to attempt the conquest of the Western Isles whose Lords still chose to give their allegiance to the kings of Norway.

This task, interrupted by his death, was resumed by his son Alexander III who, when scarcely more than a boy, launched his first raids against the Hebrides. Disturbed at these encroachments on his domains, old King Hakon of Norway decided to retaliate and in the summer of 1263 assembled a great fleet with which he sailed for Scotland. By opening negotiations with the Norwegians, Alexander managed to delay giving battle until October. This was the season of autumn gales and these, as he had hoped, played havoc with Hakon's fleet as it lay in the Firth of Clyde. In the end the Norwegians fought their way ashore at Largs in Ayrshire, where, in the course of a rather confused engagement, they were defeated on land as well as at sea and withdrew in disorder. Old Hakon himself died at Kirkwall on his way home to Norway and his successor Magnus signed a peace under which the Hebrides now became part of Scotland, though remaining in practice an independent kingdom under the Lords of the Isles, who for their part paid no more heed to their Scottish than they had to their Norwegian overlords. Orkney and Shetland were left for the time being in Norwegian hands.

The remainder of Alexander's reign was both peaceful and prosperous. His marriage to Margaret, the daughter of the English King Henry III, secured peace with England, while in 1283 the marriage of their daughter Margaret to King Eric of Norway set the seal on the Peace Treaty of twenty years before between Scotland and Norway and established, after four centuries of strife, a friendly relationship between the two countries which has lasted ever since. Meanwhile, at home trade improved, the revenue increased, law and order were maintained, education, within its limits, prospered, more building was done, both domestic and ecclesiastical, and for most people life became less disagreeable than it had been.

Had Alexander III lived longer, Scotland might have been spared many misfortunes. But in 1286, while he was on his way from Edinburgh to Kinghorn, his horse came down with him in the darkness and he was killed. His first wife, Margaret, both his sons and his daughter, the Queen of Norway, had died before him. A second wife, Yolette de Dreux, whom he had married the year before his death and to whom he was hurrying home when he was killed, had as yet borne him no children. The heir to the throne of Scotland was his grandchild Margaret, the infant daughter of the King of Norway.

Alexander had not long been dead and the little Queen was still in Norway when Edward I Plantagenet of England, a formidable, ruthless man, who had been King since 1272, came forward with the proposal that Margaret should marry his son. In 1290 a treaty of marriage was signed at Birgham and a ship sent to fetch little Margaret, with a consignment of sweetmeats and raisins on board as a present from the English King.

The Treaty of Birgham provided that Scotland should remain a separate and independent kingdom and when Edward proposed that English troops should garrison a number of castles in southern Scotland, the Scots indignantly rejected his suggestion. But it was already clear enough what he had in mind.

The plans of all concerned were, however, now thrown out by the news that the little Queen had died in the Orkneys on her way over from Norway. This laid the succession open to more than a dozen claimants. Of these the two strongest were Robert de Brus or Bruce and John de Bailleul or Balliol. Both were nobles of Anglo-Norman origin with estates in England as well as Scotland. Both were descended on the distaff side from David I's youngest son. And both were personally well known to King Edward I, in whose army they had fought. With so many and such formidable candidates in the field, trouble seemed certain.

Already in October, at the first rumours of the little Queen's death, William Fraser, the Norman-descended Bishop of St Andrews, foreseeing difficulties, had written privately to Edward suggesting that he should come to Scotland to keep the peace and to judge who had the strongest claim to the throne. He also took the opportunity of hinting that John Balliol was likely to prove a docile and amenable neighbour. Edward came and in November 1291, in the Great Hall of Berwick Castle, after much apparent deliberation with eighty Scottish and twenty-four English auditors, announced that the crown had been awarded to Balliol.

The reasons for this choice were clear. Balliol, it is true, had a strong claim to the throne. But Edward also had reason to believe that he would do as he was told. Nor did the English King lose any time in making his demands known. They were that Edward himself should have feudal superiority over Scotland and that Balliol should pay homage to him; that Balliol should, when necessary, come to London to answer any charges brought against him by his own subjects; and finally that Balliol should contribute to English defence costs and join him in his forthcoming invasion of France.

Balliol, not a strong personality, was to go down to history as a non-entity – the Toom Tabard or Empty Coat. But Edward's terms proved too much even for him. Repudiating his allegiance to Edward, he concluded an alliance with France and early in 1296 prepared to invade the north of England.

Edward was waiting for this. His plans were made. Two days after Balliol entered England, he crossed the Border into Scotland. He was met by large numbers of Scottish nobles, many of whom owned estates in England and were therefore his vassals. They had come to do homage to him. Amongst them were Balliol's rival, Robert Bruce, and the latter's old father. On hearing this, Balliol seized all Bruce's lands in Scotland and gave them to his own brother-in-law, Red John de Comines or Comyn. The Scots, as so often, were deeply divided among themselves.

Edward next marched on Berwick, at this time the most prosperous city in Scotland, and sacked it, at the same time massacring large numbers of the inhabitants. He then moved on to Dunbar, where, supported by Robert Bruce and other Scottish nobles, he met and utterly defeated Balliol, inflicting terrible slaughter on the Scottish force. Balliol now renounced his crown and after spending three years in the Tower of London withdrew to his estates in France, where he died in 1313.

Edward, meanwhile, continued his relentless progress through Scotland, taking possession of Edinburgh, Stirling, Perth, Elgin and numerous other castles as he went. In August 1296 he returned to Berwick. Here some two thousand Scottish nobles and landholders were compelled to do homage to him and to add their names to the 'Ragman's Roll', a document recognizing him as King. He then left for London, carrying off with him the ancient Crowning Stone of the Scottish kings which Fergus of Dalriada had brought from Ireland seven centuries earlier, and leaving an English Viceroy and English officials to take charge of the administration and English garrisons to occupy the chief strong points. *Bon hosoigne fait qy de merde se deliver'*, was his rude, soldierly comment. The conquest of Scotland was complete. Or so it seemed.

CHAPTER TWO

'NOT FOR GLORY, NOR RICHES, NOR HONOUR, BUT ONLY FOR THAT LIBERTY'

For some months all was quiet. Then in the spring of 1297, a young Scottish knight from the south-west named William Wallace became involved in a brawl with some English soldiers in the market place at Lanark. With the help of a girl he made good his escape. But the girl – some say she was his wife – was caught and put to death by the Sheriff of Lanark. Wallace resented this. That night he killed the Sheriff and so became an outlaw. Within weeks he was leader of a fast-spreading movement of national resistance. Such movements often spring from small beginnings.

The extent of this movement was forcibly brought home to the English in September 1297, when at Stirling Bridge a large, lavishly equipped and overconfident English army under Edward's Viceroy, Surrey, was completely annihilated by a hard-hitting Scottish force led by Wallace and including warriors from all over Scotland. Wallace was now master of southern Scotland. But his triumph was short-lived. At Stirling Bridge he had lost his ablest lieutenant, Sir Andrew de Moray, and now he was to make the mistake, disastrous for a guerrilla, of allowing himself to become involved in a pitched battle against superior forces. In July 1298 he was heavily defeated by Edward himself at Falkirk and never again commanded an army in the field. For another seven years he avoided capture, but in 1305 he was finally caught by the English, taken to London, submitted to a form of trial in Westminster Hall and barbarously executed. For seven years already Edward's armies had ravaged Scotland, using their superior strength to crush any remaining opposition. With Wallace's death it seemed as though resistance in Scotland must finally be at an end.

Robert Bruce

But again appearances were misleading. Amongst the Norman-descended nobles who had paid homage to Edward nine years earlier and served him or seemed to serve him more or less loyally in one capacity or another at different times since, was Robert Bruce, the eighth of his name since the Norman Conquest and the son of John Balliol's chief rival for the throne of Scotland at Berwick in 1291. Despite his long record of service to Edward, Bruce for various reasons of his own, was growing restive. So, too, was John Balliol's nephew, Red John Comyn, now leader of the rival Balliol faction and, like Bruce, a claimant to the throne. So was another Norman noble, Sir Simon Fraser of Tweeddale, who had already been out with Wallace.

Resistance to a foreign occupier is by its nature a complex and secret phenomenon. Evidence is hard to come by and often misleading. Personal motives are varied and involved. The line of demarcation between collaboration and resistance, between treachery and heroism, is not always clearly drawn. Things, in short, are rarely what they seem.

A meeting, presumably to discuss plans for fresh resistance to the English, was arranged between Bruce and Comyn at the beginning of 1306 in the Greyfriars Kirk at Dumfries. Just what passed at the meeting is not known. It seems probable that mutual charges of treachery were made. The ownership of land was also in dispute. All that is certain is that there was a quarrel between the two potential resistance leaders and that Bruce stabbed Comyn and left him dying in the church.

By the standards of the day there was nothing very unusual or indeed particularly disturbing in the murder of one great noble by another. What lent special significance to the incident was that it had occurred in a church and so amounted to sacrilege. This meant that Bruce had at one blow not only involved himself in a blood-feud with the Comyns and their many powerful supporters, but had also incurred immediate excommunication by the Church, an essential ally in any enterprise of the kind he was contemplating. His position was precarious in the extreme.

A lesser man might have decided to lie low and let things blow over. Bruce went to Scone and on Palm Sunday, the 27th of March 1306, raised the Royal Standard and had himself crowned King of Scots. Two days later the crown was again ceremonially set on his head by Isobel of Fife, Countess of Buchan. It was her brother's right to crown the King but he dared not do so. She did.

Edward's reply was to send a strong English army to Scotland under Aymer de Valence. On 26 June Bruce was heavily defeated at Methven. His troops were scattered and he himself became overnight a hunted outlaw. The brave Countess of Buchan, who had crowned him, was caught by the English and kept in a cage. Of his other allies, the Earl of Atholl and Simon Fraser were hanged, drawn and quartered, and Fraser's head was put beside Wallace's shrivelled skull on London Bridge.

In these adverse circumstances the great Norman noble showed astounding resilience. He spent the ensuing months in hiding in Arran and Rathlin Island and the Hebrides, in Kintail and Kintyre, in Orkney and possibly in Norway. In the spring of 1307 he returned to find devastation and widespread demoralization. Two of his brothers, who landed in Galloway, were caught and killed. But Bruce and his followers persisted and on Palm Sunday 1307 a first victory followed a year of unmitigated defeat. His principal lieutenant, Sir James Douglas, famous as the Black Douglas and henceforth to be the terror of the English, recaptured his own castle of Douglas from the enemy and utterly destroyed it. Gradually Bruce gathered round him more and more valuable allies: from the east the Celtic Earls of Lennox and Atholl; from the west Angus Og, the ancestor of Clan Donald, and the progenitors of the Campbells and Macleans. Soon other Scottish victories followed: a successful guerrilla action at Glentrool and an encounter at Loudon Hill, where Bruce showed conclusively that his spearmen had the measure of the English heavy cavalry. The English redoubled their efforts and in June Edward I, now a sick man, himself set out for Scotland at the head of a great army with which to subdue his former ally and liege. On 7 July 1307 Edward died at Burgh-on-Sands. With his dying breath he ordered that his bones were to be borne at the head of his army in a leather bag until Scotland had been crushed. But his son Edward II was not the man to carry out his father's injunctions.

For Bruce and for Scotland Edward I's death proved a turning point. Edward II, weak and harassed by domestic preoccupations, soon abandoned his father's project of a major campaign and withdrew, leaving the English garrisons in Scotland to manage as best they could. Bruce now pushed northwards. By the beginning of 1309, after a winter campaign against the Comyns in the north-east and a summer campaign against their allies, the Macdougall Lords of Lorne, during which he seized the Macdougall stronghold of Dunstaffnage, he controlled most of Scotland north of the Forth and Clyde. Later that year, after triumphantly holding a Parliament in Fife, he was secretly recognized as King by the King of France. In 1310 the Church in Scotland came out on his side despite his renewed excommunication by the Pope. By 1311 he was able to invade and devastate northern England, sacking Durham and Hartlepool. During the next three years he drove the English from Perth, Dundee, Dumfries, Roxburgh and Edinburgh, leaving Stirling alone in foreign hands.

It was only now that Edward II really bestirred himself. With a large, lavishly equipped army, he marched north to the relief of Stirling. And there he found Bruce waiting for him.

Bannockburn

The two armies met on midsummer day, the 24th of June 1314, by the Bannock Burn below Stirling. Bruce was outnumbered three to one, but he had chosen his ground carefully. His army, with only a handful of light cavalry and no archers to match the English, was drawn up on higher ground than his opponents. The heavily armoured English knights thus found themselves forced to advance through the waterlogged meadows which bordered the Bannock Burn – 'the evil, deep, wet marsh', as one writer has called it – while the English archers, for their part, had no room to deploy. The battle was joined at sunrise. Long before noon the English were in full flight and their King was making for Dunbar and the border as fast as his horse could carry him.

Henceforward the English made little attempt to keep a hold on Scotland. In 1318 Berwick, their last strongpoint, had fallen and the Scots were free of them. Though the war was to drag on for another fourteen years, its battles were fought outwith Scotland. Bruce now turned the tables on the English, invading and devastating their country as they had devastated his. He also carried the war over to Ireland, whose people, encouraged by what had happened in Scotland, had in 1316 bestowed the Crown of Ireland on his brother Edward. And when in 1322 Edward II in exasperation attempted another invasion of Scotland, he was chased back into Yorkshire, losing his personal baggage in the process.

Nor was Edward much more successful in the spiritual field. Pope Clement V, who had excommunicated Bruce in 1310, was dead, and Edward now invited his successor Pope John XXII to confirm the excommunication. His action provoked a strong reaction from the nobles, clergy and commons of Scotland. Meeting at Arbroath in April 1320, they addressed to the Pope a notable declaration, in which they proclaimed their devotion to Bruce and to liberty. 'We fight', they wrote, 'not for glory, nor riches, nor honour, but only for that liberty which no true man relinquishes but with his life.' And of Bruce: 'By the Providence of God, by the right of succession, by those laws and customs which we are resolved to defend even with our lives, and by our own just consent, he is our King.' 'Yet Robert himself,' they continued, 'should he turn aside from the task he has begun and yield Scotland of us to the English king or his people, we should cast out as the enemy of us all, and we should choose another king to defend our freedom; for so long as an hundred remain alive we are minded never a whit to bow beneath the yoke of English dominion.'

After receiving this most unequivocal message, the Pope seems to have shown himself rather more forthcoming towards Scotland, and, though still hesitating to recognize Bruce as King, eventually agreed to annul his excommunication. Edward II had failed again. In 1327 he was finally deposed by his wife Isabel and her lover Mortimer and his place as King taken by his young son Edward III.

Further English attempts at invasion came to nothing, only provoking vigorous counter-attacks. The English were by now growing tired of the war. A number of earlier efforts at mediation had failed, but a fresh English envoy was now sent to Norham to sue for peace and in May 1328 a Treaty of Peace between the two countries was signed at Northampton, recognizing Scotland as an independent kingdom and Robert Bruce as her King. At the same time Bruce's baby son David was married to Edward III's little sister Joan.

Just over a year later, in June 1329, at the age of fifty-three, Bruce died at Cardross, some say of leprosy. Human experience shapes human character. The impact of events on the individual cannot be left out of account. Bruce had been transformed by the hazards and hardships, the setbacks and triumphs of the past twenty years which he shared with the ordinary people of Scotland. From an Anglo-Norman noble, an apparently loyal servant of the English King, he had, in twenty years or so, become a Scottish national hero, a leader who by his courage and his will to win had united the people of Scotland as never before and given them a new sense of nationhood.

Now he was dead, leaving an only son, David, aged five years old. His daughter Margery had married a noble of Breton descent, Walter fitzA-lan, the Hereditary High Steward of Scotland, also known as Walter the Steward or Walter Stewart or, to give the name its later form, Stuart. At a Parliament held at Cambuskenneth in 1326 and attended for the first time on record by all three Estates, the barons, clergy and representatives of the burghs, it had been decreed that the succession should go first to David and then, in the event of his death without heirs, to Margery's son Robert Stewart. But the future was far from assured.

Most of the men who had shared Robert Bruce's triumphs and achievements were by now either dead or did not long survive him. His brother Edward Bruce and Walter the Steward were both dead. James Douglas was killed fighting in Spain in 1330, while carrying his master's heart on Crusade in fulfilment of a vow. In 1331 little David was crowned King as David II and Bruce's nephew, Thomas Randolph, Earl of Moray, a man of strong character and a good leader, became Regent.

But already trouble was brewing. In August 1332, urged on by Edward III of England, a number of Scottish nobles, who had been deprived of their lands for siding with the English against Bruce, landed in Fife. Their purpose was to put the Toom Tabard's son, Edward Balliol, on the throne. Moray moved to meet them, but died before the battle was joined. He was succeeded as Regent by the Earl of Mar, another of Bruce's nephews. But

Mar was at once defeated and killed in a night attack on Dupplin Moor. The invaders now marched on Scone, where they crowned Balliol king.

It was a situation which invited English intervention. Balliol, intent on appeasement, at once offered Edward III the shire of Berwick as a free gift. But, before he could do anything else, some of his angry subjects under James's brother Archibald Douglas and Andrew Moray of Bothwell had driven him across the border in his shirt and one boot. In the summer of 1333, however, Edward III marched on Berwick in strength, dispersed a French fleet sent to relieve it, heavily defeated the Scots at Halidon Hill and took Berwick. Seeing which way things were going, large numbers of Scottish nobles and clergy now promptly changed sides and joined the enemy, with the result that the Lowlands of Scotland were easily overrun and garrisoned by the English, who filled them with their own merchants, settlers and clergy.

In this confused and dangerous situation David II, now aged ten, and his little English wife, Joan, were sent to France for safety and the Regency entrusted to Bruce's seventeen-year-old grandson, Robert Stewart. The latter, much to his credit, now rallied such resistance as he could and drove the English garrison out of Bute. In 1339, with the help of a French expeditionary force, he captured Perth. By 1340 he had cleared Scotland north of the Forth. And in 1341 he was able to bring his young uncle David back from France and hand over to him the government of the country.

The English were by now fully engaged in France with the Hundred Years War. This gave the Scots a badly needed respite. In addition to Perth, Stirling and Edinburgh were recaptured and Randolph's daughter Black Agnes won lasting fame by her resolute defence of her castle of Dunbar. But in 1346 the French were defeated at Crécy and the King of France appealed to his ally for a diversion. Accordingly in October David II, who was far from being a worthy son of his father, set out with an army for England. There he was soundly beaten at Neville's Cross and himself taken prisoner by the English. David spent the next twelve years in England at the Court of Edward III. He had never been happier, finding that he greatly preferred the easy life of the English Court to the cares and burdens of kingship in Scotland.

In David's absence Robert Stewart once more became Regent. In 1355 the French, again hard-pressed, again asked the Scots for a diversion. This time it was more successful. Berwick was recaptured and the English badly beaten by William Douglas at Nesbit Muir. Returning from France, Edward III retaliated by invading Lothian, but, though he caused some devastation in the Lowlands, in the end he was forced to withdraw from Scotland with his troops hungry and demoralized.

Edward now tried a new approach. Instead of again attempting to invade Scotland, he made a ten years' truce and, in return for a crippling ransom of 100,000 marks, handed King David back to his subjects. Scotland was in a bad way. David was a useless king. The payment of his ransom debased the coinage and strangled trade. The resulting economic crisis coincided with a period of plague and floods. Across the Channel the war was going badly for France. Demoralization set in. Soon there were those who counselled capitulation to the English. King David, who cared nothing for Scotland, set himself at their head and, returning to England, where he had many friends, made a private arrangement with Edward under which the latter's younger son was to become his heir.

Robert II

But this arrangement was angrily rejected by the Scottish Parliament and when David's deplorable reign ended with his death in 1371, the kingdom passed, not to the English prince, but to Robert Stewart, the King's nephew and former Regent, who assumed the throne as Robert II, the first Stewart king.

Robert had shown himself an adequate Regent, but he proved a weak king. He came, it is true, of a noble family, but one that was no nobler than half a dozen others, was of Norman origin and did not possess the authority or prestige that flowed from eight centuries of kingship. Henceforward a new peril threatened Scotland, that of strife between the nobles and the Crown. It was to be our country's bane through the centuries to come.

Robert sought to give Scotland peace and prosperity. The English, fortunately for him, had their hands full in France. But the national economy was still strangled by continuing payments on the dead King's ransom and the peace was continually disturbed by the brawling of the great nobles amongst themselves. 'In those days', wrote a contemporary, 'there was no law in Scotland; but the great man oppressed the poor man and the whole country was one den of thieves. Slaughters, robberies, fire-raising and other crimes went unpunished, and justice was sent into banishment, beyond the Kingdom's bounds.' Yet another feature of the reign was continual border-raiding which devastated the whole Border region and culminated in 1388 in the major battle of Otterburn, or Chevy Chase as it came to be called, between the Douglases and the Percys of Northumberland.

In 1390 Robert II died. His son, Robert III, who succeeded him, had been kicked by a horse five years earlier and never fully recovered his health. A well-meaning cripple, he leaned as heavily as his father had done latterly on his younger and more resolute brother, the Duke of Albany. Once again the peace was disturbed by the bickering of the great nobles amongst themselves.

In 1399, Robert III virtually abdicated on the grounds that 'sickness of his person' unfitted him for 'restraining trespassers and rebellers', and for the next twenty-five years Scotland was ruled by Regents. The first of these was Robert's elder son, David Duke of Rothesay. But in the spring of 1402 he was carried off to Falkland and disappeared. Some said that he had died of dysentery; others that his uncle Albany had contrived his disappearance. In any case he did not reappear and Albany again assumed control, this time as Regent, with his son Murdoch to help him.

The heir to the throne was now Robert III's younger son, James. As rumours were current that the Regent was plotting to hand him over to the English, Robert decided in 1406 to send James to France for safety. But, by ill fortune, the ship in which he was travelling was seized by English pirates from Norfolk. These took him to London and delivered him to the King, Henry IV, who held him as a hostage. The shock killed poor crippled Robert, who died a month later. Little James was now duly proclaimed King James I, but he was destined to spend the first eighteen years of his reign in the hands of the English. Meanwhile his uncle Albany ruled in his stead, and made, as James was the first to notice, very little effort to secure his release. The great nobles, needless to say, made the most of the opportunities presented by this prolonged interregnum, expanding and consolidating their estates, assembling private armies, and building up what amounted to independent principalities of their own.

The Douglases

Of the great lowland families, none surpassed the Douglases, whose power soon came to rival that of the Crown. James, the founder of the family fortunes, had won great glory as one of Bruce's captains. His successor had been made Warden of the Marches and Lord of Galloway by David II. In 1358 an Earldom had been bestowed on the Douglas of the day, and thereafter, by clever marriages, the Douglases had further increased the extent both of their connections and of their possessions. By the end of the fourteenth century, the fourth Earl, who was Robert III's son-in-law, possessed lands stretching over Galloway, Douglasdale, Annandale, Clydesdale, Lothian, Stirling and Morayshire. The thousands of fighting men he could muster, toughened by constant border-fighting against the Percys, constituted a power factor that no one, least of all the Crown, could safely ignore.

In the north-west, the Macdonald Lords or, as they styled themselves, Kings of the Isles, continued to enjoy the status of autonomous monarchs, paying little or no heed to the central government of Scotland. Together with their neighbours and kinsmen the Macleans, those 'Spartans of the North', as Andrew Lang has called them, and the Lords of Lorne and Argyll, the Macdonalds had fought with Bruce against the English at Bannockburn. But they had done so as allies rather than as subjects and the Lord of the Isles was now formally allied with the King of England by a series of treaties dated 1392, 1394 and 1398 and signed as between sovereign states. In 1408 this alliance was again renewed when Henry IV of England sent a special embassy to Oxford-educated Donald of the Isles for this purpose.

In addition to the Isles, the Macdonalds, whose power had been greatly strengthened by Bruce's defeat of the Macdougalls a hundred years earlier, already held sway over much of the western seaboard. An opportunity now presented itself for Donald to extend his dominions still further. In 1411 his wife's niece, the young Countess of Ross, entered a convent and renounced her Earldom and estates. With these in his possession, Donald could become master of most of northern Scotland. A counter-claim was, however, advanced on behalf of the Regent Albany's son, Buchan, who, as it happened, was also an uncle by marriage of the Countess. Enraged by this and encouraged by promises of help from his ally Henry IV of England, Donald, supported by the Macleans under their Chief, Red Hector of the Battles, marched in strength across Scotland with the object of seizing and sacking Aberdeen. After a preliminary skirmish with the Mackays and the Frasers (now removed from the Borders to north-east Scotland), the Islesmen encountered at Harlaw a mixed force sent to meet them by the Regent and led by Alexander Stewart, Earl of Mar, Sir James Scrymgeour, the Royal Standard Bearer and Constable of Dundee, Sir Alexander Ogilvy, Sheriff of Angus, and Sir Robert Davidson, the Provost of Aberdeen, supported by the armed burgesses of the city. The ensuing battle – the Red Harlaw, as it came to be called – was savage in the extreme and, though militarily indecisive, was nevertheless followed by the withdrawal westward of Donald and his allies, leaving Red Hector dead on the field of battle.

Had things gone otherwise, had the Islesmen achieved their aims, the future course of Scottish history would have been altogether different. As it was, Donald remained quiet until his death in 1423, while the English, who had done nothing to help their ally, now made a truce with Albany. The year 1411, meanwhile, had been marked by a different but important event, the founding of Scotland's first university at St Andrews, to be followed in due course by Glasgow and Aberdeen. Side by side with Scotland's fame as a nation of fighters, a Scottish tradition for learning and the arts was also beginning to grow up, a tradition that, fostered in the first place by the Church, brought in its train increasingly fruitful links with Europe and with European places of learning.

Two years later, in 1413, Henry IV of England died and was succeeded by his son Henry V, who, at once seizing the opportunity offered by the civil war then raging in France and by the King of France's madness, attacked France with spectacular success. In 1420 the Treaty of Troyes gave him more than half of France, with the reversion of the rest on the King's death.

But Charles, the French Dauphin, had not surrendered. He now called on Scotland for help. By the beginning of 1421 twelve thousand Scottish troops had arrived in France under Albany's son, Buchan. By the end of March they had turned the tide. At Bauge Henry's brother Clarence was defeated and killed. In 1422 Henry himself died. 'That', he said of the Scots as he lay dying, 'is a cursed nation. Wherever I go, I find them in my beard.' Buchan now became Constable of France and Commander-in-Chief of the French armies, and Douglas was rewarded with the Duchy of Touraine. *Sacs à vin* and *mangeurs de mouton* the French peasants called the Scottish soldiers, impressed by their capacity for food and drink no less than by their fighting qualities.

In 1420 the Duke of Albany had finally died and his place as Regent had been taken by his son Duke Murdoch, a feeble creature by comparison with his father and his brother Buchan. James I, now twenty-nine, was still in England, having spent the whole of his boyhood and youth there. But the way was at last open for his return to Scotland. Old Albany was dead. Henry V was dead. James was on good terms with the Regents who ruled England on behalf of little Henry VI. He was also in love with Henry's cousin, Lady Joan Beaufort, the daughter of the Earl of Somerset. The English, after their experiences in France, were anxious for peace with Scotland. They hoped that James might help them to this end. An agreement was negotiated and in 1424, having married Joan Beaufort, James returned to his kingdom, taking his bride with him.

James I and his Reforms

Having thus at last entered into his inheritance, James lost no time in asserting himself. He possessed great gifts and had been given a good education in England. He had also learnt something of military matters on his visits to the English army in France and of statecraft from personal observation of the methods of those astute and enterprising monarchs Henry IV and Henry V. Furthermore, he had a revengeful and vindictive side to his nature. On his return to Scotland, he found the authority of the Crown weakened, the power of the great nobles dangerously inflated, the administration chaotic, and poverty, lawlessness and pestilence abounding. He took immediate and drastic action. In 1425, as a first step, the Regent Albany, his father-in-law and his two sons were arrested and executed and all their considerable properties seized by the Crown.

The Highlands as usual were stirring. In 1427 James summoned the Highland Chiefs to a Parliament and arrested forty of them. While most were later released, some were put to death. The Highlanders were disgusted by this double-dealing on the part of the King. A year later, to show his resentment, Alexander of the Isles marched on Inverness with 10,000 men and burned it to the ground. James managed to defeat him in battle. But in 1431 the Western clans were out again under Alexander's cousin Donald Balloch of Islay, who again soundly defeated the Earls of Caithness and Mar at Inverlochy, where Caithness was killed. James now once again took command himself, and, thanks to superior numbers and armament, succeeded for the time being in restoring the situation and pacifying the Highlands.

There was trouble, too, in the Lowlands. Again James took vigorous steps to quell it, imprisoning Douglas and driving the rebellious Earl of March into exile. In a dozen years forfeiture and reversion were to give the Crown the Earldoms of March, Fife, Mar, Buchan, Ross and Lennox. Strathearn and Atholl were held by the King's uncle. Douglas and Angus were his neighbours, Moray and Crawford his kinsmen. The balance between the Crown and the nobles seemed well on the way to being restored.

As though to underline this point, the King dressed splendidly, spent lavishly and made Linlithgow Palace into a magnificent royal residence. In 1428, after an unsuccessful attempt to come to terms with England, he formally renewed the Auld Alliance with France and sent a fresh Scottish contingent to fight for Charles VII and Joan of Arc against the English. It was a popular move. 'Nothing', wrote Aeneas Sylvius, the future Pope Pius II, who visited Scotland at this time, 'pleases the Scots more than abuse of the English.' Aeneas, for his own part, was pleased by the Scottish women, whom he found 'fair in complexion, comely and pleasing, though not distinguished for their chastity'.

James meanwhile had busily embarked on a far-reaching programme of social and legislative reform. 'If God give me but the life of a dog', he had said on first returning to Scotland, 'I will make the key keep the castle and the brackenbush the cow.' Within a week of his coronation, Parliament was at work on a mass of new statutes, and attendance by the greater and lesser barons was energetically enforced. *Rex Legifer*, they called him, the Law-giver. He even considered the idea of a second chamber on English lines. Not only did he provide for the maintenance of law and order; he regulated the finances of the country; raised new taxes; and introduced a whole range of no doubt badly needed but not necessarily popular reforms. Poaching was prohibited. Salmon fishing out of season was forbidden. Rooks and wolves were to be kept down; football discouraged;* pease and beans planted; hostelries built in the burghs; archery encouraged and improved. James also intervened vigorously in matters ecclesiastical, thus quickly bringing himself into conflict with the Holy See and, incidentally, carrying his point.

It was in the nature of things that such an active king should make enemies. James made three dangerous ones: his uncle, Atholl, his Chamberlain and cousin, Robert Stewart, and Robert Graham, the Tutor of Strathearn, who bore the King a grudge for his treatment of his nephew. Together, these three plotted to kill him, and in Perth, on 20 February 1437, they carried out their plot, stabbing him to death in the presence of his Queen. Joan Beaufort took a terrible revenge on her husband's murderers, but the exceptionally savage and ingenious tortures she inflicted on them, unheard of even in Scotland, could not bring the dead king back to life.

James's son, who now came to the throne as James II, was only six years old. Once again there was a Regency. And once again the great nobles took charge. Parliament was powerless without a strong king and the practice of delegating business to small committees – the Committee of Articles in particular – made it easy for a group of determined men to gain control. The Regent and, as it happened, the next heir to the throne, was the immensely powerful Earl of Douglas. But Douglas died in 1439, leaving two young sons, and the Regency passed to Sir William Crichton, who had been Master of the Household to James I and Keeper of Edinburgh Castle.

Crichton feared the immense power of the Douglases and in November 1440 he saw a chance to break it. Summoning the young Earl, a headstrong

---

*   Act of 1424: 'Item it is statut and the King forbiddis that na man play at the
    fut ball under the payne of iiij d [fourpence].'

boy of fourteen, and his younger brother to dinner with the little King in the Great Hall of Edinburgh Castle, he caused to be placed before them the symbolic Black Bull's Head, betokening death. He then murdered them both. 'Edinburgh Castle, towne and toure,' sang the poet,

> *God grant thae sink for sinne!*
> *And that even for the black dinoir*
> *Earl Douglas got therein.*

The vast Douglas estates were now divided up and for a time the power of the Douglases was eclipsed.

In 1449, James II, now nineteen, took control of affairs. He was to rule Scotland for just eleven years. During these loyally supported by Crichton and by his own cousin, Bishop Kennedy of St Andrews, a man of exceptional integrity and strength of character, James was to show himself in many ways his father's son. But he had other things to attend to besides administrative reforms. An alliance, highly dangerous to the Crown, had come into being between the young Earl of Douglas,* who was negotiating with the English, the Earl of Crawford, known as 'Earl Beardie' or the 'Tiger Earl' and at this time the most powerful man in the east, and, last but not least, John of the Isles, still smarting under the affronts which his father Alexander had suffered at the hands of the Scottish Crown in the last reign.

James made some effort to conciliate Douglas. But Douglas rejected his advances. Indeed, he went out of his way to provoke him, while his allies, the Islesmen, again seized Inverness. Finally, in 1452 the King, recalling perhaps a similar scene from his early childhood, invited Douglas to dine with him at Stirling Castle. Douglas came under a safe conduct and over dinner the King stabbed him to death with his own hand. 'The Earl', was the tactful judgment of Parliament, 'was guilty of his own death by resisting the King's gentle persuasion.'

---

* On his murder in 1440, William, the fourteen-year-old sixth Earl, had been succeeded by his great-uncle, James the Gross, the seventh Earl, who was believed by some to have connived at his great-nephew's murder and who in 1443 was in turn succeeded by his son William as eighth Earl.

The Douglases Broken

For a time it seemed as though the dead man's four brothers might, with English help, successfully defy the King. But James by his conduct of affairs had won the confidence of his subjects and when in 1455 he forced an issue and marched in strength to meet the rebels, he was abundantly justified by the outcome. James Douglas, the murdered man's heir, fled first to the Isles and thence to England, and at the Battle of Arkinholm his three brothers were defeated and killed. The power of the Black Douglases was thus finally broken and Parliament decreed the forfeiture of their vast estates. Crawford, the 'Tiger Earl', and John of the Isles had already come to terms with the Crown. The kingdom, for the time being, was at peace.

The English, having been decisively defeated in France, were now in the throes of civil strife and their loyalties divided between the rival Houses of York and Lancaster. James, who had made a temporary truce with Henry VI, chose this moment to intervene on his side against the usurper York. The stronghold of Roxburgh, which had been in English hands since 1346, was held by a partisan of York's. In the summer of 1460, James laid siege to it and, as he was watching his guns bombarding it, one of them burst and killed him. A few days later Roxburgh was taken by the Scots and that historic stronghold utterly destroyed.

Scotland was now once again ruled over by Regents. For a short time the Queen Mother assumed the Regency on behalf of her nine-year-old son, James III, but in 1462 her place was taken by Bishop Kennedy, who the following year negotiated a truce with the English, still preoccupied with the Wars of the Roses. Kennedy, however, died in 1465 and was succeeded as Regent by Lord Boyd, an ambitious lesser noble. In 1469 Boyd arranged for the young King's marriage to the daughter of the King of Norway, who brought as her dowry the Orkneys and Shetlands, which thus became part of Scotland. After the wedding, James, now eighteen, himself assumed control of affairs. His first move was to rid himself of Boyd, whose growing influence he resented.

James III did not, however, justify his early promise as a man of action. Though in many ways a gifted individual, he was unsociable and morose, a poor horseman, more interested in architecture, astrology and necromancy than in affairs of state and preferring the company of a group of intelligent and gifted favourites to that of his nobles. This did not endear him to the latter and his reign was punctuated by the usual plots and counterplots, while the English, despite a peace treaty signed in 1474, as usual tried to fish in troubled waters. In all this an active part was at first played by the King's more prepossessing brothers, Albany and Mar, and later by Archibald Douglas, Earl of Angus, head of the Red Douglases, 'who rose upon the ruins of the Black' and had by now replaced the Black as chief menace to the Crown.

In 1479 James, anxious for his crown, imprisoned both his brothers. Mar died mysteriously in prison in his bath. But Albany, having killed his guards, made a spectacular escape from Edinburgh Castle on a rope and, finding his way to London, there assumed the style of King of Scots. Three years later he joined an English army which was preparing to invade Scotland. James set out for the borders to meet the invaders but at Lauder was overtaken by a number of his own nobles. These were led by Archibald Douglas who, while the others hesitated, earned by his forthright approach to the monarch the name 'Bell-the-Cat'. Having hung a number of the King's favourites from the bridge at Lauder, Douglas and his friends now returned to Edinburgh, taking the King with them. There they were joined by Albany who, reconciled with his brother, briefly assumed the Regency. The English, for their part, contented themselves with capturing Berwick and then went home, no doubt thinking it wiser to leave the Scots to themselves. Albany eventually fled the country and was killed at a tournament in France. But the King's authority had been badly shaken.

In 1488 a fresh group of conspirators, again led by Archibald Douglas and by Lord Home, and supported this time by Colin Campbell, first Earl of Argyll and Chief of Clan Campbell, managed to lay hold of James's young son, whom they proclaimed King in place of his unpopular father. James hesitated, sought to come to terms with the rebels, called upon them to disband their troops and in the end fled to Stirling, where he found the city gates closed in his face. There was nothing for it now but to stand and fight. On 11 June 1488 the opposing armies met at Sauchieburn, south of Stirling. In the course of the rather half-hearted fighting that ensued James's horse bolted and threw him. Badly injured by his fall, he called for a priest, and a passer-by, who claimed to be one, stabbed him to death as he lay helpless in the kitchen of a mill.*

---

* There is an old tradition, accepted as authentic by Sir Iain Moncreiffe of that Ilk, that this quick-thinking regicide was none other than William Striveling or Stirling of Keir, a local notable, later to be knighted by his victim's son.

CHAPTER THREE

'THEY SPEND ALL THEIR TIME IN WARS AND WHEN THERE IS NO WAR, THEY FIGHT ONE ANOTHER'

James's heir, who now succeeded to the throne as James IV, was fifteen years old. For a time Archibald Douglas exercised a kind of regency and a circular was sent to the Courts of Europe giving a tactful account of the Battle of Sauchieburn, 'whereat the father of our Sovereign Lord happinit to be slane'. Meanwhile Douglas and his fellow-conspirators reaped to the full the rewards of their victory. It is from this time that dates the rapid rise to power of the Argyll Campbells, while Hepburn of Hailes, a minor laird, was rewarded for his services by the titles of Earl of Bothwell and Lord High Admiral.

The young King himself was not without misgivings, remorse even, at the way in which he had been brought to the throne, for the rest of his life he wore an iron chain round his body as a penance. Nor was he one to let himself be ruled by his nobles. When civil war broke out again in the following year, James took the field at the head of his own troops, soundly defeated the rebels, and promptly restored order.

James IV

James IV was to prove the ablest and most popular of all the Stewart kings, a ruler of energy, intelligence and charm and a born leader of men, whose love for the good things of life was as intense as his religious fervour and the vigour with which he pursued his kingly duties. 'He had', wrote the great scholar Erasmus, who was tutor to one of his many bastards, 'a wonderful force of intellect, an incredible knowledge of all things.' And Pedro de Ayala, the Ambassador of Ferdinand and Isabella of Spain and a constant companion of the King's at the card-table, was impressed by his self-confidence, his physical courage, his religious devoutness and his gift for languages, including the Gaelic. 'The King even speaks', he wrote, 'the language of the savages who live in some parts of Scotland and in the islands.' The people of Scotland, for their part, liked James's ostentation, his open-handedness, his friendliness, his many mistresses and his great horde of illegitimate children. For this was before the days of the Calvinist conscience.

It has been rightly said that James stood between two ages. In his reign the Renaissance reached Scotland and its years were marked by a true flowering of learning and of the arts. It was also a period of peace and prosperity and of progress and expansion in a whole range of different fields. In literature this was the age of Robert Henryson and his *Testament of Cresseid*; of William Dunbar's *The Thistle and the Rose*; of Gavin Douglas's translation of the *Aeneid;* and of Blind Harry's popular epic *Sir William Wallace*. Music, too, became important. James himself played the lute and never travelled without his court musicians and a wide range of musical instruments. Splendid churches were built. In the towns stone began to take the place of wood in the merchants' houses and in the country the great castles ceased to be mere strongholds and took on some of the magnificence of palaces, Falkland, Linlithgow and Craigmillar amongst them. And Ayala was able to tell his King and Queen of the fine furniture and charming gardens and of the elegance of the great Scottish ladies, whose headdress, he said, was 'the handsomest in the world'. Education, though still the privilege of the few, increased its impact. More books were imported and in Edinburgh in 1507 a first printing press made its appearance. King's College, Aberdeen, came to join

St Andrews and Glasgow as Scotland's third university. A thriving trade, based mainly on Middelburg, grew up with the Low Countries. Scottish raw materials, hides, wool and salted fish were exported against imports of manufactured goods and luxuries from abroad.

The Clan System

Meanwhile in the north-west, beyond the Highland Line, life went on much as it had for five hundred years or more. Here what happened in Edinburgh or in the Anglicized Lowlands had very little relevance. In the Highlands the hold of both Church and State was tenuous in the extreme. Here a different system, different loyalties and different standards prevailed. In Gaelic *clann* meant children. The chief was the father of his people. He was, in theory at any rate, of the same blood as they were. He had power of life and death over them (of which he made full use). And he commanded, by one means or another, their absolute loyalty. His land, in a sense, was their land; their cattle were his cattle. His quarrels (and they were bloody and frequent) were their quarrels. In its essence, the clan system was patriarchal rather than feudal, an ancient Celtic concept which bore but little relation to the more recent central monarchy, but had its origin rather in the early Norse and Irish kingdoms of the west, from whose kings and high kings the chiefs of most of the great clans traced their descent.

To the Highlander, land, the wild barren land of the Highlands, cattle, the stunted little black beasts that somehow got a living from it and from which he in turn got a living, and men, men at arms to guard the land and the cattle, were what mattered. The clan lands belonged by ancestral right to the chief and were subdivided by him among the members of his family and the men of his clan. The cattle were the most prized possession of chief and clansmen alike, the source of their livelihood and social standing and the source, too, of unending strife. In time of war the chief and those of his own blood led the clan in battle and, when he sent out the fiery cross, it was the duty of the men of the clan to follow where he led. In war and peace alike he had absolute power over them, being, by ancient custom rather than by any feudal charter or legal right, both law-giver and judge. The clan had its foundation in the deeply-rooted

Celtic principle of kindness, a mixture of kinship and long tradition, far stronger than any written law. As father of his people, the chief stood midway between them and God, settling their disputes, helping them when they were in need, protecting them and their cattle against their enemies. *Buachaille nan Eileanan* was the Gaelic title of the Macdonald chiefs, the Shepherd of the Isles.

With his chief the humblest clansman shared a pride of race scarcely conceivable to a stranger. All who bore their chief's name liked to believe themselves – and often were – descended, as he was, from the name-father of the clan, from Somerled, from Gillean of the Battleaxe, from Calum Mor, from Olaf the Black or Gregor of the Golden Bridles, and, through them, from countless generations of Norse or Irish kings. 'Though poor, I am noble,' ran an old and constantly repeated Maclean saying; 'thank God I am a Maclean.' And Cameron of Lochiel could boast with conviction that his clan were 'all gentlemen'. 'Almost everyone', the English Lieutenant Edward Burt was to write in amazement some centuries later, 'is a genealogist.'

Little wonder, then, that from their mountain or island fastnesses the great chiefs and chieftains of the north and north-west, surrounded by their loyal clansmen, should through the ages have paid but little heed to the pronouncements of kings or parliaments or officers of state from south of the Highland Line, regarding these only as potential allies or enemies in their own, more personal struggles for power. Which is why, in following the twists and turns of Highland history, it is important to think, not in terms of a clan's loyalty or disloyalty to this or that monarch or dynasty or government, but rather of a system of ever-shifting alliances and conflicts of interest between a number of independent or semi-independent minor kingdoms and principalities. For this is what in fact the clans were.

James, like his predecessors, made an attempt to tackle the recurrent problem of the Highlands and Islands. In 1462, during the previous reign, John, Lord of the Isles, had in his turn concluded an alliance with Edward IV of England, the Treaty of Westminster-Ardtornish. The Estates had subsequently sought to forfeit him, but James III had formally restored the Lordship to him and had hopefully created him a Lord of Parliament.

1 Chamfrain of engraved and beaten
bronze, perhaps as early as 200 BC.
This strange piece of armour protected
the faces of horses that drew the war
chariots of Celtic chieftains.

2 The Papil Stone, from Shetland
(Pictish, early 9th century): the bird-men
typify Pictish obsession with myths
and monsters.

3 Entangled animal figures and
interlocking spirals on this Pictish
cross-slab of the 8th century recall
the style of the roughly contemporary
Lindisfarne Gospels.

1

2

3

4

4 St Margaret, Queen of Malcolm III
Ceann Mor, in a 15th-century
illumination. Under her influence
and Malcolm's, Court life became more
civilized, and English fashions and
customs were introduced. She ordered
the rebuilding of the Monastery of
Iona and for her benefactions to the
Church was canonized in 1251.

5 The Monymusk Reliquary, in which
the remains of St Columba were taken
by King Kenneth MacAlpin from Iona
to Dunkeld.

5

ALCOLOHVS d
ſalutem. Nou
quandam ab
pro ſalute an
Sʒ poſtqm di
· uenerabil mei
locuſ ille non e
ſita eſt ſup ripam fluminis Tuede. in loco qui dr kelcho
pau ſubiectione libam ee conceſſit. Ita ſalicet ut abbas &

6

7

6 David I and his grandson, 'Malcolm the Maiden', who succeeded him at the age of eleven as Malcolm IV. Miniature from the Charter of Kelso Abbey, 1159.

7 Part of a set of chessmen carved from walrus ivory (Scandinavian, 12th century), found on the island of Lewis in 1831. The king (*right*) is about four inches high.

8

8 'The Ragman's Roll.' In this copy, on
28 August 1296, one Richard of Horseley
signed an oath of allegiance to 'nostre
Seigneur le Roi d'Engleterre' (Edward I)
in Norman French. Some two thousand
Scottish nobles and landowners were
forced to do likewise.

9 'The Arbroath Declaration' of 1320,
bearing the seals of all the barons
subscribing to its defiant terms: freedom
for Scotland and Robert Bruce for king.
It was executed in duplicate; one copy
was conveyed to Pope John XXII at
Avignon, the other kept in Scotland.

9

10

11

10 Robert Bruce died in 1329, barely a
year after securing Scottish sovereignty.
He gave this sword to Sir James Douglas
in token of his last injunction, to go on
Crusade to the Holy Land 'and thair
bury my hart'. Douglas died on the way.

11 Siege of Perth by the Earl of Mar, a
nephew of Bruce who in 1332 was briefly
Regent for the infant King David II. Just
nine days after his election he was slain
at the battle of Dupplin Moor. Woodcut
from Holinshed's *Chronicles* (1577).

12

13

12 This twelve-foot pennant in sage-green silk is the standard of the Douglases, whose power rivalled that of the Crown. Traditionally held to have been carried at the Battle of Otterburn in 1388, it bears a lion passant and St Andrew's cross; the motto 'Jamais areyre' (*jamais arrière*) refers to the Douglas claim to lead the vanguard of the Scottish Army into battle.

13 Hermitage Castle, Roxburghshire, most formidable of the Border strongholds, belonged to the Douglases from 1341 until the late 14th century.

14 View of St Andrews, seat of Scotland's first university, which was founded in 1411. The Scottish traditions of learning and the arts would grow to match their fame as warriors.

14

15

15 Two groats of James III. The first
is unusual in showing the King in
half-profile – a Renaissance device.
The fleur-de-lys on the other symbolizes
the long-standing French alliance.

16 James III: detail from a triptych by
Hugo van der Goes at Holyroodhouse.
He was a cultured man with a taste for
archaeology and the occult, and for like-
minded favourites, but as a king he was
ineffective and suspicious. In 1469 he
married Margaret, daughter of King
Christian I of Denmark and Norway, who
brought as her dowry the Orkneys and
Shetlands – joined to the Scottish Crown
just a few hundred years ago.

16

18

17

17 Device of Andrew Myllar, who, in partnership with Walter Chepman, received a royal patent to set up Scotland's first printing-press in 1507. The device, a pun on Myllar's name, works his initials into the form of a Greek alpha and omega.

18 Portrait, believed to be of James IV (r. 1488–1513), the ablest and most popular of the Stewart kings. In his reign the Renaissance reached Scotland and the arts flourished. (16th century, Flemish school.)

19 'Queen Mary's Harp', a finely decorated Celtic instrument of c. 1500.

19

John himself, who was peacefully inclined, might have given no further trouble. But his bastard, Angus Og, who had married Argyll's daughter, took a different view and declared war both on the King and on his father, thus splitting the western Highlands in two and, incidentally, starting a prolonged feud between the Macdonalds on the one hand and the Macleods and Mackenzies on the other. At the Battle of the Bloody Bay off Mull, Angus Og in 1480 decisively defeated his father and the latter's chief lieutenants, Maclean of Duart and Maclean of Ardgour, taking all three prisoner. Angus Og was, even for the age, an unusually violent and bloodthirsty man and was only prevented from dispatching his cousin Ardgour on the spot by the timely intervention of Macdonald of Moidart, who was reluctant to see a congenial neighbour obliterated. 'If Maclean were gone', said Moidart, 'who should I have to bicker with?' And for once Angus Og relented. After this Angus Og kept the western Highlands in a turmoil until in 1490 his throat was finally cut by his own harper.

In the following year, the feud between the Isles and the Scottish Crown flared up again. Old John's nephew, Alexander of Lochalsh, setting out from Lochaber, seized the royal castle of Inverness and ravaged the lands of the Mackenzies. The latter, however, defeated him heavily in a great battle at Park and in 1493 the Estates, on discovering that John of the Isles had again been intriguing with the English, finally forfeited the Lordship and annexed it to the Crown. In 1494 old John surrendered and entered a monastery at Paisley. He died four years later, a broken man, in a common lodging-house in Dundee.

James IV now did something that none of his predecessors had done. He made a series of visits to the Isles and the western Highlands, armed and escorted, it is true, but coming as a friend rather than as an invader, making himself known to the chiefs, whose language, as we have seen, he had actually learnt, and feasting and hunting with them. In the hope of keeping them occupied and improving their economic position, he even sought to encourage fishing and shipbuilding. But nothing much seems to have come of this somewhat optimistic project. 'The Scots', reported that shrewd observer Ayala, 'are not industrious and the people are poor. They spend all their time in wars, and when there is no war they fight one another.'

In the end, James, finding the response to his overtures disappointing, reversed his policy, exchanging his patriarchal approach for a more feudal one. Charters were revoked and Huntly and Argyll were made Lieutenants of the Isles and given powers where necessary to feu land to new holders.

This attempt to impose feudal overlords was a mistake. The tutelage of the King's Lieutenants was resented. In 1501 there was another uprising, under John of the Isles' young grandson, Donald Dubh, Black Donald, the son of Angus Og. This culminated in 1503, when the victorious Macdonalds, with the help of the Macleans, again seized and burned Inverness. It was not until 1506 that young Donald was finally hunted down and made a prisoner. In the hope of keeping order, the King now established a number of strategically placed strongpoints throughout the Highlands, at Tarbert and Urquhart, at Inverlochy and Loch Kilkerran. At the same time he greatly strengthened his fleet and substantially increased the number of Sheriff's and Sheriff's Courts.

Meanwhile southern Scotland was for the time being at peace and relatively united. The burghs were more prosperous than ever before. Learning, culture and the arts were making some progress. The outlook for the future seemed hopeful. But appearances were misleading.

Having achieved a measure of peace in his own country the King turned his attention to foreign parts. In the shifting pattern of European alliances, Scotland, her prestige higher than ever, now held, in a sense, the balance of power. James's purpose was to maintain this balance and so prevent a recurrence of the disastrous wars which had ravaged Europe during the past century. Amongst other ideas he nurtured a romantic plan to unite Christendom in a latter-day crusade against the Turks, who, having captured Constantinople, were now sweeping on through the Balkans in an advance which was only to be checked before the walls of Vienna. With this end in view and in furtherance of his active foreign policy, he built a great fleet, for which vast quantities of timber were felled in Fife and at Luss on the shores of Loch Lomond. The *Great Michael* was, or so James believed, the mightiest warship in Europe and Sir Michael Wood and Sir Andrew Barton and his brothers were among the most famous sea-captains of their day.

Basically everything, as usual, depended on Scotland's relationship with her southern neighbour. History showed that a hostile Scotland could hamstring England. For a time James's relations with England had been strained owing to his support of the Yorkist pretender, Perkin Warbeck. But in 1501, at the age of twenty-eight, he had finally agreed to marry Margaret Tudor, the twelve-year-old daughter of Henry VII, a Welsh upstart who in 1485 had usurped the English throne. In February of the following year he signed with England a treaty of perpetual peace – 'a good, real, sincere, true, entire and firm peace, bond, league and confederation on land and sea, to endure for ever.' It was even sponsored by the Pope, who undertook to excommunicate whichever sovereign first broke his pledged word, and in August 1503 James married little Margaret at Holyrood amid scenes of unparalleled splendour, which dazzled, as they were intended to, the grudgingly admiring visitors from south of the Border.

But Scotland's new alliance with England did not mean the end of her Auld Alliance with France. On the contrary, in the years that followed James sought consistently to use these two connections to restrain his allies from attacking each other, thus earning the name of *Rex Pacificator*, the Peace-Bringer. Then, in 1511, the Pope, the King of Spain and the Doge of Venice formed what they called the Holy League against France. Their declared aim was her partition. They were joined first by the Emperor and then by James's brilliant but bellicose young brother-in-law, who had recently succeeded to the throne as Henry VIII of England.

France now stood alone save for Scotland. In July 1512 James, convinced that France's survival was essential to the stability of Europe, formally renewed the Auld Alliance. To the last he sought to mediate between the hostile powers. But it was too late. By April 1513 a European war was in progress and a couple of months later France, attacked on both sides, was in deadly peril. In response to French appeals for help, James sent an ultimatum to Henry VIII. But Henry replied insolently, asserting that he was 'the verie owner of Scotland' which James 'held of him by homage'. Clearly Scotland's own survival was at stake. Mustering the most splendid army a Scottish king had ever commanded, James crossed the Tweed at the head of his troops on 22 August.

Flodden

For a couple of weeks the campaign went well. Four English castles fell to the Scots. Then on a wild afternoon at the beginning of September the two armies met near Flodden Edge under Branxton Hill. For a time it seemed as though the Scots might win the day and at first Lord Home's borderers drove back the English division which faced them. But the English foot soldiers were better armed, their bills outmatching the Scottish spears. The Scots stood their ground and were killed where they stood. In the end the battle became a massacre. The King was slain and with him the flower of Scottish chivalry. Nine earls and fourteen lords, the chiefs of many of the great Highland clans, James's natural son, Alexander, Archbishop of St Andrews, the Bishop of Caithness, the Bishop of the Isles, the Dean of Glasgow and the Provost of Edinburgh and thousands of Scotland's best young men all perished on that day and their followers with them. Their untimely end is commemorated in the most moving of all laments: *The Flowers of the Forest are a' wede away*.

After the battle James's body was taken to his brother-in-law, but Henry denied it burial and no one knows what in the end became of it. In his own country there were those who believed that their King was still alive and would one day return to them.

The situation in which Scotland now found herself was extremely precarious. Her King was dead and with him the best of her leaders. Her army had been wiped out. Her only ally, France, was in mortal danger. Across the Border, her old enemy England was triumphant and more aggressive than ever. Her new King, James V, was a baby who could barely walk. Queen Margaret, who now assumed the Regency, had the faults of the Tudors without their brains, and was in any case of doubtful loyalty. Such nobles as had survived Flodden were, with her encouragement, intriguing among themselves. No wonder that an English visitor to Scotland at this time rejoiced at the 'myschefe, robbery, spoiling, and vengeance' which he saw everywhere and prayed God that it might 'continewe'.

But within a year or two things, though still confused, had taken a turn for the better. In 1514 Margaret had forfeited the Regency by marrying the Earl of Angus, head of the powerful Red Douglases, and had been succeeded as Regent by the French-educated and French-speaking Duke of Albany, the son of James Ill's ambitious and adventurous brother, who had arrived from France in 1515, determined to continue the traditional policy of a French alliance. France, meanwhile, had been saved from destruction by the divisions of her enemies. The balance had thus been partially restored.

During the years that followed, Albany, supported by the Estates and bolstered by the French alliance, formally renewed in 1517, headed the National or French Party. Against him, at the head of the English Party, stood Angus and Margaret, who were now plotting with Henry VIII to kidnap the little King and carry him off to England. When their plans finally failed, they fled across the Border, though Margaret, after quarrelling with her husband, returned in 1521 to join Albany. Her brother Henry VIII, meanwhile, continued to interfere whenever he could in Scottish affairs and to intrigue against Albany, who in 1524 finally gave up the Regency and returned to France.

Albany's former opponents now started to quarrel among themselves. Angus returned from England and the young King was, in the phrase of a contemporary, 'coupit from hand to hand'. In 1526 James, having reached the age of fourteen, was declared ready to govern. In fact he was to all intents and purposes a prisoner of the Douglases. These, under Angus, had recently routed and slaughtered their rivals the Hamiltons, under Arran, in a pitched battle in the streets of Edinburgh, long to be remembered by its citizens as 'cleanse the Causeway'. They were now masters of the situation.

But two years later, early one summer morning in 1528, James escaped from his captors disguised as a groom, and reached Stirling where some relatively loyal supporters awaited him. 'I vow', said James, after he had escaped from the Douglases, 'that Scotland will not hold us both.' He was as good as his word. After a sharp clash, Angus was driven across the Border into England, where, needless to say, he was well received by Henry VIII, always glad to welcome disaffected Scots. James, meanwhile, having made a truce with the English, set to work to restore law and order in the Borders and elsewhere. There were, as usual, signs of trouble in the north and north-west, but here also, the young King, thanks to a conciliatory policy, met with a measure of success.

Europe meanwhile was in turmoil. In 1517, four years after Flodden, Martin Luther had nailed his Theses to the church door at Wittenberg. Soon the Continent was to be split into two armed camps. *Cujus regio, ejus religio* was the order of the day. Every sovereign sought to impose his own religion on his own dominions and as often as not on his neighbour's as well. Scotland, once again key to the balance of power, was eagerly sought after. Henry VIII offered James his daughter in marriage. The Emperor Charles V pressed the claims of his sister. Even the Pope proffered his formidable niece, Catherine de Medici. In the end, in 1537, James married Madeleine, the daughter of François I of France. But barely six months later she was dead.

The next year James took another French bride, Marie de Guise-Lorraine. But the two sons she bore him died in 1541. The English, meanwhile, were becoming ever more aggressive. Having himself broken with Rome in 1534, Henry VIII was set on making Scotland Protestant and so turning her against France. But James resisted this. Then in 1542 some Irish chiefs offered James the Crown of Ireland. This gave Henry the pretext he was looking for. Sending his troops across the Border, he followed it up by formally proclaiming himself Lord-Superior of Scotland. James, already ill and at odds with his nobles, replied by invading England. But his nobles refused to march. On 24 November 1542 James's little army, mutinous and feebly led by his favourite, Oliver Sinclair, was defeated at Solway Moss. Sick at heart, the King rode to Falkland and there, two weeks later, received the news that his wife had borne him a daughter. To the dying man this was the last straw. Remembering how the Crown had come to his family through Margery Bruce, 'It came with a lass', he said, 'and it will gang with a lass.' Then he 'gave one little laughtir' and fell back dead. The baby girl, who had been christened Mary, was at once proclaimed Queen.

Mary Queen of Scots

Mary Queen of Scots was less than a week old when she succeeded to the throne in 1542. The outlook was disturbing. By one means or another her great-uncle, King Henry VIII of England, now the principal protagonist of Protestantism in Europe and the sworn enemy both of France and the

Pope, was determined to make himself master of Scotland. Ten years earlier he had wanted James V to marry his daughter. Now he sought to win the little Queen as a bride for his sickly son, Edward.

A treaty of marriage was duly negotiated with Arran, the Regent and heir to the throne, who was inclined to favour an English rather than a French connection. But Marie de Guise, the clever and determined young Queen Mother, and her unprincipled but extremely able adviser, Cardinal David Beaton, had other plans. Little Mary was carried off by the Cardinal and crowned Queen at Scone, while the Estates, who rightly distrusted Henry, were without difficulty persuaded to repudiate the treaty of marriage.

Henry VIII's answer was to invade Scotland. During the summer of 1544 Edinburgh and the Borders were laid waste and burnt and appalling atrocities perpetrated by Henry's soldiers. 'Put all to fyre and swoorde,' ran the Privy Council's instruction, 'burne Edinborough towne, so rased and defaced when you have sacked and gotten what ye can of it, as there may remayne forever a perpetuel memory of the vengaunce of God.' This Rough Wooing, as it came to be known, left in southern Scotland a legacy of hatred for the English which was to endure for centuries. Even the Douglases felt less affection for the English when they found their lands devastated and the tombs of their forefathers destroyed.

Meanwhile in the north-west Henry had found an ally in Angus Og's son, Donald Dubh, Black Donald of the Isles, who, escaping from prison in 1545 after some forty years of captivity, raised, with the help of the Macleans, a force of 8,000 men and 180 galleys to fight against the Government of Scotland and thus show for all to see how little the power of the Isles had been affected by the forfeiture of fifty years before. 'Auld enemys to the realme of Scotland', the Islesmen proudly called themselves.

But the power of the Isles had flared up for the last time. Donald Dubh died the same year in Ireland, leaving no successor. The Islesmen quarrelled over the manner in which Maclean of Duart, as Treasurer of the Isles, had distributed the funds raised to equip the expedition, and the Macdonalds fell out amongst themselves. Henceforward the western clans split along new lines of cleavage and at long last began to show themselves more willing to come to terms with the House of Stewart.

In January 1547, death came to Henry VIII of England. But the Duke of Somerset, as Regent for the young Edward VI, continued Henry's policy, sending a fresh army to Scotland which was to inflict a disastrous defeat on the Scots under Arran at Pinkie Cleugh later the same year.

Scotland, meanwhile, had turned to France for help. For the Scots the choice lay more clearly than ever between a connection with Catholic France and one with Protestant England. It was a choice fraught with religious, social and economic, as well as national and political implications. In Scotland, each cause had its adherents. The latest turn of events had driven the Scots for the time being into the arms of France. But it was, for a variety of reasons, an alliance that had come to lack stability.

It was now thirty years since Martin Luther had first published his Theses. Since then Zwingli had founded his Reformed Church and Calvin produced his *Institutes of the Christian Religion*, while in 1534 Henry VIII of England, for reasons not entirely theological, had in his turn embraced Protestantism.

Corruption in the Church

To Scotland the Reformation was to come later. Nowhere at this time was the Church more corrupt or degraded. 'Pilates rather than Prelates', Pope Eugenius IV had called the Scottish Bishops. And Archibald Hay, a relative of Cardinal Beaton, had found it necessary to warn him that priests were being ordained 'who hardly knew the order of the alphabet', while others 'come to the heavenly table who have not slept off last night's debauch'. The poet William Dunbar, himself a Franciscan friar, also had something to say about the private life of his spiritual superiors:

Sic pryde with Prelatis, so few till preiche and pray,
Sic hant of harlottis with thame, baith nicht and day.

Though most parish priests were miserably poor, there were eye-catching exceptions. Parson Adam Colquhoun of Stobo lived, we are told, with his mistress Mary Boyd and their two sons, James and Adam, in luxurious ostentation in Glasgow in a manse in the Drygate full of gold and silver, damask and silk, carved and gilded furniture and feather beds, with a striking clock and, in the bedroom, a parrot in a cage.* When Adam died in 1542 his nephew Peter claimed this desirable inheritance, but the parson's two sons, having been formally legitimated in 1530, were duly awarded his entire fortune, including, of course, the parrot. The Bishop of Moray, for his part, provided for all nine of his children at the expense of the Church, while the bastard daughters of rich prelates were much in demand for their dowries. Even Scottish nuns, if we are to believe the reports of Cardinal Sermoneta, 'go forth abroad surrounded by their numerous sons, and give their daughters in marriage dowered with the ample revenues of the Church'. Alexander Stewart, a bastard of James IV, was made Archbishop of St Andrews at the age of eleven as well as Abbot of Arbroath and Prior of Coldingham.

Such a system was, needless to say, not without its advantages to those in authority. In Scotland, the Church was immensely rich, controlling considerably more than half the national wealth. The Scottish Crown in particular received lavish ecclesiastical subsidies from the Pope. And had not His Holiness, at the King's request, obligingly provided priories and abbeys for no less than five of James V's bastards while they were still infants? But for the sincerely religious it offered cold comfort. Everywhere fewer people attended Mass and more churches crumbled into disrepair. 'A great many of the parish churches,' reported the Archbishop of St Andrews, 'their choirs as well as their naves, were wholly thrown down ... others were partly ruinous or threatening collapse ... without glazed windows and without baptismal font.'

Successive Provincial Councils, warned by what had happened in England, made some efforts to restore the situation. The root of the trouble, they declared, was 'the corruption of morals and profane lewdness of life in churchmen of almost all ranks, together with crass ignorance of literature and of all the liberal arts.' And this they sought to remedy by statutes: statutes encouraging the clergy to learn to read and to preach in person at least four times a year; statutes laying down 'that neither prelates nor their subordinate clergy keep their offspring born of concubinage in their company nor suffer them directly or indirectly to be promoted in their

---

* 'A bird, viz. ane parrok.'

churches, nor under colour of any pretext to marry their daughters to barons or make their sons barons out of the patrimony of Christ.'

But already it was too late. Though Parliament had banned them, English translations of the Bible were now beginning to be smuggled across the border; they had an immediate, a profound effect. At last people were coming to learn more about the true nature of Christianity; the impact was revolutionary. Everywhere signs of active discontent with the Church became more and more discernible. Soon, by one of those mysterious processes that occur at such times, a spontaneous popular movement of dissent had sprung into being. Of the critics, some, like the good Bishop Dunbar of Aberdeen, desired reform from within. Others aimed at more drastic changes. Neither group in the event received much practical encouragement from the authorities, whether ecclesiastical or secular.

Of the protagonists of Protestantism in Scotland, one of the earliest and most notable was Patrick Hamilton, a rich young scholar of noble birth and unusual charm. From visits to Paris and to Marburg he had come back to St Andrews a convinced adherent of the new doctrines. On orders from Archbishop James Beaton he was arrested and invited to recant. When in 1528 he refused to do so, he was burnt at the stake outside the Chapel of St Salvator – slowly, for the technique had yet to be perfected. 'My Lord, if you burn any more,' a friend said to the Cardinal, 'let them be burned in cellars, for the reek of Master Patrick Hamilton has infected as many as it blew upon.'

He was right. Patrick Hamilton's death and the courage with which he met it left a lasting impression on many people in Scotland. Soon the new ideas were spreading through the country like wildfire. Nor were the motives of all concerned purely spiritual. To the religious zeal of the reformers were added the greed of many nobles for the rich Church lands and the political enthusiasms of the Anglophile faction.

As a member of the Council of Regency and also a close friend and adviser of the Queen Mother, David Beaton, Abbot of Arbroath and Bishop of Mirepoix in Languedoc, was in a position of great strength. A dissolute man of great experience and ability, he had succeeded his uncle James as Archbishop of St Andrews and had with French support also become a Cardinal. Having successfully resisted the attempts of the

English to gain control of the little Queen and of Scotland, he and the Queen Mother had next turned their combined energies to the task of consolidating the French connection, while at the same time seeking to check the ever-rising tide of Protestantism in Scotland.

After Patrick Hamilton's death, many of the Protestant leaders had taken refuge abroad. George Wishart, one of the most prominent, had returned to Scotland in 1544, when the persecution of the Protestants was at its height, to resume his preaching and face the consequences. He was accompanied wherever he went by a fervent, grim-looking young priest with a black beard, carrying a large two-handed sword – Father John Knox.

Knox and the Covenant

The Rough Wooing was in full swing. It was a time of tension and war, of plots and counter-plots, of mayhem and assassination. Henry VIII had generously offered a thousand pounds for the murder of Cardinal Beaton. John Knox, for his part, had more than once publicly expressed approval of murder, always provided it was from the right motives. Early in 1546 Wishart was arrested on charges of collaboration with the English and participation in a plot to murder the Cardinal. Knox, who had been his constant companion, had been loath to leave him when danger seemed to threaten him. But Wishart had sent him away. 'Return', he said, 'to your bairns. And God bless you. One is sufficient for a sacrifice.' In March, Wishart, having been convicted of heresy, was duly burned in the Cardinal's presence at St Andrews.

Two months later, in May 1546, the plot to murder Cardinal Beaton was put into effect. His castle at St Andrews was seized by a band of Protestant noblemen and the Cardinal stabbed to death and thrown from his own window. 'Fie! Fie!' were the prelate's last words. 'All is gone.' No one was better pleased to see him go than his old enemy, Henry VIII. An important obstacle to his designs was now out of the way.

The Cardinal's assassins now barricaded themselves in the Castle, with John Knox as their rather reluctant chaplain, and, appealing to the English for help, held out there until July 1547, when the Castle was finally reduced with the help of the French fleet, which had arrived off St Andrews at the request of Marie de Guise. Having captured the Castle, the French dispatched to the galleys such prisoners as they took, including young John Knox. The English army, sent by the Regent Somerset, arrived too late to save the garrison, but at Pinkie, six miles outside Edinburgh, managed, as we have seen, to inflict a crushing defeat on the Scots, who, we are told, 'fled ... like beasts'. In 1549, however, under the Treaty of Boulogne, which ended hostilities between England and France, the English also undertook to withdraw their forces from Scotland.

Until now little Queen Mary had been in Scotland. From Inchmahome Island in the Lake of Menteith she had been moved, for safe keeping, first to Stirling Castle and then to Dumbarton Rock. Now in 1548 she was sent to France, to become, it was decided, the bride of the Dauphin and thus yet further to strengthen the traditional bonds linking Scotland to France. On hearing that agreement had been reached the French King, it is said 'leaped for blitheness'. 'France and Scotland', he declared, 'are now one country.'

In Europe the Protestant movement seemed on the wane. The Council of Trent, by which the Vatican was seeking to regain the initiative, had begun its deliberations. The English had been chased out of France and were withdrawing their troops from Scotland. Their King, Edward VI, though reliably Protestant, was sickly and the succession far from assured. In France Henri II was preparing to crush the Huguenots. The Emperor was getting the best of the Protestant Princes in Germany. In Scotland, finally, Marie de Guise had won over Arran by having him made Duc de Châtelhérault and in 1554 had herself assumed the Regency. Meanwhile Arran's half-brother, John Hamilton, had succeeded Beaton as Archbishop and, however belatedly, embarked on a programme of Church reform.

But in 1549 John Knox had been released from the galleys by his French captors. The hardships he had endured had done nothing to damp his enthusiasm or diminish his energy or conviction. He had first crossed to England, where he had met Archbishop Cranmer, served as Chaplain to Edward VI and been offered a bishopric. In 1553, on the accession of Mary Tudor to the English throne and England's abrupt reversion to Roman Catholicism, he had gone to Germany and thence to Geneva, where he came strongly under the influence of Calvin. In 1555, fuller than ever of the new ideas and fiercely eloquent, he returned to Scotland. His first target for attack was the Queen Mother, whom he resented not only as a Roman Catholic, but as a woman. The Bishops cited him, but finally decided to drop the charge. His impact was formidable. Even Marie de Guise herself was half fascinated by him. In 1556 Knox went back to Geneva, where Calvin had now set up a model state on Calvinist principles, and there attended to the spiritual needs of the local English community. In 1559 he was to return to his own country for good.

Already, despite Marie de Guise, the Protestant movement in Scotland was now rapidly gaining ground. The numbers of active Protestants were increasing and they were becoming more demanding. In 1557 a powerful group of nobles led by Argyll and Morton drew up the document which was to be known as the First Covenant and for which signatures were sought all over Scotland. In this the Lords of the Congregation, as its sponsors were called, pledged themselves to 'establish the most blessed word of God' and to 'forsake and renounce the congregation of Satan', in other words to break with Rome and set up a reformed national Church. In particular, they insisted on the Communion in both kinds, on the public exposition of the Scriptures and the holding of religious services in the vernacular on the lines laid down by the new English Book of Common Prayer. They won widespread popular support. But neither Parliament nor the clergy would meet their requests. And there were signs that the Regent, now sure of help from France, was preparing to take a more intransigent line.

Oflate, the burning of Protestants as heretics had become much less frequent. In April 1558, however, the Catholic hierarchy, possibly feeling that things were going too far, decided to make an example of Walter Myln, an aged priest of eighty-two, who was accordingly sent to the stake at St Andrews. But the event aroused so little enthusiasm locally that in the end the Archbishop's servants had to burn him themselves for want of volunteers. He was, as it turned out, the last Protestant to be burned in Scotland as such.

A few days later, at a magnificent ceremony in the Cathedral Church of Notre Dame de Paris, the fifteen-year-old Queen Mary was married to the Dauphin of France. The two countries were now more closely linked than ever. Henri II graciously granted French citizenship to all Scots who came to France and Frenchmen in Scotland were accorded reciprocal privileges. An eventual union of the crowns and the virtual conversion of Scotland into a province of France seemed probable. Indeed before her marriage the young Queen had already signed documents placing her kingdom in pledge. In Scotland, however, many viewed the course events were taking with apprehension and murmured louder than ever against the Queen Mother.

It now became clear that Marie was proposing, with all the resources of the State behind her, to suppress the Covenant by force. Soon feeling in Scotland ran high. Early in 1559, in response to pressing requests from the powerful Protestant faction, John Knox returned. His sermons were more stirring and inflammatory than ever. He seemed possessed of an almost daemonic power. All over central Scotland, in Perth, at St Andrews, in Stirling and Linlithgow, excited mobs, inflamed by his eloquence, set to work breaking up churches, smashing altars and destroying religious statues and pictures. The scene seemed set for civil war.

In November 1558, meanwhile, had come the news that the Catholic Mary Tudor was dead, leaving the English throne to her Protestant half-sister, Elizabeth. The Scottish Protestants could once more hope for help from England. Moreover Queen Elizabeth's personal interests were very much involved. In July 1559 Henri II died and Mary's husband François succeeded to the throne of France. No sooner had he done so than he proceeded to quarter the arms of France with those not only of Scotland but also of England thereby openly announcing his claim to both crowns. For in Roman Catholic eyes Elizabeth was only the natural daughter of Henry VIII and Mary, as the grand-daughter of Henry VII, could rightfully claim the throne of England as well as that of Scotland. It was a warning which Elizabeth Tudor knew how to take and which was greatly to influence her subsequent attitude towards her young cousin.

Encouraged by the renewed triumph of the Reformation in England and by the prospect of English support, the Scottish Protestants redoubled their efforts. All the churches in Perth were sacked and the Mass forbidden on pain of death. The Queen Mother now sent the Earl of Argyll and Lord James Stewart, Mary's own half-brother, to reason with the rebels. But all they did was themselves to join the insurgents and, though Knox himself spoke chidingly of the rascal multitude', still more churches were sacked. Marie could only appeal for more help from France.

It was in these circumstances that Elizabeth of England opened negotiations with the Scottish Protestants. She did so reluctantly, for she disapproved of rebels on principle and, as a woman, particularly disliked John Knox and the title of his latest work, *The First Blast of the Trumpet against the Monstrous Regiment of Women*. 'To promote a woman', ran one passage, 'to bear rule, superiority, dominion or empire above any realm, nation or city is repugnant to Nature; is contumely to God.' Knox, for his part, was no more enthusiastic. But neither party had any doubt in their minds that France's claims to the thrones of England and Scotland must be firmly rebutted. Accordingly the astute Maitland of Lethington was sent to London to negotiate the Treaty of Berwick and early in 1560 an English fleet appeared in Scottish waters; soon the Queen Mother's French forces, sent by the Guises to support their sister, fell back on Leith. Here, besieged by an Anglo-Scottish army four times their size, they bravely held out for another six months.

The year 1560 marked a turning point in Scottish history. In June, Marie de Guise died. Her death removed from the scene a powerful influence on affairs. Early in July the Treaty of Edinburgh recognized Elizabeth as Queen of England and provided for the withdrawal from Scotland, not only of all English, but of all French troops. In effect it put an end to the Auld Alliance and ensured the ultimate victory of Protestantism in Scotland. It also marked the first step towards ultimate union with England.

Protestantism Prevails

In August Parliament was called. By successive statutes, the authority of the Pope in Scotland was abolished and the celebration of the Latin Mass forbidden. And now John Knox, who had seen his ideas triumph, was, with five others, given the task of formulating the creed and the constitution of the new Church. These were embodied in *The Confession of Fayth and The First Book of Discipline* to which was later added *The Book of Common Order*, to be known as 'Knox's Liturgy'. These documents were to provide for a time the foundation for Protestant worship in Scotland.

Compared with other countries, the Reformation in Scotland had made few martyrs. In all, seven Protestants suffered death by law before the Reformation and two Catholics after it. The majority of the Catholic clergy either joined the new Church or retired on pensions, while their flocks for the most part followed suit. In the old Church corruption and decay had more than done their work. It fell apart almost of its own accord. The time for killing was to come later, when the finer points of Protestant doctrine were ripe for debate. But, whereas in England the Reformation had been a matter of botched-up compromises and equivocal half-measures, in Scotland it was radical. Calvin's relentless logic saw to that. Henceforth the Church of Scotland was governed not by a hierarchy of Bishops and Archbishops, but by Kirk Sessions of lay elders and later by district Presbyteries, possessing the power to ordain the Ministers. The General Assembly of the Kirk, meeting once or twice a year to settle questions affecting the Church as a whole, soon became a forum for Scottish opinion on secular as well as on ecclesiastical matters. Provision was made, too, for a new national system of education. Every parish, in theory at any rate, was to have its school, an ideal that in practice long remained unfulfilled.

Under the influence of Knox and, indirectly, of Calvin, the early Kirk was austere in character. With time this austerity increased still further. Soon Christmas and Easter were no longer observed and Knox's liturgy was abandoned in favour of spontaneous prayer. Singing was unaccompanied. The churches were unadorned. Holy Communion, which Knox had intended should be central to the life of the Church, was celebrated less and less frequently. Throughout Scotland the influence of parish ministers became paramount in lay as well as Church matters and Kirk Sessions exercised widespread influence. Though there were notable exceptions, austerity became the keynote of Scottish life, both social and religious.

It was to this austerely Protestant Scotland, the Scotland of John Knox, that Mary Queen of Scots returned in August 1561. Her husband had died in the previous December. No longer Queen of France, she was still Queen of Scotland. And now, young, beautiful, light-hearted, high-spirited, highly-sexed, impulsive, French in education and outlook, a devout Roman Catholic and a widow at eighteen, she came to claim her inheritance. Clearly the situation was fraught with the most explosive possibilities.

From the first, Mary let it be known that, while she had no intention of abandoning her own faith, she equally did not intend to impose it on her subjects. Indeed she went out of her way to surround herself with Protestant nobles and advisers; she wished to reign as Queen of Scots and not as leader of a faction. But this was of no great help to her. The Protestant divines were scandalized by Mass being celebrated in Holyroodhouse, not to mention what they regarded as the frivolous conduct of the Queen and her Court. They were equally dismayed when the Protestant nobles who had seized the rich properties of the old Church kept them for themselves instead of letting them be made over to the new.

Then in 1565, Mary fell in love with, or at any rate decided to marry, her worthless cousin, Henry Stewart Lord Darnley, a not very intelligent, teenaged Roman Catholic of notoriously bad character, four years younger than herself. On 29 July 1565 they were married according to the Roman Catholic rite and Darnley was proclaimed King. They had not been married for twelve months when Darnley became jealous of the influence of the Queen's Italian secretary, Riccio, and, with some friends, murdered him in her presence. This greatly distressed Mary, who was six months pregnant. It also turned her against her husband. In 1567 came the news that Darnley's house at Kirk o' Field, near Edinburgh, where the Queen had sent him to convalesce from a distressing, some said disgraceful, disease, had been blown up and his body found amid the wreckage. On closer inspection, he proved to have been strangled.

No one ever discovered just who had murdered Darnley. But it was obvious to all that James Hepburn, fourth Earl of Bothwell, the Lord High Admiral, a bold, reckless Protestant of considerable charm, but of the most deplorable reputation, was heavily implicated. Eight weeks later Mary married him according to the rites of the Protestant Church.

Abdication of Mary

Whatever its motivation, this further error of judgment alienated both Protestants and Catholics alike and finally cost Mary her throne. Scotland was in turmoil, a prey to intrigue and violence. Within a month the Protestant Lords had raised an army on the pretext of saving the Queen from Bothwell and at Carberry Hill had successfully taken her from her followers. After being led, in a short red petticoat, through the streets of Edinburgh amid derision, Mary, who was still only twenty-four, was in June 1567 forced to abdicate in favour of her baby son, who was immediately crowned King as James VI. The sermon on this occasion was preached by John Knox. Bothwell escaped to Norway and Mary's Protestant half-brother, James Stewart, who was one of James V's more intelligent, if devious, bastards and had been made Earl of Moray, was now appointed Regent. He was, and remained, in close touch with the English Court.

After Carberry Hill Mary was held for some months a prisoner in Lochleven Castle. Thence in 1568 she escaped by boat, with the connivance of the Hamiltons who had plans of their own for her and, taking her to Hamilton Palace, again helped her to raise an army. But again she was defeated, this time at Langside by her half-brother, Moray. In desperation she now crossed the Solway and in May 1568 threw herself on the mercy of the Queen of England, who, never for a moment forgetting her cousin's claim to the English throne, promptly imprisoned her. 'Strike or be stricken,' was Elizabeth's motto. 'Strike or be stricken.'

CHAPTER FOUR

'THE GREAT MARRIAGE DAY OF THIS NATION WITH GOD'

The years that followed Mary's abdication and flight were troublous ones for Scotland – years of disquieting signs and wonders. 'In this time', we read in the *Diurnal of Occurrents* for 1570, 'there was ane monstrous fish in Loch Fyne, havand greit ein in the heid thairof, and at sumtymis wald stand abune the watir as heich as the mast of ane schippe; and the said had upoun the heid thairof two crowins, the ane abuve litel and the dounmaist crown mekill: quhilk was reportit be wyse men that the same was ane signe and taikning of ane suddain alteration within the realm.'

It was a safe enough conclusion for the wise men to draw. While James VI, who had been barely a year old at the time of his coronation, was growing up under the care of his learned but disagreeable tutor George Buchanan, who methodically thrashed and overworked him, the country was once again ruled by a succession of Regents. Mary's supporters, meanwhile, the 'Queen's Lords', who were working for her return, had seized Edinburgh Castle and were holding it against all comers. The first two Regents, Moray and Lennox, were murdered one after the other. Mar died in office. It was not until 1573 that the next Regent, Morton, a sworn enemy of the Queen, succeeded, with the help of heavy cannon brought from England, in capturing the Castle and ousting its garrison. Then in 1578 Morton himself was overthrown and two years after that, in 1581, impeached and executed on the charge, strange to say, of having, fourteen years before, murdered Darnley.

Morton's removal was the work of Esmé Stewart, Seigneur d'Aubigny, a fascinating Franco-Scottish cousin of the little King's, for whom the latter had formed a sentimental attachment and whom he now created Duke of Lennox and Lord High Chamberlain of Scotland. This was the first of a series of such attachments which persisted throughout the reign and did nothing to improve the image of the monarchy.

While publicly repudiating his own Roman Catholicism, it now became Lennox's purpose to make a Catholic of James and use him to head a Catholic rising in Scotland and England, with French and Spanish help. In this he was frustrated by a group of strongly Protestant nobles led by the Earl of Gowrie and by Morton's nephew Angus, who in 1582, with the aid of English funds, kidnapped the King, in what was known as the Raid of Ruthven, and took over the government of the country themselves. Lennox now fled back to France and died there a few months later. Much relieved, the General Assembly approved the raid and in Edinburgh a great concourse sang the 124th Psalm: 'Our soul is escaped as a bird out of the snare of the fowlers.'

James VI of Scotland

In 1583, however, James, who was now seventeen, escaped from Ruthven and from his captors and, accompanied by a single servant, made his way to St Andrews where he proclaimed himself King in fact as well as in name. One of his first actions on assuming power was to execute the Earl of Gowrie, who had held him prisoner at Ruthven and had since again sought to get him into his power. Seventeen years later the pattern was, strangely enough, to repeat itself when, in mysterious circumstances, yet another kidnapping, or alleged kidnapping, of the King was followed by the sudden demise of yet another Earl of Gowrie, the son of the first.

Despite a promising start, the young King had difficulty in controlling his nobles and his favourites and the early years of the reign were further marred by civil strife and by the brawling of the Catholic and Protestant factions and various combinations and permutations of the two. But, though the experiences of his childhood and youth, going right back to the prenatal impact of Riccio's murder, might have been enough to unbalance a stronger character, James, for all his faults and foibles (which were considerable and included a persistent obsession with witchcraft and witches), was to grow up a man of taste, education and intelligence who, as a monarch, lacked neither shrewdness nor political skill.

Like others of his line, James VI aspired not to be the leader of this faction or that, but 'universall King'. Some of his subjects, notably the Ruthvens, thought him too generous in his treatment of the Roman Catholic Earls of Huntly, Erroll and Angus, whose rebellions constantly disturbed the north of Scotland at this time, and whose assassination of the Bonny Earl of Moray, a popular Protestant, was blamed by many on the King, who let Huntly off with no more than a week's imprisonment. But James, quite apart from his personal convictions, had very good reasons for remaining a Protestant. So long as he did so, and so long as he stayed on reasonably good terms with his cousin Elizabeth of England and with her powerful Secretary, Sir Robert Cecil, he had every reason to hope that on her death he would succeed to the English throne, a rich prize by any standards. And so in 1585 he concluded an alliance with England and when in 1587, after holding her a prisoner for nineteen years, Elizabeth finally executed his mother Mary for alleged complicity in a plot to assassinate her, he made a formal protest, but did no more, though his subjects, impulsive as ever, and enraged by what they regarded as an insult to Scotland, loudly clamoured for war against the hereditary enemy. With Robert Cecil, in particular, James henceforward kept up a constant secret correspondence and received from him much useful advice and encouragement.

In 1589 James travelled to Oslo to marry Anne of Denmark, a suitably Protestant princess. But there was no money to celebrate their homecoming in what he considered suitable style. 'For God's sake,' he wrote to a well-disposed minister, 'take all the pains ye can to tune our folks well now against our homecoming lest we be all shamed before strangers. Thus recommending me and my new rib to your daily prayers, I commit you to the only All-sufficient.'

The principal problem that now faced James was that of the Kirk. The issue was no longer the old religion or the new, but just what form the new religion should take, and in particular whether the Church should be governed, as in England, by bishops appointed by the Crown or by

Assemblies of ministers and laymen. For the Scottish Reformed Church had a very different tradition from the English. It had come into being not thanks to the Crown, but in spite of the Crown. And that tradition persisted.

Though a convinced Protestant, James was no Presbyterian. Indeed, presbytery stood for everything he most disliked. He himself was strongly attached to the idea of episcopacy. 'No Bishop,' he would say, 'no King.' And he was equally strongly opposed to any suggestion of interference by the Church in the affairs of the State.

In 1581 *The Second Book of Discipline* had been declared authoritative by the General Assembly. This represented a success for the ideas of Andrew Melville, the religious leader on whose shoulders the mantle of John Knox had fallen after the latter's death in 1572. But while Melville equalled Knox in zeal and vehemence, his theological views went a good deal further than those of his predecessor. He was in particular more strongly opposed to episcopacy than Knox had ever been and even maintained that Church Courts should instruct civil magistrates in their jurisdiction, quoting divine authority in support of this view. In other words he claimed that the Church should direct the affairs of the State and not vice versa. He did not even accord the King the respect which James felt was his due. 'God's sillie vassal', he called him, to his face.

In 1584 James, who saw in bishops (who were appointed by him) a convenient means of enforcing his own will, retaliated by inducing Parliament to pass statutes confirming the appointment of bishops and forbidding Convocations of ministers save by leave of the King. These measures encountered immediate and vigorous opposition and in the end James was forced to give way. Though bishops of a kind still held office, Presbyteries, Synods and General Assemblies were once again allowed to meet.

There ensued, under the aegis of Andrew Melville, a fresh trend towards extreme Calvinism. Opposition to episcopacy increased still further and, as part of the reaction against a formal liturgy, extempore prayer began more and more to replace the forms of worship provided for in the Book of Common Order. But these opinions were by no means universally held. A strong body of Protestant opinion, led by Archbishop John Spottiswoode and strongly supported by the King, took the opposite view. I am verily persuaded', wrote Spottiswoode, 'that the government episcopall is the only right and Apostolique form. Paritie among ministers is the breeder of confusion, as experience might have taught us, and for these ruling elders, as they are a mere human devise, so they will prove, if they find way, the ruin both of Church and estate.' The religious conflict inherent in these two opposing Protestant views was to grow in violence throughout the seventeenth century, colouring this whole period of Scottish history, and persisting scarcely diminished until our own times.

James I of England

Meanwhile for James the fulfilment of all his dearest wishes was at hand. At the end of March 1603 came the long-awaited news that Elizabeth of England had died and that he had been declared her heir. Robert Cecil had not failed his friend. On 5 April James set out for London. Though he continued to speak broad Scots for the rest of his life, he was only once again to return to Scotland.

James thoroughly enjoyed the new life which now began for him. He liked the pomp and the luxury, the flattery of the obsequious English courtiers and the rich magnificence of the English Court. He liked the way the English did things. And, above all, he liked the Church of England with its abundance of bishops and its elaborate ritual.

As for the affairs of Scotland, he would ideally have favoured a union of the two Kingdoms as well as of the two Crowns and, whenever he could, used the name Great Britain to cover both, while the new joint flag bore the name of Union Jack. In 1607 the Estates, after due debate, passed an Act of Union. But in the end no treaty was signed. James's English subjects had no wish to merge their identity with that of their northern neighbours and viewed with abhorrence the idea of a joint Parliament. 'The Scots', said Sir Charles Piggott, Member of Parliament for Buckinghamshire, censoriously, 'have not suffered above two Kings to die in their beds these two hundred years.' And so the Union was rejected.

Henceforward James's orders went forth in writing from Whitehall to the Scottish Privy Council, and by them and by the Committee of Articles, who to all intents and purposes now controlled Parliament, were promptly carried out. 'This I must say for Scotland,' was his comment, 'here I sit and govern it with my pen. I write and it is done, and by a Clark of the Council I govern Scotland now, which others could not do by the sword.'

Not that James was opposed to the use of armed force against his compatriots when he considered it necessary. It was his ambition in particular to pacify the Highlands, where the old Celtic culture still persisted and the clans pursued their ancient feuds without much regard for what happened further south. This he sought to do largely by issuing Letters of Fire and Sword, which authorized one or more clans to deal with their erring neighbours in the manner they thought best – generally a very rough one. The method, it must be admitted, was not ineffective. Thus, orders came from London for the extirpation by their hereditary enemies of the notorious Clan Gregor, the destruction of their homes, and even the extinction of their name, which the remaining survivors of this operation were no longer allowed to bear. At the King's behest, too, the Macdonalds of Islay suffered frightful punishment, while his own cousin, Patrick Stewart of the Orkneys, or Earl Pate, as he was known, he had publicly hanged. Finally in 1608 Maclean of Duart and a number of chiefs of the other Island clans were invited on board one of the King's ships for the purpose of hearing a sermon, and then, by a characteristic stratagem, carried off and imprisoned. The following year, after they had been released on giving pledges of future good behaviour, they were summoned to a kind of peace conference under Andrew Knox, the able new Bishop of the Isles, and invited to sign a document entitled the Statutes of Iona. These were intended to discourage, amongst other things, begging, drinking and the use of firearms and also committed the signatories to reduce the numbers of their own entourage, to dispense as far as possible with the services of clan bards and to send their sons to be educated in the Lowlands. It also placed on a more regular footing relations between the chiefs and the Scottish Crown. The chiefs duly signed the document set before them and for a time things were quieter in the north-west. Henceforward, in particular, no more was heard of the claims of the Lords of the Isles to be independent sovereigns. The days when the Macdonalds could look to Westminster for support were past. James played the Macleans off cleverly against them and they now took their place among the other western clans as equals and not as overlords, and suffered, as did their neighbours, from the rapid rise to power of the Campbells of Argyll, who now emerged more and more as the agents of the central Government and the protectors of the Lowlands against the warlike clans of Lochaber and the west.

James also had a rod in pickle for the Presbyterians. For some years after 1603, the General Assembly was not allowed to meet. Then, in 1606, Andrew Melville, with seven other Ministers, was on some pretext summoned to England, rigorously interrogated, imprisoned for three years in the Tower of London and then forbidden ever again to return to Scotland.

Five Articles

Having thus removed the principal obstacle to his designs, James now increased the powers and numbers of the Scottish bishops. By 1610 there were eleven bishops and two archbishops, one of whom was John Spottiswoode. For the time being the King did not seek to interfere with the prevailing form of congregational worship, which was perhaps why the opposition to his religious policy was not more widespread. In 1617, however, he decided to take matters further still and himself set out for Scotland for the first time for fourteen years. The appearance in the Chapel Royal of Holyrood of carved heads of the Saints, of an organ – a 'Kist o' Whistles', as the disgusted citizens called it – and of surpliced choristers was not popular. Nor were the Five Articles which the King now sought to impose: that Holy Communion should be received kneeling; that the festivals of the Christian year should be observed; that confirmation should be administered by bishops and not by ministers; that private baptism and private Communion should be allowed in case of serious illness.

But James was determined to have his way. A General Assembly was summoned to meet in Perth in 1618 and the Five Articles pushed through. They met with widespread and vigorous opposition, and a systematic boycott throughout most of Scotland. Men would walk miles rather than take Communion in a 'kneeling' church. The dispute was to be a long drawn out one.

But James's life was now approaching its end. By 1624 he was mortally ill and the control of affairs had passed to the last of his male favourites, the Duke of Buckingham, and to his son Charles, who had become heir to the throne on the death of his elder brother Henry. In 1625 James died and Charles I began his ill-fated reign.

Charles I

Charles had been born a Scot and was accordingly regarded by his English subjects as a foreigner. But he had left Scotland when he was three and did not return there until 1633, the eighth year of his reign. He thus had but little understanding for Scottish affairs or Scottish opinion. Neither the Highlands nor the Lowlands, with their diverse and highly individual traditions and social systems, meant much to him. A devout Anglican and Episcopalian like his father, he disliked what he knew of the Kirk and of Presbyterians. He also shared his father's distrust of democratic assemblies, whether Scottish or English, and, like him, believed profoundly in the Divine Right of Kings, especially as applied to himself. He did not, however, possess his father's natural caution nor his statecraft. His chief duty towards Scotland, as he in all sincerity saw it, lay in bringing the Scottish Kirk into line with the Church of England. And this he now set out to do.

As a first step he decreed in 1625, by the Act of Revocation, the restoration to the Church of the Church lands and tithes which had been distributed among the nobles – the Lords of Erection, as they were called – at the time of the Reformation, his purpose being to make adequate provision for the maintenance of the Scottish clergy. This no doubt well-meaning measure earned him the distrust of the nobles without winning him the support of anybody else, and, even when a compromise solution was eventually arrived at, the early suspicions still lingered. An outright demand in 1629 that religious practice in Scotland should conform to the English model further alienated all sections of opinion in Scotland and further increased his unpopularity. Nor was this all.

In 1633 Charles came to Scotland to be crowned, accompanied by William Laud, his new Archbishop of Canterbury. The Coronation Service was held in St Giles's with candles, crucifix, genuflecting bishops and full Anglican rites. Edinburgh was made a bishopric with St Giles's for Cathedral. Archbishop John Spottiswoode was appointed the King's

Chancellor for Scotland. Ministers were advised to wear surplices. The General Assembly had not met since 1618 and presbyteries were now threatened with dissolution. Soon feelings were running high and the word 'Popery' was on men's lips.

It was in this atmosphere that the King and Laud raised the most explosive of all questions, that of the liturgy. They had by now begun to realize that the English Prayer Book, unaltered, could never be acceptable to the Scots and a Commission was accordingly appointed to draw up a Revised Prayer Book for Scotland, its purpose being to take the place of extempore prayer.

The new book was read for the first time in St Giles's on 23 July 1637 amid scenes of violence and disorder which soon developed into a regular riot, in which the female members of the congregation, egged on according to tradition by a certain Jenny Geddes, played a leading part. Before long the resulting disturbances had reached such a pitch that the Privy Council were obliged to shut themselves in Holyroodhouse to escape from the mob, while the Bishop of Brechin, for his part, found it advisable to conduct Divine Service with a pair of loaded pistols laid in front of him in full sight of the congregation. On receiving in London the Privy Council's report of what was happening, the King, who by now had many other no less serious cares and preoccupations and but little time to devote to Scottish affairs, simply sent back instructions that all who had protested against the Prayer Book should be punished and its regular use enforced.

In Edinburgh, meanwhile, opposition to the Prayer Book was becoming daily more formidable and better organized. During the autumn and winter of 1637 a committee was formed in Edinburgh known as the Tables. It included the Earls of Montrose and Rothes, Lord Warriston, an eminent lawyer, some influential ministers, in particular Alexander Henderson of Leuchars, and numerous other notabilities, both clerics and laymen. Known to be in sympathy with them were Lord Lorne, heir to the Earl of Argyll, and Sir Thomas Hope, both Privy Councillors.

But the King, oblivious as usual of the strength and fervour of the opposition he had aroused and as usual out of touch with opinion in Scotland, persisted stubbornly in the course on which he had embarked. To the petitions against the Prayer Book now coming in from all over the country, backed by men of the utmost weight and substance, he responded by sending orders that the petitioners should be dispersed and punished. Finally in February 1638, before leaving for Newmarket to hunt, he issued from London a proclamation, to be read in public in Edinburgh and other cities, summoning the nobles who had resisted the Prayer Book to submit to the King's will and conform.

The National Covenant

This brought matters to a head. There were angry demonstrations at the Mercat Cross. The Tables recalled the Lords of Congregation, and on 28 February and the two days that followed several hundred representatives of the nobles, the gentry, the burghs and the clergy flocked to Greyfriars Kirk in Edinburgh to sign a document which had been drawn up by Lord Warriston, Alexander Henderson and others, and which was to be known as the National Covenant. 'The great Marriage Day', Warriston called it, 'of this Nation with God.'

The Covenant was a skilfully drawn-up document, calculated to attract the maximum of support. It incorporated the Negative Confession of 1581, which specifically condemned a number of characteristic Catholic doctrines, and also appended a whole catalogue of Acts confirming it. It showed how these had been contravened by the latest 'inovations' and protested against their violation. And it ended with a pledge on the part of the signatories to maintain 'the true religion' and, it may be observed, 'His Majesty's authority'. For the leaders of the movement did not want, at this stage at any rate, to come out openly against the King, but only to convey to all and sundry the impression that he was badly advised.

Soon mounted messengers were carrying copies of the Covenant all over the Lowlands and thousands of signatures were being collected. The countryside was in a ferment. National feeling was deeply aroused. In the eyes of many the Covenant possessed more than purely theological significance. It was also a defence 'against our poor country being made an English Province'. And so opposition to the Covenant was vigorously discouraged and ministers who refused to read it from the pulpits were in due course deposed.

During the summer of 1638 contact of a kind continued between London and Edinburgh. But Charles suffered, as he was bound to, from being an absentee sovereign and his Commissioner, the Duke of Hamilton, an unpopular figure at the best of times, carried but little weight. Already the Tables had become the *de facto* government of Scotland.

The King, now thoroughly alarmed, had already told his English Privy Council in July that he would have to use force. In order to gain time, however, he now agreed to a meeting of the General Assembly in Glasgow. This was called for November 1638, and at once got down to business. The Assembly knew its own mind. All bishops were deposed or excommunicated, the Prayer Book, roundly condemned as 'heathenish, Popish, Jewish and Arminian', was abolished and a Commission set up to investigate abuses. To this the King simply replied that none of the Assembly's decisions were valid because they had been reached in the absence of his Commissioner, who had walked out at an early stage in the proceedings. An open breach was now inevitable.

Meanwhile, in Scotland enthusiasm for the Covenant was growing. In the east this was largely inspired by the young James Graham, fifth Earl of Montrose, whose influence extended through Stirlingshire, southern Perthshire, parts of Angus and even into Aberdeen, where Episcopalianism and resistance to the Covenant were most deep-seated. In the west, the Covenant's chief supporter was Archibald Campbell, eighth Earl of Argyll, the powerful Chief of Clan Campbell, a convinced Calvinist, deeply distrustful of the King.

All that summer arms had been coming into Scotland from abroad and Scottish soldiers serving overseas had been returning to their own country 'in gryte numbers upone hope of bloodie war'. In Alexander Leslie, the 'old, little, crooked soldier' who had fought against Wallenstein in Germany and eventually succeeded Gustavus Adolphus in command of the Swedish Army, the Covenanters had an outstanding and experienced general. The King, for his part, was in a less favourable position. He had an inefficient administration, no standing army and no general worthy of the name.

In the early summer of 1639, however, Charles, having somehow assembled a poorly trained force of some twenty thousand men, moved to the Border. At Berwick he came face to face with a far better trained, better disciplined and above all better commanded force under Sandy Leslie. Neither side wanted to fight and the First Bishops' War, as it was called, was eventually brought to an end by the so-called Pacification of Berwick, under which the King agreed that all disputed questions should be referred to another General Assembly or to Parliament.

The new General Assembly's first move was at once to re-enact all the measures passed by the Glasgow Assembly. Parliament, when it met, went further still, defying the King and his Commissioner, abolishing episcopacy and ultimately freeing itself from royal control. In particular, steps were taken to ensure that the Committee of Articles, by which the King had long controlled Parliament, should cease to be a mere tool of the Sovereign.

A Second Bishops' War followed speedily. This time the Scots under Leslie and Montrose crossed the border and quickly captured the important English cities of Newcastle and Durham. Once again the King, whose disorderly rabble had melted away before the Scottish onslaught, was obliged to negotiate. For this purpose and also in order to raise funds, he found it necessary to summon his English Parliament, something which, to all intents and purposes, had not been done for more than ten years. It was to prove a fateful step. For the Parliament which at his behest now assembled in Westminster was to be the famous Long Parliament.

By summoning Parliament Charles gave his English enemies the chance for which they had long been waiting. The King's Government at once came under severe attack and his chief supporters, Strafford and Laud, were impeached and in due course executed. Civil war threatened.

It was now the autumn of 1641. In the hope of winning Scottish support Charles came to Scotland, where he distributed a number of titles, making Leslie Earl of Leven and promoting Argyll to Marquess, and as part of a package deal, accepted all the decisions of the General Assembly of 1638 as well as those of the Scottish Parliament of 1641. Finally he formally gave Parliament the right, of which it had long been making full use, to challenge the actions of his ministers.

Civil War

Events were by now fast reaching a climax and in August 1642 came the news that civil war had actually broken out in England between the

King's forces and those of Parliament. The Scots at first held aloof. The principal purpose of the Covenanters was not political but theological. They were concerned to secure the suppression of episcopacy and the establishment of presbytery, not only in Scotland, but in England and Ireland as well. And they were prepared to give their support to whichever party promised them this. They were also far from agreeing amongst themselves.

In the Kirk, meanwhile, extremist tendencies were gaining the upper hand. To read passages from the Bible at funerals 'bred', it was now held, 'debosherie'. To repeat the Lord's Prayer in public was a sign of Popery. To take cognizance of Christmas or Easter was a special abomination. At the same time it began to appear to Montrose and others that the newly created Marquess of Argyll was exploiting the situation to further his personal interests and consolidate his personal power. Montrose, while remaining a Presbyterian and an upholder of the Covenant, accordingly now took his place at the head of the Moderates and with some of his supporters signed a pact at Cumbernauld, reaffirming both his belief in the Covenant and also his loyalty to the King.

In England, meanwhile, one Royalist victory had followed another until, in the summer of 1643, the Parliamentary leaders, facing defeat, decided in their turn to go to Scotland for help. The English Parliament had one considerable inducement to offer the Scottish Covenanters. While on the whole satisfied with the state of religion in Scotland, the latter had the gravest doubts about the religious practices of their English and Irish neighbours. Moreover, although they had deeply resented the King's attempts to bring Scottish religious practice into line with that of England, they saw nothing wrong in seeking to reverse the process. Negotiations were accordingly opened and in the autumn of 1643 an agreement known as the Solemn League and Covenant was signed by representatives of the Scottish Covenanters and of what was left of the English Parliament. Under the terms of this strange document the Covenanters undertook to attack the Royalist forces from the north – this in return for the sum of £30,000 a month and an undertaking that there would be 'a reformation of religion in the Kingdoms of England and Ireland in doctrine, worship, discipline and government, according to the Word of God and the examples of the best reformed churches, and that popery and prelacy should be extirpated'. In the eyes of the Scottish signatories there was no necessity further to define the phrase 'the best reformed churches'. It could only mean one thing.

The English now set out to fulfil their part of the bargain by summoning the Westminster Assembly. This was a mixed body of clergy and laymen, including eight Scottish delegates, and was entrusted with the exacting task of establishing uniformity of worship in Scotland, England and Ireland. Ironically enough, this predominantly English body, while leaving but little trace of its deliberations in England or Ireland, was to have a lasting influence on Scottish religious thought and practice. To this day the Westminster Confession of Faith serves as the basis for Presbyterian worship in Scotland. It is also interesting to recall that the original version of the metrical psalms, which have since played so large a part in Scottish life, also came from England, having been produced by the then Provost of Eton, a Cornish Member of Parliament named Francis Rous.

For Charles the conclusion of the Solemn League and Covenant meant serious trouble. Early in 1644 a Scottish force of 26,000 men crossed the Tweed under the command of David Leslie, a distant kinsman of Alexander's. And in the following July, largely thanks to Scottish help, the Parliamentary forces, now re-organized under Oliver Cromwell, were able to inflict a heavy defeat on the Royalists at Marston Moor in Yorkshire.

At this critical juncture, however, the King gained a new ally. For some time past Montrose had been finding himself less and less in sympathy with his fellow Covenanters – least of all with Argyll. Making his way to the Highlands, he proceeded in the summer of 1644 to raise a force which consisted mainly of Highlanders, but also included a contingent of mercenaries and Scottish expatriates from Ireland and a few Royalist lairds from the Lowlands. At the head of this oddly assorted army, with no artillery and very little cavalry, he set out to win Scotland for the King, who in return made him a marquess.

Advancing in September on Perth, he utterly defeated a much larger force of Covenanters under Lord Elcho at Tippermuir and captured the city. Lord Elcho's troops, who had been assured that the Holy Ghost had promised them victory and advanced into battle to the incongruous cry of 'Jesus and no quarter', now fled in confusion. A couple of weeks later Montrose entered Aberdeen, a rich prey for the hungry Highlanders, who on this occasion seem to have conducted themselves with less than their usual chivalry, while the Irish contingent murdered and looted with characteristic gusto. He next turned westwards through the hills into Campbell country, and, with the ready help of the Macleans and the Macdonalds, always glad of an opportunity to pay off old scores and ready to sink their own differences in such a good cause, swooped on Argyll's stronghold of Inveraray, burning it to the ground and causing its noble occupant to rise abruptly from his dinner-table and take refuge in a boat in the middle of Loch Fyne. In February 1645 Montrose won yet another victory at Inverlochy, when, after an arduous march through the snowy hills, he once more routed the Campbells and their Covenanting allies and again forced their Chief to leave his followers to their fate and make off by boat. 'I have traversed all the north of Scotland up to Argyle's country,' he wrote to Charles next day, 'who durst not stay my coming, or I should have given your Majesty a good account of him ere now. But at last I have met with him, yesterday, to his cost .... I departed out of Argyleshire, and marched through Lorn, Glencow and Lochaber, till I came to Loch Ness, my design being to fall upon Argyle before Seaforth and the Frasers could join him. My march was through inaccessible mountains .... I was willing to let the world see that Argyle was not the man his Highlandmen believed him to be, and that it was possible to beat him in his own Highlands.' Continuing his triumphant progress, Montrose went on in March to storm the walled city of Dundee; in May he smashed the Covenanters at Auldearn near the Moray Firth; in July he routed them at Alford outside Aberdeen; finally in August he again defeated them at Kilsyth and occupied Glasgow.

Montrose and his Highland allies had covered themselves with military glory. But they had so far failed to win the support of the Lowlands or for that matter to relieve Cromwell's pressure on the King's forces in England. In June 1645, at the height of Montrose's victorious progress through Scotland, the Royalist forces in England had suffered a disastrous defeat at Naseby. In September David Leslie, returning from England with a Covenanting force of four thousand seasoned troops, surprised, out-generalled and heavily defeated Montrose at Philiphaugh.

It was Montrose's first defeat. During the months that followed he still hoped to restore the King's fortunes in Scotland. Then in May 1646 came the news that Charles had surrendered to the Scottish army at Newark in England and that it had been made a condition of his surrender that Montrose should disband his followers and leave Scotland. Disillusioned and depressed, he took ship to Norway.

The Scots in England now found themselves in some perplexity. Their primary purpose in signing the Solemn League and Covenant with the English Parliament had been to secure England's conversion to Presbyterianism. They were only indirectly concerned with the quarrel between King and Parliament.

But it was growing ever clearer that, despite the Solemn League and Covenant and despite the deliberations of the Westminster Assembly, the establishment of Presbyterianism in England was becoming an increasingly remote possibility. Power in England was passing more and more into the hands of the Army and of its master, Oliver Cromwell. And neither Cromwell nor his Army were at all interested in turning England Presbyterian. Nor, despite the valuable services they had rendered, had the Scots received the monthly payments due to them under the agreement. Had the King declared his readiness to establish the Presbyterian religion in England, they would have been prepared at this stage to change sides and fight for him. But this the King declined to do. And so in return for a promise of £400,000, they handed him over to the English Parliamentary Commissioners and went back to Scotland. 'Traitor Scot', jeered the English, 'sold his King for a groat.' But the Covenanters, for their part, indignantly rejected the suggestion that they had behaved in any way dishonourably.

No sooner had the Scots handed over King Charles, than they began, rather characteristically, to have doubts about the wisdom of their action. They wondered, in particular, whether the English Parliament might not now seek to diminish the King's authority and whether things might not after all have been better otherwise. They accordingly sent secret emissaries, among them the wily Earl of Lauderdale, to resume contact with Charles, now more or less a prisoner in the Isle of Wight, and also to sound him out once again about the topic that was ever uppermost in their minds.

The result of these soundings was an agreement, arrived at towards the end of 1647 between the King and the representatives of the Scottish Parliament and styled the Engagement, under which the Scottish signatories, who became known as the Engagers, undertook to send an army to England to support the King in return for a promise from the latter to give Presbyterianism a three years' trial in England.

And indeed in the summer of 1648 a Scottish army, commanded by the Duke of Hamilton, actually set out for England to restore the King's position. It reached Preston in Lancashire, where it was heavily defeated by Cromwell and Hamilton himself captured and executed. What remained of the army surrendered, without having done anything to improve its own or the King's position.

Charles Executed

The Engagement had always been strongly opposed by the more extreme Covenanters, the anti-Engagers or Whigs, as they were known. Taking the disaster of Preston as their cue, they now marched on Edinburgh from the south-west, where their strength lay, and overthrew the Government. This left their leader Argyll to all intents and purposes master of Scotland. Under Argyll's auspices, Cromwell now came to Edinburgh and there received a hero's welcome. Before leaving, he let it be known that he did not wish anyone who had fought for King Charles to hold any office in Scotland. In January the Scottish Parliament obediently gave effect to his wishes by passing a measure known as the Act of Classes. A few days later news reached Scotland that the King had been executed in Whitehall.

The news of the King's execution by the English was received in Scotland with dismay. Even Argyll is said to have been disturbed by it and Montrose, when he heard of it in exile in Brussels, fainted from the shock. To all sections of opinion, even those most strongly opposed to Charles's policies, it seemed unbecoming that Scotland, through English action, should be left without a king. Accordingly Argyll now established contact with the dead King's eighteen-year-old heir, Prince Charles, and, as a first step, had him proclaimed King in Edinburgh.

Montrose meanwhile had also offered the new King his services and had received from him the assignment of invading on his behalf the north of Scotland. The enterprise was ill-fated from the outset. Crossing to Orkney and thence to Thurso, Montrose assembled a mixed force of foreign mercenaries, Orcadians and local recruits. This was easily dispersed at Carbisdale in Ross-shire and Montrose himself handed over to his enemies by Macleod of Assynt, 'ane of his auld acquentance', who was awarded for this service £25,000 Scots. An eyewitness from the enemy camp, the Reverend James Fraser, later chaplain to the Covenanting Lord Lovat, has described how he was brought to Beauly as a prisoner, 'upon a little shelty horse, his feet fastened under the horse's belly with a tether and a bit halter for a bridle …. Yet, with a majesty and a state becoming him, kept his countenance high.'

At the instance of Argyll Montrose was now taken to Edinburgh, put on trial as a traitor to the King he had served so loyally, and in May 1649 hanged and quartered. He met his unpleasant fate with a calm dignity which won the respect even of the Edinburgh mob who had flocked in their thousands to watch him die. 'I never saw', wrote an Englishman in the crowd, 'a more sweeter carriage in a man in my life. I should write more largely if I had time: but he is just now a turning off from the ladder; but his countenance changes not.' Of Argyll it is recorded that, as the cart bearing Montrose approached his house, he turned away from the balcony on which he had been standing and went indoors.

With Montrose gone, Charles II became entirely dependent on Argyll and bound, if he wanted to come to Scotland as King, to comply with the latter's wishes. The strongest pressure was brought to bear and in the end the young man agreed, though doubtless with certain mental reservations, to accept both Covenants and in the summer of 1650 arrived in Scotland to claim his Kingdom.

Cromwell's answer was at once to invade Scotland. At Dunbar he out manœuvred and utterly routed a Scottish army under his former ally, General David Leslie. 'The Lord', was his pious comment when he saw the relative positions of the two forces, 'hath delivered them into our hands.' He then occupied Edinburgh.

But Cromwell's failure to fulfil the terms of the Solemn League and Covenant still rankled and the Covenanters were still reluctant to deal with him. Even now they would not admit defeat. On New Year's Day 1651 Charles II was crowned King by Argyll at Scone and, in spite of opposition from the more extreme Covenanters, the Act of Classes was formally repealed. Men who had fought for Charles I were now no longer debarred from fighting for his son and by the summer of 1651 David Leslie had assembled a sizeable army with which to guard the approaches to Stirling.

But again disaster overtook the Scots. At Inverkeithing, near North Queensferry, a Scottish force composed of both Highlanders and Lowlanders, thrown in to check Cromwell's progress northwards, found themselves heavily outnumbered by an English army under General Lambert. The bulk of the Lowland cavalry under Holborn of Menstrie turned and fled. The Highlanders, mainly Macleans, stood and fought. Of eight hundred Maclean clansmen who took the field under Hector Maclean of Duart, seven hundred and sixty were killed, including Duart himself and two of the sons of Maclean of Ardgour. 'Another for Hector' the clansmen are said to have cried as they died beside their Chief. It was rumoured afterwards that Argyll, for reasons of his own, had ensured that no reinforcements should reach them. However this may be, the way was now open to Cromwell, who marched on Perth and soon controlled the country both to the north and to the south of the Forth.

Battle of Worcester

Outmanœuvred in Scotland, Leslie and his main force next crossed the Border into England in the hope of winning more support there. It was a bold move, but it failed. Leaving General Monck to deal with Scotland, Cromwell himself followed the Scottish army into England, picking up reinforcements on the way. On 3 September 1651 the two armies met at Worcester and there, on the banks of the Severn, the third army the Scots had raised in as many years was heavily defeated and driven to surrender. 'The Crowning Mercy', Cromwell called it.

Among the few who eluded capture was King Charles himself, who, after various adventures, managed to make his way to the Continent, and now, in his own words 'went on his travels'. A few days earlier Monck's troops had captured the Committee of the Estates, which was all that was left of the Scottish Parliament, and had also stormed the rich city of Dundee. Scottish resistance was to all intents and purposes at an end.

CHAPTER FIVE

'ANE END OF
ANE AULD SANG'

Cromwell, now Lord Protector, spent the next year or so in stamping out such vestiges of resistance as remained and setting up in Scotland an efficient system of military government with English garrisons in the principal towns and strongpoints. Even the Highlands were temporarily subdued. In due course Scotland was formally united with England by a Treaty of Union and became part of Cromwell's Commonwealth. There were no further meetings of the Scottish Parliament, but thirty Scottish Members were sent to represent Scotland in the Commons at Westminster. In return for the loss of their independence the Scots received certain economic benefits. 'As for the embodying of Scotland with England,' wrote Robert Blair, 'it will be as when the poor bird is embodied with the hawk that hath eaten it up.'

The resulting regime was probably the most efficient and orderly the country had ever experienced. 'A man', it was claimed, 'could ride all over Scotland with a switch in his hand and £100 in his pocket, which he could not have done these 500 years.' It was also, like so many efficient regimes, deeply unpopular. The English, oddly enough, were unable to understand the reasons for their own unpopularity. 'Soe senceless', wrote one of them, 'are this generation of theire owne goode that scarce a man of them showed any sign of rejoycing.'

Restoration

Prominent among the few Scots who came to terms with Cromwell was Argyll, 'that political lord', who, despite his support of Charles II in 1649, managed, with characteristic flexibility, to make himself acceptable to his successors. His luck changed, however, when in 1660, after Cromwell's death and the collapse of the Protectorate in England, Charles at General Monck's behest returned from exile and resumed his throne. Then, like his enemy Montrose a dozen years earlier, Argyll in his turn was, to his pained surprise, arraigned for treason and duly executed, though in a less barbarous manner than his rival. He, too, to give him his due, met his end with dignity and composure. 'I set the crown on the King's head,' he said. 'He hastens me now to a better crown than his.' After his execution his severed head was set on the same spike in the Tolbooth from which Montrose's had only lately been removed.

Charles II, for his part, was never again to visit Scotland. For the next twenty-five years, like his father and grandfather before him, he governed his northern kingdom through a Privy Council situated in Edinburgh and a Secretary based in London. The latter appointment was, for a start, entrusted to the Earl (later Duke) of Lauderdale, who in the last reign had been a dedicated Covenanter, but had since come to hold other views. For most of Charles's reign, as Secretary and later as Commissioner, it was he who governed Scotland.

Charles, who considered that 'Presbytery was not a religion for gentlemen' and had only signed the two Covenants in 1649 in order to secure his own coronation, had no intention of carrying out the political and religious obligations he had at that time undertaken or, for that matter, those undertaken by his father before him. He chose his Privy Council and his Officers of State without reference to Parliament, and the Scottish Parliament, when it met in 1661, was packed with reliable Royalists who lost no time in rescinding most of the measures passed since 1633. This meant, first and foremost, the restoration of James VI's method of himself choosing the Committee of Articles, which further greatly strengthened the King's position in relation to Parliament. It also had the effect, as far as the Church was concerned, of bringing back bishops and restoring the former system of patronage, under which ministers were chosen by the

20

21

22

20 John Knox preaching to the Lords of the Congregation, sponsors of the First Covenant, 10 of June 1559. They pledged to break with Rome and establish a reformed national Church.

21 George Wishart, Knox's mentor, burned at the stake in 1546.

22 John Knox's formidable personality and fierce eloquence laid the foundation for the triumph of Protestantism in Scotland – and, in turn, to closer ties with England in place of the Auld Alliance with Catholic France.

23

24

23 David Riccio, the Queen's Italian
secretary and favourite, was murdered
in her presence by her jealous, newly-wed
husband Darnley and a band of armed
men in 1565. Within two years Darnley
was strangled and Mary remarried.
Oil painting by Sir William Allan, 1833.

24 Mary Queen of Scots, in mourning
for her father-in-law Henri II of France,
two years before she arrived in Scotland.
Young, beautiful and impulsive,
she made a rash first marriage and a
disastrous second. Portrait by François
Clouet, *c.* 1559.

25

25 James VI of Scotland, I of England.
Portrait dated 1610, school of Marcus
Gheeraerts the Younger.

The high &
mighty Monarch:
CHARLES by ye grace
of GOD king of Great
Brittaine France &
Ireland Defendor of
the Fayth. etc.

EDYNBURGH

26

26 Charles I depicted on his first visit to
Edinburgh in 1633. He was crowned in
St Giles's with full Anglican rites, and
soon the word 'Popery' was on men's lips.

The Arch-Prelate of St Andrewes in Scotland reading the new Service-booke in his pontificalibus assaulted by men & women, with Cricketts stooles Stickes and Stones.

27

28

27 An etching by Wenceslaus Hollar shows a riot caused by the Revised Prayer Book for Scotland, read for the first time in St Giles's in 1637: the air is thick with flying missiles as the 'Arch-Prelate', in full canonicals, reads from the loathed book. Scotland was not to be reconciled to Anglican ways without a fight.

28 In summer 1643 the Parliamentary leaders turned to Scotland for help in the Civil War. The price: £30,000 a month and a Solemn League and Covenant to establish uniformity of worship in the three Kingdoms of England, Scotland and Ireland, according to the examples of 'the best reformed churches'.

29

30

29 Map of 'The Isthmus of Darian' (sic), or New Caledonia, which Scotland tried to colonize between 1698 and 1700. The scheme lost 2,000 lives and £300,000.

30 The Duke of Queensberry, on behalf of Scotland, presenting the Treaty of Union to Queen Anne in 1707.

31 The execution of the Earl of Derwentwater and Viscount Kenmure on Tower Hill in 1716. Many Jacobite leaders lost all in Prince James's cause.

32 Toasting glass,18th century, for drinking to 'the King over the water'.

33 Prince Charles takes leave of Antoine Walsh, who had conveyed him from Eriskay to Moidart in 1745.

31

32

33

34

34 This old cottage, on the battlefield, is the only building to survive the Battle of Culloden, where Prince Charles was decisively defeated in 1746.

35 William Augustus, Duke of Cumberland, who led the the English army at Culloden and oversaw the brutal reprisals visited on the Scots. Portrait by Sir Joshua Reynolds.

35

laird and not by the congregation. As for James Sharp, a Covenanting minister, who had been sent to London from Scotland to make representations at Court as the emissary of the moderate Presbyterians, he came back Archbishop of St Andrews and professing entirely different opinions from those with which he had set out.

The Covenanters

Under the new regulations, ministers appointed since 1649 were required to resign their charges and receive them again from their bishops and patrons. No significant changes were made in doctrine or in the order of worship and most ministers in the end agreed to the new procedure. But some three hundred, or about a third of the total number, refused to do so and left their manses and their churches rather than submit. What is more, they had, particularly in the south-west, the support of their parishioners, people of no great account, maybe, but of great steadfastness. And before long unauthorized religious services were being held in many areas by these 'outed ministers' in houses and barns and on the bare hillside.

As time went on, the Privy Council reacted with increasing severity to this open defiance of the law, while the former Covenanter Lauderdale, for his part, wished that there might be a regular rebellion, 'that so I might bring over an army of Irish Papists to cut all their throats'. Troops were sent to collect fines from those attending illegal conventicles, and armed clashes ensued. But this did not dismay the Covenanters who, as good Calvinists, knew that they were predestined to grace and so were the more eager to die for their faith. In spite of the savage punishments inflicted on them, their resistance continued unabated and as often as not they gave the Government forces as good as they got. Thus in 1679 the promising career of the unfortunate Archbishop Sharp was brought to an end when he was dragged from his coach and brutally murdered by a party of Covenanters who claimed that they had 'received a call from God to put him to death', while not long after three troops of Government horse under Graham of Claverhouse were utterly routed by a rabble of armed Covenanters.

The Government now reacted more vigorously than ever. A strong force under the King's illegitimate son, James Duke of Monmouth, was sent to deal with the rebels and at Bothwell Brig the Covenanters were heavily defeated and fourteen hundred prisoners herded into Greyfriars churchyard in Edinburgh to await their various unpleasant ends. But the resistance of the Covenanters continued as stubborn as ever, while the Government's measures of repression grew increasingly severe. At the market cross in Sanquhar the preacher Richard Cameron publicly called his followers to armed insurrection against the King and his Government. He and those who listened to him met with the fate that was to be expected. It was not for nothing that the 1680's became known as the Killing Time.

James VII

In 1685 Charles II died and was succeeded by his brother James VII, who towards the end of Charles's reign, during the Killing Time, had, as Duke of York, briefly acted as Royal Commissioner in Scotland. He was popular neither in the Lowlands of Scotland nor in England. For the first time for nearly a hundred and twenty years Scotland had a Roman Catholic monarch and his subjects, both in Scotland and England, not unnaturally suspected him of wanting to establish his own religion throughout his dominions. Nor, in that age of intolerance, did he in any way endear himself to most of them by using the royal prerogative to accord complete toleration to all his subjects, Roman Catholics, Covenanters and Quakers alike. Under Charles, opposition to the King's policy had been largely local and had come in the main from the lower orders. Under James it was more broadly based. It was also actively encouraged from Holland by James's Dutch son-in-law, William of Orange, a devious, unscrupulous man, who himself had designs on his father-in-law's throne. Attempted insurrections, under Argyll in Scotland and Monmouth in England, were unsuccessful, but in November 1688, at the invitation of the Whig leaders, William of Orange landed in England with an army. James, after much vacillation, fled to France and in February 1689 his son-in-law William and daughter Mary were proclaimed King and Queen of England and Ireland. In Scotland a Convention of Estates, which had been summoned after various preliminary soundings to decide what should be done, showed a majority for William and Mary and in April 1689 they were accordingly also proclaimed King and Queen of Scotland. As at the Restoration so now Scotland had simply followed England's example.

Dutch William

There were those, however, in the Highlands who still remained true to their legitimate monarch, greatly preferring him to a Dutch usurper. They were known as Jacobites. When William was proclaimed King, Graham of Claver house, now Viscount Dundee, rode north to raise the loyal clans for King James who had himself now landed in Ireland. A body of troops under General Hugh Mackay was sent by William to put down the Highland Jacobites. At sundown on 27 July 1689, at the head of the narrow gorge of Killiecrankie in Perthshire, the Highlanders fell upon William's soldiers 'like madmen' and almost annihilated them. But Dundee himself was killed in the battle and his troops were left without a leader. And so, after another savage encounter with the Government troops in the churchyard at Dunkeld, in which the dour followers of Richard Cameron, now formed into a regiment and known as the Cameronians, distinguished themselves by the doggedness of their defence, the Highlanders in the end faded ineffectually back into their hills and glens and left the field to their enemies. A fresh Jacobite attempt in the spring ended in disaster at Cromdale on Speyside and six weeks later the Battle of the Boyne put an end to James's Irish campaign and caused him finally to withdraw to France.

Despite the setbacks suffered by the Jacobites, Dutch William's Government and in particular his Secretary of State, Sir John Dalrymple, the Master of Stair, were still uneasy about the Highlands and sought anxiously for a means of enforcing their will there. As a first step they sent General Mackay to build and garrison a strongpoint near Inverlochy to be named Fort William. At the same time the sum of £12,000 was entrusted to Iain Glas or Grey John, the Campbell Earl of Breadalbane, an equivocal figure of doubtful loyalty to anyone – 'cunning as a fox, slippery as an eel', was the verdict of a contemporary. This money was to be distributed among the chiefs in the hope of making them loyal to William. Some accepted the bribe; others refused it. But none became any more loyal to William than they had been before.

The Government now decided to adopt other tactics. They were characteristic of the personalities involved. 'There never was trouble brewing in Scotland,' Charles II had once said, 'but that a Dalrymple or a Campbell was at the bottom of it.' This time the honours were shared between them.

I think,' wrote Stair to Breadalbane, 'the Clan Donell must be rooted out and Lochiel. Leave the McLeans to Argyll .... God knows whether the £12,000 sterling had been better employed to settle the Highlands or to ravage them: but since we will make them desperate, I think we should root them out before they can get the help they depend upon.' 'Look on', he wrote to the same correspondent next day, 'and you shall be gratified of your revenge.' Seldom has the hereditary hatred of the Lowlander for the Highlander – *mirun mor nan Gall* – found more vigorous expression.

The Government now issued a proclamation ordering the chiefs of the various clans to take the oath of allegiance to King William not later than 1 January 1692. Failing this, recourse would be had to fire and sword. The time of year was carefully chosen. 'The winter time', wrote Stair, 'is the only season in which we are sure the Highlanders cannot escape, and carry their wives, bairns and cattle to the hills .... This is the proper time to maul them in the long dark nights.'

But the mauling was not to be on the scale that the Master had hoped for. From his exile in France King James at the last moment authorized the chiefs to swear allegiance to his Dutch son-in-law. Stair was sadly disappointed. By the appointed date only two chiefs had failed to take the oath, the powerful MacDonell of Glengarry and the elderly chieftain of a minor, but notoriously turbulent, sept of the MacDonalds, Maclan MacDonald of Glencoe. The latter, partly from dilatoriness and partly through the inclemency of the weather, arrived three days late in Inveraray, the seat of the Sheriff-depute, where, owing to the absence of that officer, he was only able to take the oath on 6 January.

This gave William the opportunity for which he and his advisers were looking. At the instance of his Secretary of State, he allowed the powerful Glengarry another chance. Maclan he picked as his victim. 'If Maclan of Glencoe and that tribe', he wrote to the General commanding his troops in the Highlands, 'can be well separated from the rest, it will be a proper vindication of public justice to extirpate that sect of thieves.'

Massacre of Glencoe

And so a company of trustworthy Campbell troops, from the Earl of Argyll's Regiment of Foot, commanded, as it happened, by a relative by marriage of MacIan's, Captain Robert Campbell of Glenlyon, were sent to Glencoe and billeted in the cottages of the clansmen. The MacDonalds received them hospitably. Captain Campbell spent a couple of weeks drinking and playing cards with MacIan and his sons, while his soldiers fraternized with the clansmen. Then, on 12 February, he received from his military superior, Major Duncanson, the following instructions: 'You are hereby ordered to fall upon the McDonalds of Glencoe and put all to the sword under seventy; you are to have a special care that the old fox and his sons doe on no account escape your hands.'

That night Robert Campbell and two of his officers accepted an invitation to dine with MacIan. Meanwhile a force of four hundred Government troops moved to block the northern approach to the glen and four hundred more to close the southern. At five in the morning of 13 February Glenlyon and his troops started to carry out their instructions. Parties of soldiers went from cottage to cottage, slaughtering the sleeping MacDonalds and setting light to their houses. MacIan himself was shot by one of his guests of the night before. A Campbell soldier gnawed the rings from Lady Glencoe's fingers with his teeth. A child of six, who clung, begging for mercy, to Glenlyon's knees, was promptly dispatched. As the massacre proceeded, snow began to fall. Some of the inhabitants of the glen were able to escape in the confusion. Others died in the snow.

King William and Stair had succeeded in their object, which was to make an example of a Jacobite clan and establish a measure of control over the Highlands. But, in spite of their efforts to hush things up, the affair gave rise to unfavourable comment, not only in the Highlands, but in the Lowlands and even in England, and in the end William was forced to dispense with the services of his Secretary of State. In due course, however, Stair was rewarded with an earldom, while Campbell of Glenlyon was promoted to colonel. King William, for his part, despite documentary evidence to the contrary, loftily disclaimed any previous knowledge of the affair.

In Church matters, too, the new King, though reassuringly Protestant, found himself confronted with a number of problems. Most Scottish Episcopalians were opposed to him on dynastic grounds, while many Presbyterians suspected him of being half-hearted in his attitude towards 'prelacy'. A settlement had finally been reached in 1690 under which bishops and patronage were abolished, the Westminster Confession re-adopted, Episcopalian ministers driven out and the Presbyterian system re-established in its entirety. But William's not unreasonable plan for a wider and more comprehensive solution was doomed to failure.

Nor did William's reign do much in other ways to improve feeling between Scotland and England. The massacre of Glencoe, while doubt-less winning him the admiration of the Whigs, had sullied his reputation in the Highlands. Soon disillusionment with the Dutch monarch and his London-based advisers was to spread to the commercially minded Lowlands as well. And for very good reason.

Under the English Navigation Act, goods could only be imported into English ports in English ships or in ships belonging to their country of origin. This was a serious obstacle to the expansion of Scottish overseas trade. So were the virtual monopolies established by the English East India and Africa Companies. At every turn the Scottish trader found his way blocked by privileged English competitors.

The Darien Scheme

In June 1695 a project was launched, designed to redress the balance and give Scottish merchants a better chance. At the instance of an enterpris-ing operator from Dumfriesshire named William Paterson, who amongst other things had helped to found the Bank of England and to give North London its efficient new water supply, an Act was passed by the Scottish Parliament establishing The Company of Scotland Trading to Africa and the Indies. The capital of the new Company was to be £600,000 of which half was to be subscribed in Scotland and the rest in England and elsewhere. And one of its first aims was to gain control of what Paterson called 'the Door of the Seas, the Key of the Universe', namely the narrow isthmus of Darien, linking North and South America. Here goods for India could be transhipped and replaced by goods from India, and the long journey round the Cape of Good Hope or Cape Horn thus avoided. It would also give Scotland something she had lacked since Charles I had sold Nova Scotia to the French within a dozen years of its foundation, namely a colony of her own.

The necessary £300,000 had soon been subscribed in London and good progress was being made when it became known that King William personally disapproved of the project. At this stage the English subscribers hastily with drew and Paterson was left to find the balance of his capital elsewhere. He turned to Holland and Hamburg; but here too William brought pressure to bear. In the end the scheme was launched with a capital of some £400,000, almost entirely subscribed in Scotland and representing a high proportion of the nation's cash resources. And in July 1698 Paterson and three ships with 1,200 emigrants on board set sail from the Port of Leith for Darien, or New Caledonia, as the proposed colony was to be called. The colonists carried with them a cargo including 4,000 periwigs, some bob wigs and blue bonnets and a great many Bibles, as well as large quantities of serge, huckabacks and gridirons. They seem to have had no knowledge of the climate of the Isthmus or of its malarial marshes. Nor do they appear to have realized that it belonged in fact to the King of Spain, with whom King William was at this moment seeking to conclude an alliance.

Paterson and his party reached Darien in November. Without waiting to hear how the first expedition had fared, a second and then a third group of settlers set out. By the summer of 1699 pestilence had killed a quarter of the members of the original expedition. The remainder, as a result of inadequate provisioning, faced starvation. On appealing to the English colony of Jamaica for provisions, they were told that King William had expressly forbidden his colonial officials to help them in any way. There were rumours, too, of an impending Spanish attack. No trade had been done at all. In July 1699 Paterson himself and the fever-stricken survivors of the ill-fated first expedition finally set sail for home. Long before they reached their destination almost half had died of the fever they carried on them.

It was thus that when the second Darien expedition arrived a few weeks later, they found the bravely named Fort St Andrew abandoned and just enough survivors still left to tell them of the disaster that had overtaken them. They themselves stayed long enough to catch the pre-vailing pestilence and to lose one of their two ships by fire as she lay at anchor. Then they too left, huddled in a single ship – *The Hopeful Binning of Bo'ness.* By the time they reached the inhospitable shores of Jamaica, nearly half their number had died of fever.

Meanwhile, at the end of September 1699, a third expedition had set out with another 1,300 prospective settlers. Fever was not their only problem. They had barely had time to man the defences of Fort St Andrew before the Spaniards attacked them in strength from land and sea. After stubbornly defending themselves for more than a month, they finally surrendered. The Spaniards were so impressed by their courage that they allowed those of them who could still stand to march out with flags flying and drums beating. But they insisted that they should leave Darien. And once again the journey back brought more deaths and the loss of another ship.

The Darien Scheme had been a disaster. Two thousand Scottish lives and three hundred thousand Scottish pounds had been lost. And the responsibility, as far as Scotland was concerned, lay fairly and squarely with William of Orange and the English. By the time William died in March 1702 and was succeeded by his sister-in-law Anne, hatred for England had reached new heights and in the months that followed, a number of other deplorable incidents still further exacerbated relations between the two countries.

Such was the background against which, from both sides, feelers were now surprisingly enough put out for union between the two countries. At first sight the prospects of success could not have seemed less favourable. But to many Scots it had by now begun to appear that their country's only hope of economic survival lay in some kind of deal with their southern neighbours, which would admit them to the trading privileges at present exclusively enjoyed by the English and which the English were at present most reluctant to share. Nor did such a deal need to be entirely one-sided. The Scots, as it happened, possessed one important bargaining counter.

Queen Anne, who had succeeded to both thrones on her brother-in-law's death, had given birth at one time or another to seventeen children, but the last survivor of these, the little Duke of Gloucester, had died two years earlier. She therefore had no direct heir.

The Whig statesmen now in power in England feared nothing more than the possibility of a second Stuart restoration. For one thing, England was predominantly Protestant, while James Edward, the son of James VII and II, who since his father's death in 1701 was legally King, was, unlike his two half-sisters, Mary and Anne, a Roman Catholic. The Whigs were also profoundly opposed to the Stuart concept of the monarchy, which did not at all correspond to their own ideas. In 1701 an Act of Settlement had accordingly been passed through the English Parliament, designed to ensure that on Anne's death the English Crown should go, not to James Edward, but to a German princess, the Electress Sophia of Hanover, grand-daughter, through the female line, of James VI and I. Having achieved this, it now remained for the Whigs to make certain that 'the backdoor' as the Bishop of Salisbury put it, should be 'shut against the attempts of the Pretender Prince of Wales', in other words that, independently of what happened in England, there should be no Stuart restoration in Scotland. Which, so long as Scotland remained a separate country, was always a possibility.

Act of Security

The potentialities of this situation were not lost on the Scots. In 1704 the Scottish Parliament passed by a substantial majority an Act of Security. This provided that Parliament should name the successor to the throne of Scotland within twenty days of the death of the reigning sovereign. This successor was to be a Protestant and a descendant of the House of Stuart, but was not to be the occupant of the throne of England, unless Scotland were given equal trading rights and liberty in government and religion. It also provided, rather pointedly, for a military force to be trained for the defence of the country. Further measures removed foreign policy from the control of the Sovereign and provided for the duty-free import of French wines. These measures acquired added significance from the fact that England was now at war with France.

Queen Anne's Whig ministers at first advised her to withhold her consent from the Act of Security, which needless to say, had aroused great indignation in England, but in the end agreed that she should grant it for fear that otherwise the Scots might retaliate by allowing French warships to use Scottish ports. In March 1705, however, the English Parliament responded with the Aliens Act. Under this all Scotsmen were to be treated as aliens, especially for trading purposes, unless Scotland accepted the Hanoverian succession by Christmas.

Within a month tension between the two countries was further heightened by the execution on Leith sands, at the behest of the Edinburgh mob, of an English sea-captain called Green and two of his crew, accused, wrongly as it happened, of having piratically seized the Scottish ship *Speedy Return* somewhere off the Malabar coast. The execution took place despite urgent entreaties from Queen Anne and in the teeth of all the available evidence. But such considerations weighed less with the Scottish Privy Council than did the menaces of the Edinburgh mob. The two countries now seemed close to war.

But the English Government, already at war with France, did not want war with Scotland as well. The alternative was some sort of accommodation. And so in the summer of 1705 the young Duke of Argyll, who had distinguished himself fighting for the English under Marlborough in the Low Countries and whose family and clan were not handicapped by a record of undue loyalty to the Stuart cause, was dispatched to Edinburgh as the Queen's Commissioner, with the task of persuading the Scottish Parliament to authorize negotiations for a Treaty of Union. After some weeks of acrimonious debate Parliament finally gave their consent and in April 1706 thirty-one Scottish Commissioners, for the most part sound Whigs, and including the newly created Earl of Stair, were sent off to London to open negotiations with an equal number of English Commissioners.

In the negotiations that followed, the Scottish Commissioners sought to retain Scotland's national Parliament, in other words to make the proposed union a federal one. But the English rejected a federal solution from the start, insisting that the Scots must pay a higher price for commercial equality with England. In the end it was agreed that there should be a combined British Parliament to which Scotland should contribute sixteen representative Peers and only forty-five Members of the House of Commons as against more than five hundred English Members. It was also agreed that Scotland should bind herself to accept the Hanoverian succession. In return the Scots would receive 'full freedom and intercourse of trade and navigation'. Financially, Scotland was to be awarded the sum of £398,085 *10s 0d*, to be known as the Equivalent, partly in return for taking over a share of the English National Debt and partly as compensation to the shareholders in the Darien Company. Finally the Scots were to retain their own legal system and the special rights of the Royal Burghs. On all flags the emblems of both countries were to be united.

Such, in its main outlines, was the Treaty which was submitted to the Scottish Parliament when it met in October 1706. To allay Presbyterian fears that an English-controlled Parliament might saddle Scotland with an Anglican Church, a Bill of Security had been drafted, affirming that the Church was 'to continue without any alteration with the people of this land in all succeeding generations'.

Even so it seemed on the face of it improbable that the Treaty would gain acceptance. In Parliament the Country Party, who opposed it, outnumbered the Court Party, who were in favour of acceptance. Outside Parliament, public opinion was thoroughly hostile. Mob violence and agitation against the Treaty threatened at any moment to develop into open insurrection. The Duke of Queensberry, now High Commissioner, was chased down the Canongate to Holyrood by an angry crowd who stoned his coach. 'His Grace', we are told, 'was constantly saluted with curses and imprecations as he passed through the streets, and if Parliament sat till towards evening, he and his guards were all well pelted with stones … so that often he and his retinue were obliged to go off at a top gallop and in great disorder.' The Duke of Hamilton, on the other hand, who was believed to head the opposition to the Treaty, was cheered whenever he showed his face. In the end three regiments of soldiers had to be called in to keep order. In Glasgow things were even more out of control and the Provost was obliged to hide from the angry crowd in a folding bed. And further disorders broke out in other parts of the country.

But characteristically enough, the opponents of the Treaty, even at this critical juncture, were unable to agree among themselves or to act in unison. The Jacobites, for their part, totally rejected the Treaty and Lord Belhaven spoke movingly of 'our ancient Mother Caledonia … sitting in the midst of our Senate waiting for her own children to deal the fatal blow'. But when the time for voting arrived, an important section of the opposition, the so-called *Squadrone Volante*, at the last moment decided to vote with the Government, while the Duke of Hamilton, who had proclaimed his intention of staging a mass walkout by the opposition, found, when it came to the point, that he was suffering from toothache and could not be present.

Union

And so, while the mob roared outside and rumours of insurrection were rife, article by article the Treaty became law, reaching its final stages in January 1707 after the Act of Security had duly been incorporated in it. From all sides petitions against the Union poured in, 'fit' in Argyll's telling phrase, 'to make kites'. Meanwhile, from south of the Border came the news that Argyll's former comrade at arms and commander, Marlborough, was moving his cavalry northwards in strength. And gradually the protests and disorders subsided.

In the English Parliament the Treaty met with no opposition and on 6 March received the Royal assent. On 25 March the Scottish Parliament met for the last time to conclude a few routine transactions. 'The public business of this session now being over,' said Queensberry in a final speech, 'it is full time to put an end to it.'

And so, in this rather humdrum manner, Scotland was deprived of her sovereignty. 'There's ane end', said Lord Seafield, the Lord Privy Seal, 'of ane auld sang.' The Crown, the Sword and the Sceptre were wrapped in linen and stowed away in a box in Edinburgh Castle, and the Duke of Queensberry rode in triumph into London, where he received a pension of £3,000 a year and an English dukedom. The toothache-stricken Duke of Hamilton, on the other hand, had to wait four years for his. 'We are bought and sold,' sang the Jacobites, 'for English gold.' And they were not far wrong.

Scotland's Parliament had existed as a democratic legislature for less than twenty years. It is arguable that, had it survived longer, the native genius of the Scottish people might have found in it a means of expression not to be vouchsafed to them at Westminster, where their representatives would perforce always be in a minority.

CHAPTER SIX

'THE KING OVER THE WATER'

Although many of those responsible for the Treaty of Union doubtless believed at the time that they were acting in Scotland's best interest and saving her, if not from war, at any rate from economic disaster, the Union was from the start unpopular. It soon became more so. 'I never', reported the English agent Daniel Defoe, 'saw a nation so universally wild. ... It seems a perfect gangrene of the temper.'

The Whigs were now in control and, from the working of the new British Parliament, it soon became all too evident that the Union was not to be one of equal partners. Much of the trouble concerned fiscal matters. 'Have we not bought the Scots, and a right to tax them?' an English member inquired with characteristic forthrightness. And Scottish Members who objected were told that Scotland was 'now but a county of Britain' and that 'now she is subject to the sovereignty of England, she must be governed by English maxims and laws'. Over ecclesiastical questions, too, there were indications that, despite the Act of Security, the position of the Presbyterians was not as secure as they had hoped, so that they, too, began to entertain doubts about the Union. Soon, discontent with the Union permeated all classes and all parts of the country and when in 1713 a motion to repeal the Union was submitted to the House of Lords by Seafield and Argyll, who had both played such an important part in bringing it about, it was only defeated by four votes.

It was only natural that in these circumstances, the Jacobites, who since James VII's death in 1701 had regarded his son James Edward as the rightful King and hoped for his return on his half-sister Anne's death, if not sooner, should have felt encouraged. 'The Jacobites', wrote Parson Wodrow of Eastwood in 1710, 'are mighty uppish ... they talk their King will be over, either by Act of Parliament or by invasion by August next.' 'They boast mighty,' he added acidly, 'which I hope will ruin their cause.' Already many of the Tory leaders and even some Whigs, in England as well as in Scotland, were in touch with James at his Court in France and when Anne fell ill in 1714, a Jacobite coup seemed likely. In the event, however, this was averted by swift action on the part of the Whig Administration. On Anne's death she was at once succeeded by George of Hanover, son of the Electress Sophia, who had narrowly predeceased her cousin, and on 5 August 1714 George was publicly proclaimed King in Edinburgh. The following night the Duchess of Argyll gave a great ball at Holyrood to celebrate the occasion.

Had James been prepared to turn Protestant or had he and his supporters shown greater initiative, there seems little doubt that he could now without much difficulty have become King. George I was not only personally unattractive, but took little interest in his new subjects and had nothing in common with them, not even language. Politically, he was a Party monarch, relying exclusively on the Whigs to whom he owed his throne and deliberately cold-shouldering the Tories. When, with James's permission, the Highland Chiefs generously sent him an address of acceptance, George promptly rejected it. It was scarcely the way to win their allegiance. Meanwhile, even in the Lowlands discontent with the Union was rife and there were many who drank to the health of 'The King over the Water'. For the new dynasty the outlook was far from healthy.

James Edward

When James VII had died in 1701, Louis XIV of France, then on the brink of war with England, had promised to help his son. And in March 1708, less than a year after the Union, a sizeable French fleet had escorted James Edward to within sight of the Scottish coast. But an encounter with vessels of the English fleet had deterred the French commander and, despite James's entreaties, for he did not lack personal courage, the expedition had returned to France without ever putting him ashore.

Now, seven years later, in 1715, there was again talk of a Jacobite rising. This time there was less hope of help from France. In 1713 the Treaty of Utrecht had put an end to hostilities between France and England and, on the death of Louis XIV two years later, power passed to the Regent d'Orleans who was still less disposed to give active help to the Jacobites. But James Edward, who was now twenty-seven and had spent nearly all his life in exile, decided to make the attempt notwithstanding. In the summer of 1715 he accordingly wrote from France to the Earl of Mar, with whom he had for some time past been in correspondence, calling on him to raise the Clans without further delay.

Lord Mar, or Bobbing John, as he was known to his contemporaries, had been a supporter of Queensberry and one of the signatories of the Treaty of Union. At the beginning of the new reign he had hastened to declare himself the 'faithful and dutiful subject and servant' of King George. But he had been disappointed by the latter's cool response and had accordingly established contact with the exiled Court. On receiving James's letter, he disguised himself as a workman and, going down to the London docks, boarded a collier for Scotland. Arriving towards the middle of August, he first summoned his friends and neighbours to a great *tinchal* or hunting party on the Braes of Mar and there acquainted all concerned with what was afoot. Three weeks later, on 6 September, he publicly proclaimed James VIII and III as King and raised the old Scottish standard at Castletown in Braemar, when, to the dismay of the superstitious spectators, the ornamental golden ball on the flagpole suddenly fell to the ground. At the same time Lord Mar publicly declared that the Union had been a blunder, by which Scotland's 'ancient liberties were delivered into the hands of the English'.

Raising the Clans

At first the rising prospered. No fewer than twelve thousand armed Jacobite clansmen rallied to the standard under their chiefs and many of the northern towns declared for King James. By mid-September Mar had without difficulty captured Perth and from this point of vantage issued a number of resounding proclamations. Between him and the English border there lay only two thousand government troops based on Stirling and commanded by the Duke of Argyll.

But, whatever his qualities as a politician, Mar was no kind of military leader. Having once captured Perth, he stayed there for week after week, missing the opportunity for swift action against an enemy who was outnumbered and unprepared. Elsewhere individual clans made independent sorties. The MacGregors tried unsuccessfully to storm Dumbarton Castle while the Macleans and some of the Macdonalds marched on the Campbell stronghold of Inveraray in an unsuccessful attempt to repeat their exploits of Montrose's day. But this time there was no Montrose; there was not even a Dundee. And, after some indecisive exchanges with Argyll's brother, Islay, they withdrew to Strathfillan.

At last, learning early in November that the border Jacobites were stirring (Kenmure on the Scottish side and Derwentwater and Forster on the English), Mar dispatched his most experienced commander, Mackintosh of Borlum, with two thousand men, to make contact with them, while he and the rest of his force stayed on in Perth. Old Borlum, as he was known, had seen some service in the French Army, and now, on his own initiative, made a quick dash for Edinburgh. He was, however, headed off by the no less experienced Argyll, and so continued southwards, joining Kenmure and Forster at Kelso. Thence their combined force struck south across the Border to Preston in Lancashire, where, thanks to the stupidity and inaction of the English Jacobites, they were soon forced to capitulate.

Mar, meanwhile, was still in Perth. When Argyll had left Stirling unprotected in order to save Edinburgh from Borlum he had, it is true, advanced as far as Dunblane, but only to fall back once more on Perth when Argyll returned. In the north, meanwhile, Lord Lovat, Chief of Clan Fraser, returning from France, where he had been in touch with King James, had raised his clan and seized Inverness Castle on behalf of King George, thereby regaining to some extent the confidence of the English Court and Government, who up to then had, like everyone else, regarded him with suspicion. Such Frasers as had joined Mar accordingly now deserted, as did many of the Gordons, who were in due course followed by their Chief's son, Huntly. The Jacobite situation in the north was fast deteriorating. Soon the Whig clans, Sutherlands, Frasers, Mackays, Rosses and Munroes, were in more or less complete control there.

The news was now received that strong reinforcements of Government troops from Holland were on their way to join Argyll and, in the second week of November, Mar and his main force once more slowly advanced in the direction of Stirling. Argyll moved to meet him and on the morning of 13 November the two armies met at Sheriffmuir, a mile or two to the north of Dunblane.

At the outset of the engagement that followed, the Macleans and Macdonalds, on the right of the Jacobite line, threw off their plaids and charged the enemy with the claymore. For them something else was at stake besides just the future of this dynasty or the other. They were fighting once again for their existence as clans against their hereditary enemies, the all-pervading Campbells. 'Gentlemen,' said Maclean of Duart, a veteran of Killiecrankie, placing himself at the head of his Clan and looking across to where Argyll had drawn up his troops over against them, 'this is a day we have long wished to see. Yonder stands MacChailein Mor for King George. Here stands Maclean for King James. God bless Maclean and King James. Gentlemen, charge.' In the ensuing encounter the enemy's infantry were routed. But such was the enthusiasm of the clansmen on the right that they hardly noticed that their own centre and left had in the meanwhile been broken by Argyll's cavalry and driven back to Allan Water. In the event, neither side saw fit to risk a second round. Argyll now fell back on Dunblane, while Mar once again withdrew to Perth.

Militarily the battle had been indecisive. But in a wider sense it had been a defeat for the Jacobites. Argyll still held Stirling, thus blocking the way to England, whence the news soon arrived of the Jacobite surrender at Preston. The longer Mar sat at Perth, the worse his position became. His Highlanders, with nothing to do and little hope of plunder, faded back into the hills in ever larger numbers. Meanwhile Argyll's army had been joined by reinforcements from Holland as well as by the troops released by the Jacobite surrender at Preston. From being themselves heavily outnumbered, the Government forces now outnumbered their opponents by nearly three to one. Only heavy snow stopped them from at once attacking in strength.

Such was the situation when on 22 December 1715 James Edward landed at Peterhead. But 'Old Mr Melancholy' was not the man to restore a situation that was already as good as lost. He himself was suffering from fever and ague, while some gold sent him by the Spaniards had been lost at sea off Dundee. 'For me', he told his officers with gloomy resignation, 'it is no new thing to be unfortunate, since my whole life from my cradle has been a constant series of misfortunes.' It was not a speech to raise the spirits of already disheartened men. Nor did his cold, reserved manner endear him to those he met.

At the end of January 1716 came the news that Argyll was advancing to the attack, and to their utter dismay Mar's Highlanders now learned that it was their leaders' intention to abandon Perth and retreat northwards. Worse still, on reaching Montrose, James Edward and Mar, slipping away, secretly took ship to France. When the remaining Highlanders reached Aberdeen, a message was read out to them from James advising them to shift for themselves.

Having had this warning, the London Government now took what they considered the necessary measures to prevent another rising. Hundreds of Jacobites were sent to the plantations, two of the leaders who had failed to escape abroad were executed, and nineteen peerages and a number of estates were forfeited. An attempt was also made to disarm the clans, but this was only partly successful. Those clans whose loyalty was to London duly handed over their weapons, while the others turned in any obsolete weapons they no longer needed and hid the rest for future use. The Union was now more unpopular than ever and even those Scots who supported the Hanoverians had come to resent the Government's attitude to their country.

The Jacobites, meanwhile, had found a new ally in Cardinal Alberoni, the all-powerful Minister of the King of Spain, and in 1719 it was agreed that Seaforth and the Earl Marischal, with two frigates and three hundred Spanish soldiers, should land on the west coast of Scotland to raise the clans, while a force of twenty-seven ships and five thousand soldiers sailed for England. But once again the Jacobites were dogged by ill fortune. A storm scattered the larger expedition before they could land. The party destined for Scotland duly landed on the shores of Loch Alsh and marched as far as Glenshiel. But here they found themselves confronted both by sea and by land with greatly superior Government forces. The Spaniards surrendered, while the Earl Marischal and the Scottish Jacobites who had joined him took to the hills and dispersed. On the other hand, some six thousand muskets that were landed seem in due course to have found their way into the hands for which they were intended.

Pacifying the Highlands

The Government, for their part, persisted with their measures for the pacification and subjection of the Highlands. The native Gaelic or 'Irish' tongue, as they called it, had in particular long been a target for English and (more especially) Lowland Scottish reformers. Already in 1695 an Act had provided for the 'erecting of English Schools for rooting out of the Irish language and other pious uses' and in 1720 we are told that the design of the Society for the Propagation of Christian Knowledge was 'not to continue the Irish language, but to wear it out, and learn the people the English tongue'. A new and more stringent disarming Act was passed in 1725 and many Highlanders actually abandoned, for the time being, their habit of always carrying arms in public.

Meanwhile, General Wade, who had been appointed Commander-in-Chief for Scotland, embarked on a ten-year programme of military road-building, designed to penetrate the more important regions of the Highlands and link the strategic strongpoints of Fort William, Fort Augustus and Fort George. These roads which, when completed, covered 260 miles, gave the central Government a far greater measure of control over the Highlands than ever before and, by opening them up, did as much as anything to destroy the old order which still prevailed there. At the same time, a number of Independent Highland Companies, recruited from Whig clansmen and later formed into a regular regiment known as the Black Watch, were raised by General Wade, in the first place for police duties. The command of one of these companies was entrusted for a time to Lord Lovat, but later, much to his disgust, withdrawn.

In 1727 George II had succeeded George I. But there had been no change in the Government's attitude to Scotland and relations between Scotland and England showed no signs of improvement. Up to 1725 Scottish affairs had been handled in Whitehall by a separate Secretary for Scotland. Now, under the long premiership of Sir Robert Walpole, they passed into the province of the Home Secretary, while for most purposes executive power resided with Argyll or Forbes of Culloden, the Lord Advocate and later Lord President. Friction, of one kind or another, was constant. Resentment at taxes on malt and taxes on salt led to various outbursts of rioting in the cities. Smuggling became a patriotic duty, the excisemen public enemies and smugglers popular heroes. Finally in 1736 there was a major scandal, when a certain Captain Porteous, who had been sentenced to death by a Scottish court for firing on an angry crowd protesting at the public execution of a well-known smuggler, but subsequently reprieved, was taken from prison and hanged by 'persons unknown', acting, we are told, 'with the greatest secrecy, policy and vigour'.

To this rough justice Queen Caroline, who was acting as Regent during her husband's absence in his native Hanover, and the Government in London reacted with a Bill of Pains and Penalties. This required the City Charter of Edinburgh to be destroyed, the City Guard disbanded, the Netherbar Port demolished and the Provost imprisoned. And it was only thanks to the intervention of Argyll with Queen Caroline, who in her German way had taken what had happened as a personal insult and announced her intention of 'making Scotland a hunting ground', that these outrageous penalties were not in fact enforced, a heavy fine being exacted from the City in their place.

None of this did anything to endear the House of Hanover to their Scottish subjects. And now tensions were building up in Europe which were to involve Britain in war, first with Spain in 1739 and then the following year with France. By 1742 a British army, the newly raised Black Watch with it, was fighting in the Netherlands and once again there was reasonable hope that a Jacobite rising might enjoy the active support of powerful allies.

Prince Charles Edward

The Jacobites had another asset. In James's elder son, Prince Charles Edward, they had at last a potential leader, a young man of energy, courage and personal magnetism, more than ready, if the chance offered, to fight for his rights and those of his house. In January 1744 Prince Charles took leave of his father in Rome and set out for France.

The French were at this moment planning to invade England with a sizeable fleet and an army of ten thousand men assembled at Dunkirk under the famous Marshal Saxe. In March the invasion fleet was dispersed by storms and the whole project had to be abandoned. In May of the following year, however, the French soundly defeated the English and Dutch at Fontenoy and Charles's hopes rose again. 'May I not trust', he wrote to Louis XV of France, 'that this signal victory which Your Majesty has just won over your enemies and mine (for they are one and the same) has resulted in some change in affairs; and that I may derive some advantage from this new blaze of glory which surrounds you?'

But this did not evoke from Louis the ready response that Charles had hoped for. Nor did the Scottish or English Jacobites show any great readiness to rise of their own accord. To Charles it now became evident that the best hope lay in bold action on his own part. Only thus could the reluctant Jacobites be persuaded to rise and the doubting French be convinced that his cause was worthy of support. And so, with money raised by pawning his mother's rubies, he fitted out a frigate, the *Dutellir* or *Doutelle* and a ship of the line, the *Elizabeth*, and with these set sail in July from Nantes for Scotland. After a sharp encounter with an English warship off the Lizard the *Elizabeth* was forced to put back into port, but the *Doutelle* escaped her pursuers and on 2 August 1745 Prince Charles, with seven supporters, landed on the Island of Eriskay in the Outer Hebrides.

The reception that greeted him was not encouraging. Macleod and Macdonald of Sleat, for all their past professions of loyalty, refused to have anything to do with him, while Macdonald of Boisdale anxiously urged him to go home. 'I am come home,' the Prince replied tersely and set sail with his seven companions for Moidart, where Macdonald of Clanranald at once rallied to his colours.

The news of his landing filled the mainland Jacobites with concern. Cameron of Lochiel, always a fervent supporter of the Stuarts, begged him in his turn to abandon the enterprise. But without success. 'Be the issue what it will,' Charles replied, 'I am determined to display my Standard and take the field with such as may join it. Lochiel, whom my father esteemed the best friend of our family, may stay at home, and learn his Prince's fate from the newspapers.' To this there could be only one answer. 'I'll share the fate of my Prince,' said Lochiel, 'and so shall every man over whom nature or fortune hath given me any power.' And so on 19 August, in Glenfinnan, before some nine hundred assembled Camerons and Macdonalds, the Standard was raised and James VIII and III once more proclaimed King.

From Glenfinnan the Prince boldly set out for Edinburgh, gathering support as he went. Soon nearly three thousand clansmen from the west had joined him, Camerons, Macleans and Macdonalds. On receiving news of what was happening, Sir John Cope, the English Commander-in-Chief, avoiding an engagement with the Prince's force in the Pass of Corryarrick, withdrew northwards towards Inverness, leaving open the way to the capital.

Having captured Perth, the Highlanders marched on Edinburgh. It was now mid-September. At Coltbridge they met two regiments of Government dragoons and routed them. In the city itself there was panic. The City Guard and Volunteers melted away, and when the Netherbar Port was opened to let a coach pass through, a party of Camerons rushed the sentries and gained control of the sleeping city. Next day King James VIII was proclaimed at the Market Cross and Charles entered Holyrood in triumph, 'met' we are told, 'by vast multitudes of people who by their repeated shouts and huzzas express'd a great deal of joy to see the Prince'. Only a few took a less enthusiastic view, speaking of 'a Popish Italian Prince, with the oddest crew that Britain could produce, with plaids, bagpipes, and bare buttocks ... tag, rag and bobtail'.

Prestonpans

General Cope, meanwhile, was at Aberdeen. The Frasers and the great Whig clans of the north had not, as he had hoped, rushed to his support; they were waiting to see what happened. Not wishing to be cut off completely, Cope rather shamefacedly piled his soldiers into some ships and, landing them at Dunbar, marched on Edinburgh. At Prestonpans he encountered the Prince who had come out to meet him. As often before, the regular infantry could not withstand the violence of the Highland charge. The thin red line wavered and broke; the Government artillery missed their opportunity; and Cope's two regiments of dragoons once again sought safety in flight. 'They ran', Charles wrote to his father, 'like rabets.' Meanwhile, leaving his troops to surrender to the insurgents, John Cope galloped into Berwick ahead of the advance party with the news of what had happened. 'The first general in Europe', it was afterwards said of him, 'who had brought the first tidings of his own defeat.'

His victory at Prestonpans gave Charles a high opinion of the troops under his command and of their potentialities. It also brought him fresh reinforcements. But he failed to follow up his advantage and lingered on in Edinburgh for more than a month, while George II's Government, now seriously perturbed, brought back more and more Dutch and English regular troops from Flanders and sent them to join old General Wade, now a Field-Marshal, at Newcastle. In London, meanwhile, a new verse had been added to the recently composed National Anthem and was sung nightly at Drury Lane to loud applause:

God grant that Marshal Wade
May by thy mighty aid
 Victory bring.
May he sedition hush
And like a torrent rush
Rebellious Scots to crush.
 God Save the King.

Charles had hoped for active French support. Supplies came from France, and money, but no men. Further delay was impossible. In a letter to his father written from Edinburgh in October Charles put his own strength at eight thousand, and three hundred horse. 'With these, as matters stand,' he wrote, 'I shall have one decisive stroke for't. ... I must either conquer or perish in a little while.' Again his best hope lay in boldness. At the beginning of November he crossed the border and started his advance on London.

Charles would have liked to begin by attacking Wade in Northumberland, but, on the pressing advice of Lord George Murray, his Lieutenant-General, he finally agreed to advance instead by way of Carlisle into Lancashire, where it was hoped that he would be joined by large numbers of English Jacobites. In the event this hope did not materialize. Though he met with no resistance to speak of in England, where the inhabitants were relieved to find that the Highlanders were not cannibals, as they had been led to expect, he was joined by only two or three hundred English recruits, mostly from Manchester, while already some of his Scottish troops, feeling homesick, were beginning to desert.

Wade, meanwhile, was threatening Prince Charles from the north-east with one army; George II's fat young son, the Duke of Cumberland, was advancing through the Midlands to meet him with another; while a third, of doubtful quality, was drawn up at Finchley for the defence of the English capital; in all some thirty thousand regular troops against no more than five thousand badly equipped Highlanders and a couple of hundred men from Manchester.

By the beginning of December the Highland army had reached Derby and there Charles held a council of war to decide on his next move. He was now only 130 miles from London. He had not suffered a single setback. In the English capital there was panic. The Bank of England was paying in sixpences and George II was getting ready to go back to Hanover. It was a moment when boldness offered the best, if not the only, hope of success. Counsels of prudence could only be counsels of despair. Charles, realizing this, wanted to continue his advance. 'I can see nothing', he said, 'but ruin and destruction to us in case we should retreat.'

But his advisers, led by Lord George Murray, only saw the obvious dangers of advancing further and in the end it was they who won the day. The decision was now taken to withdraw to the Highlands, where a new campaign, said Lord George, could be launched in the spring. At this Charles, in Lord Elcho's words, 'fell into a passion and gave most of the Gentlemen that spoke very Abusive Language and said that they had a mind to betray him.' For all this, on 6 December 1745 his army began their long march north and soon Horace Walpole in London was able to say that he was no longer afraid of 'a rebellion that runs away'.

On 19 December the Highlanders reached Carlisle and the following day crossed the Esk and were back once more on Scottish soil. But not necessarily, they found, on friendly territory. Dumfries was openly hostile and Glasgow not much better. In the Highlands, it was true, more clans had come out for the Prince, so that his numbers were again on the increase. But Seaforth (more accurately, Lord Fortrose) and his Mackenzies had joined the Hanoverian clans of the north, Sutherlands, Macleods, Mackays and Munroes. Lord Lovat, on the other hand, his interest aroused by the prospect of a Jacobite Dukedom, was now veering to Prince Charles, despite the urging of his old Whig friend Forbes of Culloden to do nothing of the kind.

In January 1746 Charles, continuing his march north, advanced on Stirling with seven or eight thousand men. At Falkirk he met the English General Hawley with a rather larger force of Government troops. Again the shock tactics of the Highlanders put the regulars to flight. But the battle was not decisive and again Charles did not follow up his advantage. Instead, he raised the siege of Stirling and, moving further north beyond the Tay, established his headquarters at Inverness. Once more frustration and inactivity took their toll; morale sagged and numbers dwindled.

All this time the Government had been bringing back more and more troops from Flanders. These were sent to Scotland and assembled at Aberdeen under the Duke of Cumberland, who spent six weeks there in careful preparation. In April 1746 Charles learned that Cumberland, with a well-armed, well-trained and above all, well-fed army, twice the size of his own, was advancing on Inverness.

Culloden

On receiving this news, Charles made an effort to rally his troops and in the end gathered some five thousand hungry, ill-equipped Highlanders on Culloden Moor outside Inverness. The site was essentially unfavourable to the semi-guerrilla tactics of the Highlanders, though well suited to regular troops. On 14 April Cumberland's army, having crossed the Spey, pitched their camp twelve miles away, outside the town of Nairn.

On the night of 15 to 16 April, Lord George Murray, who quite rightly 'did not like the ground' and hoped that surprise might help to redress the balance between the two armies, proposed a night attack on Cumberland's camp. But the plan miscarried. The Highlanders, who had only eaten one biscuit apiece the day before, spent half the night wandering about in the dark without ever finding the enemy. By the time they had made their way to their camp, they were completely worn out and slept where they dropped. At daybreak Cumberland gave his well-fed, well-trained and well-rested regulars the order to attack and the starving and exhausted Highlanders were dragged from their sleep by the sound of the enemy's drums beating to arms.

Cumberland began his attack with a heavy artillery barrage to which the Highlanders could make no effective reply. After this had lasted for an hour, and more and more gaps began to show in their ranks, they began to grow restive and the Prince told Lord George Murray to give the order to charge. The Macdonalds, who traditionally claimed the right of the line, had been placed on the left and were therefore disgruntled. In the centre the Camerons, Clan Chattan, the Macleans and the Maclachlans came first to the shock. 'They came running upon our front line like troops of hungry wolves,' a soldier of the Royal Scots from Ayr wrote to his wife next day. But this time the Hanoverians were ready for the Highland charge. 'Nothing', says Colonel Whitefoord of the Fifth Marines, 'could be more desperate than their attack or more properly received.' Having broken through Cumberland's first line and engaged the second, the Highlanders found themselves caught between two fires and died by hundreds on the Hanoverian bayonets.

With the regular English and Lowland Scottish Regiments stood four companies of Argyll's men – his 'brave Campbells', as Cumberland called them. And now the enemy cavalry were charging down on the Jacobites. '*Allein*', said old Maclean of Drimnin, on learning from his son Allan that his other son Lachlan was dead, '*comma leat misse, mas toil leat do bheatha thoir'n arrigh dhuit fhein*' – 'Do not think of me, take care of yourself if you value your life.' Then, with his wig and bonnet gone, the old man, who had once served in the Royal Navy, turned to face the enemy. 'It shall not be for naught,' he said, and, cutting down the first English dragoon who came at him, managed to wound another before three more rode up out of the smoke and finished him off. On the left, meanwhile, the Macdonalds, outflanked by the English cavalry, had been mown down by grapeshot before they could come to grips with the enemy. Already all over the field the English troopers were riding down and butchering the Highland wounded.

Prince Charles, it is said, watched the rout of his army with tears in his eyes. When it was complete, he let himself be led from the field by one of his officers. 'There you go for a damned cowardly Italian,' was the blunt Lowland comment of Lord Elcho, who himself lived to publish a valuable account of his experiences during the Rising.

For the next five months Prince Charles, with a price of – £30,000 on his head, wandered, a Runted fugitive with sometimes only two or three companions, through the western Highlands and Islands. The £30,000, he was assured by the poor Highlanders he encountered, could be no temptation to them, because anyone who earned it would be ashamed ever to show himself in the Highlands again. And so, thanks to the loyalty and resourcefulness of his friends and possibly to the half-heartedness of some of those who were supposed to be searching for him, he was never captured by the Government troops with whom the whole area was now swarming. From South Uist, where he first took refuge, he made his way across to Skye and thence back to the mainland. Through all the hazards and hardships of those strenuous months, Charles showed unfailing courage and cheerfulness and won the hearts and devotion of all he met. It was in a sense his fulfilment, something that had never been after a portrait by vouchsafed him before and never would be again. At last on 19 September 1746 he was, with difficulty, picked up by a French frigate from the shores of the same sea-loch where he had landed fourteen months before, and thence carried safely back to France, to spend the rest of his life as an unhappy exile. *Bliadna Thearlaich*, Charlie's Year, as the Highlanders called it, was over.

CHAPTER SEVEN

'FOR A' THAT'

The Rising of 1745 gave the Government in London a nasty fright. 'I tremble with fear,' wrote Cumberland, 'that this vile spot may still be the ruin of this island and our family.' It also offered them and their friends in Scotland the opportunity they had long been seeking for a final reckoning with the Highlanders. In Cumberland they found the ideal instrument for this task. He carried it out with characteristically Teutonic thoroughness and gusto.

After Culloden no quarter was given. Hundreds of Jacobite wounded were, on the Duke's express instructions, shot as they lay on the field of battle. Some, where it was more convenient, were burned alive. Such prisoners as were taken were treated in such a way that they died by hundreds. Meanwhile detachments of Government troops, both Scottish and English, were sent out into the territory of the clans who had been, loyal to Prince Charles to hunt down the fugitives, loot and burn the houses, drive away the cattle and devastate the country. When the Provost of Inverness, a good Whig, came to plead for better treatment for his countrymen, he was kicked downstairs. And when Forbes of Culloden, who in his way had done more than anyone to further the Hanoverian cause in the Highlands, appealed for less brutality, he was dismissed by Cumberland as 'that old woman who spoke to me of humanity'. In May 1746, to crown his triumph, the Duke received an official address from the General Assembly of the Church of Scotland which praised his conduct and valour in the most effusive terms and even spoke of the 'public blessings' conferred by his family 'on mankind'.

The Government followed up Cumberland's victory with a series of acts of policy designed to prevent any risk of a Jacobite revival by crushing the spirit of the Highlanders and destroying the Highland way of life. The Episcopal Church, which was suspected of favouring the Jacobite cause, was more deliberately and methodically persecuted than ever. Most of the Jacobite leaders who had not died in battle or escaped abroad were tried and executed and hundreds of clansmen were sent to the plantations. Even the aged Lovat, who with less than his usual flexibility had brought his Clan in at the last moment on the losing side, was taken to the Tower of London and, like his ancestor four centuries before, beheaded, a fate which he met with commendable dignity and courage. As he was being taken to the place of execution, the throng of spectators was so great that one of the stands collapsed and a number of people were killed. 'The more the mischief, was the old man's characteristic comment, 'the better the sport.'

Disarming the Clans

Meanwhile the lands of the Jacobite chiefs were forfeited and a determined attempt was made to destroy the clan system once and for all. A special Disarming Act was evolved by Lord Hardwicke, the Lord Chancellor, whose son Joseph had been present at Culloden as Cumberland's *aide-de-camp*. This Act, which was passed in 1746, imposed severe penalties not only for carrying or possessing arms, but for wearing the kilt, plaid or any other tartan garment. Even the pipes were prohibited as 'an instrument of war'. At the same time, the heritable jurisdictions of the chiefs were abolished and various other measures taken to break their power and destroy their old patriarchal relationship with their clan. The Government's policy led in the long run to large-scale emigration and drew from Dr Samuel Johnson, who was certainly not unduly prejudiced in Scotland's favour, the acid comment that 'to govern peaceably by having no subjects is an expedient that argues no great profundity of policy'. His words recalled, perhaps consciously, the speech which seventeen centuries before Tacitus had put into the mouth of the Caledonian hero Calgacus, '*solitudinem faciunt, pacem appellant*'.

But for all this, something of the old spirit lingered on. Spies sent out by Lord Albemarle, now Commander-in-Chief in Scotland, reported that the Macleans, Grants of Glenmoriston, Macphersons, Macdonells of Glengarry and Camerons, were all eager 'to do it again', if only help could be obtained from France. On 15 May 1752 Campbell of Glenure, while engaged in evicting tenants from the forfeited Jacobite lands of Lochiel and of Ardshiel in Appin, was shot dead in broad daylight by a marksman who, thanks to good planning and the widespread sympathy his action commanded, got clean away, though the Duke of Argyll and a Campbell jury saw to it that another, innocent man was hanged in his place. And even as late as 1770 secret agents were to report to Argyll that the Macleans were once more 'stirring'.

But by now there was no longer any real hope for the Jacobite cause. Prince Charles, since 1766, in his turn, 'King over the water' and now belatedly a Protestant, was living in a rented Italian palace with the Royal Arms of Great Britain painted in the entrance hall and on the roof a weathervane, which to this day still bears the Royal cypher CRIII, a pathetic, rather drunken elderly gentleman with a disagreeable, unfaithful German wife and no legitimate child. His only comfort besides the bottle was his natural daughter Charlotte, Burns's 'bonie Lass of Albany', on whom he bestowed much affection and the title of Duchess of Albany and who, though she never married, managed to bear three children to the Archbishop of Bordeaux. Sometimes, we are told, a visitor or a member of Charles's entourage would sing *Lochaber no more* or some other Jacobite song and tears would come to his bleary eyes at the memories it recalled.

Reconciliation

On Charles's death in 1788 he was succeeded as head of the House of Stuart by his younger brother Henry, Cardinal York, who by entering the Church had effectively destroyed the prospects of his dynasty, but nevertheless now assumed the style of Henry IX. In 1807 he, too, died. Twelve years later a fine marble tomb was erected to the two brothers and to their father in St Peter's by the generosity of their distant relative and legal successor, King George III of England, now mentally disturbed and almost on his own deathbed. In 1822 the latter's ebullient son, George IV, his plump limbs draped in what he had been told was the Royal Stuart tartan, paid a state visit to Scotland, the first member of his own family to do so since his great-great-uncle William Duke of Cumberland nearly eighty years earlier and the first reigning monarch of any dynasty since Charles II's brief though eventful sojourn in 1650. He was greeted with enthusiasm by Sir Walter Scott, who for his part was wearing Campbell tartan and by many others, and was entertained in tremendous style by Lord Hopetoun, whose father in his day had taken the trouble to ride out in his coach to welcome the conquering Duke of Cumberland on his return from Culloden.

But any previous neglect by its monarchs of the northern part of the United Kingdom was to be more than made up for by the assiduous attention it subsequently received from George IV's indomitable niece, Queen Victoria, who with her brightly kilted consort, Prince Albert of Saxe-Coburg-Gotha, regularly spent her summer holidays there, describing them day by day and in great detail in her *Journal of Our Life in the Highlands*. 'We were always', she wrote in an explanatory footnote, 'in the habit of conversing with the Highlanders with whom one comes so much in contact in the Highlands. The Prince highly appreciated the good-breeding, simplicity, and intelligence which make it so pleasant and even instructive to talk to them.' And again: 'The view was so beautiful over the dear hills; the day so fine; the whole *so gemiithlich.*'

It was a tradition that was to be happily continued by Victoria's successors. In the years that followed, the Crown, most appropriately, was to serve as the strongest link between Scotland and the rest of the United Kingdom, while by his marriage to the daughter of an ancient Scottish family King George VI was to bring to his dynasty a stronger native strain than it had enjoyed since James VI and I had rumbled south in his state coach with his bag of golf clubs slung behind. Again, in the present reign the Queen, by more than once attending the General Assembly of the Church of Scotland and by taking up residence each year at Holyroodhouse, has stirred the imagination and roused the enthusiasm of her Scottish subjects, who thus see Edinburgh once more playing its proper role as capital of their country.

Advantages of the Union

In 1707 the most attractive thing to Scotland about the Union with England had been the economic advantages she hoped to derive from it. But it was some considerable time before these began to be felt. Indeed the immediate effect of the Union was to make things worse for Scotland than they were already. By the middle of the eighteenth century, however, a flourishing trade had been built up in tobacco shipped from the American colonies for re-export to the Continent. Big fortunes were made by the swaggering red-cloaked 'tobacco lords' and Glasgow was soon the biggest tobacco port in Great Britain. At the same time a flourishing new linen industry grew up and linen became Scotland's most important export.

With the American War of Independence, however, the situation changed. The Americans were now free to sell their own tobacco anywhere in the world and the profitable tobacco trade collapsed. Much of the available capital thus released was to go into building up the new cotton industry, which in its turn superseded linen and dominated the Scottish economy for the next hundred years.

By the end of the eighteenth century the simple, mainly rural economy of Scotland had been replaced by a more complex one. People no longer necessarily lived from the produce of their own districts. In the Clyde Valley and elsewhere, industrial areas, accompanied by corresponding concentrations of population, were beginning to grow up.

For another sixty years cotton remained dominant. Then, in the 1860's, the American Civil War cut off supplies of raw cotton and the cotton industry collapsed as suddenly as the tobacco trade had done ninety years before. From textiles, the emphasis now shifted to heavy industry, and stayed there. As the nineteenth century went on, iron, steel, coal, engineering and shipbuilding in particular played an ever more dominant part. Before long Clydeside was leading the world in shipbuilding. Great fortunes were made and soon the ornate residences of the new rich lined the Firth of Clyde. But, as later generations were to discover to their cost, the basis of the economy was now dangerously narrow and had lost much of its earlier flexibility.

At the time of the Union Scotland, and the Highlands in particular, had possessed comparatively few roads. With increasing economic development, better means of transport became a necessity. And soon a regular system of roads covered the country. In the Highlands General Wade's strategic roads, built originally for military purposes, served as the starting-point for a more comprehensive road system. At the same time bridges were built and canals dug, the Forth and Clyde and the Caledonian being the most important. Scottish inventors and Scottish engineers led the world and in the 1840's, following the invention of the steam engine by James Watt of Greenock, Scotland was struck, like the rest of Great Britain, with railway mania and the road and canal systems were supplemented by a railway network which soon linked all the principal towns with each other and with the rest of the United Kingdom. In 1802 the *Charlotte Dundas* and in 1812 the *Comet* put Scotland as far ahead in steam navigation as in shipbuilding. Up to the time of the Union, the Scottish economy had been primarily agricultural, and despite growing industrialization, agriculture still remained of the utmost economic importance. Here, too, important changes were taking place. Old-fashioned methods of farming were discarded and new, more up-to-date methods introduced in their place.

The Drift from the Highlands

In the Highlands, the developments which followed the Union and the Risings of 1715 and 1745 were less happy. By the legislation with which they sought to break the clan system and by destroying the old patriarchal links between the chief and his clan, the London Government had succeeded in turning the surviving chiefs, whether Jacobite or Whig, into mere landed proprietors, some, though by no means all of whom no longer felt the same sense of responsibility for their clansmen and dependants as formerly, but, in difficult times, were more concerned with making their estates pay. The easiest method of doing this, most of them found, was to turn them over to sheep farming. For this large areas of land were required and so, in many parts of the Highlands, farms were cleared and taken over and tenants dispossessed and evicted, those responsible sometimes expediting matters by burning the houses of any who were slow to leave. Some of those thus thrown on the world turned, where they could, to crofting or fishing. Others emigrated to America or enlisted in the newly formed Highland regiments. Thousands more drifted into the already overcrowded cities and industrial areas. Beginning in the second half of the eighteenth century, the process, justified as often as not by reference to the most progressive Liberal principles, continued for the best part of a hundred years, culminating in the notorious Sutherland clearances which continued well into the reign of Queen Victoria. Soon in the glens little heaps of stones amid the grass and nettles were all that remained of what once had been sizeable *clachans* and townships.

But while, after an initial increase, the population of the Highlands eventually dwindled, that of the cities and industrial areas increased by leaps and bounds. From 1,608,420 in 1801, the population of Scotland as a whole had grown by 1911 to 4,760,904. To the thousands of uprooted Highlanders were added in the 1840's vast numbers of starving Irish immigrants, driven from their homes by the potato famine and ready to accept any standard of living and any wage that would feed them. Low wages and long working hours were the rule. The expanding industries could absorb any amount of cheap labour. In the first forty years of the nineteenth century 350,000 people moved into the Clyde valley. From 12,000 at the time of the Union, the population of Glasgow rose to 77,000 in 1800 and to over 200,000 by 1830. By 1931 it had reached a million. That of the other industrial towns increased in like proportion. The result of this sudden growth was fearful overcrowding and appalling living conditions with disastrous consequences for the health and general well-being of the population. Nor was any serious attempt made to improve things until well into the second half of the nineteenth century.

In the course of the hundred years that followed the Union, while Scotland was being completely transformed economically and socially, the political life of the country remained to all intents and purposes at a standstill. At times after 1707 the responsibility for Scottish affairs was officially entrusted to a Secretary for Scotland and at others to the British Secretary of State in charge of Home Affairs. But in practice power in Scotland resided with a political manager or boss, sometimes a private individual, who, owing to his personal influence and power of patronage, found himself able to manipulate the votes of the forty-five Scottish Members in the Westminster Parliament.

Of the latter, thirty represented the counties and the remaining fifteen the sixty-five royal burghs. The country franchise was still based on the medieval concept that Parliament was an assembly of the King's tenants, a system which made it possible to produce new voters at will by legally subdividing Crown tenancies without the lands involved ever changing hands. Even so the number of actual voters in Scotland remained small. With a total of 235 voters in 1781, Ayrshire possessed the largest electorate of any Scottish county. The Sheriffdom of Bute, on the other hand, could only boast 12. In 1788 the total for the whole country was under 3,000.

The system of franchise obtaining in the royal burghs bore even less relation to democracy. The burgh Members were not elected by the burgesses nor, save in the case of Edinburgh, directly by the town councils, but by delegates appointed for the purpose by groups of four or five burghs. The wholesale redistribution of population which followed the Industrial Revolution still further exaggerated the defects of the system. Large new centres of population, such as Paisley and Greenock, which were not royal burghs, had no representation at all, while three of the fifteen burgh Members were returned by the Fife Burghs, several of which had long ceased to be more than hamlets.

Such a system clearly lent itself to corruption and manipulation. The London Government had in its gift innumerable appointments, benefits and preferments, both at home and overseas, the promise of which, at a time when the ballot was not secret, was more than enough to swing this voter or that in the desired direction. 'Has a family to provide for', 'Sons in the army', 'His son wants a Kirk' are significant notes on a list of country voters for 1788. And the small total number of votes made the task of the party manager even easier.

Henry Dundas

During the earlier part of the eighteenth century Scotland was managed in the Whig interest by two successive Dukes of Argyll and later in that of the Tories by the most famous manager of all, Henry Dundas, first Viscount Melville, who in effect governed Scotland for thirty years. From Lord Advocate, Dundas, who became the close friend and political ally of William Pitt the younger, went on to be President of the Board of Control for India, Treasurer of the Navy, Home Secretary and Secretary for War, all of which offices in turn provided him with ample opportunities for patronage both at home and abroad and enabled him to keep the great majority of the forty-five Scottish Members and their constituents happy and loyal to the Tory cause. Only once, at the beginning of his career in 1778, when he sought to secure the passage of a Bill relieving Scottish Roman Catholics of some of the disabilities imposed on them, did he find that he had overreached himself and was obliged to bow before the storm of indignation which his proposal aroused.

Though less popular with those he passed over, Dundas achieved some useful reforms. His connection by marriage with a great west Highland family may have given him some understanding of Highland problems and he certainly tried, however belatedly, to right some of the wrongs which the Hanoverians had inflicted on the Highlands. Thanks to him, Lord Hardwicke's preposterous Act of 1746, proscribing Highland dress and the playing of the pipes, was finally repealed in 1782, and in 1784 most of the forfeited Jacobite estates were returned to their rightful owners.

Already during the Seven Years War the elder Pitt had taken the controversial step of raising a number of Highland regiments, recruited from clansmen who barely a dozen years before had fought for Prince Charlie at Culloden. I sought', he said, 'for merit wherever it was to be found. It is my boast that I was the first Minister who looked for it and found it in the mountains of the north. I called it forth and drew into your service a hardy and intrepid race of men …. They served with fidelity as they fought with valour and conquered for you in every part of the world.' To Lord Hardwicke, on the other hand, he cynically commended his decision on other grounds, namely that 'not many of them would return'. Thus his policy served a double purpose. It provided King George II and his heirs with some of the finest soldiers in the world. And at the same time it denuded the Highlands of manpower and so removed a potential threat to the House of Hanover.

In 1805 Dundas, now First Lord of the Admiralty, was impeached for peculation. Although he was duly acquitted and restored to the Privy Council, his position was never again quite the same. On his death in 1811, however, he was succeeded by his son, who managed Scotland in his stead until his own death sixteen years later, when the task fell to a succession of less remarkable Lord Advocates.

In such circumstances it was perhaps not unnatural that the Scottish people should have sunk into a state of political apathy. 'When we had a King, and a Chancellor and Parliament men o' oor ain', says one of Sir Walter Scott's characters, 'we could aye peeble them wi' stanes when they werena guid bairns – but naebody's nails can reach the length o' Lunnon.' When a Scottish interest was directly attacked by some tax or other, there was an occasional display of resentment, which usually took the form of riots. Otherwise, the task of running the country was readily left to the manager of the day and his forty-five followers, who, for their part, were glad enough to do as they were told and accept the appropriate reward. Indeed one of the few recorded complaints from a Scottish Member was that the Lord Advocate of the day was not tall enough. 'The Scottish Members', he explained, 'always vote with the Lord Advocate, and we therefore require to see him in a division. Now, I can see Mr Pitt, and I can see Mr Addington, but I cannot see the Lord Advocate.'

It was in this frame of mind that the fact of the Union, once so bitterly and so widely resented, came during the next hundred years or so to be generally accepted. But from this it was a long step to active Scottish participation in the political life of Westminster.

Only twice in the second half of the eighteenth century did informed Scottish opinion concern itself with questions of external policy. One occasion was the American War of Independence, when Scottish opinion, ignoring the generally subservient attitude of its parliamentary representatives, showed itself on the whole sympathetic to the colonists. The other was the outbreak of the French Revolution, when the new ideas found a ready response in Scotland. On both occasions, it was only natural that parallels should be drawn between the political rights of Scotsmen and those of Americans and Frenchmen. And the sympathy shown in Scotland for the ideas of the French Revolutionaries was strong enough to provoke savage reprisals from the authorities. Thus, Thomas Palmer, a minister of religion, was sent to Botany Bay for seven years and Thomas Muir, an advocate, sentenced to fourteen years' transportation, the judge in each case being the notorious Lord Braxfield. With the onset of the

Napoleonic Wars, however, and the rumoured threat of a French invasion, the Scots, many thousands of whom were now fighting for King George III in various British regiments and in the Royal Navy, began to feel increasing solidarity with their English neighbours.

Meanwhile, though Scottish politics were stagnant and Scotland was denied the means of political self-expression, the second half of the eighteenth century and the beginning of the nineteenth witnessed a great flowering of literature and of the arts and of the intellectual life of the country in general. Edinburgh, though now no longer the capital of an independent state, became one of the great literary, intellectual and artistic centres of Europe. This was the age of David Hume and Adam Smith, of Allan Ramsay and Raeburn, of David Wilkie and the Nasmyths, of Robert Adam and his brothers, of Macpherson's *Ossian* and the Celtic Revival, of Robert Burns and Walter Scott. Scotland might no longer be independent, but in men's minds her sense of nationhood was as strong as ever. 'Is it not strange', wrote David Hume in 1757, 'that, at a time when we have lost our Princes, our Parliaments, our independent Government, even the Presence of our chief Nobility, are unhappy in our Accent & Pronunciation, speak a very corrupt Dialect of the Tongue in which we make use of; is it not strange, I say, that, in these circumstances, we shou'd really be the People most distinguish'd for Literature in Europe?'

But Robert Burns and Walter Scott did more than spread Scotland's fame abroad throughout the civilized world. They helped to restore to the Scots themselves the self-confidence and self-respect which the events of the past century had done so much to destroy, to dispel the unhappy feeling of inferiority and lost identity which had followed the Union. In particular both writers helped to create a new, popular image of Scotland and the Scots, which, though not always very closely related to reality, certainly served to put our country and nation back on the map. To such an extent that, from being regarded as uncouth barbarians inhabiting an insalubrious region north of the Tweed, the Scots soon became in the popular imagination paragons of all the virtues, at once fearless heroes and shrewd, merry, honest, hospitable folk with their hearts in the right place and their heads screwed on the right way, while Scotland and the Highlands in particular became the goal of innumerable enthusiastic sightseers from all over the world. Soon every Englishman was busy finding himself a Scottish great-grandmother and the children of half Europe were tricked out in fancy tartans *à la Lucia di Lammermoor*.

In Burns's poems, with their stress on tolerance and broadmindedness and their strong emphasis on human nature with all its virtues and all its shortcomings, the Scots could see themselves with new pride as 'men for a' that', as human beings more human than most, warm-hearted and open-handed to a fault, great drinkers and lovers and sturdy fighters for freedom and the rights of man. Sir Walter, for his part, gave Scotland back her history, a history of which all could be proud and in which all could see themselves and their forebears in a dramatic and romantic, if occasionally somewhat idealized light. Soon, with the help of Macpherson's *Ossian*, the Ettrick Shepherd and a generation of neo-Jacobite poetesses, was born, in place of the harsh, bloodstained reality, a happy many-hued mythology of Celtic heroes, Robert the Bruce, Mary Queen of Scots, Rob Roy, Bonnie Prince Charlie and Flora Macdonald, which, at some slight cost to the cause of historical accuracy, has held the limelight ever since.

Meanwhile, the building of Britain's growing Empire offered the people of Scotland new scope for their special energies and talents. Sir Walter Scott had spoken of 'the national disposition to wandering and adventure', and the part played in this by the Scots was certainly out of all proportion to their numbers. 'A race of men', wrote James Barrie, 'the wind of whose name has swept the ultimate seas.' In every continent the lead was taken by Scottish explorers, soldiers, sailors, administrators, diplomats, merchants, engineers, missionaries, and doctors, who found abroad the opportunities that were denied them at home. This was the age of Mungo Park, of David Livingstone, of Colin Campbell, of Abercrombie and of innumerable others. And Scotland's part in this gave her in the long run a feeling of ever greater unity with the rest of Britain and of shared responsibility for the Empire she had helped to build.

Church Affairs

In Church matters, while the moderates in the Church of Scotland gradually came to accept their position as members of the Established Church, the Evangelicals found it less easy to reconcile themselves to the control of a Parliament the vast majority of whose members were neither Scottish nor Presbyterian. Trouble arose in particular over the question of patronage, which had been restored shortly after the Union and was not finally abolished until 1874. At the General Assembly of 1842 matters came to a head over Parliament's right to intervene in the affairs of the Church and in 1843 over four hundred ministers, more than a third of the total number, walked out of the Assembly and of the Established Church, followed by a like proportion of their parishioners, and, abandoning churches, manses and stipends, formed the Free Church of Scotland under their leader Thomas Chalmers. In 1900 the Free Church joined the so-called United Presbyterians to form the United Free Church, which could now muster 1,700 ministers as against 1,400 in the Church of Scotland. Finally in 1929, after the virtual abdication by the Westminster Parliament of its right to interfere in Church affairs in Scotland, a union was effected between the Church of Scotland and the United Free Church on terms satisfactory to both, thus uniting the great majority of Scottish Presbyterians in one Church.

The Episcopal Church, meanwhile, had been kept alive as a separate denomination by those members of the Church of Scotland who refused to accept the Settlement of 1690, and had, owing to the attachment of many of its adherents to the Jacobite cause, been vigorously persecuted throughout the eighteenth century. The penal laws against it were finally repealed in 1792, by when it had in Scott's words been reduced to 'the shadow of a shade'. But, though its numbers now increased, its membership was never to amount to more than a very small percentage of the total population.

As for the Roman Catholic Church, it had by the end of the seventeenth century virtually become extinct as an organized body in Scotland, its numbers dwindling to a few thousands, who lived for the most part in the remoter western Highlands and Islands, to which the influence of the Reformation had as yet scarcely penetrated. Partly as a result of missions from the continent of Europe there was some increase during the eighteenth century and by 1800 the total had reached about thirty thousand. During the nineteenth century, however, the number of Roman Catholics was enormously increased by large-scale Irish immigration, until in the

36

37

38

36 Signature of Charles Edward on a
letter to his banker, *c.* 1773. His father
being dead, he signs 'Charles R.',
King Charles III.

37 The Crown of Scotland, last used at a
coronation when the Marquess of Argyll
placed it on the head of Charles II on
New Year's Day, 1651.

38 Marble tomb in St Peter's, Rome,
of James III, Charles Edward, and
his brother Henry. It was paid for by
King George III.

39

40

41

42

43

44

39 'Walking the cloth', a primitive
method of fulling cloth with bare feet,
in Pennant's *Tour in Scotland* (1774–6).

40 Power-loom weaving – an early form
of industrialization (1835).

42 The pioneering paddle steamer
Comet (1812).

41 Steam-paddle tug *Charlotte Dundas*.

43 James Watt in his workshop. His
separate condenser gave the steam-
engine real power for the first time.

44 Opening of the Glasgow and Garnkirk
Railway, 1831. View from St Collox,
looking south-east

45

46

45 Eviction of tenant-farmers went on all over the Highlands, from the 1760s onwards, as farms were cleared to make way for the easier profits of sheep.

46 Glasgow, a town of 12,000 at the time of the Union in 1707, had reached a million by the unlovely 1930s. View from the Necropolis.

47

48

49

47, 48 David Hume (*top left*) and Allan
Ramsay (self-portrait, 1776). By the end
of the 18th century, Edinburgh was one
of the great cultural capitals of Europe.

49 The Academy of Fine Arts, Glasgow.
Its foundation in 1753 formed part of a
general flowering of the arts in Scotland
in this period.

50

51

52

50 Sir Walter Scott with his friends:
he gave Scotland back her history.

51 Robert Burns gave Scots a new idea
of themselves.

52 Robert Louis Stevenson, novelist.

53

54

53 Hunger marchers of the great depression. Scottish contingent in the march of protest against the Means Test, passing through Croughton, Northamptonshire, 22 October 1932.

54 The newest Covenant in Scottish history: in 1950 over a million and a quarter Scots signed this Covenant demanding a measure of self-government for Scotland.

55

56

55 The economic resurgence of Glasgow: the redeveloped Princes Square shopping centre reopened in 1988.

56 Mrs Ewing, the newly elected Scottish Nationalist M.P. for Hamilton, leaving to take her seat in the House of Commons, 16 November 1967.

57

58

57 The debating chamber of the new Scottish Parliament building, its seats set in half-moon shape beneath hanging beams and a boat-shaped roof. The costs of the building, estimated originally at £40 million, would eventually rise to more than £400 million.

58 SNP leader Nicola Sturgeon with her predecessor, Alex Salmond. Her charismatic performances in televised debates, together with the turmoil following Britain's vote to exit the European Union, have kept Scottish independence firmly on the agenda.

Glasgow area it amounted to nearly one-third of the population – a third who distinguished themselves from the city's native Scottish inhabitants in a number of other ways besides religion. These differences and divergences were in due course to find ready expression on and around the football field, where the massively attended contests of Celtic and Rangers have become an increasingly important feature of our national life.

With the passing into law of the Scottish Reform Bill of 1832, which followed the stormy passage of the English Act of 1832, Scottish politics acquired a new vitality. Thanks to the creation of eight new burghs, the number of Scottish Members in the House of Commons was increased from forty-five to fifty-three. Edinburgh and Glasgow were now given two Members each and some of the new centres of population were at long last represented in Parliament. At the last election before the Reform, just thirty-nine electors had voted in Edinburgh. At the first election that followed it the number of voters under the extended franchise was over nine thousand.

Scots at Westminster

Following the reform of Parliament and the reorganization of local government which accompanied it, the people of Scotland began to take more interest in politics. The old system of management by political bosses came to an end, and there was a wholesale change in the political complexion of the Members of Parliament that Scotland sent to Westminster. Under the Dundas regime all but six out of forty-five had been Tories. In the reformed Parliament forty-four out of fifty-three were Liberals. This Liberal ascendancy in Scotland was to last for the best part of a century. At only one general election between 1832 and 1917 did Scotland fail to return a majority of Liberal Members to Parliament. And as lately as 1922 twenty-eight out of the seventy-four Scottish Members were still Liberals. After this the fortunes of the Liberal Party in Scotland declined rapidly, until by the middle of the present century there was only one Scottish Liberal Member of Parliament. Nor has the promise of a second Liberal revival as yet been fulfilled.

The Reform Act of 1832 had enfranchised the middle class. Those of 1868 and 1885 further widened the franchise, while also increasing the number of Scottish Members to sixty and seventy-two respectively. In 1918 this was brought up to seventy-four and universal male adult suffrage introduced.

By the end of the eighteenth century, the Scottish cotton weavers had formed a trade union and during the first half of the nineteenth century strikes were organized in a number of industries in protest against the atrocious working conditions then prevailing. It was not, however, until the second half of the century that the trade-union movement took shape. In 1886 the Scottish Miners' Federation was formed with James Keir Hardie as its secretary and by 1892 there were 150,000 trade-union members in Scotland.

Side by side with the trade-union movement came the rise of the Scottish Labour Party. This was founded as an autonomous political body in 1888 by Keir Hardie and by R.B. Cunninghame Graham, a romantically minded writer and landowner. Its programme included, at that time, the nationalization of land, the abolition of the House of Lords, the disestablishment of the Church and Home Rule for Scotland. It was later merged in the British Labour Party, but, although it lost its separate identity, the Scottish section of the Party was to act as a vitalizing influence to the Party as a whole during the 1920's and 1930's. In 1922, despite a decisive Conservative victory in England, Labour won thirty out of the seventy-four Scottish seats. Henceforth, with the decay of the Liberal Party, political power in Scotland was, over the years, to be more or less evenly balanced between the Conservative and Labour parties.

During the early part of the nineteenth century numerous influences combined to strengthen the connection between Scotland and England. Increased trade, improved communications, constant coming and going across the border and movement of population, intermarriage, loyalty to the same monarch, common victories, common sacrifices in a common cause, the influence achieved by individual Scots in every field of British life and, in return, the gradual spread to Scotland of English ideas and fashions and habits, all tended to break down the barriers which divided the two peoples. While it certainly could not be said that Scotland had been assimilated to England or vice versa, many of the old differences between them were beginning to disappear.

Already Scotland was a very different place from what it had been at the time of the Union. 'There is', wrote Sir Walter Scott in 1814, 'no European nation, which, within the course of half-a-century or a little more, has undergone so complete a change as the Kingdom of Scotland.' And as the nineteenth century progressed this became truer than ever. In the Highlands, in particular, the Gaelic language was, thanks to English but more still to Lowland Scottish influence, fast dying out, the number of native Gaelic speakers dropping from more than 250,000 in 1891 to 95,000 in 1951.

Equally, though Sir Walter's own influence continued long after his death to manifest itself in baronial castles and romantic novels and ballads, there were in Scotland no signs of any fresh national revival in the arts or in literature, comparable to that earlier flowering. Individual Scots, it is true, made names for themselves. In literature, Carlyle and Stevenson. In the arts, a handful of competent painters, Sir John Watson Gordon, a painstaking follower of Raeburn, Sir James Guthrie, the founder of the Glasgow school, McTaggart, MacWhirter and others. In architecture, 'Greek' Thomson, who adorned Victorian Glasgow with tenements and shops, merchants' offices and Presbyterian churches, all in a spirit of the purest classicism; Robert Lorimer, who stuck conscientiously to the historical, not to say baronial manner; and Charles Rennie Mackintosh, whose vigorous originality and skilful use of traditional themes in a functional context won him a bigger reputation in Europe than in his own country. But of a new Scottish renaissance there was no sign.

Nor were there, for a century or so, many signs of serious discontent with the Union or of a vigorous nationalist or separatist movement. It was not until 1853 that the first stirrings of a new Scottish nationalism manifested themselves in the foundation of a National Association for the Vindication of Scottish Rights. This attracted some little support. Well-attended meetings were held and we learn that by 1880 Home Rule was 'distinctly and loudly mentioned'. So much 'so that in 1885 the London Government once again thought it advisable to appoint a special Minister with the title of Secretary for Scotland to take charge of Scottish affairs.

But this did not satisfy the advocates of Home Rule, who continued to demand self-government. At one time or another both the Liberal and

Labour Parties committed themselves to Home Rule for Scotland and during the next fifty years or so various Home Rule Bills and resolutions were introduced. But though launched with a wealth of good will and good intentions, they made little progress towards the statute book. In 1907, however, a modest move was made in the direction of autonomy, when a Scottish Committee of the House of Commons was set up in which Scottish Members could deal with Scottish Bills.

The outbreak of war in 1914 made Scotland's own problems seem less immediate and for the next four years Scottish soldiers, sailors and airmen fought bravely on all fronts for Great Britain and also for the concept of a British Empire so largely built by Scots. During these four years some seventy-four thousand Scotsmen gave their lives, a heavy toll for so small a country, as the War Memorials in every town and village in Scotland testify.

The peace and the economic depression that followed it brought a wave of disillusionment. Scotland, too dependent on heavy industry and textiles, both now suffering from severe foreign competition, was harder hit than England and suffered even worse unemployment. At the height of the slump in 1931 as many as 65 per cent of the shipyard workers on the Clyde were unemployed. Agriculture, too, was depressed. The result was widespread suffering and demoralization on a scale which was to deprive Scotland of some of the best elements in the country and to lead in the long run to dangerous and continuing depopulation. In Scotland it was widely felt that these misfortunes were due to London's neglect of Scotland's interests and the result was a revival of the Home Rule Movement. It was, in the words of Sir Robert Horne, 'the natural outcome of the sense of defeatism and humiliation engendered in the depression'.

London's answer was to promote the Scottish Secretary to be a Secretary of State with Cabinet rank and wider powers. This was in 1928. In 1939 these powers were further extended, when the functions in Scotland of the Departments for Home Affairs, Health, Agriculture and Education were vested in him. In the same year the headquarters of his Department were moved to St Andrew's House in Edinburgh, leaving only a small subsidiary staff in London. In 1951 provision was made for a Minister of State who was to act as deputy to the Secretary of State and to be based in Scotland. At the same time the number of Parliamentary Under-Secretaries of State was raised to three, each with specific functions.

In these ways Scotland achieved an ever greater measure of administrative independence. But the aim of the Nationalists was political independence. In 1934 two nationalist groups had merged to form the Scottish National Party. Five years later the Second World War broke out and the National Party's aspirations were temporarily eclipsed. Once more Scotland bore her full share of Britain's burden and once more tens of thousands of Scotsmen gave their lives in the common cause.

Though he was to be defeated at the General Election a few weeks later, the return to Parliament for the first time of a Scottish Nationalist candidate in April 1945 showed that Scottish Nationalism was not dead. The vast increase in the central power of the State (and therefore of London) caused by the war and fostered by the Labour Government of 1945 was bound to provoke a reaction in Scotland. However soothing it might sound to some English ears, the Socialist assertion that the 'gentleman from Whitehall knows best' had a far less reassuring ring north of the Border. In 1948 the scope of the Scottish Standing Committee was somewhat extended. But in the same year a fresh wave of Scottish Nationalist feeling culminated in the launching of a Scottish Covenant, calling for a Scottish Parliament within the framework of the United Kingdom, to which hundreds of thousands of signatures were appended all over Scotland. In 1950 the successful removal by the Nationalists of the Stone of Scone to Scotland from Westminster Abbey aroused grudging admiration even in England. And two years later the next reign was heralded all over Scotland by the merry crack of exploding pillar boxes in protest against the new Royal Cypher, ERII, held by many to be insulting to Scotland.

For a time rather less was now heard of the Scottish National Party. But there was still an undercurrent of feeling in Scotland that insufficient attention was paid to Scottish affairs in Whitehall and that Scottish interests would be better served by increased devolution. This feeling was reinforced by the fact that ever since the war the unemployment figures for Scotland, under Labour and Conservative Governments alike, though better than between the wars, had even so run at approximately double the level for the United Kingdom.

The Labour victories of 1964 and 1966 and the consequent return to Socialist policies and increased centralization engendered as usual a strong recrudescence of Scottish national feeling and led in 1967 to the overwhelming victory at a by-election in the Labour stronghold of Hamilton of a Scottish Nationalist candidate, who, while the Union Jack was publicly burned by her supporters, declared amid scenes of enthusiasm that it was her aim to see Scotland seated at the United Nations between Saudi Arabia and Senegal. Though it was argued at the time that this was no more than a protest vote, it was a protest vote on a scale which made a powerful and in some ways salutary impact on the whole political scene and gave the old-established political parties serious food for thought. Soon a variety of committees and commissions were busily enquiring into the advisability of a further measure of devolution for Scotland.

Once again, economic grievances and a feeling that Scotland was not getting a fair deal had contributed to this reaction and it was freely claimed by the Nationalists that Scotland would enjoy greater prosperity as an independent State than as part of the United Kingdom. This in spite of much evidence to the contrary and a worldwide trend towards larger, rather than smaller, economic units.

But the problem was not purely economic. Great Britain was passing at this time through a difficult period in her history, a period of change and frustration and disquiet. And this was reflected in a mood of growing disillusionment with politics and politicians. The issues of the day were neither clear-cut nor readily comprehensible and to some people there seemed little to choose between the big London-based political parties. It was to this section of the electorate in particular that the simple, easily grasped slogan 'Scotland for the Scots' made an immediate and powerful appeal. It caught the imagination and aroused the emotions, which was all that it was required to do. Its precise implications could always be worked out later, though to most Scots the idea of an independent but diminished Scotland solemnly taking her seat at the United Nations 'between Saudi Arabia and Senegal' had as yet no great appeal.

Finally, the factor which, a hundred years earlier, had done as much as anything to make the Union acceptable to Scotland was now absent. In the century and a half that had followed the Union, Great Britain had become the heart of a great and expanding Empire, an Empire to which its citizens, whatever their race, were proud to belong, an Empire that offered unlimited opportunities for men of parts, opportunities of which the Scots had taken their full share. Now this was no longer so. Britain had become a small country with big problems and a waning confidence in its own ability to solve them, a country which, as a distinguished American somewhat acidly observed, had 'lost an Empire and not yet found a role'. It was not so much that the Scots had suddenly discovered that they loved their own country more or took more pride in it. It was simply that some of them now took less pride than formerly in belonging to Great Britain, that the Union Flag no longer had quite the same meaning for them as in the days when so many of them had willingly died for it. Whether or not this particular mood persisted, would largely depend on Great Britain's ability to recover her old self-confidence and find her place in the modern world, and so rekindle in the Scots (and for that matter in the English) the wider patriotism of former years.

It could, I think, be said that, during the ensuing quarter of a century, though the Scots did not escape the worldwide recession of the 1990s, things on the whole did not go badly for Scotland. In the industrial field, the trend away from heavy industry to new, more widely diversified light and science-based industries continued. In what came to be known as Silicone Glen, science-based industry helped to fill the gap left by the continuing decline of ship-building, steel and coal, while Eastern Scotland enjoyed a new prosperity engendered by a rapidly emerging oil industry based on Aberdeen and Dundee. Scarcely less important, the United Kingdom's entry into the European Common Market in 1973 served to attract a substantial amount of investment to Scotland, not only from Europe, but from North America and Japan, and led to the establishment of numerous new enterprises in different parts of the country.

It is as yet too early to say what the ultimate effect of Great Britain's entry into the Common Market will be on Scottish farming. So far the Highlands and Islands have undoubtedly benefited from the subsidies and subventions available to marginal farmers, while the community as a whole has gained by the general improvements which membership has made possible. But it will take time to assess the overall impact of the radical changes it brought with it.

Of the political parties, many individual members of both the Conservative and Labour Parties showed themselves reluctant to accept the European concept wholeheartedly. The Liberal Democrats had fewer doubters, while the Scottish National Party, having at first rejected it completely, eventually came round to it with all the enthusiasm of converts, realizing perhaps that logically it was a good deal easier to make a convincing case for Scottish independence within Europe than outside it. And twenty years on, Mrs Winnie Ewing was not slow to make a name for herself at Strasbourg as the Member of the European Parliament for the Highlands and Islands.

One notable new development in Scotland has been the remarkable change that has taken place in the city of Glasgow. While Edinburgh remains in its essence Scotland's capital, Glasgow reflects even more directly the country's well-being and state of mind. For far too long, Glasgow, in the eighteenth and nineteenth centuries the focal point of Scotland's burgeoning prosperity, has in our own century demonstrated all too clearly the inescapable fact of her economic depression, accompanied as this has inevitably been by heavy unemployment and a consequently lowered morale. But now, all of a sudden, Glasgow has taken on a new look, clearly manifesting itself in every kind of way.

The initial impetus, it is only fair to say, came between 1980 and 1984 during the term of office of Lord Provost Michael Kelly, who first launched the imaginative catchphrase GLASGOW'S MILES BETTER as part of a far-flung scheme to put Glasgow back on the map. The improvement was to continue under his successors. In 1990 Glasgow was designated the Cultural Capital of Europe. In 1983, to universal acclaim, H.M. the Queen opened at Pollok the magnificent Burrell Collection, for which a suitable site had, after much discussion, at long last been found. At the same time Glasgow's existing amenities were strikingly improved. New buildings went up everywhere. The old buildings were imaginatively restored and refurbished. The city's communications by rail, road and air were markedly improved. And, most important of all, the morale, attitudes and frame of mind of the people of Glasgow improved out of all recognition.

Politically, the main change in Scotland during the second half of the present century was a marked decline in the fortunes of the Scottish Conservative and Unionist Party, accompanied by a corresponding improvement in those of the Scottish Labour Party and to a lesser extent of the Liberal and Nationalist Parties.

Throughout the whole period, agitation continued for a greater measure of 'devolution' for Scotland. Under the Heath administration of 1970–74, the Tory Government, in the hope presumably of winning more Scottish votes, developed a new-found enthusiasm for devolution, meaning, apparently, some kind of Scottish National Assembly; this enthusiasm was not shared by all their supporters. Nor, indeed, by the Scottish Labour Party, who, under the firm leadership of the late Willie Ross, for the most part eschewed the idea and continued to do so after Labour came back to power in 1974. In March 1979, however, a referendum was held on a proposal for a Scottish Assembly put forward by the Labour Government of the day, with the proviso that it would only be taken forward on condition that it obtained the support of at least 40 per cent of the electorate. In the event, only 33 per cent voted for the proposal and 31 per cent against, while 36 per cent did not vote at all. Thus, the idea was dropped.

With the advent to power, in 1979, of Mrs Margaret Thatcher, the Tories' enthusiasm for devolution vanished as quickly as it had come. It soon became abundantly clear that she had no intention whatever of redeeming her predecessor's pledge to endow Scotland with some kind of Parliament. Nor were there signs of a change of policy in this respect when in 1990 John Major succeeded Margaret Thatcher as Prime Minister and Leader of the Conservative Party, with Ian Lang as Secretary of State for Scotland.

Meanwhile, a Scottish Constitutional Convention met in late 1990 to study the whole question of devolution and constitutional reform. This enjoyed the active support of the Scottish Labour and Liberal Democrat Parties, but was firmly boycotted by the Tories, who in principle remained opposed to increased devolution, and by the Scottish National Party, who declared that they were only interested in outright independence. A number of distinguished figures in the public life of Scotland took part in the Convention's proceedings which, though inclined to be inconclusive, aroused considerable interest.

All over the world the abrupt disintegration of the Soviet Union in 1991, and the events which accompanied it, produced a sudden resurgence of nationalist feeling, notably in Yugoslavia, where it quickly led to savage internecine strife between races which had until recently been living on reasonably good terms with each other.

With nationalism of one kind or another rampant worldwide, it was perhaps only to be expected that the Scottish National Party should feel the wind of change blowing from Eastern Europe and beyond. 'If the Lithuanians can do it, so can we,' cried Mrs Winnie Ewing's daughter-in-law, Margaret. And it was expected by many that the Nationalists would make substantial gains in the forthcoming General Election, indeed that independence might at last be within Scotland's grasp.

There the matter stood when John Major, having succeeded Margaret Thatcher as Prime Minister, went to the country in April 1992. During the election (which he was widely expected to lose, especially in Scotland), neither the Prime Minister nor Ian Lang, his Secretary of State for Scotland, made any promises of increased devolution, but resolutely upheld the principles of the Union. 'A solitary Scotland', said John Major, 'means a solitary England alongside Wales and Northern Ireland. Two proud nations. Divorced. Marginalised. Diminished. In place of Great Britain a little Scotland and a lesser Union.' Both Labour and Liberal Democrats, on the other hand, while apparently remaining unionist in principle, expressly promised a Scottish Parliament, while the Nationalists started planning, perhaps rather prematurely, to leave the United Kingdom.

In the event, John Major won the 1992 election more easily than many had expected and, though in Scotland the overall balance remained heavily weighted against the Conservatives, their results were on the whole better than they had been at the previous General Election. Nor did the Nationalists, while winning 20 per cent of the vote, do anything like as well as they had expected. Which clearly showed the degree of conviction carried by the Prime Minister's robust defence of the Union, for which a large number of Scots, while deeply conscious of Scotland's nationhood, still felt intense loyalty.

That demands for an increased measure of devolution for Scotland will continue seems probable. What at the time of writing is hard to ignore is the continuing anomaly of a Conservative administration governing Scotland from Westminster, when in Scotland it has the support of no more than 11 out of 72 members of Parliament and a much smaller proportion than the Labour Party of the votes cast in Scotland as a whole. So far the Government have, wisely, I believe, done no more than promise to 'take stock', though what this will amount to is as yet not clear.

Meanwhile, what has been happening elsewhere in the world should be sufficient warning of the dangers of controversy run rife and of pre-cipitate action based on supposed political advantage. Yugoslavia is a case in point. Scotland has not always been the peaceful, relatively unified country it is now. Nor are the interests of the Highlands and Islands, the Central Belt and the Lowlands necessarily always identical even today.

It is at any rate conceivable that, in pursuit of the somewhat nebulous concept of devolution, some future government may choose to embark on a far-reaching programme of constitutional change, in which case they may well find themselves on a slippery slope. It is to be hoped that Scotland will in any event not be burdened with an additional tier of government. That she might actually be relieved of one is perhaps too much to hope for, though there could be a case for replacing the regions by a national assembly which in Europe would be able to deal directly and on equal terms with, say, the German Länder.

Whether change, if it comes, will bring great benefits to the average Scot or be much appreciated by him or her remains to be seen. What is important is that the problem, which must inevitably affect the rest of the United Kingdom as deeply and directly as it does Scotland, should not become a political plaything to be bandied about between the parties, but should, when the time comes, be approached with due deliberation and, both main parties having changed their ground on the subject at least once, with as wide a measure of consensus as possible. Important, too, that whatever changes are introduced should catch people's imagina-tion and strengthen their sense of Scottish nationhood within the Union.

CHAPTER EIGHT

'THE SETTLED WILL OF THE SCOTTISH PEOPLE'

In December 1992, less than ten months after the return of a Conservative Government at Westminster, 25,000 Scots marched through the streets of Edinburgh to demand more democracy. It was an early sign that, whatever had happened in London, support for devolution north of the border had not disappeared. Those who argued that a sound economy and growing prosperity would distract the peoples' attention from constitutional change, found that interest in reform was, if anything, growing.

Conscious of the need to respond to popular feeling, the Government announced various measures to reflect Scottish interests more closely. A new Secretary of State, Michael Forsyth, revived the Scottish Grand Committee, a somewhat moribund Westminster institution, and held meetings throughout the country, with ministers travelling north to debate current issues. More dramatically, he brought back the Stone of Destiny, the symbol of Scottish power which had been removed to England by Edward I in 1296, and housed it in Edinburgh Castle.

Neither of these gestures, however, proved sufficient to meet the growing pressure for change. Surveys examining the complex question of Scottish identity found that the Scots felt themselves increasingly to be less British and more Scottish. The findings suggested that, as memories of war and empire receded, so the ties that had bound generations of Scots to the notion of Britishness were loosening.

The Scottish Constitutional Convention (see p. 137), though spurned by the Conservatives and the Scottish National Party, nevertheless claimed to reflect mainstream opinion within Scotland, something the Labour leader, John Smith, had once termed 'the settled will of the Scottish people'.

From it emerged a proposal for a fully legislative body, elected by proportional representation to ensure that it would not be permanently dominated by Labour, the largest party in Scotland. It was to have a limited ability to levy income tax – no more than 3p in the £ was suggested. This was immediately labelled 'the tartan tax' by the Tories, who predicted it would lose votes and sabotage the Scottish economy. The idea survived, however, to be incorporated into a commitment from both Labour and Liberal Democrats that, if they won power, Scotland would once again have a tax-raising Parliament in Edinburgh.

This, then, together with dire warnings from Conservatives that it represented the slippery slope towards separation and the break-up of the United Kingdom, was the issue that came to dominate the General Election of 1997. It resulted in a massive Labour victory and the rout of the Tories in Scotland. They were left with not a single seat at Westminster and controlled not a single Scottish council. The Scottish Nationalists had fared better, and now made up the principal opposition. But the outcome was a triumph for supporters of devolution, not independence.

Labour's pledge to hold a referendum on the devolution issue was delivered in September 1997, following publication of a White Paper which set out the terms of Home Rule. Two questions were to be put, one asking whether voters wanted a Scottish Parliament, the second asking whether they wanted it to have tax-raising powers. For once, the SNP and Labour parties campaigned together, with support from the Liberal Democrats. Only the Conservatives, with backing from some leading figures in business, sought a 'No No' vote under the slogan 'Think Twice'. The result was an overwhelming response of 74 per cent in favour of the parliament and 63.5 per cent in support of its tax-raising powers. Unlike the 1979 referendum, which had revealed a country of divided views, particularly in the Highlands and the Borders, this time there was almost universal support for a Scottish Parliament across the country, with only Orkney and Shetland voting against the tax-raising element.

The Scotland Bill, which outlined the powers that would be extended north, began with the ringing declaration: 'There shall be a Scottish Parliament.' It went on to define the areas where Westminster would continue to exercise control – foreign policy, defence, the major aspects of the economy, social security, ethical matters such as abortion, and broadcasting. All the rest would be devolved to Scotland. It represented a substantial shift of power between the two countries, certainly the most significant since the Act of Union. And though the new Prime Minister, Tony Blair – anxious not to undermine the Union – had once warned that the new Parliament would not exercise any greater control than an English parish council, the reality was very different.

Opposition to the Bill now came only from diehard Unionists, mainly English MPs, who still viewed it as the thin end of a very dangerous wedge. The veteran Labour MP Tarn Dalyell, who had once posed a fundamental objection to the new parliament in a form known famously as 'the West Lothian Question' remained unconvinced. It would, he said, be absurd for Scottish MPs at Westminster to be able to legislate on English matters, while English MPs would have no say over matters in Scotland. He believed the new constitutional model was fundamentally unstable – 'a motorway without exits to independence' he termed it.

The West Lothian question never was answered – it was simply put to one side, at least partly because even the Scottish Conservatives were reluctant to address it. Realising that if they were ever to regain their support in Scotland they would have to jump on the devolution band-wagon rather than continue to oppose it, they began to recast themselves as a purely Scottish party 'wrapping themselves in tartan' as a derisive opponent put it.

For the SNP there was a different kind of dilemma. As the Scottish elections, set for May 1999, approached, those who remained dedicated to the idea of independence as soon as possible, viewed the new Parliament as a diversion from the ultimate goal. It should be used purely, they argued, as a platform for expressing SNP policies.

The party's leader Alex Salmond, however, a former banker and a shrewd tactician, argued that it made better sense to work within the parliament, and to ensure it delivered policies which would benefit the new Scotland. Then, when Scots voters realised what it had managed to achieve, the SNP would be able to claim that, with independence, even more might be gained.

At the same time, he positioned the Nationalists on the left, pledging to raise an extra penny on income tax, to be spent on health and education. It was not a strategy that seemed to work: 'Spend a penny for Scotland' was not judged an election-winning slogan, or perhaps the Scots were cannier than some of the forecasters had predicted. When the results of the first democratically elected Scottish Parliament were declared, the SNP found themselves in second place with 35 seats, trailing behind Labour's 56. The Conservatives, gaining from the PR system, were in third place, with 18, while the Liberal Democrats came fourth with 17.

The new Scottish Parliament could hardly have been more different in composition from its largely unelected 292 year old predecessor. For a start, nearly half its members were women. There were three independents, including a Scottish Socialist, and Britain's first ever elected member of the Green Party. The lack of a single party majority meant that it would be governed by a coalition, between Labour and the Liberal Democrats. There was a Presiding Officer, or Speaker, a First Minister rather than a Prime Minister, and a collection of ministerial posts, with titles unfamiliar to a British constitution. A new system of members' committees was set up, giving them power not only to scrutinize legislation, as at Westminster, but to initiate it – a significant transfer of power from the government (or Executive as it was now called) to ordinary members (or MSPs – Members of the Scottish Parliament).

One thing had not changed. Just as in 1639, when the old Parliament House on the High Street was still being completed, the building in which the new members were to sit was not ready in time. A heated debate over where the new chamber should be sited had resulted in the commissioning of an entirely new building at Holyrood, close to the ancient Palace of Holyroodhouse. Since even the foundations of this ultra-modern structure, designed by an architect from Barcelona, had not been laid, the first session of the Scottish Parliament was convened in the specially converted quarters of the Assembly Hall on the Mound, traditional meeting place of the General Assembly of the Church of Scotland.

In a notably informal atmosphere, at 9.30 a.m. on 12 May 1999, Dr Winifred Ewing, the veteran Scottish Nationalist, and at 69 the 'mother of the house', announced simply: 'The Scottish Parliament, adjourned on the 25th day of March, 1707, is hereby reconvened.' The 129 new members took their oaths, pledging their loyalty to the Queen, thus demonstrating that they remained subjects of a United Kingdom rather than a separate Scotland. Some, however, affirmed the oath, rather than swearing on the Bible; the Socialist member, Tommy Sheridan, raised a clenched fist rather than an open palm; and Mr Salmond prefaced his words by saying that for the SNP, 'loyalty is with the people of Scotland, in line with the sovereignty of the people'.

Two months later, on 1 July, Queen Elizabeth and the Duke of Edinburgh, together with the Prince of Wales, journeyed north for the official opening of the parliament, which took place in glorious sunshine in front of a crowd of many thousands, clutching flags and lining the streets of the capital. The proceedings inside the Assembly Hall were broadcast on giant screens outside, and overhead there was a fly-past by the Red Arrows and a Concorde jet. There had been much discussion about what form the ceremony should take, whether simple or elaborate. In the event, a compromise was reached: the scarlet-clad Household Cavalry clattered up the Royal Mile behind the royal carriage, but in modest numbers. The Scots Heralds, in their traditional costumes, were on hand, but only a few. The Duke of Hamilton, Scotland's premier duke, bore in the Scottish Crown, but dressed in day kilt and jacket. The Queen wore royal purple, but woven into a modern coat and skirt. In handing over a newly designed mace, she paid tribute to 'the grit, determination and humour, the forthrightness and above all the strong sense of identity of the Scottish people'.

The new First Minister, Donald Dewar, spoke of 'a moment anchored in our history', then went on to deliver these thoughts on the parliament: 'Today, we reach back through the long haul to win this parliament, through the struggles of those who brought democracy to Scotland, to that other parliament dissolved in controversy nearly three centuries ago. Today, we look forward to the time when this moment will be seen as a turning-point: the day when democracy was renewed in Scotland, when we revitalised our place in this United Kingdom.'

It would be hard to argue that, in its first full year, the Scottish Parliament fulfilled that pledge. The early months were spent wrangling over minor internal matters, such as members' allowances and the cost of the new building at Holyrood. The first piece of genuine legislation – an emergency measure – involved closing a loophole which allowed dangerous psychopaths to walk free from mental hospitals. The early standard of debate was uninspiring, and even the sparring matches between the First Minister, Donald Dewar, and the opposition leader, Alex Salmond, failed to match the cut and thrust of Prime Minister's Questions at the House of Commons.

But those who had predicted that Scottish politics, once detached from the 'mother of parliaments' at Westminster, would gradually sink to a parochial level were proved wrong. A series of issues, apparently minor in themselves, but of great potential significance, demonstrated that the shift in power from London to Edinburgh had been genuine, and that a new agenda was beginning to emerge north of the border that would, over the years, profoundly alter the centuries-old relationship between Scotland and England.

A commitment by the Liberal Democrats to abolish tuition fees for students in Scotland became an early test of the coalition government and a challenge to United Kingdom legislation. There was strong pressure from ministers in London to prevent the introduction of a measure that would give Scottish students advantages denied to their English counterparts, but in the event a compromise law was framed which would indeed change the way in which higher education in Scotland was financed and students were supported. A spirited debate on the Act of Settlement, which denies the succession of Roman Catholics to the British throne, showed that the Parliament was fully prepared to take on issues outside its immediate remit, and thus influence matters south as well as north of the border. A furious controversy broke out over the abolition of Section 28 of the UK Local Government Act, which forbade the promotion of homosexuality in schools. Again a compromise was reached, this time between the conservative and the liberal positions; and once more, an issue which affected all of Britain was decided separately in Scotland.

Not all of this reflected well on the new Scottish Executive and its First Minister Donald Dewar. The opposition parties, particularly the SNP, seized on a series of mishaps to make political capital and undermine the standing of ministers. These included the resignation of a succession of political advisers and the departure of the Lord Advocate to become a judge, just as a major international trial was about to take place in the Netherlands – a trial conducted under Scots law of the two Libyans suspected of involvement in the infamous Lockerbie air disaster of 1988, when Pan Am jumbo jet Flight 103 exploded in mid-air over the little borders town, killing all 259 people on board as well as 11 people on the ground. After a trial lasting 31 weeks, Abdelbaset Mohmed Ali al-Megrahi was found guilty and sentenced to life imprisonment. At the same time a row was rumbling over the escalating costs of the new Parliament building, threatening further trouble.

But whereas the new Parliament was clearly showing signs of the slings and arrows that go with any democratic institution, there was little to indicate that the Scottish people were of a mind to regret their decision and put the clock back. Polls showed that while they remained dissatisfied with what had been achieved so far, they neither wished to revert to their former state within the Union, nor to embrace the challenge of full independence. For the first time since 1707 the Scots had charge of their own affairs. It was now up to them to make the best use of it.

CHAPTER NINE

'WE SHALL CARRY IT CAREFULLY AND MAKE THE NATION PROUD'

Scotland's new parliament had been in existence for barely 15 months when, on 10 October 2000, tragedy struck. The First Minister Donald Dewar, walking from his official residence, Bute House in Edinburgh, suffered a brain haemorrhage, after falling on the pavement outside. Taken to a hospital in the city, he died the next day. His health had not been good, and only six months earlier he had undergone heart surgery. But he had insisted on returning to work, where he had faced not only a punishing schedule but also, briefly, a bruising encounter in parliament with the new leader of the Scottish National Party, John Swinney.

His loss was mourned throughout Scotland and beyond, because he was seen as the man who had delivered devolution and steered the new parliament through its difficult early days. Widely described as 'the father of the nation', he was one of the few Scottish politicians of stature who had willingly turned his back on the House of Commons and devoted himself to Scottish affairs. Even the previous leader of the Scottish National Party, Alex Salmond, had decided to step down and return to UK politics in London.

Dewar's untimely death left a political void. As the Queen, paying tribute to his contribution, noted: 'His passion for Scotland and all things Scottish was renowned, and his contribution to the historic process of devolution in recent years has been immense'. His task, however, had not been an easy one. After the initial enthusiasm for a new political era had worn off, the ruling Labour–Liberal Democrat coalition found itself under attack, not so much for any major blunders, as for failing to deliver on the high ideals and ambitions of devolution. Expectations that the mere existence of a Scottish Parliament would boost the economy, transform the education and health of the nation, and ensure a higher quality of administration, were, perhaps inevitably, not met. Instead, its members were criticized for the manner in which they debated the nation's affairs, while the Scottish Executive found itself open to the charge of incompetence.

Nowhere was that more graphically exemplified than by the spiralling costs and ongoing delays in the construction of the still unfinished parliament building. Both the architect, Enric Miralles, as well as the location and design had been personally championed by Dewar, who had assured the public that its cost would be only £40 million, and also that it would be occupied by the summer of 2001. But as its elaborate structure and complex design became increasingly apparent, it emerged that both were a gross underestimate. Miralles himself died in July 2000, shortly after estimates of the cost had risen to £195 million. By the end of 2002, that figure had reached £325 million, and the project had become the focus for furious debate by members of the Scottish Parliament, continuing to sit in temporary accommodation in the Church of Scotland's Assembly Hall. A strong faction within the parliament urged that work should be abandoned, but to have done so would have been a national humiliation, and, after commissioning an architectural report, which concluded that the project remained viable, the decision was taken to press on, while a wider inquiry was set up to examine the reasons for its massive expense.

By the time that inquiry, headed by Lord Fraser of Carmyllie, a former Conservative minister, reported in July 2004, the final cost was thought to have reached £430 million, more than ten times the original estimate (in fact it was later calculated at £414.4 million). Lord Fraser's report was a damning indictment of the management, supervision and political accountability of a major public project; Dewar himself, however, was cleared of direct responsibility for the fiasco.

The report went some way towards clearing the air, and when, later that year, the Queen travelled north to open the new building, where the 129 Members of the Scottish Parliament (MSPs) sat in the dramatic setting of a half-moon-shaped debating chamber with suspended beams and high ceilings, the light streaming in through its boat-shaped roof, there was a sense that it was time to move on, and accept that, whatever past controversies, this was now the seat of Scottish democracy. What went on inside would prove to be more important than its construction.

As Scotland's national poet, Edwin Morgan, said in verses composed for the opening:

*What do the people want of the place? They want it to be filled with
thinking persons as open and adventurous as its architecture.
A nest of fearties is what they do not want.
A symposium of procrastinators is what they do not want.
A phalanx of forelock-tuggers is what they do not want.
And perhaps above all the droopy mantra of 'it wizny me' is what
they do not want.*

Dewar was succeeded as First Minister by Henry McLeish, a former professional footballer and academic who represented Central Fife, first as MP and later MSP. While lacking Dewar's warmth and charm, he was seen as a safe pair of hands, marking out his devolution credentials by declaring an intention to seek increased powers for the Scottish Parliament.

Already the country was growing used to measures that further widened the policy gap between Scotland and England. While the British Prime Minister Tony Blair was driving through reforms of English hospitals and schools, introducing more competition and private enterprise, Scotland continued to keep faith with state ownership and management of health and education, maintaining hospitals under the control of local authorities, and schools within the comprehensive system. With tuition fees abolished for Scottish students, a further step was taken towards improving the welfare of the nation's citizens by offering free care for the elderly, a measure judged too expensive by the UK government, but introduced north of the border at an initial cost of £125 million a year.

That Scotland could afford – at least for the time being – expensive policies paid for by the state was due to the rising value of the block grant from Westminster, which funded the public sector. Over the first decade of devolution, the grant more than doubled in cash terms and increased by 60 per cent in real terms, taking its value from around £18 billion a year to just under £30 billion. A formula, established by a previous Labour Treasury Secretary, Joel Barnett, ensured that any rise in UK funding led to Scotland benefiting from a relatively larger increase, based on the size and distribution of its population. Although the disparity was intended to disappear in time, it still meant that public expenditure per head of population was 25 per cent higher in Scotland than in England, leading to accusations from some English MPs that the Scots were over-subsidized. However, the principal effect of devolution was a growing lack of interest south of the border in Scottish affairs. Coverage in the media declined, knowledge of Scottish politics faded, and at one stage, embarrassingly, a Labour minister even mistook the name of the new First Minister of Scotland, despite the fact that they were both members of the same party.

The tenure of Henry McLeish lasted barely a year before a minor scandal over his office expenses led to his resignation. He was succeeded by a fellow Labour MSP, Jack McConnell, a former mathematics teacher, who was to pursue the process of introducing measures specific to Scotland, such as a ban on smoking in enclosed public spaces and the so-called Fresh Talent Initiative, designed to encourage immigration, as Scotland's own birth rate continued to decline. The Scottish parliamentary election of 2003 brought no great political change, and the Labour–Liberal Democrat coalition continued to exercise power. It was notable, however, that Labour control of local authorities, once ironclad, had steadily weakened. With the introduction of proportional representation, the party found itself having to share or even cede power at local level, a revolution that would once have seemed unthinkable.

Meanwhile, opinion polls continued to indicate that there was an appetite throughout the country for the Parliament to be given more powers, and though this stopped well short of independence, there was criticism of Labour's strong links with the party at Westminster, which were seen as a barrier to further autonomy. Scots were beginning to identify themselves increasingly as 'Scottish' rather than 'British', the concept of the Union was weakening, and, despite some change of outlook, the party that had been such a dominant influence in the country for more than 50 years was still seen to be controlled from London rather than Glasgow.

That control was personified by Gordon Brown, Chancellor of the Exchequer and later Prime Minister, whose Scottish credentials were unquestioned, but who was seen in Scotland as representing the vested power of a Westminster parliament, and who argued powerfully for a rekindling of the concept of Britishness. His approach was out of tune with the Scottish mood, and did little to boost the standing of his party in Scotland. Meanwhile, in 2004, Alex Salmond had been once more elected leader of the Scottish National Party, and though he initially continued to represent his constituency of Banff and Buchan at Westminster, while his deputy, Nicola Sturgeon, led the party in Scotland, he was to stand again for the Scottish Parliament in the election of 2007. By far the most charismatic politician in Scotland and, arguably, in Britain, Salmond was regarded within the SNP as a 'gradualist' – one of those who believed that independence could be achieved by stages rather than by storming to power. By dint of personality and persuasion, he had steadily converted the party from a single-issue protest movement into a convincing and electable body.

When, therefore, in 2007, Scotland prepared once again to go to the polls, Salmond was able to present the SNP not only as a party with solid and convincing policies, but also one that stood unequivocally for the Scottish interest. An eloquent and persuasive speaker, he was able to inject that spark of excitement and enthusiasm into Scottish politics that had been so markedly absent in the Labour era, and there was a surge of support for the Nationalists, which took them, narrowly, to power. When the final count took place, the SNP found itself with a single seat majority in the Scottish Parliament.

It was a profound shock, not just in Scotland, but throughout the United Kingdom. At a stroke it knocked the Labour Party from its posi-tion of unquestioned power, and demonstrated at the very least that Scotland was determined to seek even more control over its own affairs. Above all, it elected to government a man whose ambitions were to make Scotland independent. As one member of the royal family, Prince

Andrew, commented: 'an election in Scotland has rattled the timbers of the concept of the Union'.

That Salmond was forced to govern the nation with a minority administration, unable to command the support of rival parties for any of his more controversial policies, was less important than the mere fact that he was wielding power. As he put it himself in his acceptance speech: 'The nature and composition of this third Scottish Parliament makes it imperative that this government will rely on the strength of its argument in parliament and not the argument of parliamentary strength.'

Over the next four years, despite his inability to push through measures such as a local income tax, minimum pricing for alcohol and, most notably, a bill that would have introduced a referendum in Scotland on independence, Salmond won support for his budgets and pledged a freeze on council tax, which proved widely popular. He was also able to demonstrate the competence of his ministers, notably his deputy, Nicola Sturgeon, and also the Finance Secretary, John Swinney, while opposition parties struggled to regain their lost momentum.

In September 2008, however, an economic crisis of global dimensions brought down some of the world's greatest financial institutions, including Scotland's two major banks, the Royal Bank of Scotland (RBS) and the Bank of Scotland, the latter having been amalgamated with the Halifax Building Society, to become HBOS. In just one day in October, more than £90 billion was wiped off the value of Britain's companies, and though the Prime Minister, Gordon Brown, promised to do 'whatever it takes' to halt the panic, in the course of that week the world's financial system came closer to absolute collapse than at any time since the 1930s.

HBOS was rescued thanks to a takeover by a rival bank, Lloyds TSB, bolstered by a government bailout of £11.5 billion for HBOS and £5.5 billion for Lloyds. RBS, which had once been the world's largest company by assets (£19 trillion) and the fifth largest bank by stock market value, lost more than £24 billion, and was only saved from bankruptcy by an injection of – £20 billion of government funds. As the Chancellor of the Exchequer, Alistair Darling, later recalled, the bank had been just two hours from collapse. Its chief executive, Sir Fred Goodwin, once hailed for his entrepreneurial skills, was forced to resign.

The banking collapse was not only a major setback for the Scottish economy, leading to the loss of thousands of jobs, it was also a blow to national pride. For Salmond, who had once boasted that an independent Scotland could be part of 'an arc of prosperity' stretching from Ireland through Iceland, to Scandinavia, it was a reminder of the harsh reality that Scotland, like any other country, was subject to the vagaries of the global economy. Both Ireland and Iceland had been brought down by the collapse of their own financial institutions, and Scotland's banks had only been rescued thanks to the intervene tion of a UK government.

Over the next three years, however, the Scottish economy, while still performing marginally less well than the rest of the UK, remained on course, buoyed up by some of its traditional industries, such as whisky and tourism, but also through more traditional manufacturing activities, which had never entirely disappeared, such as engineering, electronics, ship-building and the emerging importance of renewable energy. Salmond said it was his belief that the power of its wind and waves could transform Scotland into 'the Saudi Arabia of renewable energy'.

The Scottish Labour Party, in the meantime, had seen one of its brightest stars, Wendy Alexander, a close ally of Gordon Brown, replacing Jack McConnell. She was instrumental in introducing a commission, headed by Sir Kenneth Caiman, to review the provisions of the 1998 Scotland Act and determine what new powers might be given to the Scottish Parliament. Although opposed by the SNP, the commission was approved, and went on to recommend giving the Parliament a limited ability to raise or lower income tax in Scotland, as well as greater borrowing powers. This fell short of the full 'fiscal independence' that some had argued for, but was a step in that direction, and formed part of a new Scotland Bill, presented to the Westminster parliament.

Although undoubtedly gifted with intellectual powers, Wendy Alexander struggled to take the party or the country with her, and, in 2008, after a minor row over her acceptance of a party donation from a Jersey-based financier, she resigned, to be replaced by Iain Gray.

The only event that threatened the credentials of the SNP government was a decision to release Abdelbaset Mohmed Ali al-Megrahi, the Libyan agent who had been convicted of the 1988 attack on the Pan Am airliner over Lockerbie, and sentenced to life imprisonment (see p. 146). The Libyan government had put enormous pressure on the British government to have al-Megrahi returned, and various UK ministers had supported them; the Prime Minister, Tony Blair, had negotiated a prisoner transfer agreement with the Libyan leader, Colonel Muammar Gaddafi. However, it was widely recognized that this was a matter for the Scottish government, under whose judicial system al-Megrahi had been tried and convicted (albeit in a court in the Netherlands).

Salmond made it clear that there was no intention of returning the Libyan under the transfer deal; it was pointed out that there was an appeal against his sentence outstanding, which made his return illegal. However, it emerged that al-Megrahi was suffering from prostate cancer, and in August 2009, it was announced by Kenny MacAskill, Cabinet Secretary for Justice, that he would be returned to Libya on compassionate grounds.

The decision provoked fury from the relatives of those who had died in the atrocity, and was attacked by Conservative ministers. Both Salmond and MacAskill argued that the release was justified for humanitarian reasons, since they had been told that al-Megrahi had only three months to live. They were subsequently embarrassed when the Libyan was given a hero's welcome on his arrival in Tripoli, and went on to live for more than two years.

But the affair did little to dent Salmond's popularity, and, with Labour seemingly unable to reform, the SNP had political momentum behind it as the next election to the Scottish Parliament in May 2011 approached. At Westminster, a coalition government, formed by an alliance of Conservatives and Liberal Democrats, had introduced harsh economic measures to combat the financial downturn, and these had begun to have a severe impact on the public sector in Scotland, where jobs had been lost and services cut.

Salmond went into the election maintaining that Scotland needed more powers to tackle the economic crisis. His argument was that Scotland was being unfairly penalized by policies introduced by an unsympathetic London government. At the same time, he presented a version of independence that was deliberately designed to appear as unthreatening as possible to the Scottish people. He said that an independent Scotland would retain the monarchy, share armed services and diplomatic representation, and remain, for the time being, within the sterling area; he spoke of a 'social union' between the nations north and south of the border. He also promised a referendum on independence, but not immediately – he intended to steer the country through the economic turmoil before presenting the voters with a choice.

Whether it was the appeal of this message, disaffection with Labour or the unpopularity of the coalition government in London, by the time it came to the May elections, the mood in Scotland had undergone a transformation, and voters swung overwhelmingly to the Nationalist cause. When the votes were counted, it emerged that Salmond had achieved what had once seemed unimaginable – an overall majority in the Scottish Parliament, with 69 seats to Labour's 37. The Conservatives managed to win 15, but the Liberal Democrats, punished for their association with the Tories in London, had been reduced to just five seats.

Landing by helicopter on the manicured lawns of an Edinburgh hotel, Salmond hailed his triumph as 'a victory for a society of people and a nation'. He also said that, although the SNP had 'a majority of the seats', it did not have 'a monopoly on wisdom', and he promised to govern responsibly, representing not just those who supported independence, but the majority who remained to be convinced. 'I will govern for all of the ambitions for Scotland and all the people who imagine that we can live in a better land', he promised, adding 'This party, the Scottish party, the national party, carries your hope. We shall carry it carefully and make the nation proud.'

Whether that promise was fulfilled remained to be seen. What was undoubtedly true, however, was that Scotland was now on a new course that would take it into uncharted waters, remodelling not just the nation itself, but quite possibly the constitution of the United Kingdom as a whole.

CHAPTER 10

'SHOULD SCOTLAND BE AN INDEPENDENT COUNTRY?'

The possibility that Scotland might hold a referendum on the independence of the nation had once seemed not only remote but, to many English parliamentarians, unthinkable – it might, after all, lead to the break-up of the United Kingdom. The SNP's victory in the election of 2011, however, made that prospect unavoidable. The party had given a firm commitment in its manifesto that one would be held, and, though its leader Alex Salmond held back until he had negotiated some further powers for the Scottish Parliament, he made it clear that, in his view, the referendum should take place in the second half of his new government's term of office.

First, approval had to be sought from the British government. The Scottish parliament had no formal powers to stage a binding referendum, since that was a constitutional matter reserved to Westminster. Some Tory backbenchers urged the prime minister, David Cameron, to refuse permission; but he realised that to do so would play into the hands of the Nationalists, who would regard such a refusal as denying them their democratic rights.

On 15 October 2012, the so-called Edinburgh Agreement was drawn up and signed by Mr Cameron and Mr Salmond, laying down that a referendum should be held, and a subsequent Order in Council was approved by both parliaments, at Westminster and Holyrood. The vote was set for 18 September 2014. There had been much debate about the question on the ballot paper, with Mr Salmond suggesting there should be three options, one urging the status quo, one for independence, and a third for greater powers in Scotland, short of full separation. Mr Cameron was clear, however, that there should be just one question, which was finally approved by the Electoral Commission. It read simply: "Should Scotland be an independent country?".

Two campaigns were launched, one for independence, called Yes Scotland, the other, for the continuation of the Union, known as Better Together. Key issues fiercely debated over the next two years concerned the sustainability of the economy, the nature of a Scottish currency, border security, defence, joining the EU, the exchange of intelligence, and membership of NATO. Perhaps the most fraught was whether, in the event of independence, Scotland would continue to use the pound sterling, join the Euro, or create its own currency. The decision to keep the pound in the short term was attacked by unionists as incompatible with full independence, since major decisions on such matters as interest rates would still be determined by the Bank of England. The Yes campaign said, by contrast, that it would offer Scotland much-needed stability in the early years of independence.

For many people, however, the debate hinged on something deeper – the question of whether they felt themselves committed to a 300-year-old union that had served Scotland well in the past, or to the independent status that would reflect the ambitions of a nation rediscovering its separate identity. Communities, even families, found themselves divided, with some undecided right up to referendum day. Two days before the vote, the tabloid *Daily Record* published a front-page commitment from the leaders of the pro-union parties, entitled The Vow, promising to give Scotland greater powers in the event of a No vote.

When results came in, 55.4 per cent had voted against independence, and 44.7 per cent in favour. There was a turnout of 84.6 per cent – the highest since mass franchise was introduced after the First World War. Only four areas voted Yes (Dundee, Glasgow, North Lanarkshire and West Dunbartonshire) but they contained over 20 per cent of the Scottish electorate.

In the aftermath of the referendum, Mr Salmond announced his resignation as leader of the SNP, and was succeeded by his deputy, Nicola

Sturgeon, a rising star in the party since her election as a member of the Scottish Parliament in 1999. Mr Salmond had predicted that, in the event of a No vote, independence would be put back for a generation. Instead, however, in the aftermath of the vote thousands of Scots began signing up to join the SNP, hoping to force another referendum. The party's membership doubled from 25,000 to more than 50,000, making it the third largest party in the UK. By March 2015 the total had passed 100,000, meaning it entered the general election of May 2015 as a movement two-thirds the size of the Conservatives and half the size of Labour. The election saw the SNP win all but three seats in Scotland in an unprecedented landslide, gaining a total of 56 seats and becoming the first party in 60 years to win 50 per cent of the Scottish vote. Labour, once predominant in Scotland, suffered its worst ever election defeat, losing 40 of the 41 seats they were defending.

The stunning victory meant that independence remained a live debating point in Scotland. In the aftermath of the referendum, a commission, headed by Lord Smith of Kelvinside, had recommended greater powers for the Scottish parliament, including decisions on altering tax bands, and increasing the country's borrowing powers; they were described as the greatest constitutional change since devolution, but the SNP continued to insist that independence remained its central goal.

Gradually, however, questions were being asked about more immediate issues, such as the SNP's competence as a government, and whether it had delivered improvements on core issues including education, the economy, and the National Health Service. In the Scottish elections of 2016, the party lost its overall majority at Holyrood, and the Conservatives, once a minority party, made significant gains under a new and charismatic leader, Ruth Davidson.

Significant as these movements were, they were eclipsed by the impending referendum on Britain's membership of the European Union in June 2016. The commitment to hold a vote had been made by the prime minister, David Cameron, and he had campaigned to remain within the EU; north of the border, most parties backed this position. Against expectations, however, when votes were cast, a majority of almost 52 per cent in Britain supported a decision to leave, and negotiations on what was to become known as Brexit, began to take place. In Scotland 62 per cent had voted in favour of remaining, and the outcome illustrated starkly the contrast between opinion north of the border and that in the rest of the United Kingdom. It strengthened the views of many within the SNP that Ms Sturgeon should use the European vote to advance again the case for a second referendum on independence; but when, in June 2017, the prime minister Theresa May held a surprise election to strengthen her hand in the EU negotiations, the SNP lost seats to the Tories, and was forced to admit that hostility to a second referendum might have been a factor in the result.

With deep uncertainty over Britain's future relations with Europe, Ms Sturgeon held off committing herself to another vote on independence, saying that she preferred to await the outcome of Brexit negotiations. Scotland's future seemed likely to be determined not at Holyrood, but in the corridors of power at Westminster and in Brussels.

LIST OF ILLUSTRATIONS

1 Torrs chamfrain, unique Celtic bronze mask, possibly as early as 200 BC. Horns are also Celtic, added at a later date, making a false reconstruction. National Museum of Antiquities of Scotland, Edinburgh. *Photo Malcolm Murray.*

2 Papil Stone, found at an early ecclesiastical site on the island of Burra, Shetland. Pictish, early 9th century. *Crown copyright, reproduced by permission of the Ministry of Public Building and Works, Edinburgh.*

3 Aberlemno cross slab. Early Pictish sculptured cross, 8th century. *Crown copyright, reproduced by permission of the Ministry of Public Building and Works, Edinburgh.*

4 St Margaret, Queen of Scotland. Illumination from 15th-century manuscript, possibly written at Bourges for a Scottish lady. *By courtesy of the Trustees of the British Museum*, MS. Add. 39761, f. 93b.

5 Monymusk Reliquary in the shape of an early Irish church, 8th century. *National Museum of Antiquities of Scotland, Edinburgh.*

6 David I and Malcolm IV Miniature from the Charter of Kelso Abbey, 1159. By kind permission of the Duke of Roxburghe. *On loan to the National Library of Scotland, Edinburgh.*

7 Walrus ivory chessmen, from island of Lewis. Probably Scandinavian, 12th century. By courtesy of the Trustees of the British Museum. *Photo Edwin Smith.*

8 Detail of 'the Ragman's Roll', 28 August 1296. *Crown copyright, reproduced by permission of the Controller of H.M. Stationery Office. Public Record Office, London, c. 47/23/5.*

9 'The Arbroath Declaration', letter of the barons to Pope John XXII, 6 April 1320, with seals of barons. *Scottish Record Office, Edinburgh. Crown copyright, reproduced by permission of the Controller of H.M. Stationery Office.*

10 Bruce sword, inscribed with initials of Bruce, 'KRB', and Douglas, ILD', with instructions to Douglas to bury Bruce's heart in the Holy City. Dated 1320. Disputed authenticity. By kind permission of Rt Hon. Sir Alec Douglas-Home, Douglas Castle.

11 Perth besieged by the Earl of Mar, c. 1332. Woodcut from Holinshed's *Chronicles*, vol. I, 1577. British Museum.

12 The Cavers Standard of the Douglas family. *National Museum of Antiquities of Scotland, Edinburgh.*

13 Hermitage Castle, Roxburghshire. *Photo Edwin Smith.*

14 View of St Andrews. Engraving from *Theatrum Scotiae*, John Slezer, 1693. Mace of the Faculty of Arts, 1418. *By permission of the Librarian, St Andrews University.*

15 Coin of James III, obverse, probably

earliest Renaissance-type portrait outside Italy, c. 1485. *National Museum of Antiquities of Scotland, Edinburgh.*

Coin of James III. Reverse, showing three pellets with an annulet, crown and fleur-de-lys in angles of cross. *National Museum of Antiquities of Scotland, Edinburgh.*

16 Portrait of James III. Detail from altarpiece, ascribed to Hugo van der Goes, 1476. *Reproduced by gracious permission of Her Majesty the Queen.*

17 Andrew Myllar's printing device. *Reproduced by permission of the Trustees of the National Library of Scotland, Edinburgh.* F.7, d.27, p. 168.

18 Portrait, called James IV, Flemish school, 16th century. *National Gallery of Scotland, Edinburgh.*

19 'Queen Mary's Harp', c. 1500. *National Museum of Antiquities of Scotland, Edinburgh.*

20 *The Preaching of Knox before the Lords of the Congregation, 10th June* 1559. By Sir David Wilkie, 1832. *By courtesy of the Trustees of the Tate Gallery.*

21 George Wishart being burnt at the stake, St Andrews, March 1546. Woodcut from Holinshed's *Chronicles*, vol. I, London, 1577. British Museum.

22 Portrait of John Knox, by Hondius, after the Beze, *hones* version of 15 80 from a painted portrait. British Museum.

23 *The Murder of Riccio*, by Sir William Allan, 1833. *National Gallery of Scotland, Edinburgh.*

24 The 'Deuil Blanc' portrait of Mary Queen of Scots, probably painted in 1559 by François Clouet. *Scottish National Portrait Gallery, Edinburgh.*

25 Portrait of James VI and I, 1610, school of Marcus Gheeraerts the Younger, now

attributed to J. de Critz. *By courtesy of the Trustees of the National Maritime Museum, Greenwich.*

26 Charles I at Edinburgh. Engraving by Cornelius van Dalen, probably executed in 1638. British Museum.

27 The Arch-Prelate' of St Andrews assaulted while reading the new Revised Prayer Book for Scotland imposed on the Scottish Kirk by Charles. Scene in St Giles's, Edinburgh, 1637. Etching by Wenceslaus Hollar for *Sight of the Transactions of these latter yeares*, John Vicars, 1646. British Museum.

28 A Solemn League and Covenant for Reformation, as published in London, 25 September 1643. Top left panel illustrates English nobles, gentry and clergy solemnly taking the Covenant. Engraving by Wenceslaus Hollar.

29 Map of Darien. From 'A letter giving a description of Darien by an unknown person' sent to the Marquess of Tweeddale, 1699. British Museum.

30 Duke of Queensberry presenting the Treaty of Union to Queen Anne. Anonymous engraving. British Museum.

31 Execution of Jacobite Lords, Tower Hill, 1716. Anonymous line engraving. *Scottish National Portrait Gallery, Edinburgh.*

32 Jacobite toasting glass, 18th century. *Victoria and Albert Museum, London.*

33 Antoine Walsh taking leave of Prince Charles on the shores of Loch nan Uamh, 1745. Contemporary drawing. *Scottish National Portrait Gallery, Edinburgh.*

34 Cottage on the site of the Culloden battlefield. *Photo Edwin Smith.*

LIST OF ILLUSTRATIONS

INDEX

INDEX

countries, the partners they work with in the UK, and their growing legion of customers."

James Niven, Triodos Bank

"Provides a lively and important reminder that fair trade provides consumers with a way to take individual positive action in solidarity with the poor."

Benedict Southworth, Director, World Development Movement

"While fair trade is complex, *50 Reasons to Buy Fair Trade* has untangled the issues and lays them out clearly in excellent easy-to-read chapters."

Stefan Durwael, Executive Director, International Fair Trade Association

"This book is illuminating, accessible, and above all, empowering."

Jeremy Seabrook, author of Consuming Cultures: Globalisation and Local Lives

"This timely and well-researched publication confronts those doubtful of the effectiveness of fair trade as an instrument for sustainable development with substantiated evidence. Litvinoff and Madeley's extensive overview of the advantages inherent to the logic of fair trade contributes dearly to the cause of increased justice in international trade."

Dr Frithjof Schmidt MEP, European Parliament Rapporteur on Fair Trade

"Fresh and clear as a see-thru mint. If this doesn't persuade you to support fair trade, nothing will."

Anuradha Vittachi, OneWorld.net

"In showing how buying fair trade products can support a range of social and environmental goals, *50 Reasons* reminds us that trade is simply the interaction between all of us and reflects our level of consciousness as humans today. Litvinoff and Madeley show us a range of reasons for thinking, living and, yes, shopping, as one people on one planet. Those of us who have the knowledge and opportunity to do something about the fragmentation between people and nature that exists in mainstream commerce no longer have any option but to change it, and ourselves."

Dr Jem Bendell, Senior Strategic Advisor, World Wide Fund for Nature

"A first-class guide, without ducking the issues, to why being a smart consumer makes sense. Whether you're a fair trade fanatic or wondering whether to start, this book will give you lots of new reasons to be a smart consumer. Buy it and help change the world through the way you shop."

Richard Bennett, General Secretary, BOND; former Chair, Make Poverty History

"Miles Litvinoff and John Madeley have done a service in writing this book. It will, I hope, make a contribution to a world where the people who produce goods that enhance our lives receive a return that also enhances theirs."

Wendy Craig, actor

Praise for *50 Reasons to Buy Fair Trade*

"A lively, accessible and inspiring survey of how fair trade is bringing new hope to poor producers around the world."

Paul Chandler, Chief Executive, Traidcraft

"The best and most comprehensive guide around to the principles and practice of fair trade."

Joanna Blythman, food writer and campaigner

"A wonderfully inspiring and uplifting book, which demonstrates the power of the personal choices we make as consumers. *50 Reasons to Buy Fair Trade* not only offers 50 powerful reasons to choose fairly traded goods, but also tells us some of the compelling stories behind the products. And while each of the stories is very different, the message remains the same: fair trade changes lives. The fair trade movement is one of the great success stories of our time – and this book bears witness to its growing strength and importance."

Dr Caroline Lucas, Green Party MEP for South-East England

"This well-researched, balanced and inspiring book is a great guide to how and why the empowered individual can make a difference. … This book educates and empowers – the WTO board should read it and learn from it."

Craig Sams, founder of Green & Black's

"This book captures the spirit of our times. We live in a risky and divided world and though as an individual you can't do everything, you can do something – or, as this book shows, 50 things. This book is a celebration of social justice."

Ed Mayo, Chief Executive, National Consumer Council

"Want that really pithy example to convince a sceptic you are right when it comes to the way the world is headed for oblivion but doesn't have to be? It's here. Want to be surprised by how much you can make

a difference? Try this book. Eloquent voices from around the world will compel and provoke you, reason by reason, to act differently!"

Pauline Tiffen, founder of Cafédirect and the
Day Chocolate Company

"*50 Reasons to Buy Fair Trade* is a extensively researched piece of work that defies all myths that fair trade doesn't work."

Wendy Martin, Editor, New Consumer magazine

"Buying fair trade goods is one of the most direct ways a consumer in the North can help some of the poorest people in the world to get a decent price for their products. As *50 Reasons to Buy Fair Trade* shows, fair trade's impact goes much wider, forcing governments and corporations to rethink the way they do business."

Duncan Green, Head of Research, Oxfam

"Quietly, against the odds, fair trade has emerged as a powerful social force. But there are even more powerful forces against it: not just nasty, thoughtless companies or people, but all of us desiring things on the cheap. Sometimes we don't know what lies behind the goods; sometimes we bury our heads, denying the hidden costs, pretending we don't know. This book gives powerful reasons why that tension in modern consumer culture cannot go on and why the fair trade movement is not about being 'worthy' or wallowing in guilt, but about changing what we do and injecting justice into what otherwise easily becomes a brutal world."

Tim Lang, Professor of Food Policy, City University, London

"Buying fair trade is one of the most practical actions consumers can take against exploitation by the multinationals. This highly readable book shows how and why."

Patricia Barnett, founder and Director, Tourism Concern

"Fair trade allows people to act – to use their power as consumers to make a difference. *50 Reasons to Buy Fair Trade* will encourage many more to join them, and that's good news for producers in developing

50 Reasons to Buy Fair Trade

Miles Litvinoff and John Madeley

Pluto Press
London • Ann Arbor, MI

For

Gillian and Stephen

Cecilia

and fair trade producers around the world

First published 2007 by Pluto Press
345 Archway Road, London N6 5AA
and 839 Greene Street, Ann Arbor, MI 48106

www.plutobooks.com

British Library Cataloguing in Publication Data
A catalogue record for this book is available from the British Library

Hardback
ISBN-13 978 0 7453 2585 9
ISBN-10 0 7453 2585 8

Paperback
ISBN-13 978 0 7453 2584 2
ISBN-10 0 7453 2584 X

Library of Congress Cataloging in Publication Data applied for

10 9 8 7 6 5 4 3 2

Designed and produced for Pluto Press by Curran Publishing Services, Norwich
Printed and bound in the European Union by Antony Rowe Ltd, Chippenham and
Eastbourne, England

Contents

CONTENTS

Contents

CONTENTS

CONTENTS

CONTENTS

Goods produced under conditions which do not meet a rudimentary standard of decency should be regarded as contraband and not allowed to pollute the channels of international commerce.

President Franklin D. Roosevelt,
message to US Congress, 1937

Acknowledgements

We are grateful to the following for their help and advice:

Sergio Allard, Richard Armstrong, Tricia Barnett, Simon Billing, Felicity Butler, Paul Chandler, Mark Cherrington, Atif Choudhury, Tony Cook, Maria José Cordoba, Wendy Craig, Barbara Crowther (special thanks for enhancing the accuracy of the text), Cathi Davis, Chris Davis, Janixce Florian, Heather Gardner, Christine Gent, Xavier Gomez, Dave Goodyear, Colin Hopkins, Regina Joseph, Silver Kasoro-Atwoki, Harriet Lamb, Jamie Lloyd, Bente Madeira, Tatiana Mateluna Estay, Blanca Rosa Molina, Terry Mollner, Maranda St John Nicolle, Veronica Pasteur, Shailesh Patel, Abi Pettit, Andy Redfern, Craig Sams, Kate Sebag, Issaka Sommande, Arsene Sourabie, Annabel Southgate, Joel Uribe, Luis Villaroel, Nicola Ward, Helen Yuill, Roger van Zwanenberg.

Any errors or omissions in the book are of course our own.

We and the publishers would also like to thank the various fair trade organisations for permission to use the trademarks, logos and symbols that appear on the cover of the paperback edition of this book

Miles Litvinoff and John Madeley

About the authors

Miles Litvinoff writes and edits on human rights, sustainable and international development, and corporate responsibility. His *Earthscan Action Handbook for People and Planet* and *Young Gaia Atlas of Earthcare* were shortlisted for awards, and he was general editor of the *World Directory of Minorities*. He is also a manager in the NGO sector and has worked in Africa, Asia, Eastern Europe and Latin America. He previously taught environment studies with the Open University and has supported fair trade for 20 years.

John Madeley is the author of eight books and many other publications and articles on economic and social development issues, especially international trade, transnational corporations, food and agriculture, and human rights. His interest in fair trade spans three decades. He was a member of the Council of Reference of Traidcraft when it was set up in 1979. He has travelled in over 50 developing countries and seen some of the poverty of people who produce for the mainstream trading system.

Introduction

When we arise in the morning ... at the table we drink coffee which is provided for us by a South American, or tea by a Chinese, or cocoa by a West African; before we leave for our jobs we are already beholden to more than half the world.

Martin Luther King

We are beholden to people across the world – many of them the very poorest – who supply products that we value so highly. Yet how much do they receive for them? In most cases, it's a pittance, and most of us feel that's not right. Those sandals we picked up for a fiver – well, that made us feel uneasy. How much could the woman or man who made them have earned?

We don't want the poor to get screwed like this. The question is, how to put it right? More and more of us want to know how we can buy goods which have given the producer a fair return. And in the mid to late 1990s we increasingly began to buy food, drink, craftwork and other products which do that – goods that have been traded fairly.

Fair trade is a success story of our time. In the first five years of this millennium the number of fair trade products we could buy increased by over 15-fold. Originally it was just handicrafts. Then it spread to coffee and chocolate, and on to include a widening range of foodstuffs. Today we can buy far more. Fair trade clothes, bedlinen, shoes, furniture, flowers, carpets, footballs, wine and fruit juice are all available – and they are great quality!

WHAT IS FAIR TRADE?

Fair trade is trade with a difference. It's a way for us to help the world's poor every time we shop. With fair trade, producers in poor countries receive a decent return – a fair and stable price or wage for their products. And also in many cases they get extra money – a premium – to invest in their business or community. Buying fair trade products is a way of taking practical action to bring about a better, more generous world. It can help make poverty history.

[1]

Many fair trade products carry the Fairtrade Mark. This is awarded by an organisation called Fairtrade Labelling Organisations (FLO) International to products that meet internationally agreed fair trade standards. FLO is the umbrella organisation of "national initiatives" in 21 countries across Europe, Japan, North America, Mexico, Australia and New Zealand. The Fairtrade Foundation is its UK member.

Fair trade products also come from fair trade organisations like Traidcraft and People Tree that belong to the International Fair Trade Association (IFAT). This is a network of 270 fair trade organisations in more than 60 countries, from every continent, which adhere to fair trade principles.

There are other initiatives that are close to fair trade in spirit, such as Rugmark carpets and community-based tourism. Our book covers these too.

The need for fair trade is clear. The mainstream international trade system is failing the world's poor. Since 2001, and the launch of the Doha Development Round of world trade negotiations, member countries belonging to the World Trade Organization (WTO) have talked about changing world trade to benefit the poor. But wealthy countries, notably European Union countries and the United States, have refused to make the changes needed. The poor are left to wait. All this makes fair trade more crucial than ever.

The poor cannot eat talk. They need real, lasting benefits. The fair trade system can provide these benefits. The great thing about fair trade is that it works for poor people. Fair trade provides a viable alternative to the mainstream trading system.

As dramatic as the growth of fair trade has been, and for all its increasing influence, it still represents only a small fraction of world trade. Most producers of fair trade coffee, for example, still have to sell a lot of their crop on non-fair trade terms.

Fair trade has huge potential. It can influence and change the world trade system and help poor people and communities work their way out of poverty. But for this to happen, it needs to keep on growing. The more fair trade goods we buy, the more people can sell under a fairer system. *50 Reasons to Buy Fair Trade* gives 50 powerful and different reasons for buying these products. The Reasons show, very directly, how fair trade works for the benefit of children, women and men in developing countries and what people in developed countries can do to give it more impact.

HEAR PEOPLE TALKING

In most of the Reasons in this book, we hear people in the fair trade system doing the talking. They tell us in their own words about the difference that fair trade makes to them, to their families, to their communities. Many of them are poor, some very poor. But they are all clear that fair trade means a better life.

Nicaraguan coffee grower Blanca Rosa Molina tells us that the fair trade system "makes the difference between whether my family eats or does not eat".

Cecilia Mwambebule, who grows tea in Tanzania, tells us that with fair trade "we have been able to do many things. We have primary schools, secondary schools. ... Our schools are very important. Now we have tables and chairs, and real floors and windows to keep the wind and dust out."

For Dominican banana farmer Amos Wiltshire, fair trade "has made a huge difference to the families, the farmers concerned and to the economy as a whole. ... Fairtrade is a shining light."

And Shailesh Patel, fair trade cotton project manager for Agrocel in India, tells us that "Fair trade saves farmers' lives. It prevents suicides."

Did you know that around three-quarters of the world's footballs are made in and around the city of Sialkot in Pakistan? We hear of how fair trade footballs have made a big difference to the families who stitch them.

We hear of how the "social premium" included in the price of Fairtrade-certified products helps small-scale farmers and other low-income producers raise the quality of their produce, make the land more productive, improve the local environment, support community education, health services and women's rights, and deliver a host of other benefits.

[3]

Whether it's fair trade mangos from Burkina Faso, one of Africa's poorest countries, Rugmark-labelled carpets from Pakistan, or fair trade wine from Chile, this book shows the many connections between buying fair trade and helping low-income people all over the world.

WIDER ISSUES

Our book also looks at wider issues. Fair trade alone will not solve all the world's poverty, although its growth could make a significant contribution for many people. We talk about the need for trade justice, the importance of respect for human rights, and achieving the Millennium Development Goals. And we highlight how fair trade has helped trigger a wave of consumer awareness. How it has even led to transnational corporations making some improvements.

The role of the transnational corporations in fair trade is controversial. There is a big debate about whether a product from a company such as Nestlé should be awarded Fairtrade certification. We look at both sides of the argument.

Some transnationals talk about ethical trade. But fair trade goes further. Ethical trade means companies trying to ensure that workers or farmers in developing countries who make or grow their products have decent working conditions. Fair trade goes beyond ethical trade, because it guarantees fair terms of trade and fair prices, supports and encourages workplace democracy and co-operatives, and enables people to take more control over their own lives.

Today there's an important debate about food miles and climate change, about global versus local, the environmental costs of air transport, and the negative impacts that big supermarkets can have on local economies. For a more sustainable world, we need to buy local produce where we can, and have supply chains that are less oil dependent. What sense is there in flying apples across the world when we can grow them in the UK? Fair trade does not address these issues – and it's not intended to.

Where fair trade does contribute to sustainable development is in those goods that cannot easily be, or are not currently, produced locally in the global North. Most fair trade produce comes from tropical regions that Western countries have exploited for so long, and most people living in those regions need our solidarity. So if we're buying their tea, coffee, cocoa or bananas, we can make it fair trade every time.

THE FUTURE

There are growing doubts as to whether the mainstream international trading system – dominated by corporations whose overwhelming concern is to make big profits – can change enough to help the poor. By contrast, the verdict on fair trade is loud and clear. Shah Abdus Salam, executive director of the non-governmental organisation Development Wheel in Bangladesh, puts it like this:

> Only Fair Trade can ensure better and sustainable livelihoods for the marginalized artisans in the world. [The] Fair Trade movement can enhance market access for the southern poor and distress[ed] producers and [help] to establish ethics in the business in the world.

Harriet Lamb, director of the UK's Fairtrade Foundation, says the first ten years of the Fairtrade Mark have proved that consumer choice, "once derided as trivial, individualistic and apolitical, can wield positive power".

It's people like us buying the products that has made fair trade a success – and will make it even more so. Fair trade products are for everyone. Most compete on price and are widely available in supermarkets. Recognition of the Fairtrade Mark is growing. One in every two people in the UK now recognises the Mark across all age groups from 16 to 64. It's especially encouraging that recognition has grown fastest among younger people aged 16 to 34.

When you buy fair trade, your purchases can help to redress the income balance. You can help change the world. We end the book with a look into the future – a future where there can be more hope for poor people.

This book does not pretend to be an exhaustive list of reasons to buy fair trade. You may have others. If so, please write to us c/o Pluto Press, 345 Archway Road, London, N6 5AA, or email: 50reasons@phonecoop.coop. We would be delighted if readers can help us turn our 50 reasons into 100.

In the Appendices at the back of this book, we give information about where to buy fair trade (shops and suppliers), the Fairtrade Towns movement, and leading UK and international fair trade organisations and campaigns.

We feel excited about the future of fair trade. If you are new to fair trade, a whole new world awaits. If you're an old hand, we hope that in these pages you will discover even more reasons to buy the goods that help poor people.

Miles Litvinoff and John Madeley
August 2006

1. Back a system that benefits the poor

The mainstream trading system is failing the poor. Fair trade offers partnership in place of exploitation.

Trade is as old as humankind itself. At its most basic, trading takes place because people have different skills and abilities and find it worthwhile to exchange with people who have other skills and resources. Nations began to trade for much the same reason.

International trade has enabled people to enjoy a vast range of goods and has raised the living standards of many communities. But it has long been marked by greed, indifference and the oppression of those whose trading skills, resources and circumstances are relatively poor. Trading skills in an unfettered "free" market have led to the amassing of wealth for some, who gain a dominant position over others. The mainstream trading system is today failing the poor. While some gain, many lose.

The trade that has increased living standards has also caused people to go hungry and starve. During Ireland's famine of 1845–9, for example, which killed almost a million people, large landowners routinely exported food to Britain as poor peasants dropped all around them. Today food is still being exported from countries where there is gross hunger and people are dying as a result.

Substitute developing countries for Ireland, transnational corporations for large landowners, and the Western world for Britain, and little has changed. The system continues to fail the poor.

As international trade widened, economists developed the theory of comparative advantage. This holds that output will be maximised and all will gain if each country specialises in producing those goods and services for which it is best suited, and then trades them with other countries. For a variety of reasons a country may be able to produce something at a lower cost than another country. It may have a better climate, or its workforce may have special skills, for example.

[7]

But the theory is deeply flawed. Clearly, not all countries have gained from international trade. Countries that produce industrial goods – notably Western nations – have fared better than those specialising in primary produce, notably developing countries. Divisions between industrialised and primary-producing countries are widening rather than narrowing. Some 300 years ago, there was little difference in income levels across countries. At the start of the twenty-first century the difference across countries was 100 to 1.

The economists' theory has failed. Whereas people in Western countries buy more manufactured goods as incomes increase, many developing countries are less and less able to earn enough from selling their commodities to buy the manufactured goods they need.

"FREE" TRADE TODAY

In the last 20 years of the second millennium, international trade went even more severely wrong. Trade liberalisation – the reduction of barriers to trade to bring about "free" trade – began to work against millions of the poor, intensifying their poverty. The liberalisation had been underway for manufactured goods since the late 1940s, but the big move came under the structural adjustment programmes of the World Bank and International Monetary Fund, introduced in the early 1980s. Developing countries had to agree to these programmes if they wanted aid, investment and, more recently, debt relief. Trade liberalisation was a central feature.

More recently the World Trade Organization, set up in 1995, has given a further push to liberalisation. The Geneva-based WTO makes the rules that govern trade. With 149 member countries (in July 2006) the WTO has the task of enforcing the agreements that emerged from the Uruguay Round of world trade talks which ended in 1993. There are four main agreements – the Agreement on Agriculture, the General Agreement on Trade in Services, and agreements on Trade-Related Intellectual Property Rights (TRIPs) and Trade-Related Investment Measures (TRIMs).

The WTO presents itself as a forum for members to negotiate over trade liberalisation. In practice it is a trade liberalisation juggernaut which has been ceded enormous power by its members. It uses that position to further the cause of liberalisation, chiefly to the benefit of those who stand to gain most from that process – in practice, transnational corporations. The WTO's first director-general, Renato Ruggiero, said in 1998:

> We stand at the very beginning of a whole new phase of internationalism. We are living through a time of deep and rapid transition towards a very different world. [We have] an opportunity to reaffirm our political will to move towards a better system of global governance ... shaping the institutions of an increasingly borderless economy. The great promise of the new global age demands nothing else.

The vision is therefore one of a borderless world economy, of global governance, based on the "free" trade system. A snapshot of what has happened to developing countries since the early 1980s and the coming of significant trade liberalisation is revealing. Developing countries were growing at about 3 per cent between 1960 and 1980, but they grew at only about 1.5 per cent between 1980 and 2000, as University of Cambridge economist Ha-Joon Chang points out. He says:

> During the last 20 years, African economies have been shrinking (at a rate of about 0.8 per cent per year versus a 1.6 per cent growth rate before), while Latin America has been basically stagnant (growing at 0.3 per cent vs 2.8 per cent before).

Only in parts of Asia, notably South Korea, Taiwan, Indonesia and China, has there been any significant reduction in poverty, and those countries have made extensive use of trade restrictions. They have not followed the classic trade liberalisation route.

There is clear evidence from developing countries that the poorest peoples and communities have lost ground under trade liberalisation. Small-scale farmers are an example. The last 20 years have seen a huge increase in food imports into developing countries.

[9]

Millions of small-scale farmers have been unable to compete and have been driven into bankruptcy. "The relentless pursuit of trade liberalisation, privatisation and deregulation", said the Make Poverty History campaign, "has continued in the face of mounting evidence that they entrench and do not overcome poverty. The impact on poor people and our collective environment has been disastrous."

A world without barriers may sound a good idea, but the reality is that in today's economic world there are huge disparities of power. In the twenty-first century, it is companies not countries that trade. In a "free" trade, no-barriers system, the poor swim in the same economic stream as the corporations. Putting a tiddler into the same stream as a shark can have only one outcome – and it's not good for the tiddler. The poor cannot be expected to survive, let alone gain, in a system where they have no say, control, power or influence.

The corporations have been described as "instruments of a market tyranny that is extending its reach across the planet like a cancer ... destroying livelihoods, displacing people, rendering democratic institutions impotent, and feeding on life in an insatiable quest for money". The worst aspect of this is that it hits hardest at the most vulnerable people. Throughout the developing world people are working in poor countries for less than a dollar a day to make goods such as clothes and toys for the Western world. Often these goods carry prestigious brand names and sell for high prices. But wages for the people who make them are rock bottom and working conditions are often appalling. "Free" trade does not free the poor from poverty. In the mainstream trading system, the poor lose.

Fair trade, which helps the poor rather than reinforcing their poverty, is gaining support the world over and offers important hope to millions of impoverished people. In the fair trade system, the poor gain.

The rest of this book will show just how much.

2. Pay small-scale farmers a fairer price

Fair trade raises incomes of small-scale farmers and boosts local economies. The fair trade farm-gate price is the key to a better life for hundreds of thousands of families.

Agriculture is the biggest economic sector in most developing countries, and hundreds of millions of people earn a living as small-scale farmers. For decades there has been an oversupply on world markets of widely traded agricultural commodities like coffee, sugar and tea – and often an undersupply of more varied local produce for local needs. This market glut has resulted in falling prices and dwindling incomes for Southern growers. Variations in the weather, crop diseases and other factors also make farm-gate prices rise and fall unpredictably.

Twenty-five million farmers in 50 developing countries depend on coffee as their main or only crop, roughly half of them operating small family farms. Many small-scale coffee growers are geographically isolated or lack transport to take their produce to market, so they have to sell to traders and moneylenders (see Reason 21). In the case of exported coffee, the middlemen often sell to a mill for processing first, and the costs at each stage cut part of the price paid to the original grower. In addition, having to hire seasonal labour at harvest time can easily double a coffee grower's production costs.

When we buy coffee in a supermarket, only a small fraction of the retail price goes to the producer. No surprise, then, to hear from Oxfam that two-thirds of the world's coffee growers live in absolute poverty. With the international coffee agreement's collapse in 1989, prices fell below the cost of production for many farmers. Supermarkets, coffee shops and large transnational brands like Kraft and Nestlé carried on making big profits, while many debt-burdened growers could hardly scratch a living. In the words of Nicaraguan coffee farmer Mario Perez: "We practically had to give away our harvest."

Low and unstable coffee prices have had a terrible impact on the lives of small-scale farmers and their communities. There have been reports of increasing social unrest, robberies, suicides, mounting household debt, children withdrawn from school by parents, families unable to afford hospital fees – and in Colombia and Haiti growers turning in desperation to illegal drugs cultivation. In Nicaragua thousands of coffee workers held a "March of the Hungry" to the capital in mid 2003. It's said that 14 of the marchers died on the way.

Prices have been falling for banana producers too. The world banana trade – worth more than £5 billion a year – is dominated by five transnationals: Dole, Del Monte, Chiquita, Fyffe's and Noboa. They have driven down costs by sourcing supplies from large Latin American and West African plantations that pay rock-bottom wages, where working conditions are abusive and the fruit is drenched dangerously with pesticides. The smaller independent banana growers – such as hillside farmers in the Caribbean – have been unable to compete on price and have lost market share. As Dominican grower Amos Wiltshire puts it: "The economy went down to zero. ... Everything was going haywire: increasing crime, youth violence, ... delinquency. ... Husbands couldn't maintain their families."

Faced by this downward price spiral, "free" trade seems to have nothing to offer small-scale Southern farmers except more of the same. But fair trade does have an answer: a fair minimum price.

BETTER INCOMES FROM FAIR TRADE

Fairtrade certification guarantees minimum prices for producer organisations. The minimum price is based on local economic conditions and covers production costs, plus provision for household members to enjoy a decent living standard, and the cost of farm improvements and compliance with fair trade standards, including the cost of belonging to a farmers' co-operative.

Fair trade buyers pay this "floor price" – plus, for all Fairtrade-certified produce, a "social premium" (Reason 4) – when world market prices are low. But they pay the going world market rate when it rises above the "floor". In recent years the floor price paid to producers for Fairtrade-certified arabica coffee has averaged $1.21 per pound, compared with an average world market price of 70 cents a pound.

The fair trade market for bananas – second in retail value worldwide only to coffee – works similarly. The floor price takes account of the fact that smaller-scale banana growers use fewer pesticides than large plantations, and so have higher production costs because more handwork is needed, and that they have higher organisational and transport costs. In 2005 the minimum fair trade export price for Ecuadorian bananas was $0.13 per pound – roughly double the non-fair trade market rate.

The additional benefit to producers for Fairtrade-certified produce worldwide was an estimated $100 million in 2004–05. Every study made has found income higher for producers who sell to fair trade markets than for those who don't. Fair trade farmer co-operatives are estimated to earn between 25 and 60 per cent more than they would without fair trade.

How do the producers feel about it? Nicaraguan fair trade coffee grower Bertilda Gamez Peres says:

> There are big advantages. ... We get more money for our crop. We didn't make enough money to live on before. Now we get a better price and the money comes directly to us. I can buy more food. I can help support my daughter at university ... and take care of my son.

Costa Rican farmer Guillermo Vargas, who visited the UK in 2002, recalled:

> For my grandfather and my father, both coffee farmers, nothing changed. Between 1950 and 1988, nothing got better. We knew we had good coffee, but working on our own, trading as individuals, we could do nothing. Then, in 1988, we decided to form a co-operative. It gave us strength to negotiate a better price and we were able to sell to Fairtrade. When we found that one thing had gone well by acting together, we tried other things.

For Amos Wiltshire, a Dominican banana producer, fair trade "has

[13]

made a huge difference to the families, the farmers concerned and to the economy as a whole. ... Fairtrade is a shining light ... the saviour of the farmers in Dominica."

Fair trade farmers and their families benefit by being able to invest in their smallholdings and homes and pay for schooling and health services (rarely entirely free in developing countries). But the wider community also gains from the "multiplier" effect of more money earned and spent locally. New jobs get created, and local governments have more tax to spend (Reason 48).

On a broader scale, influenced by the success of fair trade in raising coffee producers' incomes, banana companies like Fyffe's and Dole are looking into ways to source and market fair trade or other forms of "socially responsible fruit".

3. Buy products you can trust

There are now over 2,000 Fairtrade-certified products – and even more fair trade goods besides!

When you buy a fair trade product, you want to know that it's the genuine thing. You want to know that it's a product you can trust. There are two main ways you can do this.

PRODUCTS THAT CARRY THE FAIRTRADE MARK

The Fairtrade Mark is your guarantee that a product has been carefully checked and certified. It's an independent label that appears on products as a guarantee that disadvantaged producers are getting a better deal.

Coffee was the first product to be certified Fairtrade – in the Netherlands in 1989. The Dutch label is called Max Havelaar, after a best-selling nineteenth-century book about the exploitation of Javanese coffee plantation workers by Dutch colonial merchants (see

Reason 11). After this first initiative, other national labelling initiatives soon followed, some using the same name, others introducing new ones like TransFair, Fairtrade Foundation and Rättvisemarkt. They all started individually, and each chose for its market the Fairtrade consumer label it wanted on the products.

In 1997, 17 national initiatives together founded a worldwide organisation, Fairtrade Labelling Organisations International (FLO). And they recognised the need for a single mark. This came into being in 2002 as the "International Fairtrade Certification Mark". FLO is responsible for setting international fair trade standards, for certifying production and auditing trade according to these standards, and for the labelling of products. Its Fairtrade Mark is both a certification mark and a registered trademark. FLO is now made up of members in 20 countries (Appendix 3).

A product qualifies for the Mark when FLO standards and procedures are met. They need to be met by producer groups, traders, processors, wholesalers and retailers. There are two sets of standards for producers, one for small farmers and one for workers on plantations and in factories. The first set applies to smallholders organised in co-operatives or other organisations with a democratic, participative structure. The second applies to organised workers whose employers pay decent wages, guarantee the right to join trade unions and provide good housing where relevant. This applies, for example, to plantation workers (Reason 7). The FLO standards stipulate that traders have to:

- pay a price to producers that covers the costs of sustainable production and living
- pay a premium that producers can invest in development
- partially pay in advance, when producers ask for this
- sign contracts that allow for long-term planning and sustainable production practices.

Fair trade is ultimately about development, so FLO's standards distinguish between minimum requirements, which producers must meet to be certified Fairtrade, and "progress requirements" that encourage producer organisations to continuously improve working conditions and product quality. Progress requirements also include improving the environmental sustainability of activities and investment in organisational and producer or worker development.

FLO gives credibility to the Fairtrade label by providing independent, transparent and competent certification of social and economic development. The four main aspects of certification are:

- ensuring the producer groups conform to the standards
- ensuring that Fairtrade benefits are used for social and economic development
- auditing FLO-registered traders to make sure that the fair trade price reaches the producers
- ensuring that the label is used only on products coming from Fairtrade-certified producers.

To ensure that producer groups comply with fair trade standards, FLO works with a network of independent inspectors who regularly visit all producer organisations to monitor traders' and retailers' compliance with Fairtrade conditions. A specially developed trade auditing system checks that every Fairtrade-labelled product sold to a consumer has genuinely been produced by a certified producer organisation which has been paid the fair trade price. Finally, there are specific fair trade standards for each product that determine such things as minimum quality, price, and processing requirements that have to be complied with.

FLO guarantees that products sold anywhere in the world with a Fairtrade label marketed by a "national initiative" conform to fair trade standards and contribute to the development of disadvantaged producers and workers.

The Fairtrade Mark therefore gives you a fivefold guarantee. It guarantees:

- a fair and stable price to farmers for their products
- extra income for farmers and estate workers to improve their lives
- a greater respect for the environment
- a stronger position for small farmers in world markets
- a closer link between consumers and producers.

There are now over 2,000 Fairtrade-certified products on the market. They include coffee, tea, chocolate, cocoa, sugar, bananas, apples, pears, grapes, plums, lemons, oranges, satsumas, clementines, lychees, avocados, pineapples, mangoes, fruit juices, quinoa, peppers, green beans, coconut, dried fruit, rooibos tea, green tea, ice cream, cakes and biscuits, honey, muesli, cereal bars, jams, chutney and sauces, herbs and spices, nuts and nut oil, wine, beer, rum, flowers, sports balls, rice, yoghurt, babyfood, sugar body scrub, cotton wool and cotton products.

And these are only some of the fair trade goods available. There are a great deal more beyond the certified range.

PRODUCTS FROM IFAT MEMBERS (INTERNATIONAL FAIR TRADE ASSOCIATION)

You can also buy fair trade goods from organisations that you trust: registered members of the International Fair Trade Association (IFAT). IFAT is made up of over 270 organisations in 60 countries (see Reason 11). Many of its members date back to the 1960s and 1970s, and they started to meet in 1985. To qualify for membership, organisations have to meet the requirements of IFAT standards, and to be registered they have to have completed the assessment process.

In January 2004 IFAT launched the "Fair Trade Organization Mark". This is an organisation mark rather than a product mark, and recognises that a whole organisation produces, imports, distributes or sells fair trade, and has poverty reduction at its core. It is used equally in both South and North. The FTO Mark recognises and unites fair trade organisations, enabling them to campaign for trade justice with greater power.

The FTO Mark guarantees that the organisation using it is registered with IFAT, and all such organisations must prove that they:

- trade honestly
- pay a fair price
- work with people who are marginalised
- exchange and build skills

- promote greater equality and empowerment for all
- protect children's rights
- respect the environment.

IFAT registration involves a three-part monitoring process: self-assessment, peer review and then external review. There is one standard for both North and South, developed and developing countries. This was established by the members and is constantly revised by them. It is not only a standard but also a tool for each FTO to ensure that it is reaching its own poverty-reducing objectives.

IFAT-registered organisations must generate the majority of their income through the sale of fair trade products. In addition, fair trade networks – such as the British Association of Fair Trade Shops (BAFTS) – and support organisations such as Shared Interest, a bank dedicated to fair trade (Reason 47), also qualify to join IFAT.

IFAT is a democratic organisation, with a majority of members from the South. It holds a global conference every two years, alternating in venue between the North and South. In the UK there are 18 members, including Bishopston Trading, Café Direct, Day Chocolate Company, People Tree, Shared Earth, Tearcraft, Traidcraft, Tropical Wholefoods and Twin Trading. Products from FTOs include clothing, jewellery, giftware, homeware, baskets, rugs, furniture, tablecloths, bedding, packaging, glassware, ceramics, embroidery, essential oils, tea, coffee, mangos and many other food products.

Among the best known UK IFAT members is People Tree, which sells "fair trade fashion" via mail order and online. People Tree clothes are made by fair trade producers at every stage – from the cloth to the final product. The company buys from farmers who grow natural fibres such as organic cotton, from handloom weavers who work in small-scale co-operatives, and from artisans who make and stitch the clothes. It is committed to supplying customers with "healthy, safe and attractive products with good service, together with information about the background of the products, producers and lifestyle alternatives".

Another major IFAT member is Traidcraft, which describes itself as "the UK's leading organisation dedicated to fighting poverty through trade". Established in 1979, Traidcraft is "a pioneering and

[18]

successful trading company (Traidcraft plc), offering the widest range of fairly traded products available in the UK". These include food, wine, fashion and crafts. It also has a development charity (Traidcraft Exchange) specialising "in making trade work for the poor" (Reason 46). The company has almost 300 different products, sourced from more than 100 producer groups in some 30 developing countries. The products are sold through a mail order catalogue, online (which is growing in popularity), and through a nationwide network of around 5,000 "fair traders" – volunteers who sell fair trade products from stalls at their church, school, university or at local events.

Products sold by IFAT member organisations can be bought with the confidence that producers receive a fair return. Consumers can trust these organisations – challenging poverty is their purpose.

4. Help producers believe in tomorrow

The "social premium" included in the price for Fairtrade-certified products may be small. But it makes a major difference when the rural poor put the money to work. And it benefits both young and old.

Millions of small-scale farmers and plantation workers in the global South are trapped in a cycle of poverty. With just enough money coming in to survive today – sometimes not enough – they are unable to think about tomorrow. Many are burdened with debt and saddled with despair.

There may not be any quick fixes. But fair trade has a medium-term remedy: the social premium. This is the extra money – on top of the guaranteed price or fair plantation worker wage – that goes to the producer community when you buy Fairtrade-certified produce. Year on year, social premium spending on community projects helps give rural producers a better future.

How much is it worth? For coffee, the current fair trade price of US$1.26 per pound paid by coffee importers includes a social premium of 5 cents. For the consumer, the premium represents about 2 per cent of the shelf price – say 5p on a £2.30 227g pack of Café-direct medium-roast ground coffee. With Fairtrade bananas it's more. For most produce the premium averages about 10 per cent of the price the importer pays.

For the producers, who spend it with great care, this money can go a long way. The Mabale Growers Tea Factory, for example – jointly owned by 1,000 small-scale Ugandan tea farmers – earns about US$30,000 a year by way of the premium. And this is based on selling only 5 per cent of its output to Teadirect and other fair trade brands. "Fair trade is significantly contributing towards the social improvement of our community and providing a better future for our youngsters," says Silver Kasoro-Atwoki, Mabale director and board member.

Under fair trade rules, the premium is saved or invested by the growers' co-operative or the plantation "joint body" of elected workers' representatives and management. It's paid directly into a special bank account, and there's a collective decision on how to use it.

Producer co-ops and plantation workers invest their premiums in a host of social projects: from building and equipping schools, clinics and community centres to paying school or medical bills; from installing water supplies, toilets and electricity to financing organic conversion; from small start-up business loans for income diversification to funding workers' pension schemes; from tree planting to women's empowerment projects.

PUTTING THE PREMIUM TO WORK

Here's how fair trade banana growers are making the most of the premium.

Leneff Hector, a St Vincent grower, told the Fairtrade Foundation: "We decided, before we use the premium for anything else, to help our schools – our producers, nurses and teachers of tomorrow." Besides supporting local schools and providing education scholarships, Windward Islands growers have invested in supporting health clinics, refurbishing community centres, upgrading local roads and small loans for on-farm improvements.

Ghanaian banana growers have used the premium to reduce herbicide use – providing more work in manual weeding – and to pay year-end bonuses. They plan to invest future premiums in organic production and a social and environmental action plan. Costa Rican growers have used the premium to pay for advice from an agronomist and environmental specialists, and for repairs to housing. "Before when it rained we couldn't transport our bananas from our fields. With the improved roads, we can," says fair trade banana farmer José Alama, who belongs to the Valle del Chira co-operative in Piura, Peru. His association of 182 small-scale growers are using the premium to improve the roads around their smallholdings and to pay for an office computer, desks, accounts books and a phone line.

Tea and coffee producers make equally good use of the premium. Tea pickers in Herkulu, Tanzania, who supply tea for Teadirect, are building a maize mill. This will save local women a 15 km walk. Their ideas for future use of the premium include paying school fees, buying sewing machines and building a technical college to train local youngsters in vocational skills. Sivapackiam, a Sri Lankan tea picker, represents fellow workers on the workers' and managers' "joint body" that decides how to use the premium on her estate: "A year ago, we didn't have any electricity in our houses," she recalls:

All the members of the joint body got together and discussed how we could pay to install it. Some money came from the Fairtrade premium and we each took out a loan. With electricity, my children can study at night. In the morning I can iron their clothes and we can use a hotplate for cooking. I am happy that fair trade helps me support my family.

The Nilgiris tea estate in the West Ghats mountains, southern India, employs more than 3,000 people. Here workers used the premium to start a pension fund. Jointly run by estate workers and managers, the scheme is a rarity in India, where few manual workers can retire with any financial security. Workers like Manickam – who picked tea for 41 years – can retire when they are 58 and receive a pension of up to 1,200 Rupees (£15) per month for the next 15 years. This can be crucial, because retired tea pickers usually have to leave the plantation where they were living and rarely receive any social security payments.

At Mabale in Uganda, the premium has been invested in training and plant husbandry. Growers are steadily producing more and better-quality tea, obtaining higher prices for the tea that they have to keep selling to non-fair-trade markets until fair trade demand grows larger.

More than 3,500 small-scale coffee growers belonging to Costa Rica's Coocafé co-operative association supply fair trade coffee to Europe and the United States. The foundation they set up with the social premium in the mid 1990s supports soil restoration, tree planting and environmental education. They have also used the money to maintain local primary schools and to fund secondary school and university scholarships for hundreds of farmers' children, as well as to provide plots to landless families.

5. Make trade more democratic

International trade is mostly undemocratic, controlled by large corporations. Fair trade spreads power and enables more people to have control over their lives.

Countries don't trade, companies do. Especially large companies. Around two-thirds of international trade is between transnational corporations (TNCs). Defined by the United Nations as "an enterprise with activities in two or more countries with an ability to influence others", transnational corporations are mostly public companies owned by their shareholders. The corporations are large, powerful and unaccountable to anyone but their shareholders. They are unelected and undemocratic and they make the mainstream trading system undemocratic.

TNCs are large. In 1999, 51 of the world's 100 largest economies were corporations, 49 were governments. To put this in perspective, General Motors is bigger than Denmark and over three times the size of New Zealand. The top 200 corporations' combined sales are bigger than the combined economies of all countries except the largest ten.

Their numbers are increasing rapidly. In the early 1990s there were an estimated 37,000 TNCs with 170,000 foreign affiliates. "By 2004", says UNCTAD, "the number of TNCs had risen to some 70,000 transnational corporations with at least 690,000 foreign affiliates." The foreign affiliates therefore increased fourfold in little over a decade.

TNCs are widespread, involved in every sphere of economic activity in virtually every country, and they are powerful. Their size, usually with the protection afforded by company law and governments, gives corporations power to make the rules. They can dictate terms to national governments – dangling jobs and foreign earnings as the carrot – and have taken full advantage of the move towards privatisation to influence government policy. TNCs have also used their power to influence international trade negotiations, often secretly. Although they work locally in developing countries, key decisions affecting what they do may be taken thousands of miles away in their head office in New York, London, Paris or other capital cities.

TNCs are not subject to international regulation. The United Nations tried for 17 years, from 1975 to 1992, to draw up a code of conduct for them. It had to abandon the attempt. The corporations were powerful enough to stop it.

TNCs dominate markets. Several million small-scale coffee farmers sell into a market where just four companies buy 40 per cent of global output, and similar structures apply in cocoa, bananas, soya and many other products.

[23]

In most developed markets, retailing has also become extremely consolidated. In Britain the "Big Four" supermarket chains account for over 70 per cent of all food sales. Globalisation offers buying companies operating at this scale huge benefits as they can seek the best deals from anywhere in the world, whereas producers, especially smallholders, are limited in their ability to find new customers.

TNCs resist attempts to make them more democratic. In mid 2006, for example, Parliament debated a Bill to reform company law. Campaigners urged that the Bill should include a clause that would hold company directors accountable for the social and environmental impact of their company's activities. They also pressed for a clause that would require companies to monitor and report on their social and environmental impacts. The Confederation of British Industry, the main UK business lobby group, were successful in persuading the government not to support such changes. The Bill does however strengthen some aspects of company reporting requirements and directors' duties.

While they make noises about sustainable development, TNCs fail the sustainable development tests. Their interest lies in maximising profits in the short term, not necessarily sustaining them over the long term. TNCs have to make good profits for their shareholders, otherwise they will be judged to be underperforming and be ripe for take-over. Shareholders want their dividends, this year and TNCs have to deliver. In terms of accountability to the wider public, they are deeply undemocratic. But it does not have to be like this.

THE DEMOCRATIC ALTERNATIVE

The fair trade system is a viable and proven economic alternative. Fair trade is democratic, decentralised and transparent. Fairtrade Labelling Organisations International – the Fairtrade Foundation is the UK member – awards the Fairtrade Mark to products that qualify. For food products, one of the conditions is that the farmers democratically organise into small-farmer groups such as co-operative organisations under terms that include the following:

- The majority of the members of the organisation must be small-scale producers.
- The organisation must be an instrument for the social and economical development of the members, and in particular the benefits of Fairtrade must come to the members.
- The organisation must therefore have a democratic structure and transparent administration, which enables an effective control by its members and its board over the management, including the decisions about how the benefits are shared. There must be no discrimination regarding membership and participation.
- An organisational structure is in place which enables control by the members.
- There is a general assembly with voting rights for all members as the supreme decision taking body, and an elected board. The staff answers through the board to the general assembly.
- The organisation holds a general assembly at least once a year.
- The annual report and accounts are presented to and approved by the general assembly.
- The organisation works towards transparent planning of the business plans. Such plans will be approved by the General Assembly.
- The participation of members in the organisation's administration and internal control is promoted through training and education.
- The organisation establishes or improves internal mechanisms of members' control over the administration, such as a control committee with rights to review the administration.
- Increasingly, the organisation's policies are discussed in member meetings.
- Management actively encourages members' participation in meetings.
- There is improvement of the flow of information from board to members about the business and the organisation's policies.

Organisations are encouraged to make annual business plans, cash flow predictions and longer-term strategic plans.

In the case of products such as tea which are grown on plantations, there are of necessity differences. One of the conditions for the Fairtrade Mark for plantation-grown tea is the development of "joint bodies" which enable workers to engage in decision-making processes with management and influence social development projects on plantations (see Reason 7).

Other fair trade organisations, such as IFAT, Traidcraft, People Tree and Oxfam Trading, have requirements about democratic structures. All are a big improvement on the structure and practice of the transnational corporation.

Fair trade is democratic trade.

6. Put a human face on development

There's a lot of debate about "development". Fair trade puts many of the best ideas into practice. This small-scale Chilean honey-producers' co-operative provides a perfect example.

The setting is the small provincial town of Santa Bárbara in southern Chile. Sitting in their wooden one-storey office in a corner of the tranquil *plaza*, Joel Uribe and Luis Villaroel talk about their beekeepers' co-operative, COASBA, with quiet pride. It was Joel, an engineer by training, who founded the association in 1994 and built it up from next to nothing, using his home as an office and working unpaid to get COASBA on its feet. More recently Luis, who used to drive lorries for a living, took over from Joel as president.

Early on, COASBA's members – families who kept bees and produced honey on a small scale – were all part-timers. "Very few of us owned any land, so most had to rent a *parcela* [small plot] for their hives. None could earn a decent livelihood as honey producers," Joel and Luis recall.

Today most of COASBA's 35 members, including two women, practise beekeeping full time. Honey and bee serum are their main source of income. After years of effort invested in developing their skills and processes, Joel and Luis claim the taste, cleanliness and nutritious quality of their honey are among the best in the country. They feel they are raising standards in their industry for the whole of Chile's BioBío region.

Too often, so-called "development" has involved huge transnational companies arriving in developing countries, plundering their raw materials, undermining the local economy, wrecking the environment and people's lives – and then getting the hell out of there.

But there's another way. It's been called "people-centred development" or "development with a human face". Examples can be found all over the world, and increasingly they're linked to fair trade.

FROM DEBT TO DEVELOPMENT

COASBA has come a long way. At first, co-op members were often in debt to local moneylenders. They had to use the cheapest low-quality bulk containers to transport the honey. There was little time to spend on hygiene, pest and disease control, or breeding. Plus they had no way of knowing when they would make their next sale. That was before COASBA was introduced to fair trade by a Chilean church-based development organisation supported by the European Union.

COASBA's honey has been Fairtrade-certified for the past five years. The most obvious benefit, say Joel and Luis, is better incomes: "Co-op members get 20 per cent more for their honey under fair trade than when they sell through other channels."

All COASBA members – who between them now keep several thousand beehives, producing roughly 130 tonnes of honey a year – allocate some of their produce to be bulked up in modern stainless steel drums and sold to Apicoop, a large fair trade exporter co-operative based on the coast. Apicoop exports the honey to fair trade buyers in Germany, Switzerland, France, Italy, Spain, Belgium and the UK. In the UK it's an ingredient in Traidcraft's popular Geobars.

Joel and Luis believe they could not have developed COASBA

without fair trade. "Fair trade has helped raise earnings for beekeepers all round – not just for co-op members," they claim. Freed from moneylenders and exploitative middlemen, each COASBA member has a regular guaranteed income. The co-op pays them a decent lump sump once a year, which enables people to plan. COASBA itself retains a percentage of sales income to invest in improving production processes and for administration. This has created several new jobs, such as for Maria-José Cordoba, the young woman who runs the small office in the *plaza*.

Co-op households have raised their standard of living. Many have bought their own plot of land and improved their homes. Several now own a vehicle for transporting the honey. Some of their children are among the first from this rural community to go to university. In a region where poverty is widespread, family finances are far better than before. Crucially, the younger generation can see a future in beekeeping and in running a co-operative enterprise, rather than joining the exodus of young rural unemployed to the bigger towns and cities.

COASBA has earned a reputation for paying off its debts promptly and won respect from such bodies as the Agriculture Ministry's Institute for Agriculture and Livestock Development. Among the members there is increasing trust and mutual support. When necessary COASBA lends members money to buy equipment or medicines for their bees, with more time to repay than before. It has supported member households through periods of hospitalisation.

Professional development, advice and training are another major benefit. Maintaining and improving production standards are all important to COASBA. The co-op is a member of Chile's national network of beekeepers and prides itself on high technical and sanitary standards. Joel and Luis sense they are gaining national recognition for their produce. COASBA has recently begun to provide advisory services for local beekeepers outside the co-op, along with programmes in basic beekeeping for the local municipality.

Though it is not certified organic, Joel and Luis claim their honey is organic in all but name. They see beekeeping as essentially an ecological activity and are determined to help protect the diverse native flora of the beautiful BioBío river valley.

HONEY FROM SANTA BÁRBARA

COASBA's confidence is growing. At the heart of their future plans lies the small yet ultra-modern honey processing plant and laboratory they are building just outside the town. The new one-storey building will house facilities that, they intend, will be second to none in the whole country. Initial support for the project, begun in 1999, came from a regional non-profit foundation.

The building is almost ready and will enable the co-op to add far more value to their product. Here they will not only bulk up their honey for export but also bottle it in jars for domestic retail markets, proudly labelled "Honey from Santa Bárbara". At the front gate will be a shop selling to passers-by.

The laboratory they are installing will enable co-op members to diagnose and control diseases among their bee colonies far more swiftly than at present. Currently they have to send samples away for analysis. The laboratory will serve not just co-op members but beekeepers throughout the region. Genetic improvement and training programmes are being planned in partnership with two Chilean universities.

Joel and Luis's ambition is for COASBA to become an independent honey exporter. They foresee a day when jars labelled "Honey from Santa Bárbara" will be on sale in food shops throughout Chile, Europe and even the Middle East.

7. Ensure plantation workers earn a living wage

Plantation workers can be among the poorest of the poor. With fair trade they receive a proper wage and decent conditions.

Plantation workers. The people who work on large farm estates toil for long hours often under the hot sun. Their working conditions may be unsafe, and they are usually paid a pittance for the work they do. And when work is finished for the day their low wages cause them to live in conditions that may be an affront to human dignity. Too often they lack the freedom to join a union to defend their rights and the opportunity to participate in decisions that affect their lives on the plantation.

Under the fair trade system a proper wage is paid to workers on plantations (estates, as they are sometimes called). And there are other benefits too.

TEA

Tea is the UK's most popular drink. We sip an average of three and a half cups a day. Only in Ireland and Poland do people drink more tea.

Most tea is plucked on plantations, notably in India, Sri Lanka, China and Kenya. Tea plantations are labour-intensive, with planting, maintenance and harvesting usually carried out by hand. The crop is picked year-round in tropical areas, mostly by women with baskets or bags on their backs to carry the leaves plucked from the growing tips of the shrubs. The leaves are taken to a collection point to be weighed then transported to a nearby processing plant, as they need to be processed on the same day to retain freshness and flavour. At these plants the leaves are withered, rolled, fermented, dried and sorted.

Working under a scorching sun, lugging heavy baskets and sacks estate employees are normally paid on a piece rate system. The amount they earn depends on how much they pluck. Often they earn the statutory minimum wage – where one exists – and receive some of the lowest wages in their countries. Taking into account the fact that entire families may have to survive on one or two incomes, the per capita wage in many cases is below US$1 a day. And that is the daily income that the World Bank defines as the acute poverty line.

Workers on tea plantations often do not earn enough to have any reserve. If they lose their jobs, their very survival can be at stake. In March 2004, for example, around 800 tea workers in India were reported to have died of starvation, "with several surviving on wild roots and rats, because the closure of uneconomic plantations rendered a million labourers jobless". The report by the Indian People's Tribunal on Human Rights and the Environment, a civil rights group based in Mumbai, said that the deaths resulted from a combination of starvation, malnutrition, general debility and diseases among workers.

In many Asian plantations entire families of men women and children work together. In India, Sri Lanka and Viet Nam women account for over 50 per cent of the plantation labour force, and in Pakistan and the Philippines it is around 35 per cent. Women usually pluck the tea whereas men are responsible for preparing the land, spraying pesticides, pruning and supervision. In most cases female workers are also responsible for the majority of household tasks, such as fetching water, which can take hours.

Although the fact is usually officially denied, child labour is also common in many of the poorer tea-producing regions due to the economic conditions of the household and lack of schools. Even where it is illegal for children to work on plantations, as in Sri Lanka, their situation may not be much better as children of tea workers are sometimes sent off to the cities to work as domestic servants, leaving them even more vulnerable. A survey by the Malawi Congress of Trade Unions found that the use of child labour is a very serious problem on many tea plantations.

India's Plantations Labour Act (of 1951) sets the legal framework for the tea industry in India but has one serious omission. It does not cover occupational health hazards and safety measures for field workers. In Assam and West Bengal, pesticides are usually sprayed by untrained casual daily wage workers, mostly children and adolescents, who are illiterate and unable to read the warnings on the containers. They often use bare hands to mix these chemicals, some of which are banned, yet workers are not provided with masks, goggles, gloves, rubber boots, polythene aprons or other protective gear. Usually they are unaware of the risks, and no compulsory medical check-ups are conducted. When they sustain injuries, their medical care is highly inadequate.

The tea industry in India relies on insecticides, pesticides, herbicides and fungicides to protect the tea crop from various diseases and maintain yields. Evidence shows that workers have developed poisoning of the cardiovascular and nervous systems as well as the kidneys and liver, blindness, memory loss and premature senility. Research in Sri Lanka has shown that deaths due to the use of pesticides are common. The International Labour Organization has identified a high incidence of accidents relating to chemical exposure.

FAIRTRADE ESTATE TEA

The need for a better deal is clear. Some tea estates now qualify under the fair trade system. To qualify for Fairtrade certification for their tea, estate employers must pay decent wages, guarantee the right to join trade unions and provide good housing when relevant. Minimum health and safety as well as environmental standards must be complied with. No child below the age of 15 can be employed. Forced labour is not allowed. A premium of €0.50 to €1.00 per kg must also be paid to be invested in social, economic or environmental programmes for the benefit of the workers (see Reason 4).

"Joint bodies" must be developed which enable workers to have a say in decisions that affect them, allowing them to influence the social development projects on plantations. This means that Fairtrade tea estate workers can negotiate directly with owners and management and have a direct input into the decision-making process. The joint bodies decide how the Fairtrade premium can be invested in projects that benefit the estate community. They proportionately include women and members of minority groups.

Business development services also have to be available to help build the commercial capacity of producers. And sustainable farming methods must be implemented that are safer for humans and the environment.

Most tea gardens have received the equivalent of a few thousand or perhaps a few tens of thousand of pounds, but some in India and Sri Lanka have earned several hundred thousand pounds in Fairtrade premiums. This money is making a significant contribution to empowering workers and improving their livelihoods. An analysis of how the premium money has been allocated shows that funds are spent on a variety of projects. Some joint bodies have decided to construct schools or health centres with the help of this money. Others have acquired computers and other equipment for schools or awarded scholarships. Electricity has been installed, cattle bought, pension and loan funds established, vaccination programmes set up or forests replanted. Village roads have been improved, playgrounds built, and flushing toilets and solar lighting installed. Pensioners, orphans and people with disabilities have received financial support.

Fairtrade-certified tea is making big difference to the lives of plantation workers.

8. Empower women and girls

Women produce most of the food and craftwork and make most of the clothes in developing countries. But they're still often treated as second-class citizens. Buying fair trade is a great way to support the fight for gender equality.

Of the world's 1.2 billion people living on less than $1 a day, 70 per cent are women and girls. Women everywhere work longer hours than men for less pay and in worse jobs. When they do the same job they earn on average two-thirds of a man's wage. And they do many extra hours of unpaid work in the home, providing food, shelter, health care, education and clothing for their families, especially in rural areas.

Most women in developing countries work in the "informal" sector. Many support their families through subsistence farming or small-scale crafts production. Often with little or no land, capital, credit or technology, they have to toil all the harder. In traditional communities, women's tasks are often treated as less important than men's.

To makes ends meet, Southern women increasingly need to work outside the home. In agriculture they are often hired on low-paid seasonal contracts, working long hours and exposed to hazardous chemicals. In manufacturing, women are less likely than men to demand better working conditions. Hours of unpaid overtime may be enforced to meet just-in-time orders from international big-name companies.

Among the world's most exploited women are millions of garment workers in countries like Bangladesh, Honduras and Morocco. Oxfam says they are "burnt out by working harder, faster and over longer hours, and with few heath, maternity or union rights".

Women's poverty goes hand in hand with widespread disempowerment. Widowed, divorced or separated women may lose their home, family or means to survive. Millions of women and girls are trafficked into the sex trade.

Yet women are so much more than victims. They often offer the best solutions for poverty reduction. Their income has been shown to provide more family and community benefits than men's, with a greater proportion spent on nutrition, health and education. Women's empowerment is crucial to improving the lives of the poorest, and fair trade is an effective way to help.

HOW FAIR TRADE HELPS WOMEN

One of fair trade's main goals is to promote women's development opportunities by valuing and rewarding their work fairly and empowering them in organisations. According to internationally agreed fair trade standards, women should have the same opportunities as men to train, develop skills, apply for job vacancies and seek leadership roles, and their gender-specific health, safety and cultural needs must be taken into consideration. This all means better opportunities for uneducated, widowed and divorced women and for single mothers.

Fair trade rules also require women workers to be well represented on the "joint bodies" and committees that decide how the fair trade social premium is spent (see Reason 4). This often gives women a chance to speak in public for the first time. Greater self-reliance and participation in a co-operative or committee enhance women's self-esteem and social standing. They gain leadership skills and a greater sense of freedom and security. Says Punjiben, who grows fair trade cotton in Gujarat, India, "Our voices are equally important in the committee. Our voices are strong in the decision-making process."

[34]

Traidcraft, one of the UK's biggest and longest-established fair trade companies, supports a range of women-centred projects in Bangladesh. Among its suppliers of arts and crafts products are: Aarong, 85 per cent of whose rural artisans are women; Eastern Screen Printers, which employs 30 women in printing designs onto handmade paper and jute and cotton fabrics; Jahanara Cottage Industries, which trains rural women in painting, weaving, knitting, woodcarving and basket weaving; and CORR-The Jute Works, working since 1973 with war-widowed and war-affected rural women.

In Africa, Traidcraft's food and drink supply chains also clearly benefit women. Sugar from Malawi used in GeoActive bars comes from the Kasinthula Cane Growers' Association, whose income paid for a borehole for Kapasule village, saving women a 1.5 kilometre daily trek for water. Juliet Ntwirenabo, of Igara Growers, Uganda, whose tea is sold by Teadirect and Traidcraft, chairs the growers' committee that decides how to spend their social premium. Juliet says: "Since we became Fairtrade farmers our women no longer die in childbirth being carried down the mountain to the hospital. From our Fairtrade proceeds we have built two maternity wards."

In 2005 the BBC reported on one of the women-only fair trade coffee co-operatives that have sprung up in Rwanda, where many women were widowed in the 1994 genocide. One member explained that now she could afford family health insurance, her children could see a doctor, and there was money to send even girls to school.

Nicaraguan agronomist and community organiser Janixce Florian tells a similar story. Janixce works with fair trade coffee co-operative SOPPEXCCA and visited the UK during Fairtrade Fortnight 2006. Of the co-op's 650 members, 190 are women, and fair trade has enabled many of them to participate in workshops for the first time.

Women have proved excellent quality coffee growers, Janixce says, in one case winning a national prize three years running. Some women members so impressed visiting US buyers that their women-only coffee is now marketed under the brand name "Las Hermanas" (The Sisters). Some of the husbands have become jealous, but the women know how to handle them.

Kuapa Kokoo, the large and well-known co-operative in Ghana that supplies cocoa to the Day Chocolate Company (Reason 44) and Traidcraft, runs a range of women's income generation projects. These include production and marketing of vegetables, soap and palm oil.

Just as deprivation gets passed down across generations, so does empowerment. Women strengthened by fair trade bring up daughters with higher expectations. Teenager Rijayatu Razak, daughter of Kuapa Kokoo members, is an example of how fair trade is changing girls' outlook. Able to go to secondary school only as a result of fair trade's social premium, Rijayatu won an essay competition and visited the UK one Fairtrade Fortnight. She says:

> At school I have started my own co-operative for girls only. We think that it is not fair that the girls have to do all the housework while the boys can ride around the village on their bicycles and play football. We think the work should be equal between the girls and the boys.

9. Bring hope to coffee growers

An expansion of the market for Fairtrade-certified coffee offers hope for coffee growers – not least the basic hope of eating.

When Nicaraguan coffee grower, Blanca Rosa Molina is asked about the difference that selling through the fair trade system makes, her reply is both simple and devastating. "It makes the difference between whether my family eats or does not eat," she says.

Blanca farms three hectares of land in the Matagalpa region in the north of Nicaragua. The country is one of the world's main coffee growing countries and coffee is its primary export crop. Blanca is president of the Cecocafen co-operative of some 1,200 coffee producers. Like other members of the co-operative, she sells about a third of her coffee in the Fairtrade-certified system.

Now 47, life for Blanca began the hard way, as it did for many other generations in Nicaragua. Her parents were workers on a large coffee plantation in Matagalpa. At the age of six, Blanca joined her parents at work in the fields. Aged 11, she left home to work as a maid in Managua, the capital city.

But things were to change dramatically when the Nicaraguan revolution was won in 1979. Agricultural reform laws were introduced and land was redistributed to the landless. A new phase of hope began for Blanca's family and many of her neighbours when they started to grow coffee on their own land in Matagalpa. Things were good for a while.

But the volatility of coffee prices on the world market began to make their lives precarious. Throughout the 1990s prices fluctuated, but were often too low for growers to make a decent living. In the early 2000s the collapse of coffee prices continued to undermine the security of peasant farmers, and gradually eroded Nicaragua's export earnings.

In 2002, the crisis reached catastrophic proportions. Coffee prices plummeted to 30-year lows, with the result that many of the big commercial farmers could no longer afford to harvest their crop and laid off full-time and seasonal labour. It was a price fall that hit workers very hard. Thousands of out-of-work coffee workers and their families were reduced to setting up makeshift roadside camps. They only survived thanks to food donations from concerned local people and businesses.

"Most people who worked on large coffee plantations lost their jobs," said Blanca. She was fortunate. The Cecocafen co-operative had by then obtained the Fairtrade mark for its coffee. Blanca points out:

The fair trade price allows us to eat, to keep our land. It means our children can stay in school and that we can have the basic health provisions. The price has enabled me to send my daughter to university and build my house bit by bit. It's a very humble house and I am still building. I took a loan from the co-operative which has to be paid back within a year. But small producers, if they are not supplying the fair trade market, could hardly afford a house, and they have no access to credit.

Blanca has also been able to diversify production on her land, "which has given us greater food security".

EMPHASIS ON QUALITY

"We hope that fair trade increases because there are many more coffee farmers in our region who would like to sell some of their crop through this system," Blanca says. "We know the importance of producing top-quality coffee so that the market keeps growing. Only the best quality goes into Cecocafen coffee. The emphasis on quality starts at the point of selection of the seeds."

Coffee from Cecocafen goes into Cafédirect's 5065 and Percol's Nicaragua coffee. The Cecocafen co-operative distributes and markets coffee for its 1,200 members, who decide at general assembly meetings how to use the Fairtrade premium they receive.

Of the US$1.26 cents a pound that growers receive for their coffee in the Fairtrade certification system, 5 cents is the Fairtrade premium that is used for business or community development programmes (see Reason 4).

"Fair trade is not just to benefit the individual farmers," stresses Blanca. "It's to benefit the community as a whole. Fairtrade isn't only about buying and selling. It has a very important social aspect." The co-operative has used the premium for social improvements, ensuring that children are going to school, for example, and that women are included in decision-making processes. The premium has also been invested in social projects such as water supply services, road building and buying medicines for the community. A scholarship fund has paid for further education for 70 children of co-operative members. A general credit scheme has been set up as a savings and loan programme for women. This is benefiting over 200 female members and non-members.

Blanca goes on:

> We don't just want to see farmers who are selling under the fair trade system improve their own standard of living, we want the community as a whole to benefit. So our co-operative is teaching literacy skills to both adults and children, and we have done lots of primary health education.

Community improvements are happening, she says. One community has used the premium to pay for a teacher. Others have ensured that young children receive nutritious food.

The Fairtrade premium has also been invested in processing facilities and a quality control laboratory. This has helped Cecocafen to develop and market its own roast and ground and organic coffee brands. The investment has created a new source of income for Cecocafen members, as the facilities are also hired to other producers.

When farmers become part of the fair trade system, says Blanca:

> It is easier for them to convert to organic, chemical-free production, because they have support in terms of training, advice on organic methods and so on. The coffee premium allows farmers to carry out soil and water conservation activities and helps to protect the environment.

She would like to sell more of her coffee through the Fairtrade system, "but that depends on the market expanding". Asked what her message is to people who buy coffee, Blanca says: "Buy our coffee because it is the best quality, not because we are poor farmers."

Coffee prices on the world market have recovered since the bleak days of the early 2000s, but in late 2006 were still low and fluctuating. This gives most growers an uncertain future. An expansion of the market for Fairtrade-certified coffee offers hope for an increasing number.

10. Save a cotton farmer's life

Buying fair trade pyjamas can help prevent suicides among Indian cotton farmers. Sounds far-fetched? Read on and decide for yourself.

Small-scale farmers the world over are more likely to commit suicide than many other occupational groups. Even in a rich country with all kinds of safety nets, such as the UK, farming can be an isolated, debt-burdened and stressful business. Crises like foot and mouth, added to uncertain or falling farm-gate prices, can easily lead to financial difficulties, anxiety and depression.

In developing countries the problems are usually worse. For many Southern smallholders, the global trading system and a collapse in government support have made it virtually impossible to earn a decent living on the land. Falling prices, rising costs, increasing reliance on expensive agrochemicals and irrigation, alongside years of worsening drought, crop failure, environmental problems and ill-health, have led millions of small-scale farmers into debt and despair.

Small-scale cotton farmers have had particularly severe problems – not least because cotton is unusually pest-prone and uses more insecticides than any other crop. In recent years world cotton prices have been undercut by heavily subsidised cotton from the EU (grown mainly in Greece, Portugal and Spain), the USA and China, and through increasing competition from synthetic fibres like nylon and polyester. India's cotton farmers have been among the worst hit, and suicides among them are common. The online newspaper *India Together* reported in 2005:

> The spell of suicides continues even in the harvest. The last two years have seen inadequate rainfall. The irrigation scenario is frustrating, and water resources are fast drying up. ... An unregulated open market and private usurers have tightened their noose around the debt-ridden cotton farmers.

Aged just 30, for example, Maharashtra state cotton farmer Lokeshwar Keshavrao Bhoyar took his life by jumping into his dried-up well in October 2005. Lata, his widow, is now a day labourer cotton picker, earning 2 Indian rupees (3 pence) per kilo.

Farmer suicides have been reported across the country – in Andhra Pradesh, Karnataka, Kerala, Maharashtra, Punjab and Rajasthan. And not only farmers are at risk, but their sons and daughters too. In November 2005, 19-year-old cotton farmer's daughter Neeta Pundalikrao Bhopat, a BA student, committed suicide, leaving a note that read: "My family can't make even a thousand rupees a month. And I have two younger sisters ... we don't have enough to eat. So I am ending my life."

VILLAGES AND KIDNEYS FOR SALE

Since 2001, when the trend began, whole Indian villages have been reported as being up for sale. In December 2005, villagers of Dorli in Maharashtra state put up signboards announcing: "Dorli village is for sale." Each of the village's 270 residents, including all its children, was said to be carrying a debt of 30,000 rupees (£380).

Not long afterwards, the people of Chingapur village, also in Maharashtra, announced a "human market for the sale of kidneys" and sent invitations to India's President, Dr Abdul Kalam, and Prime Minister Manmohan Singh to witness the proceedings. The villagers saw this as the only way to raise money to repay their debts.

"This village is ready to be auctioned. Permit us to commit mass suicide," read banners displayed by people living in another village, Shivani Rekhailapur, nearby.

MEET SHAILESH

If you ask Shailesh Patel, project manager at Indian fair trade cotton producers Agrocel Industries, what the main benefits of fair trade are, he replies: "Fair trade saves farmers' lives. It prevents suicides. ... Working alone, volatile prices and continuing worries are among the main causes of farmer suicides," he says.

Fairtrade-certified in 2005, Agrocel is co-owned by the Gujarat government and several small companies, and works with small-scale cotton growers in three Indian states. Shailesh's visit to London for Fairtrade Fortnight 2006 coincided with a high-profile launch of fair trade cotton by Marks & Spencer, followed by fair trade jeans later in the year.

Ganesha, Gossypium, Hug, People Tree, Traidcraft and other suppliers in the UK sell goods made from Agrocel's fair trade cotton, along with retailers and brands in continental Europe, North America and India. The range is wide: trousers, shirts, blouses, jackets, skirts, pyjamas, baby clothes, hats, bags, duvets, cushions, bed linen, soft toys, tableware, t-shirts, hoodies, yoga wear, crew tops, shorts and underwear. All Agrocel's cotton is grown by environmentally sensitive methods, and the farmers increasingly seek organic certification. The company pays producers 8 per cent above prevailing market prices. And there are plenty of other advantages for cotton farmers apart from a fair and steady price.

"With fair trade, each farmer belongs to an association," Shailesh points out. "And fair trade also brings the social premium and community development." Agrocel offers a range of support services. Its twelve centres across India support thousands of farmers by selling them good quality inputs at fair prices, providing advice and training in sustainable and organic production, arranging farmer-to-farmer skill-share programmes and seminars, and running demonstration plots.

One Agrocel programme involves encouraging cultivation of the neem tree, whose natural oil and leaves are a rich source of biological pesticide and fertiliser. Working with the neem tree, farmers can reduce their dependence on costly bought-in chemicals, as well as providing themselves with valuable off-season employment. Another Agrocel scheme is training women in handicrafts production, enabling them to improve family income. Agrocel farmer households – and others in surrounding communities – also benefit from a veterinary service for their livestock.

Agrocel began supporting organic fair trade cotton production in 1998 and currently works with 20,000 growers. It is expanding steadily as more and more farmers come to appreciate the difference its support, and fair trade, can make.

Indian cotton farmers are not the only ones to benefit. Cameroon, Mali, Peru and Senegal also supply Fairtrade-certified cotton for goods on sale in the UK.

11. Be part of a growing global movement

Link up with one of the most exciting developments for years!

The fair trade movement today is a world-wide success story. Over a million small-scale producers and workers in 580 certified producer groups in 58 countries are actively involved in the system. And the products are increasingly being used in workplaces, and sold in restaurants and hotels. They are sold in thousands of "world shops" or fair trade shops, supermarkets and many other sales points in the North and, increasingly, in sales outlets in the Southern hemisphere. Fair trade unites producers with millions of consumers in Europe, North America, Australasia and Japan with people in developing countries.

THE START

The first formal "fair trade" shop opened in 1958 in the USA, selling goods from Puerto Rico and other poor communities in the South. The earliest traces of fair trade in Europe date from the late 1950s when Oxfam UK started to sell crafts made by Chinese refugees in Oxfam shops. In 1964 it created the first fair trade organisation, Oxfam Trading. Parallel initiatives were taking place in the Netherlands and in 1967 the importing organisation, Fair Trade Organisatie, was established. At the same time, Dutch-third world groups began to sell cane sugar with the message: "by buying cane sugar you give people in poor countries a place in the sun of prosperity." These groups went on to sell handicrafts from the South.

During the 1960s and 1970s non-governmental organisations (NGOs) and socially motivated individuals in many countries in Asia, Africa and Latin America perceived the need for fair marketing organisations which would provide advice, assistance and support to disadvantaged producers. Many such Southern fair trade organisations were established, and links were made with the new organisations in the North. These relationships were based on partnership, dialogue, transparency and respect. The goal was greater equity in international trade.

Fair trade (or alternative trade as it was called in the early days) grew as a response to poverty in the South and originally focused on the marketing of craft products. Its founders were often the large development and sometimes religious agencies in European countries.

In 1973, Fair Trade Organisatie in the Netherlands , imported the first "fairly traded" coffee from co-operatives of small farmers in Guatemala. Hundreds of thousands of coffee farmers have since benefited from Fairtrade-certified coffee. After coffee, the food range soon expanded to include products like tea, cocoa, sugar, tea, fruit juices and spices.

In the 1980s, a new way of reaching the broad public was developed. A priest working with smallholder coffee farmers in Mexico and a collaborator of a Dutch church-based NGO conceived the idea of a fair trade label. Products bought, traded and sold in ways that respected fair trade conditions would qualify for a label that would make them stand out among ordinary products on store shelves, and would allow any company to get involved in fair trade. In 1988, the "Max Havelaar" label was established in the Netherlands. The concept caught on: within a year, coffee with the label had a market share of almost 3 per cent.

In the ensuing years, similar non-profit fair trade labelling organisations were set up in other European countries and in North America. From the beginning, the fair trade movement aimed at raising awareness of consumers about the problems caused by conventional trade, and at introducing changes to its rules. The sale of products went alongside information on the production, producers and their conditions of living.

FAIR TRADE SHOPS AND NETWORKS

World shops and fair trade shops continue to mobilise consumers to participate in campaigning activities for more global justice.

The first European World Shops conference took place in 1984 and marked the beginning of close co-operation between volunteers working in World Shops from all over Europe . The Network of European World Shops (NEWS!) was formally established in 1994 and represents approximately 3,000 World Shops in 15 European countries. NEWS! co-ordinates European campaigning activities and stimulates the exchange of information and experiences about development of sales and awareness raising work. In 1996, NEWS! established the European World Shops Day as a Europe-wide day of campaign on a particular issue, often with a goal at the European level. To further co-operation, the European Fair Trade Association (EFTA) was founded in 1987. EFTA is an association of the eleven largest importing fair trade organisations in Europe.

The first World Fair Trade Day, which involves the worldwide fair trade movement, was celebrated on 4 May 2002 (see Reason 45).

The International Fair Trade Association (IFAT) started in 1989 (it was originally set up as the International Federation for Alternative Trade). It is a global network of 270 fair trade organisations – and is still growing. Its membership covers five regions: Africa, Asia, Latin America, Europe and North America and the Pacific Rim. It also has regional chapters: the Asia Fair Trade Forum (AFTF), Cooperation for Fair Trade in Africa (COFTA), and the Associacion Latino Americana de Commercio Justo. IFAT's aim is to improve the livelihoods of disadvantaged people through trade, and providing a forum for the exchange of information and ideas. The British Association of Fair Trade Shops, (BAFTS) promotes fair trade retailing in the UK.

Other fair trade networks have been established, including the Ecota Fair Trade Forum in Bangladesh, Fair Trade Group Nepal,

Associated Partners for Fairer Trade Philippines, Fair Trade Forum India and Kenya Federation for Alternative Trade.

IFAT launched a fair trade mark, the FTO Mark, in January 2004 at the World Social Forum in Mumbai, India. The Mark identifies registered FTOs worldwide. It is not a product label, but sets organisations apart from other commercial businesses, "making recognisable mission driven organisations whose core activity is Fair Trade". The Mark serves as a common voice for solidarity amongst FTOs in the North and South.

To increase awareness of the Mark, IFAT began a "Global Journey", a world tour, in January 2004. Setting off from one of the poorest slums in Mumbai, members of IFAT have carried a banner with the FTO Mark through countries in which IFAT has members. Hundreds of thousands of people have since celebrated and promoted fair trade, it says. Following Asia, the Global Journey travelled to Latin America, North America and Africa. It reached Europe in mid 2006.

The fair trade movement has become more professional in its awareness-raising and advocacy work. It produces well-researched documents, attractive campaign materials and public events. It has also benefited from the establishment of European structures which help to harmonise and centralise its campaigning and advocacy work.

FLO International, IFAT, NEWS! and EFTA started to meet in 1998 and, when they work together, are known by their acronym, FINE. From its advocacy office in Brussels, FINE seeks to influence European policy-makers. It enables the four networks and their members to co-operate on important areas of work, such as advocacy and campaigning, standards and monitoring.

GROWTH

Fair trade's growth has been helped since the late 1990s through the opening of new channels, notably supermarkets. The 2005 Annual Report of FLO International tells of this growth. It shows that global sales of Fairtrade-certified products reached £758 million in 2005 – an increase of 37 per cent over 2004.

All the product lines are expanding, especially Fairtrade coffee in the United States (+70.9 per cent) and the U.K. (+34 per cent), bananas in Austria (+46 per cent) and sugar in France (+125 per cent). Non-food products did well too: sales of Fairtrade flowers, newly introduced last year in Canada, Germany and Belgium surpass the most optimistic expectations.

Globally, the number of certified producer organisations has grown by 127 per cent since 2001, to 580 groups in 58 countries, and the number of registered traders has increased by 132 per cent in the same period.

Fair trade products can now be found in 55,000 supermarkets all over Europe and the market share has become significant in some countries. In Switzerland, 47 per cent of all bananas, 28 per cent of the flowers and 9 per cent of the sugar sold are fair trade labelled. In the UK, a market with eight times the population of Switzerland, labelled products have achieved a 5 per cent market share of tea, a 5.5 per cent share of bananas and a 20 per cent share of ground coffee.

All this makes fair trade one of the fastest growing markets in the world. And it represents millions of pounds returned to disadvantaged producers around the world.

Every time you buy a fair trade product, you are part of this growing global movement.

12. Say "Nuts!" to unfair trade

It's hard to make a living from nuts whether you grow or gather them. As with most developing country crops, the terms of trade are simply unfair. Fair trade nuts offer producers a better deal.

Processed nuts are high-value foods in great demand in North America and Europe. As with other food and drink commodities, the international trade is dominated by a few large companies that make sky-high profits. World prices fluctuate depending on the size of each year's crop, weather patterns, and market conditions. But whatever the price, only a tiny fraction of the proceeds trickles down to the people at the bottom of the supply chain.

Farming, harvesting and collecting nuts provides income for millions of rural people in Africa, Asia and Latin America. Nut farmers and gatherers are among the most disadvantaged workers. They usually depend on intermediaries who buy at rock bottom prices at a time when producers are desperate for cash, and sell on the national or international market. Trickery is common. In Malawi, one of the world's poorest countries, Judith Harry recalls when she began to farm peanuts (groundnuts):

> The vendors who bought them used to bring tampered scales in order to steal. They used to buy unshelled groundnuts using a 50 kg sack for measurement, but they used to boil it first in order to enlarge it so that it carried more groundnuts than the 50 kg it was meant to hold. They always paid low prices.

Besides peanuts, Africa also produces a third of the world's cashew crop. But with most of the raw cashews exported to India and Viet Nam for roasting and peeling, small-scale African growers remain poor. Farm-gate cashew prices reached a 30-year low in 2002. Africa once had more of a cashew-processing industry, but it has not survived.

Across the Atlantic, just one part of the Amazon rainforest, spanning Bolivia, Brazil and Peru, produces all the world's brazil nuts. The tall brazil nut tree *Bertholletia excelsa* grows wild in the forest but not in cultivation, and only one local species of forest bee can pollinate it. Gathering wild brazils is exhausting and labour-intensive. The nuts have to be collected from the undergrowth after falling from the trees during the rainy season. Nut harvesters in Brazil earn well below the minimum wage.

Every now and again the market price for brazils rises, and big business moves in. As disputes break out over access to patches of forest, nut-gatherer families may be on the receiving end of violent attacks from hired workers.

Employment conditions are tough too for the largely female

workforce in the world's nut-processing industries. Poverty-level wages, insecure employment and hazardous working conditions are the norm.

NOT SLAVES ANY MORE

But there's hope. Brazils, cashews and peanuts have a corner of the fair trade market, with small-scale nut farmers, collectors and producers getting standard fair trade benefits (see Reason 3). Alternative trading organisations like Equal Exchange, Twin Trading and Traidcraft were among the first to import and sell fair trade nuts and nut butters as far back as the 1980s. Traidcraft buys brazils from the CAI Campesino co-operative in the Bolivian Amazon, which supports 300 nut-gathering families. Agrocel, a fair trade organisation in western India (Reason 10), supplies Traidcraft's cashews, and the 1,500 Zambian farmer-members of the Producer Owned Trading Company grow its peanuts.

In early 2006 Fairtrade-certified nuts went on sale for the first time in UK supermarkets: brazils in Tesco, peanuts at the Co-op. (The first Fairtrade-certified brazils were available from Equal Exchange through wholefood stores and mail order over a year earlier.) Bolivian and Brazilian brazil nut producer co-operatives supply Tesco under an arrangement set up and supported by Twin Trading and Equal Exchange. The co-ops store, transport and process the brazils, so members have more control over the supply chain and earn a bigger share of the profits than if they only did the gathering. Benedicto Gonzalez, a member of the Coinacapa co-op in Bolivia, comments, "It feels like we're not slaves any more. We have more income, more work and more dignity."

Crisis struck Coinacapa within weeks of its first shipment of Fairtrade brazils to the UK in March 2006. In heavy seasonal rains, the forest flooded. Rivers burst their banks, roads collapsed, villages were surrounded by flood water, and some people even died in the mudslides. Coinacapa persuaded the Bolivian government to provide a relief plane to airlift the nuts to the capital La Paz, for onward transportation by road and ship to the UK. But no fuel was available for the plane. Co-op members then searched for several days for an alternative route and, when the rains eventually eased, found a passable road to La Paz. "We think the actions of the Coinacapa members speaks volumes about their commitment to the Fairtrade market," said Duncan White of Twin Trading.

The Co-op launched the world's first fair trade peanuts in April 2006: roasted, salted peanuts from the National Smallholder Farmers' Association of Malawi. This organisation represents many local farmers' associations and more than 100,000 smallholders.

Peanut farmer Judith Harry chairs her local association. "I am very proud to have grown some of the groundnuts which have become the world's first Fairtrade salted peanuts," she says.

> In the future we will use the [Fairtrade] premium to start a clinic which will mean health facilities are nearer for families. We also need a guardian shelter at the hospital: somewhere for the sick and their carers and relations to stay and make meals while they wait for a chance to be seen to at the clinic.

Nuts and nut pieces are also available in a range of other Fairtrade-certified products including biscuits, chocolate and energy bars, muesli, nut butters and Divine's chocolate-coated brazils.

Divine sources its brazils from the Madre de Dios region of the Amazon in south-east Peru. There the local producer and export organisation, Candela, supports nut gatherers with credit, transport, and shelling and drying facilities, as well as buying their nuts at fair trade prices. Candela in turn gets support from the Shared Interest co-operative lending society in the UK (Reason 47).

It sounds like another good reason to be nuts about fair trade.

13. Enjoy real quality, produced with pride

For quality, today's fair trade products take some beating. They are grown and made by people who have a real stake in what they are doing.

Time for confession. When coffee that claimed to be fairly traded first appeared in Britain in the mid 1970s, you had to be a very devoted person to drink it. "It was a little bit like train-spotting but less enjoyable," was a comment of someone who tasted it. The quality left much to be desired and put some people off for years. If you were one of them remember that was 30 years ago – before the advent of Fairtrade-certified labelling. Time to leave the past behind and enjoy the present.

Today's fair trade products are in a different category altogether. For quality, they take some beating. From coffee to rugs, from tea to cotton, fair trade products are quality products. With fair trade, consumers are discovering the pleasures of distinctive origins of quality products – like organic coffee from Peru, forest honey from Zambia and mangoes from Burkina Faso.

Fair trade food products are grown by small farmers or plantation workers who take great care with their crops. They know the difference that fair trade is making to them. They know that quality sells – that the higher the quality, the more chance there is that buyers will stay buyers and will recommend the products to others. A rising fair trade market can mean a declining poverty rate, so fair trade growers feel passionately about the quality of their produce, their way of life, and the future of their families.

Take Fairtrade-certified bananas. All of them are quality-tested at least twice – at the farm and at the ripening depot. Growers are committed to reducing the use of pesticides and herbicides.

Luis is an example. He is the president of a small group of workers in Ecuador who inspect the quality of bananas supplied by fair trade farmers. Fairtrade certification requires that all workers have the right to represent themselves collectively. So the fair trade banana farmers helped the quality controllers organise themselves into a proper worker's association. Luis is proud to be part of a legally recognised group. He wants the association to evolve so that it can provide health care for members who are sick. He doesn't have any great dreams of wealth: "I just want to do all I can to help prepare my children for what tomorrow may bring."

Once a week, at the farms of each small grower, the week's crop of bananas have to be washed, trimmed, checked and packed. So, for one or two days a week, Luis and his colleagues travel to the farms and carry out spot checks on the boxes to ensure that the bananas are free of blemishes and are exactly the right size. Another group of workers double-checks the quality of the bananas at the port. Luis also has two other jobs. He is a night watchman, and works one day a week as the president of the workers' association.

And back to coffee. Few who have tasted today's Fairtrade-certified coffee have any doubts about its quality.

A WIDE RANGE

There is now a wide range of premium-quality Fairtrade-certified coffees. These include freshly roasted filter, espresso and cappucino, single origin, blends and organic.

Some fair trade coffee may cost a little more than other coffees, but prices are generally competitive and you might find bargains. Some may be on offer in your supermarket at prices which are lower than well-known brands. "Paying a higher Fairtrade price", says the Fairtrade Foundation, "gives farmers options – to invest in quality improvements and gain access to speciality markets or diversify into other crops to reduce their dependence on coffee."

"Consumers are increasingly choosing Fairtrade products because they're good in quality and help some of the poorest people in the world earn their own living," says Clare Short, the UK's former international development secretary.

Quality was very much on the mind of Silver Kasoro-Atwoki from the Mabale Growers Tea Factory Ltd in Uganda when he spoke in London at the launch of Fairtrade Fortnight 2006. He explained what Fairtrade means to tea growers in his country: "Through Fairtrade, we have been able to change our agricultural techniques to improve the quality and quantity of our teas," he said. Fair trade products are grown and made by people who have a real stake in what they are doing. Doing this connects with the people who produce with those who buy. So consumers can enjoy fair trade products – and feel good about them.

Chocaholics can especially enjoy Fairtrade chocolate (see Reason 44). Ghanaian cocoa farmers jointly own the company that makes Divine chocolate, Britain's first mass market Fairtrade bar. Whereas cocoa farmers generally are suffering because of the collapse in world prices, the farmers of Ghana's Kuapa Kokoo collective, on whom more than 100,000 people depend, are prospering from Fairtrade, with a stake in their product and directors on the board. "We're not asking for help," says Ohemeng Tinyase, Kuapa Kokoo's managing director. "We want people to feel good about our chocolate. We're the very best. That's what is important."

People are buying fair trade products in increasing quantities because they are quality products. And yes, because buyers can feel happy about their choices. When we buy fair trade we not only buy quality, we get the well-being that comes from giving practical help to people who need it.

Says Tadesse Meskela – the general manager of the Oromia Coffee Farmers Co-operative Union in Ethiopia, with members that produce Fairtrade-certified coffee – "Fair trade is not just a buying and selling process. It is creating a global family." It's a family united in benefiting from quality.

14. Send a child to school

Time and again, producers and plantation workers say how important fair trade is in helping their children get a good education.

Of the world's 2 billion children, more than 120 million girls and boys (more girls than boys) of primary-school age don't go to school. Almost half the girls in the world's poorest countries get no primary education at all, and in 19 African countries fewer than half the children complete primary school. Youngsters with a primary education are far less likely to contract HIV than those without.

Rural poverty is the biggest obstacle to children's schooling, and rural children are the most affected. Primary education is usually free in the South, but parents need money for uniforms, books, pencils, daily travel and food at school. In Ethiopia the nearest primary school can be up to 20 kilometres away. Secondary schools in developing countries are more likely to charge fees. Not surprisingly, a third of the world's children never get that far.

When the world market price of coffee, tea, cocoa, sugar or bananas drops, what we pay in the shops usually stays the same. But farmers' earnings and plantation workers' wages fall. This often leads them to withdraw their children from school, either to save the expense, or to raise family income through having the children work, or both. Hundreds of thousands of children work on West African cocoa farms instead of going to school, for example.

"We have to pay for schooling. Earlier we could cover expenses, now we can't. ... Three of the children can't go to school because I can't afford the uniform," says Ethiopian coffee farmer Mohammed Ali Indris.

In rural Uganda, teenage brothers Bruno and Michael Selugo had to leave secondary school because of the fees. "I have been sent home again and again," Bruno reveals. "They just send you away if you don't have the fees. ... Everyone used to go back to school with the money from coffee, but now ... the price is so low people are not even picking coffee." Patrick Kayanja, headteacher at Bruno's school, comments: "Much as we try to reduce the fees, the parents cannot pay."

Falling farm-gate prices also mean that many rural men in developing countries have to seek work away from home (see Reason 48). When women and children are left to tend the family farm without them, the children often have to give up school to help their mother.

EDUCATION IS TOP PRIORITY

Southern farmers, rural workers, craftspeople and their organisations say it loud and clear: children's education is top priority. Fair trade means they can put their money where their mouth is. When Igara Growers in Uganda began selling to Traidcraft and Teadirect, recalls Juliet Ntwirenabo, chair of the premium committee, "Our first priority was education. We bought exercise books, pens and pencils for four children in each family." For José Rivera Campoverde, a Peruvian fair trade coffee grower, "The higher price we get when we sell coffee on fair trade terms means that I can afford more food for my family and send my children to school properly equipped with pens and notebooks for the first time."

Farmers' organisations often use the "social premium" (Reason 4) to finance educational scholarships. Costa Rican coffee co-operative Coocafé has supported hundreds of youngsters at school and university this way. The premium pays to build and equip schools too. There are plenty of inspiring examples, and producer organisations take pride in investing to benefit the wider community, not just the producer group.

Kuapa Kokoo, a thriving Ghanaian fair trade cocoa co-operative with 45,000 farmer members, has set up schools and nurseries for non-members as well as members. Pupil attendance and education quality have improved significantly. Kuapa is reckoned to have earned about US$1 million in extra income through fair trade over eight years – equivalent to annual primary schooling costs for 245,000 children in Ghana. Apaco, an orange growers' co-operative in southern Brazil, supports a boarding school for girls from difficult family backgrounds, where the girls receive psychological support and therapy as well as a regular education. The workers' and management "joint body" on the Nilgiris tea estate in southern India has bought computers for local schools and a school bus.

"We built five primary schools," says Cecilia Mwambebule, a Tanzanian grower for Teadirect. "We ... build the schools and the government will then send teachers." Cecilia adds: "Everyone can send their children here, not just the tea farmers. The tea farmers want everyone to get education ... so everyone can benefit."

Ethiopia's Oromia coffee co-operative is building four primary schools, while the Union de Comunidades Indigenas de la Region del Istmo coffee co-op in Oaxaca, Mexico (Reason 49), has set up the region's only secondary school. Nicaraguan fair trade coffee co-operative SOPPEXCCA has constructed and fitted out several primary schools and provides secondary school scholarships, contributing to students' food, books and uniforms. One of its programmes gets parents planting trees – important in a region badly hit by Hurricane Mitch in 1998 – in return for supporting their youngsters through school.

Tea pickers interviewed on the Stockholm estate in Sri Lanka told how fair trade had benefited their children's education. One had borrowed from a small loans scheme to build a shop extension to his home and sell biscuits and sweets, and the extra income helped him keep his children in school. Other households were using the higher wages from working on a fair trade estate to keep one or more children at school up to A level, with the aim of a better job in the future.

High-street retailers Marks & Spencer proudly report that sales of Fairtrade-only tea and coffee in their Café Revive coffee shops are helping pay for 68 new schools in Ethiopia, Honduras, Peru and Sumatra. One of these, the new Ngelle Gorbitu School in rural Ethiopia, enables almost 600 children from the local community to attend school, as opposed to just 50 before.

15. Keep on making poverty history

Buying fair trade helps producers to build more sustainable businesses and overcome poverty.

I didn't have any breakfast and walked around half dizzy. The daze of hunger is worse than that of alcohol. The daze of alcohol makes us sing but the one of hunger makes us shake. I know how horrible it is to have only air in the stomach. ... I think that when I was born I was marked by fate to go hungry.

Brazilian slum dweller

Poverty is a dreadful disease and a quarter of humanity suffers from it, surviving on the equivalent of a dollar a day or less. Poverty means that people cannot afford to eat, to work, to live in dignity. It means they die young. Poverty kills an average of 30,000 children a day, ten times more than died on 9/11. Every day. One every three seconds. Poverty can and should be made history.

The Make Poverty History campaign in 2005 was one of the biggest campaigns the UK has ever seen. It brought a together a wide cross section of over 500 organisations – aid and development agencies, charities of many kinds, trade unions and faith groups among many others. And a number of fair trade organisations were members of the campaign, including the Fairtrade Foundation, People Tree, Shared Interest and Traidcraft. The aim was just what the campaign's name declared – to consign poverty to the scrap heap.

The campaign was launched in late December 2004 to press the UK government for action in three areas: on trade justice, more and better aid, and debt relief. Especially as Britain held the presidency of the G8 in the last six months of 2005, the year offered a good opportunity for the UK government to take the steps that were necessary to end poverty.

Make Poverty History campaigners pressed for trade rules to be rewritten in favour of developing countries so they can develop and build their own industries (see Reason 43). They urged that the debts of the poorest countries be cancelled in full. That debt cancellation should come without economic policy conditions such as liberalising or privatising economies. And all funding for debt relief should be additional to the existing and proposed increases in aid budgets. They pointed out that most of the funding for the debt relief delivered had so far come from donor country aid budgets, rather than being genuinely new money (Reason 29).

Pressing for more and better aid, the campaign said that without proper funding, "30,000 children will continue to die needlessly every day from causes associated with extreme poverty. ... Eight million lives could be saved every year if minimal healthcare was available in developing countries."

And again, aid should be given without economic policy conditions: "Many donors, including the UK, critically undermine the effectiveness of their aid by attaching economic policy conditions." Aid must be made to work more effectively for people in poverty. It must also be given in ways that help poor people, not donor country firms and citizens. At the moment, too much aid goes to politically important middle-income countries, rather than the poorest.

The Make Poverty History campaign generated a huge amount of public interest. Some 10 million people bought Make Poverty History wristbands. Around a quarter of a million people marched through Edinburgh in July 2005 to ask world leaders to take action to make poverty history. But leaders meeting in nearby Gleneagles responded with "a whisper to the roar of the people", as a South African campaigner said. They failed to rise to the occasion.

There was some progress on aid and debt in 2005 but not nearly enough. Aid is due to increase from $79 billion in 2004 to $130 billion by 2010. Grand pronouncements were made on debt, but it is by no means clear whether the debt cancelled will be new money, or whether it will come from aid budgets. And there were no measures for trade justice.

The campaigning must go on. While the national Make Poverty

History campaign was limited to 2005, communities around the UK are continuing to campaign locally. One example is the "Reading Campaign to Make Poverty History". Since February 2006 this has been campaigning to "end the poverty that affects 800 million people worldwide ... [and] on matters directly related to poverty, such as aid, debt relief, trade justice, armaments control and climate change".

Many of the organisations that supported Make Poverty History now have campaigns which focus on ending poverty. Continued campaigning is vital, not least to release the energies and potential of people in developing countries. For many could be making poverty history for themselves if the international economic system, especially the trade system, was not so stacked against them. Some are already doing so by supplying the fair trade market. Fair trade has proved that it can reduce poverty and promote sustainable development.

> Leaders ... would do well to take note of the success of Fairtrade as an economic model that works. It is commercially successful not despite the priorities and regulations which create a bias in favour of development goals, but rather precisely because of them.
>
> Harriet Lamb, executive director, the Fairtrade Foundation

AFRICA AND FAIR TRADE

Africa, the poorest continent, is the fastest growing region within the Fairtrade network, says the Fairtrade Foundation, with approximately 124 producers' organisations in 20 countries currently certified to Fairtrade standards. The range of products African producers are bringing to UK markets includes tea, coffee, wine, cocoa, honey, nuts and fruits.

Raymond Kimaro works for Tanzania's KNCU coffee co-operative, which supplies 20 per cent of its coffee to the Fairtrade market. He says:

> By strengthening their organisation and marketing skills, by improving health, water and education facilities, by

diversifying into new economic activity, and by improving environmental protection programmes, farmers and farm workers in Africa who supply the Fairtrade market are already working towards making poverty history for themselves. Being able to make a living from the sweat of one's labour should be a basic human right, safeguarded by governments, for all people in Africa and elsewhere.

Fair trade provides an "inspiring example" of a new partnership between developing countries and the developed world, agrees Tony Blair. Visiting cocoa farmers in Ghana, he says he had the privilege of seeing for himself "how Fairtrade in cocoa is increasing incomes and empowering local producers operating in global markets".

Fair trade is an inspiring and vital component of the ongoing and urgent task of making poverty history.

16. Make your town a Fairtrade Town

Fairtrade towns, cities, boroughs, villages, counties, universities, colleges, schools and places of worship are breaking out all over the UK and Ireland. Organise your own local initiative and spread the word.

In May 2000 Garstang Parish Council, Lancashire, voted itself the world's first Fairtrade Town, promising to use and promote fair trade products as much as possible. Local vet Bruce Crowther and the Garstang Oxfam group led the campaign, which involved the mayor, churches, headteachers and traders, as well as local dairy farmers who were protesting at the time against falling milk prices. Working with Garstang's schools, the group explored links between the slave trade, racism and fair trade.

MP Hilton Dawson tabled an Early Day Motion in the House of Commons congratulating Garstang. George Foulkes, then a minister at the Department for International Development, visited the town and gave his backing: "It is a great initiative. ... I want to try to ensure that the initiative is followed in many other towns and cities."

The first ten Fairtrade Towns were Aberfeldy, Ammanford, Chester, Garstang, Haworth, Leicester, Nailsworth, Strathaven, Stroud and Wells, and the movement has taken root across the UK. In January 2004 Fair Isle, between Orkney and Shetland off Scotland's northeast coast, became the first Fairtrade Island – followed by Jersey, Shetland and the Isle of Wight. March 2004 saw ten simultaneous Fairtrade Town declarations: Dundee, Aberdeen, Lancaster, York, Oxford, Cambridge, Portsmouth, Southampton, Leeds and Liverpool. In 2005 Manchester and Salford became joint 100th Fairtrade Towns. By mid 2006 there were 200 declared Fairtrade Towns, Cities, Boroughs, Villages, Zones, Islands and Counties around the country. Edinburgh and Cardiff are both Fairtrade Capitals. Fairtrade Fortnight 2006 saw 25 towns, boroughs, villages and zones declared Fairtrade, plus Cumbria as a Fairtrade County.

Garstang's Bruce Crowther has become national Fairtrade Towns co-ordinator for the Fairtrade Foundation and is still full of enthusiasm:

> The network of Fairtrade Towns has become a wonderful way of involving people throughout the community. ... The Towns raise awareness and sales of fair trade which both contribute to tackling poverty and improving the lot of marginalised and disadvantaged farmers.

"One of the biggest achievements," Bruce adds, "has been to crack the complex world of catering and procurement and getting Fair trade into local authorities, workplaces, schools and primary healthcare trusts."

To achieve Fairtrade status, a local council must pass a resolution supporting fair trade and agree to serve Fairtrade-certified coffee and tea in its meetings, offices and canteens. Fair trade products must be available in the area's shops, cafés and catering establishments, and used by local workplaces and community organisations. A steering group needs to be set up to ensure continuing commitment.

Well over 200 more places in the UK are working towards Fairtrade status, including (at the time of writing) Anglesey, Chesterfield, Chichester, Durham, East Sussex, Gateshead, the Isle of Man, Knutsford, Llandrindod and Builth Wells, London, Nottinghamshire, Powys, Shropshire, Welwyn Garden City, Wigan and Yeovil. The Fairtrade London Campaign, supported by Mayor Ken Livingstone, aims to increase awareness and availability of fair trade products across the capital. London boroughs of Camden, Croydon, Greenwich, Hammersmith & Fulham, Islington, Kingston, Lambeth, Lewisham and Richmond had declared Fairtrade status by mid 2006, and many others were working on it. The Welsh Assembly plans to make Wales the world's first Fair Trade Nation.

The idea has spread to Ireland too. By 2006 the Republic had eight Fairtrade Cities and Towns: Clonakilty, Cork, Kilkenny, Kinsale, Waterford, Limerick, Galway and Thurles.

UNIVERSITIES, COLLEGES AND SCHOOLS

Oxford Brookes became the first Fairtrade University in October 2003 after a campaign led by graduate students in the School of Built Environment inspired by course chair Hugo Slim. After 16 months of Fairtrade status, Oxford Brookes students and staff reckoned to have consumed 750,000 Fairtrade drinks – 11,600 packs of medium-roast coffee, 390 packs of vending coffee, 115 kg of cocoa powder, 48,000 teabags, 130 kg of espresso beans and 2,500 orange juices. They had munched their way through many thousands of fair trade cereal and chocolate bars, cookies and flapjacks.

Today the 30-plus Fairtrade Universities and Colleges include Birmingham, Bristol, Derby, Edinburgh, Glasgow, Hertfordshire, King's College London, Leeds, Leeds Metropolitan, the London School of Economics, Manchester, Nottingham, Portsmouth, Queen's University Belfast, Royal Holloway, Sheffield, City of Sunderland College,

Swansea, Warwick, Worcester College of Technology, York and the University of Wales. More are working towards the award.

Warwick University, with an active People & Planet student group, has gone further than many. Once it had achieved Fairtrade status, its students' union adopted a 100 per cent Fairtrade policy for tea, coffee, hot chocolate, sugar, fruit, fruit juice and vending machines. And more: "Staff and union officers' uniforms will now be made from Fairtrade cotton, as well as being made in factories guaranteeing International Labour Organization standards," said a university campaigner. "We can be very proud of what we have achieved. This policy will make a real difference to real people's lives."

Plenty is going on among school students and teachers too. Secondary school students in Hartlepool got the ball rolling in 2001 with co-operative-run fair trade tuck shops (see Reason 40). Shaftesbury School declared itself a Fairtrade School on Red Nose Day (11 March) 2005, as did King Edward VI High School for Girls in Birmingham, Tiffin Girls School in Kingston and 13 Liverpool schools that year.

Formal Fairtrade Schools criteria have recently been agreed, and plenty of schools get involved during Fairtrade Fortnight each March. In early 2007 the Fairtrade Foundation plans to launch its Fairtrade Schools initiative with support from the Department for International Development.

Good support also comes from many city, town and borough councils, and organisations like People & Planet, Comic Relief, the Co-op Movement, and SCIAF (the Scottish Catholic International Aid Fund). Oxfam and Leeds Development Education Centre have both produced Fairtrade handbooks for schools. Telford MP David Wright has written to every school in his constituency asking them to consider making their tuck shop or canteen fair trade. An Early Day Motion in Parliament has congratulated schools that have done this and called on the Department for Education and Skills to encourage more fair trade in schools. Ethical clothing company CleanSlate recently launched the UK's first fair trade and organic school uniform range.

PLACES OF WORSHIP

Christ Church & St Mark's in Watford, Herts, became the first Fairtrade Church in 2004, and the idea took off. By mid 2006 there were more than 2,800 Fairtrade Churches. Fairtrade Cathedrals include Coventry, St John's Portsmouth, and St Mary's Edinburgh. Both the Church of England and the Roman Catholic dioceses of Portsmouth are Fairtrade Dioceses.

Fairtrade status means a church serves fair trade tea and coffee at all meetings, commits to using other fair trade products such as sugar, biscuits and fruit, and participates actively in Fairtrade Fortnight.

The Fairtrade Foundation offers churches a range of ideas for worship, bible study and reflection and publishes criteria for becoming a Fairtrade diocese, district, synod, presbytery, association or other denominational area. Guidelines for churches are also available from Traidcraft, along with poems, prayers, studies, service ideas and other resources. Faith-based NGOs like Tearfund and the Methodist Relief and Development Fund have also help promote fair trade in churches.

During Fairtrade Fortnight 2005 the Shah Jehan Mosque in Woking, Surrey, became the first Fairtrade Mosque. The *mufti*, Liaquat Ali Amod, said: "Many here come from countries such as Pakistan. They know how difficult life can be for workers there and so they realise the importance of a fair deal."

A year later Birmingham Central Synagogue became the first Fairtrade Synagogue, and a dozen more have since achieved Fairtrade status.

17. Build confidence, reduce risk

Here's how fair trade's guaranteed minimum price reduces risk for producers.

Falling prices. Erratic prices. Both cause havoc for millions of small-scale farmers who grow crops for export. Farmers in developing countries can watch helplessly as the price of their crop swerves all over the place and, even worse, drops like a stone. As if growing crops for export wasn't risky enough anyway.

All this matters a great deal. The first and possibly only connection that millions of the poor have with the world trading system is through the crops they grow for the export market. But they have no idea how much their crops will fetch.

Take world coffee prices. The figures speak for themselves. The average price of coffee on world markets over the last 30 years has followed this pattern:

January	1976	95	US cents/lb	
"	1977	218	"	"
"	1978	192	"	"
"	1990	64	"	"
"	1995	152	"	"
"	2002	43	"	"
end-July	2006	89	"	"

These figures, from the International Coffee Organization, illustrate the astonishing variation in price. They show that the coffee price in January 2002 was only one-fifth of its price 25 years earlier.

When prices vary so much, the lives of growers are made so much harder. They cannot plan. Do they have enough money to send their children to school, to pay for healthcare? It all depends on a "free-trade" world market which is outside their control. The price is decided by the laws of supply and demand – which also decide their poverty.

The really bizarre thing about coffee prices is that the world price in July 2006 was lower than in January 1976. Inflation over those 30 years has considerably reduced the value of money. A pound in 1976 could buy what £4 or £5 can buy us today. Had it kept pace with inflation, the world price of coffee would be four to five times higher in 2006 than it was in 1976. The real price of coffee – what it can buy the grower – is only a fifth what it was 30 years ago. Growers are therefore earning massively less for their crop.

Millions of farmers continue to grow coffee, however, despite prices so low they may be less than the cost of producing the crop. But then the crop may be their only source of a cash income. Instead of reducing production when prices fall, some farmers increase their output – to try to sustain their incomes by squeezing more from their land, sometimes at the expense of quality.

Among mainstream export crops, coffee has fluctuated and fallen the most. But the prices of other important crops for growers in developing countries – including tea, cocoa and bananas – have also fluctuated and fallen drastically in the last 30 years.

It is countries as well as growers who are affected. Many developing countries depend on a small number of crops for their export earnings, and some on only one. Uganda, for example, depends on coffee for around two-thirds of its export earnings. In 1998 it was one of the first countries to have some of its debt cancelled. But the collapse in the world price of coffee more than wiped out the benefit of debt relief.

FAIRTRADE PRICE

The fair trade system is very different. Growers are guaranteed a minimum price for their crop. This is achieved by payment of a guaranteed fair price, and by reducing the number of intermediaries in the supply chain so that the growers get a larger share of the export price (see Reasons 2 and 21). The Fairtrade minimum price is calculated to cover the costs of sustainable production and a sustainable livelihood. All stakeholders, including producers and traders, are consulted in the price-setting process. There is an additional premium for investment in social, commercial or environmental development projects (Reason 4).

Take coffee. The price for Fairtrade-certified arabica coffee is 126 cents a pound. This comprises a minimum price of 121 cents a pound plus the premium of 5 cents a pound. If the international price is higher than the fair trade price then the price comprises the world price plus the Fairtrade premium, says the Fairtrade Foundation. So under the fair trade system the price paid to growers rises when world prices rise, but does not fall below the minimum price when world market prices fall. Fairtrade Labelling Organisations International (FLO) audits each transaction to ensure the price and premium for Fairtrade-certified products are paid to the producer organisation.

The producer organisation and trader sign contracts that allow for long-term planning and sustainable production practices. Producers can, in addition, request pre-financing of up to 60 per cent of the contract. This is important. Without access to this capital, co-operatives might have to take out costly loans to purchase members' coffee. And loans are frequently unavailable from local banks as many do not consider farmers' organisations to be creditworthy.

Fairtrade-certified coffee is produced by farmers who are members of village-level co-operatives, which are usually affiliated to regional co-operative societies and/or national co-operative unions. These organisations buy, collect, process, market and export coffee on behalf of hundreds or even thousands of farmers. Such services are mainly financed by a percentage taken from the selling price (Reason 40).

The Fairtrade premium is paid into the bank account of an elected committee set up specifically to administer the premium fund. The fund is reserved for investment in projects that are decided on with the agreement of co-op members (or following consultation with the workforce in the case of plantations). The committee must produce an annual premium plan and budget which is available for scrutiny by the beneficiaries and FLO.

The Fairtrade price does more than provide a higher income. It helps to give growers the encouragement to branch out. Many fair trade producer organisations have the capacity, for example, to process their commodity and so add value to it.

The great thing about fair trade is that growers can plan ahead with confidence.

18. Give someone's health a boost

Workplace health and safety, and free or affordable health-care, are things we in the West mostly take for granted. Both can be hard to come by in the global South, but not so hard for people linked up with the fair trade system.

In developing countries, poverty and ill-health often go hand in hand – including in the workplace. For low-paid people, going to work can be hazardous.

Take the banana industry. Many commercial plantations try to cut costs by using heavy doses of the most dangerous agrochemicals. The food and drinking water of many banana workers living close to plantations contain poisons from daily aerial spraying. A study in Costa Rica found 20 per cent of male banana workers sterile after handling such chemicals, and women banana packers had twice the average rates of leukaemia and birth defects. Maria, wife of a Costa Rican banana worker, gave birth to a baby with a head four times bigger than his body. "I couldn't even hold him," she said. "It's the worst thing that can happen to anyone."

Too many plantations, factories and workshops across the developing world neglect employee health and safety. For instance, scores of Bangladeshi garment workers have been killed by fires in textile factories in recent years. And overwork takes its toll as poorly paid employees, scared of losing their jobs, sacrifice their health or fall victim to accidents through tiredness.

Away from the world of work, the picture is also desperate. Ten million children die each year before their fifth birthday, many from easily preventable diarrhoea. One in 50 women in the South dies during or after pregnancy. Hundreds of millions lack access to safe drinking water, decent toilets, basic medicines or healthcare. Millions more suffer life-threatening yet treatable diseases like HIV/AIDS, malaria and tuberculosis.

Despite a host of good intentions and brave initiatives, many developing country governments have become less – not more – able to meet their citizens' health needs. Cuts in state budgets have reduced official spending on water, sanitation and health. Many services are part-privatised, their user charges beyond the means of poor people. Nicaraguan health union leader Evile Umaña described during a recent visit to the UK what happened when a local man, Cristobal Chavarria, aged 86, suffered a sudden heart collapse:

> There was no ambulance, his family had to pay a taxi. Once in the hospital, they had to provide sheets, pillows, toilet paper, soap, food ... on top of any medical requirements. The person in the next bed was already dead. ... His family brought him home after two nights [because] they could no longer bear the costs.

Evile went on:

> Hospitals are short of even basic medicines, medical supplies and the most fundamental tools. ... Many health-care professionals have to work double shifts or find other work outside their regular hours. Some take in washing and ironing, some drive taxis. ... Nicaragua is confronting rising rates of potential epidemic diseases, such as TB, AIDS, malaria and dengue.

PROMOTING BETTER HEALTH

"Fairtrade is about much more than just another packing case," says Dominican banana grower Amos Wiltshire. "It's not just that we want a healthy banana, it's that we also want a healthy banana farmer."

By buying fair trade we can support better health and safety conditions for workers, as well as a trading system that fills some of the gaps in health provision in developing countries.

One of the five basic guarantees of Fairtrade-certified farm produce is "greater respect for the environment". Fair trade growers observe legal limits on agrochemicals and have to work to reduce their use (see Reasons 25 and 27). Special standards are applied to industries like bananas, where buffer zones prevent pollution of rivers, forests, roads and water sources. On plantations and farms, in factories and work-shops, the world's network of Fairtrade certification bodies (Reason 3) ensures that health and safety standards are continuously improved. And fair trade producers really do look after their workers better, providing workplace healthcare, medical checks, health and safety equipment, improved ventilation and sanitation, and sickness benefit more often than non-fair-trade competitors.

In the textiles industry, for example, the European Fair Trade Association (EFTA) has helped fair trade producers in Bangladesh, Bolivia, Guatemala, India, Indonesia, Tanzania, Thailand and Zimbabwe eliminate use of cancer-causing azo dyes. In farming, fair trade crop production in South Africa has benefited the health of women farmworkers through reduced chemicals use. Because fair trade producer and worker households are often better off than their neighbours, they look after their own health better too.

There are wider benefits at community level. Health, like educa-tion (Reason 14), is a high priority when it comes to investing the "social premium". Kuapa Kokoo, Ghana's large cocoa farmers' co-operative, has set up a trust fund to provide and equip health centres and water boreholes for local communities. By 2003, 100,000 people – members and non-members – had benefited from free medical attention under the co-op's healthcare programme. In Ethiopia the Oromia Coffee Farmers Cooperative Union invests in community health clinics and water pumps, while Mabale Growers Tea Factory, Uganda, is building and equipping clinics and supplying medicines. Mabale also builds public toilets at roadside tea-collection points.

On Sri Lanka's Stockholm tea estate, the premium has paid for an ambulance. Before, plantation workers and their families living on the estate who needed medical attention had to walk seven kilometres to the nearest surgery. The ambulance is seen as especially important for getting pregnant women to hospital in time to give birth.

In Bahia, one of Brazil's poorest regions, members of Cealnor, a federation of fair trade fruit producers, have invested in equipment to make a nutritious juice mixture for malnourished children. Their infant health drink is now sold in local supermarkets. Nicaragua's SOPPEXCCA coffee producers' co-operative has used fair trade income to run a cervical smear test programme, a service usually too costly for rural women. It has set up voluntary primary health brigades and pharmacies providing low-cost medicines, as well as supporting a women's health organisation that is independent of the co-op.

There was no sanitation in Dolora Castillo's community in the Dominican Republic until fair trade banana farmers covered the cost of building toilets next to people's homes. The farmers are also constructing a community clinic. The Fairtrade premium has paid for women's reproductive health programmes in Bolivia, Ecuador, Guatemala, Honduras, India, Mexico, Nicaragua, Papua New Guinea and Peru. In East Timor 18,000 people have used free health clinic services paid for by fair trade. Family health insurance, largely unknown in the global South, is now provided by the Bagua Grande coffee co-operative in northern Peru with the premium. Farmer Martias Huaman comments:

> About five years ago I suffered with arthritis. I was insured
> by the co-operative through their health insurance and I was
> able to improve my health. ... Without the insurance I would
> be below the ground – I would be organic fertiliser!

19. Promote human rights

The United Nations says that every person is entitled to enjoy development in which all human rights are fully realised. Fair trade promotes human dignity, rights and freedom.

Agreed almost 60 years ago as one of the most significant documents of its time, the Universal Declaration of Human Rights remains a document of vital importance today. It was in December 1948 that the

General Assembly of the United Nations adopted and proclaimed the Declaration, which lays down five key areas of rights – political, social, economic, civil and cultural.

There is a tendency for some regions to promote certain rights over others. In the Western world the emphasis tends to be on political and civil rights. In developing countries there is more emphasis on cultural, economic and social rights, especially on enough food to eat. When you are hungry, human rights may not end with breakfast, but that is where your concern is likely to begin. If a person is dying from lack of food, other rights are academic.

The preamble of the Universal Declaration includes these words:

> recognition of the inherent dignity and of the equal and inalienable rights of all members of the human family is the foundation of freedom, justice and peace in the world ....
>
> ... the peoples of the United Nations have in the Charter reaffirmed their faith in fundamental human rights, in the dignity and worth of the human person and in the equal rights of men and women and have determined to promote social progress and better standards of life in larger freedom ...

The Declaration then goes on to say that "every individual and every organ of society ... shall strive by teaching and education to promote respect for these rights and freedoms." Article 23 of the Declaration states:

- Everyone has the right to work, to free choice of employment, to just and favourable conditions of work and to protection against unemployment.
- Everyone, without any discrimination, has the right to equal pay for equal work.
- Everyone who works has the right to just and favourable remuneration ensuring for himself and his family an existence worthy of human dignity, and supplemented, if necessary, by other means of social protection.

"Just and favourable remuneration" is precisely what fair trade is about.

Article 25 says that "Everyone has the right to a standard of living adequate for the health and well-being of himself and of his family, including food, clothing, housing and medical care and necessary social services." Again, this is totally consistent with fair trade.

Also Article 27: "Everyone has the right freely to participate in the cultural life of the community, to enjoy the arts and to share in scientific advancement and its benefits."

Fair trade makes it more likely that people will be able to participate in the cultural life of their community and also to promote its advancement.

FAIR TRADE AND HUMAN RIGHTS

Article 28 says that "Everyone is entitled to a social and international order in which the rights and freedoms set forth in this Declaration can be fully realised." An improved world trading order is again what fair trade is about. Fair trade promotes human dignity, rights and freedom. It seeks greater equity in international trade by offering better trading conditions to, and securing the rights of, marginalised farmers and workers in developing countries.

However, although the Universal Declaration of Human Rights was agreed over half a century ago, there are problems with compliance, especially among business corporations. "There is still no mechanism to ensure that non-state actors comply with these and other international standards," says Traidcraft. It points out that failure to recognise the importance of rights "in every context means that large companies who operate internationally are often in breach of basic human rights through their actions".

A significant step was taken in August 2003 by the UN Sub-Commission on the Promotion and Protection of Human Rights when it approved the UN Norms on the Responsibilities of Transnational Corporations and Other Business Enterprises with Regard to Human Rights (also known as UN Norms for Business or UN Norms). The Norms restate existing internationally recognised standards of human rights. They set out in a comprehensive way the key human-rights responsibilities of companies. They do not create new legal obligations, but codify and distil existing obligations under international law as they apply to companies. They are a credible international mechanism setting out the Universal Declaration of Human Rights for businesses. "They give clarity for companies and create a global level playing field for company behaviour," says Traidcraft.

In 2004, the UN Commission on Human Rights requested the UN Secretary General to appoint a Special Representative on the human rights responsibilities of transnational corporations and other business enterprises. The mandate of the Special Representative includes working to identify and clarify standards of corporate responsibility and accountability with regard to human rights.

Business groups are trying to get the Norms sidelined. It may be regulation rather than Norms that's needed if transnational corporations are to help not hinder the human rights of the poor. Rights for the poor can only be realised if governments and companies uphold the Universal Declaration. Fair trade both upholds and promotes human rights and is delivering "breakfast" for tens of thousands of disadvantaged people. Arturo Gomez, a founding member of a fair trade banana co-operative in Costa Rica, sums it up when he says that it has given him and others a sense of worth and confidence in the future:

> I thank God for the new system, because it has resolved our problems. But I look around me and I see my neighbours with great problems, without water, without a house, without food. Our dream is to be free, to be looked on as human beings, as people, not objects.

And this is what the Universal Declaration is all about.

20. Free child carpet workers

South Asian children are exploited every day in appalling conditions, making oriental-style rugs and carpets for export. But when you buy under the Rugmark label you can be sure no illegal under-age child labour has been used.

In factories and loom-sheds in India, Nepal and Pakistan, hundreds of thousands of children as young as five are reported as working in near-slave conditions. They are put to work weaving and hand-knotting oriental rugs and carpets for export. Labouring up to 20 hours a day, seven days a week, they are often forced to eat and sleep where they work. Sometimes they are locked in at night. Children who make mistakes or try to run away risk being beaten, deprived of food or even tortured. These child workers are usually from the poorest families, toiling to pay off their parents' debt to a money broker. Needless to say, they don't get to go to school.

Evidence of the scandal first broke in India in the 1980s. An activist campaign led by Kailash Satyarthi, who went on to front the Global March Against Child Labour, began to free the children by raiding factories to rescue them. But the freed children were soon replaced by others. Broader action was needed.

RUGMARK'S ORIGINS

A consumer awareness drive began in Germany – the biggest importer of oriental floor coverings – in 1990. Trade unions, faith groups, and human rights and consumer organisations got involved. The campaign spread to other European countries and to North America. A coalition of NGOs, Indian exporters, the Indo-German Export Promotion Council and UNICEF began to develop a consumer label certifying carpets that were made in India without exploiting child labour. The Rugmark Foundation was set up in 1994 to supervise this label.

Carpet makers who want a licence to use the Rugmark label must sign a legally binding contract committing them not to employ children under 14, to pay fair adult wages, to allow unannounced Rugmark inspections and to notify Rugmark of all sales of labelled carpets and rugs. Rugmark will certify rugs and carpets woven on family looms, where children may help their parents for an hour or two at home after school, provided such children also attend school regularly.

Rugmark trains and supervises its own inspectors and allows monitoring of certified factories and loom-sheds by independent child welfare organisations. Inspectors work in teams of two, and since 1999 those based at Gopiganj have used motorbikes for visiting up to eight village workshops a day. "The monsoon period is the worst," comments Santosh Nair. "Sometimes, the tyres spin around in the mud forcing you to go very slowly." Rashid Raza, who co-ordinates inspections in northern India from Rugmark's office in Gopiganj, points out that: "It is impossible for a Rugmark inspector to warn the weavers of a village beforehand, because he himself doesn't know when inspections will be done in that village."

The first Rugmark-certified rugs and carpets were exported from India, mainly to Germany, in 1995. By 1999 the scheme was also working in Nepal and Pakistan. There are now Rugmark offices in Germany (also covering Belgium, Luxembourg and the Netherlands), the UK, the USA (also covering Canada), India, Nepal and Pakistan. So far more than 4 million certified rugs and carpets have reached Europe and North America. Every Rugmark-labelled product carries a unique serial number so that the product's place of manufacture is traceable via a central database. This helps protect against counterfeiting.

Rugmark's licensed exporters and importers fund much of its work, paying a small tariff on the price of each certified item. Most of this money returns to the producer countries to cover rehabilitation and education costs.

REHABILITATION AND EDUCATION

Where Rugmark finds children working illegally, it takes them into rehabilitation and education centres and seeks ways to reunite them with their families. It also addresses problems that lead families to send away their children in the first place. For example, adult literacy programmes and self-help classes assist parents of former child weavers in finding new ways to earn a living.

Rugmark builds and runs its own schools and works with the state education system. Thousands of former child workers, and other children from weaving communities, have now had educational opportunities and health and nutritional care as a result of its programmes. Rugmark provides intensive non-formal literacy and numeracy training to prepare children for formal education. In Nepal the programmes are designed to take two years, but many children are said to be so motivated that they complete within eight months. Classes include mother-tongue language, maths, science, English, physical education, music and other extra-curricular activities.

Children who go back to live with their families receive different levels of support depending on need, such as help with school fees and payments for books, uniforms and other materials. Children aged over 14 get vocational training in occupations like electrical and vehicle repair, tailoring, textiles and masonry.

Unlike Fairtrade labelling, Rugmark does not guarantee minimum prices. Nor does it cover health and safety or environmental standards, partly because most carpet making in India takes place in small workshops rather than large factories. But it does certify that children have not been exploited, under-age children have not been employed, and adult workers have been paid the producer country's official minimum wage. Workers' rights organisations see this as a key step in ensuring that all such jobs go to adults who can bargain for better wages.

There has been real impact. In Nepal, the number of children in the country's carpet industry had fallen from 11 per cent of the workforce to less than 2 per cent by 2001.

As nine-year-old Maya replied when asked what it meant to her to move from a 50-hour working week in a carpet factory to the warm friendly atmosphere of Rugmark's centre in Nepal: "Now I can be free."

21. Bypass the intermediaries

Fair trade coffee is more likely to be traded directly from co-operatives to roasters such as Cafédirect.

How much of the money that we pay for coffee, bananas, sugar and similar commodities goes to the intermediaries, the people in between the grower and the consumer? It can be a sizeable proportion. While intermediaries can play a useful role, they can also exploit farmers, especially farmers who lack knowledge of prices. And there are often too many people "in the middle". Non-fair-trade coffee, for example, can change hands up to 150 times before it reaches your cup.

Fair trade goods, by contrast, are usually sold direct from co-operatives to manufacturers. Fair trade cuts down, and may even cut out, the intermediaries. The following three farmers speak of the effects of intermediaries.

SUGAR

Juan Valverde Sánchez is a sugar cane farmer in Costa Rica. Thirty-five years old, he is married, with five children.

"I guess my passion is my work. I'm always thinking about my work," he says. "In the evening, I'm thinking of what I have to do in the morning. I love farming sugar-cane. It's hard, because the sun is very hot. But you get used to it." Juan's working week consists of three days cutting cane, one day transporting the cane (by ox and pick-up), and one day processing the cane to convert it into sugar.

On processing days, Juan gets up at 2 a.m., never needing an alarm-clock. Like many of his neighbouring small farmers, he has a *trapiche* next to his house, a plant where the juice is extracted from the cane, purified and then boiled to turn it into sugar. It's a cottage industry in which all the family gets involved. The plant's furnace has to be fed with firewood and cane pulp. To conserve energy Juan processes all his cane on one long, hot day. He relaxes in the evening by watching television.

Juan sells his sugar to Asoprodulce, a local farmer's association that his father helped found. Asoprodulce in turn sells 60 per cent of its produce to the organic fair trade market. He says:

> I know that if I bring my sugar to the association they'll buy from me at a fixed price. I've got security. Whereas in the old days, selling was more difficult. Sometimes the middle-men bought sugar from one person, sometimes from another. You never knew. There were always fluctuations in the national price. There were very bad months.

Thanks to this new security, Juan has been able to buy his sugar-processing mill from his father and improve his house.

BANANAS

Renson is proud of the new home he been able to build in Ecuador for his wife and his two young children since he began selling his bananas to the fair trade market. His father now has a place of his own, in the old wooden house next door. Renson's ambition is simply to be able to carry on selling bananas in the market that gives him a fair price. "We're proud of being in Fairtrade. We can help each other and we can help our workers." He hopes to give his children the education he missed out on.

By 7.30 each morning Renson is at work on his three-hectare farm alongside his father and uncle. He and his family work at irrigating, keeping down weeds, and wrapping the growing bananas in plastic bags for protection. With a break for lunch at eleven, Renson works till four in the afternoon. Once a week, with the help of a team of local workers, boxes of bananas are scrupulously checked for size and defects, then packed into boxes for despatch to the local port.

Outside work, Renson relaxes with his family, plays for the co-operative's football team, and enjoys the social side of being in a Fairtrade registered co-operative. As well as holding weekly meetings, the farmers organise parties.

Renson is a member of the El Guabo banana co-operative, the only group of small farmers in Ecuador who, with the help of the fair trade system, manage to avoid the intermediaries and export their own bananas. For Renson, the benefits of fair trade include a stable, higher price for his crop, and the encouragement to stop using chemicals on his farm.

"The bananas are sweeter," he says. "They have a better scent. Other companies don't care how many chemicals you put on the crop." The co-operative gave Renson a loan to irrigate his land and install tanks for washing the bananas. The members of the co-operative also help each other, loaning small sums of money in times of need.

COFFEE

Guillermo Vargas Leiton is a coffee farmer and also the manager of his local farmer's co-operative in Costa Rica, which sells 100 per cent of its crops to the Fairtrade market. He is 41, married, with two daughters, aged eight and two. The older one likes to read every day and is currently working her way through the Harry Potter books.

"We want our children to continue growing coffee, to retain the love and passion for working the land and being part of nature. We don't want them to leave the land and be dependent on other people for their food," he says.

On a typical day, Guillermo wakes up at 5.30 a.m. In his job as general manager of the co-operative he has to work long hours, from about 8.30 a.m. to 7 at night. He'll start the day checking how things are going at the coffee-roasting plant, and spends the rest of the day in the office. If Guillermo gets home early, he'll spend time with the family, and watch the news. If not, he goes straight to bed.

As manager and a long-term member of Co-op Santa Elena, Guillermo is in a good position to see the benefit that Fairtrade has had for the coffee farmers "If we didn't have fair trade sales, most of the farmers would be cutting down their trees. The current price of coffee in the conventional market doesn't cover the cost of producing the coffee." He goes on:

> When I think of fair trade, I think: fair for the producer and fair for the consumer. To my mind, the two main players involved in trade are the producer and the consumer. The people in between – the middlemen – should be the bridge, facilitating the trade. They shouldn't secure all the benefits for themselves.

22. Drink to a better world

Enjoying a glass of Merlot or Sauvignon Blanc is not the most obvious way to help a poor family build a home or get their children to school. But opening a bottle of fair trade wine means doing something practical to make the world a better place.

There's a growing range of enjoyable Fairtrade-certified New World wines on the market. If you've ever wondered what makes these brands different, the award-winning Los Robles ("The Oaks") label is as good a place as any to start. Vinos Los Robles is a wine co-operative in Chile's Curicó valley, a few hours by bus south of the capital Santiago. Owned by its 67 members – small-scale and medium-size wine growers – it employs around 90 people full time and up to 250 during harvest time.

There are not many wine co-ops left in Chile. The Pinochet dictatorship disbanded most of them in the 1970s. Los Robles, established in 1943 in the aftermath of a devastating earthquake in the valley that killed thousands, is one that survived.

Los Robles's fair trade connection began in 1990 in association with Oxfam Belgium and Max Havelaar Netherlands. Fair trade links with the UK (Traidcraft), Germany (Gepa) and Switzerland (Claro) followed. Nowadays independent retailers and supermarkets are in on the act. Today, 15 to 20 per cent of Los Robles wine is Fairtrade certified and exported to Western Europe, and it's aiming for 100 per cent certification.

ECOLOGICAL AND SOCIAL FUND

The key to Los Robles's efforts to make its part of the world a better place is its Ecological and Social Fund, established in 2000 with money from the "social premium" (see Reason 4) received from fair trade importers. This fund supports an impressive range of activities that benefit not just employees of the co-operative and of its member growers but also poor farmers and their households in the surrounding towns, villages and countryside.

The fund has provided technical support and loans to enable Los Robles's members to replant and expand their vineyards with more marketable varieties, introduce drip irrigation and make other improvements. Visits are organised so that growers can exchange skills with each other.

Benefits for employees have included major pay rises for the lowest paid, help with home buying and repairs, a staff canteen, supplementary health insurance and support during personal and family emergencies. All good stuff, but nothing remarkable for any decent employer perhaps. It's when it comes to working with some of the poorest people in the surrounding communities, and the range of social partnerships that the co-op has entered into, that the approach begins to look really impressive.

In partnership with a non-governmental anti-poverty programme, Los Robles supports young graduate agronomists and social workers who live and work with local communities.

Finding that local children were often unable to get to school because private bus drivers did not want to pick them up and collect only a child's fare (lower than an adult's), the co-op drew on its Ecological and Social Fund to buy a school bus and donate it to the nearest municipality. "The school bus – that really was a fantastic gift," says Marta Aguilar Rojas, an education official with the local council:

> Having this bus has meant less absenteeism from school, and the average school attendance has gone up, because in those areas where the children had more difficulty to travel to the school, because of transport problems or poor roads, there is now no more excuse for absenteeism.

Another project involves helping groups of low-income people buy land, grow produce and build their own homes. This time the partner is a specialist housing foundation for poor rural areas. The local mayor's office and community organisations have a say in who benefits. One of the beneficiaries of the project, 29-year-old Ruth Funzalida Nuñez, who belongs to one of the housing groups, describes the benefits:

> I came to this area seven years ago. I am married, I have two children and currently live with my parents-in-law and with the hope of later getting our own little house. ... I think it is the best thing that could have happened in this area; we are a rural area, isolated, one of the lowest priority sectors, always we only got the least help, but now things are excellent. ... Two years ago we had no hope – no hope at all; with the funds we had it would have taken six years or more probably, but now we are all terribly motivated, we have done a lot of activities to raise funds and now after all this support, well, we expect to be able to start a housing development very soon. ... It is like a dream, it has been so many years; there are people who have been longer than us living with their in-laws, so it is been a great help to the area. ... Before, everything was very stressful, one almost was sick;

now it is different, we have new expectations and we can look forward to a future. ... My husband grows seasonal fruit, watermelons, melons and that sort of thing. I work with the fruit, I have a stall on the pavement and it is a big help for my family.

Los Robles also has a joint project with the University of Chile's social science faculty to support the formation of student co-operatives in local schools. The aim is to enable school students to experience democratic decision making and to address problems of low self-esteem that are common among poor rural people. One activity involves students in choosing books and materials to buy for community use.

There's plenty more. Los Robles has provided computers and printers for community IT classes for children and adults. There's a micro-credit scheme and support for local smallholders in the production and domestic marketing of chillies and olives. The co-op works with the community in lobbying for public works such as riverbank flood defences. It arranges educational outings by bus for low-income mothers and children. There's support for poorer households in paying university fees for their children too.

And the future? Plans are afoot for an English teaching programme in local schools, both as a practical skill and to raise self-esteem. The partner for this activity is the UK's University of Northumbria. Organic production is another target. And Los Robles wants to see the benefits of its social and environmental programme broadening to include all the 53,000 people who live in the surrounding municipalities. Naturally enough, the co-op – voted best Chilean winery in 2001 – wants to keep winning prizes for quality too.

UK wine lovers can choose from more than 90 different Fairtrade-certified wines from Chilean and South African producers, including a new range launched in summer 2006.

23. Transform lives

"Fair trade has transformed the lives of small farmers,"
says banana grower Regina Joseph. Here's how.

Regina Joseph grows bananas in Dominica, one of the chain of islands
in the Caribbean that make up the Windward Islands. Says Regina:

> Before the fair trade system, I was not able to sustain my
> family. Now I can help myself, my children, my community
> and my country as a whole. My life is completely changed.
> Before we could only eat what we grew. Now, in addition, I
> can buy food for the family that I could not afford before. And
> I can pay my bills and still have something in my pocket.

One of twelve children – the only girl – Regina is now the mother of
five children aged 17 to 26. Aged 43, she belongs to the Carib indigenous people's group (see Reason 49). Some 5,000 Carib people live
today on Dominica, out of the island's total population of 73,000.

Dominica was the last of the Caribbean islands to be colonised by
Europeans, due chiefly to the resistance of the native Caribs. And the
Caribs remain the only pre-Columbian population in the eastern
Caribbean. Over a hundred years ago, a 3,700 acre reserve was
earmarked for the Carib people. Regina lives in this territory, in the
east of Dominica. "We are separate, but within Dominica," says
Regina, "we don't buy land, the land belongs to us."

Regina is an active member of her community and of her Fairtrade
Group, which she previously served as treasurer. In addition, she is
their representative on the National Fair Trade Committee.

On her land, ten minutes' walk from home, Regina grows a variety
of crops planted between her banana trees for family consumption and
for sale to local and regional markets. Hot peppers are sold to two large
spice companies; traders buy her yams and tania, another root crop, and
cabbages and lettuces are sold locally. Regina has also planted a selection of fruit trees including grapefruit, oranges and coconut palms, as
well as several native tree species which fetch a good price for their

timber. Regina has never used chemicals on her farm because she believes they are a health hazard and are contrary to the Carib tradition of respecting the natural environment (see Reason 27).

Dominica's economy depends on agriculture, primarily on growing and selling bananas to the UK. While thousands of livelihoods hinge on bananas, growing them has become an increasingly precarious occupation in recent years. In the 1990s the island's banana industry was in crisis, unable to compete with lower cost, so-called "dollar" bananas grown on Latin American plantations. Many small farmers gave up. The Windward Island's share of the UK banana market has declined from 60 per cent to less than 20 per cent in the last 15 years.

Regina now sells all her bananas through the fair trade system. To qualify for inclusion in the system, the farmers organise into groups. Regina is a member of the Carib Territory Fairtrade Group, which has a chairman, vice-chairman, secretary and treasurer. Regina now serves as public relations officer.

In addition to the price per box of bananas the farmers receive, the group also receives an extra payment – the social premium – of US$1 a box.

THE COMMUNITY

Regina describes her community:

> Our group – of 50 members – discuss what to use the social premium for. But we do not see the premium as belonging to the group. Rather it's for projects that are for the good of the community as a whole. So we invite the community to have a say in how they believe the premium should be spent, what projects to go ahead with.

The first thing the community did with the social premium was to lay down roads so that they are no longer isolated and don't have to carry the bananas on their heads any longer. Transport can now reach them. They have used some of the premium to upgrade their water system, had the reservoir enlarged and water is now piped to their homes which means people have no need to go the river for water.

"In our community there are two schools and neither knew anything about computers," Regina says.

> We used some of the premium to buy each school a computer. I don't know anything about computers but my children and grandchildren will make use of them. We also used some to help towards the cost of building a hospital. And we bought a lawn mower! There's a playing field in our village and it can now be kept in good order so that people can participate in sports. There was a family whose houses were burnt. We assisted them with US$500 so that they can rebuild. We are hoping to build a resource centre, so that people in the community can go and learn different skills, like plumbing and woodwork, so that people have the skills they need to move out of poverty. So the fair trade system does not just help banana growers. It benefits the community as a whole.

Dominica has around 300 banana growers, 90 per cent of them now selling through the fair trade system. "We are inviting the remaining 10 per cent to come in," Regina goes on. "In the meantime we co-operate with them, through for example, selling them fertiliser at the lower rate that we buy it as a co-operative group." (Since this interview was conducted, all banana growers in the Windward Islands have joined the Fairtrade system.)

Infrastructure in Dominica, especially roads, is generally poor. In pre-fair trade days, Regina had to carry her 18-kilo boxes of harvested bananas on her head to the nearest road, "which, in my case, was half a mile away," she said. Regina now harvests 35 boxes of bananas every two weeks. Collection lorries can drive right up to her packhouse on harvest days, so she no longer has to carry her bananas on her head – or make the same journey to collect water for her packing operation from the roadside standpipe.

The government is constructing a new small hospital for the area, made possible by local community organisations agreeing to part-fund the project. The Fairtrade Group originally pledged Eastern Caribbean $5,000; then in February 2005 they reviewed it in the light of increased premiums earned from Fairtrade sales and took the decision to double their contribution to EC$10,000 (US$ 3,700 approx).

Regina also exports fair trade coconuts to the UK. Again she receives almost three times as much as she did before. And she is skilled in the traditional Carib handicraft of basket weaving which supplements her income. Regina has passed her skills on to her two daughters who work as self-employed artisans, selling their baskets to tourists from Carib handicrafts shops.

Her 18-year-old daughter is studying history and herbal medicine at college and is optimistic that she will be able to get a scholarship to continue her education at university.

At the end of a hectic two-week tour of the UK in 2005, ranging from visiting supermarkets to a meeting at the Treasury, Regina has a message for UK shoppers: "When you go to the supermarket, make sure you buy Fairtrade-certified bananas."

24. Give bad balls the boot

The people who sew fair trade footballs, basketballs, volley-balls and rugby balls get a living wage, decent working conditions, medical care and low-cost loans. That's a real first in the sportsball industry.

It's a little known fact that around three-quarters of the world's foot-balls are made in and around the city of Sialkot in Pakistan, whose sportsball industry employs approximately 30,000 people.

It takes close to 700 hand-stitches to make a 32-panel football, and an experienced stitcher will complete up to five balls a day. Wages are low for the men, women and children who sew the balls, mainly working for subcontractors. In the past, thousands of children as young as seven had to work long hours with their families to help make ends meet, often going entirely without any school education.

In 1997, under pressure from Save the Children, UNICEF, the International Labour Organization and others, major sportsball brands like Nike, Adidas, Reebok and Puma signed the "Atlanta Agreement", which committed them not to employ child stitchers younger than 14. The next year the world football governing body FIFA adopted a code of conduct prohibiting use of child labour for international soccer balls.

Despite reported violations, the Atlanta Agreement and FIFA code were steps in the right direction. But they caused new problems. Manufacturing of low-quality machine-made balls moved to China. In Sialkot, where most of the stitching had previously been done in family homes, the subcontractors set up stitching centres so that they could monitor the agreement. Many women – unable to leave the home to work, and prevented in Pakistan's Islamic society from working in the same room as men – lost their only source of income.

FAIR TRADE COMES TO SIALKOT

In 2002 three Sialkot sportsball manufacturers began making fairly traded and subsequently Fairtrade-certified balls. Initially for sale in Sweden and Italy, the balls are now also available in Australia, Canada, Germany, Japan, New Zealand, the UK, the USA and other countries.

Fair trade has made a big difference to the stitcher families. Pay has risen to about 50 per cent above the industry average. Wages are calculated to provide a decent income for a family as long as two adults sew fair trade balls eight hours a day. This works out at around 6,000 Pakistani rupees (£57.00) per month per family – a decent income by local standards that ensures children can go to school.

No children under 15 are allowed to work on fair trade balls. Over 15 they can work, but only part time so that they can continue their education. One of the supplier companies, Talon Sports, was an early winner of the International Labour Organization's "Without Child Labour" award.

The work is organised differently from before. Fairtrade-certified suppliers organise stitching in small village centres. Designated women-only units enable women to work without sharing the space with men. Acceptable standards of ventilation, lighting and safe drinking water availability have to be met. Workers receive information on fair trade conditions, wage rates and the monitoring system in their own language, Urdu.

The fair trade "social premium" on sportsballs is about 10 per cent of the price that the supplier company receives. "Joint bodies" of workers and management agree how to spend it (see Reasons 4 and 7). At Talon the premium covers free healthcare for all employees, including hospital costs for pregnant women. Other benefits include small-business credit schemes to enable workers to develop new sources of income, and funds for local irrigation projects and for buying school exercise books. Talon has set up nurseries in some of its production centres, where women can leave their children to be properly cared for and prepared for school while they go to work. A third of Talon's balls are now reported as sewn by women.

Talon's Fair Trade Workers' Welfare Society, which manages spending of the premium in partnership with the sewers and local non-governmental organisations, also supports a relief programme for refugees from Afghanistan.

PLAYING BALL

The range of fair trade balls now includes volleyballs, rugby balls, basketballs, and junior and mini-footballs, as well as FIFA international match ball standard footballs. Football kits and goalkeepers' gloves (not yet Fairtrade certified) are also available. In the UK, the main supplier, FairDeal Trading, reckons the balls are no more expensive than other good quality balls.

Fair trade sportsballs are becoming popular in the UK. Football clubs using them include Genesis FC, a Christian team from Loughborough who play in the North Leicestershire League. And when Royal Holloway, University of London, won University Fairtrade status in late 2005 (Reason 16), the college rugby club played its part by using fair trade balls.

Much has been achieved, but fair trade sportsballs are still just a small fraction of those made every year in Sialkot, and only a small percentage of the sewing families currently benefit. There's never been a better time to kick your old ball into touch.

25. Stamp out pesticide poisoning

Chemical pesticides poison 20,000 people a year and have been linked to Alzheimer's disease. Fair trade growers either use natural, organic pest control or are steadily reducing pesticide use.

"Aren't you afraid to eat chocolate?" The question was asked by a worker on a cocoa plantation in Brazil. The question was understandable, for the worker and his colleagues sprayed the cocoa plants with some of the world's most powerful and dangerous pesticides. These include paraquat and 2,4-D. And, inevitably, some residue from the pesticides may be there in that glamorous box of chocolates. A Friends of the Earth study of pesticides in our food found that "nearly all of the chocolate that was tested contained residues of the hormone-disrupting pesticide lindane, which has been linked to breast cancer".

Cocoa is by no means the only crop that is sprayed to try to keep pests and disease at bay. Bananas, coffee, cotton ... the list is lengthy. And it's producers who are in the front line. Spraying chemicals can have serious effects on the health of producers, including lungs, skin, eyes and nose. While more than 80 per cent of pesticides are applied in developed countries, 99 per cent of all poisoning cases occur in developing countries where regulatory, health and education systems are weakest, according to the UN Food and Agriculture Organization. In developing countries, an estimated 25 million agricultural workers may suffer at least one incident of chemical pesticide poisoning each year.

Many crops grown for export are sprayed with chemicals. Take bananas. Most of the world's bananas are grown on large plantations in Latin America, owned by transnational corporations. While these bananas are cheap for consumers they carry huge social and environmental costs. Heavy use of chemicals has a devastating effect on workers and the environment. In Costa Rica, sprayers on banana plantations use the equivalent of 65 kg of pesticides per worker per year, and poisonings are rife.

Male workers may be left sterile after handling toxic pesticides. Honduras banana grower Gilberto is one of them. "Many of my colleagues have suffered from the pesticides that we must spray on the bananas. Now they can have no children," he says. Yet companies refuse to stop using such dangerous practices.

The bananas that we eat in Britain may have pesticide residues. Also oranges, yams and sweet potato.

Pesticides use on coffee can be high, harming both people and the environment. Coffee may be sprayed with aldrin, dieldrin and endrin – pesticides so dangerous they are banned for use in most Western countries. Nicaraguan coffee grower Oscar Zamora describes his life when he grew the crop with chemicals:

Very often, poison from the chemicals I was using fell into my eyes. ... Of course if you read the ticket you know the dangers of this. The first thing it says is: 'Poison is highly dangerous. Avoid contact with eyes and your whole body.' This poisonous chemical was so strong that it burnt my eyes, and very often I would have to run to wash it off. After this there's your back: you see when I wore a knapsack sprayer to treat the coffee plants, poisonous liquid escaped and wet my entire back.

When I arrived home there was a burning feeling all over my back and I had to make myself wash – even though I was in so much pain and my skin was irritated. I made myself wash all the poisonous chemicals off because if you don't there's a risk that you may become terminally ill, for example in your lungs.

Oscar Zamora has now switched to using organic methods and is reaping the benefits. "I am now protecting my health; the consumer of my coffee can protect theirs too. They can consume a healthy, organic product; without any fear that that they are putting themselves at risk because too many chemicals are dangerous," he says.

Fair trade and organic often go hand in hand. Many Fairtrade-certified products are also certified organic. So the consumer gets a double benefit.

COTTON

The heaviest doses of agrochemicals are sprayed on cotton – it takes about a quarter of all the world's pesticide. Yet cotton takes up only 2.5 per cent of the world's cropped area. While it is cultivated in 70 countries, just four – China, the USA, India and Pakistan – account for two-thirds of cotton production. In eleven countries in Africa, cotton accounts for more than a quarter of export revenues.

Cotton production has severe impacts at the farm level on human and environmental health. Increasingly, the social impacts of pesticides use are becoming apparent – affecting food security for example.

Fair trade growers either use natural or organic pest control or are steadily reducing pesticide use. While the two systems are complementary – and many producers benefit from both – Fairtrade certification does not exclude producers who are unable to meet organic standards, as its priority is towards the most marginalised producers.

In cotton growing, organic cotton is proving to be a viable and beneficial option for farmers (see Reason 10). Organic production tends to lead to lower costs and give higher net incomes to producers; it thus contributes to poverty reduction. Organic cotton can also increase food security, through crop rotations, by placing less emphasis on growing as much cotton as possible to steer clear of debt, by having more wild foods available in a more diverse ecosystem, and more and healthier livestock. Organic cotton production, while sometimes leading to lower yields, allows farmers to intercrop food and livestock, helping achieve food security and more secure livelihoods.

In the organic sector, women cotton growers can gain increased independence within the community and as independent producers. They are also attracted by reduced health risks and increased food security.

There are also improvements to the environment when pesticide usage is reduced. Elia Ruth Zuñiga is a banana worker for an organisation called Coopetrabasur in Costa Rica. Ruth has noticed a number of changes since Coopetrabasur started working with fair trade:

> We use much less chemicals than other companies, and we manage the environment better. The bananas are almost organic. Before Fairtrade it was a lot dirtier here. Now it is clean. We have cleaned up the quadrant and we separate our waste to recycle plastics, and save our organic waste to be used as compost for the bananas.

Coopetrabasur has built buffer zones around the boundaries of the plantations so that chemical and other waste doesn't pollute rivers, walkways and living quarters.

26. Travel with respect

Community or ethical tourism, "people to people" tours – call it what you like – does more than pay a fair wage for the services people provide. It gives you a fuller experience without harming the local environment or exploiting local people.

Tourism is the world's largest service industry, employing one in ten of the world's workers. It's growing. People increasingly want to travel abroad, and low-cost flights make it easy. One billion of us will have travelled abroad by 2010.

But whoever first said "Tourism is whorism" had a point. Tourism exploits poor people and the environment mainly in poor countries for the benefit of richer people mainly from rich countries. It's dominated by large Western companies, which take most of the profits. Poor host countries have to provide plenty of clean water and electricity to hotels and tourist complexes while local people often do without.

Job creation? Yes, but how much of the money is left for wages when close to 90 per cent of the price of an average all-in foreign holiday goes to the home-country operator, airline, insurance company and travel agent? The local hotel gets only 3 per cent – and its service workers, peanuts. As Tricia Barnett, founder-director of Tourism Concern, puts it: "Cheap holidays for us mean people in destination countries earn a pittance."

Many of the cleaners, cooks, drivers, porters, receptionists and waiters who service the industry have to work unpaid overtime and without paid holidays, employment contracts or union rights. Tips may be the only way they can make ends meet. "We live thinking every day what we're going to eat and how to pay for the electricity," says a chambermaid from a 4-star hotel in the Dominican Republic. "We have to smile to the tourists, but it is not what we are feeling in our souls."

In the idyllic Maldives, voted Britons' most desired holiday destination in 2005, almost half the population lives close to the poverty line, and one in three children is undernourished.

Sometimes there's not even a low wage in it for local people. A breakdown of the proceeds of a wildlife holiday in Kenya finds that an average of 20p of every £1 spent goes to the travel agent, 40p to the airline, 23p to the hotel chain, 8p to the safari company and 9p to the Kenyan government (largely to pay for imports to satisfy tourist tastes). The Maasai, whose natural environment is the main attraction, often get nothing at all – in fact many Maasai communities have been thrown off their land to make way for safari parks.

Head for the mountains, and there's a similar pattern of exploitation. Trekking porters in Nepal and Peru often carry huge loads for very low pay without proper clothing or equipment. Nepalese porters, more likely to be poor farmers from lowland areas than hardy mountain sherpas, suffer four times more accidents and illnesses than Western trekkers, although a new trekking companies' code of conduct is beginning to change things.

Environmentally it's also pretty bad – and it's not just the air miles (see below). Western-style hotels use thousands of gallons of water a day, often in drought-stricken countries where rural women walk for hours each morning to fetch a few litres. One tourist may use as much water in a day as a rice farmer needs to grow rice for 100 days.

Waste water from hotels is destroying coral reefs in Barbados, and dive tourism also causes heavy damage to reefs. The Bimini Bay tourism development in the Bahamas has fenced off local people's access to most of the land and many of the beaches. Mangroves have been bulldozed, and the lagoon is silting up. A one-week Caribbean cruise may dump a million gallons of waste water and thousands of gallons of sewage and contaminated oil in the sea, much of it untreated.

Then there's human rights. Some of the worst impacts of tourism have been documented in Burma, where the military regime has built its infrastructure on the backs of near-slave labour.

And sexual abuse. With 13–19 million children working in tourism around the world, the UN estimates that more than 1 million youngsters are sexually abused by tourists.

As one Malaysian commented: "The raw material of the tourist industry is the flesh and blood of people and their cultures."

A DIFFERENT KIND OF TRAVEL

Growing public awareness and pressure from campaigners have led mainstream travel companies to develop responsible tourism policies, and the UK government has supported work on making tourism more sustainable and less exploitative. Some small independent operators go much further. They have found ways to give local people more control and benefits from tourism, to protect the environment and the dignity of local cultures, and to encourage more respectful visitor behaviour.

While there's no such thing yet as a Fairtrade-certified holiday, Tourism Concern and the fair trade movement are looking into what might be possible. In the meantime, variations on the idea of "tourism that benefits local people" are offered by many small companies in partnership with host communities.

Traidcraft, which has pioneered fair trade since 1979, has developed Meet the People Tours as a joint venture with the independent operator Saddle Skedaddle. These small-group holidays led by local guides include time with fair trade producers, visits to cultural sites, enjoyment of the countryside and wildlife, and eating locally produced foods. Visitors sleep in locally owned hotels and guest houses and travel by local means where possible. People who have gone on Traidcraft's tours have described them as "inspiring", "a privilege", "an amazing experience", "mind blowing", "unforgettable", "one of the most fulfilling and worthwhile experiences of my life" and "a trip of a lifetime".

Anther leader in the field is Tribes (Best Tour Operator in the First Choice Responsible Tourism Awards 2005), which has set up a charity to support social development and environmental protection among vulnerable communities.

Many more companies and holidays feature in Tourism Concern's book *The Ethical Travel Guide* and on the website Responsibletravel.com. Some have a strong eco-tourism element with support from the Worldwide Fund for Nature (WWF). The Rainforest Alliance is developing a similar approach for people travelling from the USA.

Even the hard-pressed Kenyan Maasai have benefited. Tricia Barnett of Tourism Concern tells of a community whose response to being forced from their land for a conservation park was to sell four cattle to buy a few tents. At first no visitors came, but when they began to market themselves as a community-based tourism destination, the project blossomed. Within a few years this community venture could accommodate 50 visitors at a time, owned its own vehicle, had built a pharmacy and provided travellers with talks on Maasai culture and guided wildlife walks. The proceeds have also funded a safe house where young women fleeing female genital mutilation can get an education and start a new life.

Similar projects are under way worldwide, such as the Nicaragua Solidarity Campaign's tours that enable travellers to live and work with an agricultural fair trade co-operative.

Air travel is best avoided wherever possible. It's set to become the number one source of greenhouse gas emissions and global warming. Go overland if you have the time, and go by train if you can. Africa and Asia can be reached overland with just a short journey by sea. It takes longer but is much kinder to the environment.

27. Be a friend of the earth

Environment friendly. That's fair trade! In the fair trade system, people are likely to use the higher returns and the premiums they receive to improve their environment.

Buying fair trade helps to promote more environmentally friendly farming methods. The so-called "free" trade system puts farmers and social and environmental concerns last, pushes prices down and monopolies up. Fair trade works in and through the market but puts farmers, their communities and the environment first.

Farmers who grow for the fair trade system are already likely to be growing their crops in an environment friendly way. Take coffee, for example. A two-cup-a-day coffee drinker consumes the annual harvest of 18 coffee trees every year. Coffee was traditionally grown by small-scale farmers in forested agro-ecosystems free of agrochemicals.

Since the 1970s, however, in an effort to raise production volumes, many coffee growers have adopted higher-yielding plant varieties. In addition to requiring massive deforestation of the shade trees that grow over traditional farms, these varieties require heavier applications of chemical fertilisers and pesticides – inputs that harm workers, wildlife and local water supplies. This has had devastating impacts on the environment and human communities.

By contrast, fair trade farms rely mainly on biological or organic fertilisers and natural pest control. There are clearly defined criteria requiring environmentally sensitive production on Fairtrade certified coffee, including promotion of integrated crop management, a farming system that combines traditional "low-input" techniques and modern technology. Fair trade farms traditionally "intercrop" coffee or cocoa with various kinds of shade and fruit trees. Such shaded farms can be as biodiverse as natural forest ecosystems, encouraging plants, insects, birds and mammals. And these shaded farms also protect topsoil from erosion by rain and wind. Belizean organic farmers supplying Green & Black's Maya Gold, for example, grow their cocoa under shade trees, helping protect the rich biodiversity of the Central American rain forest (see Reason 44). They produce their crop without chemical pesticides – which matters, because cocoa is the world's second most heavily sprayed crop after cotton.

Contrary to claims made by agro-industry, environmentally friendly farming is often as productive as, or more productive than, chemical and fossil-fuel-intensive production. TransFair USA reports that fair trade tea estates which have adopted organic cultivation have reversed long-term declines in yields that resulted from intensification and technification.

Just as important, organic and near-organic produce tastes better too.

FAIR TRADE AND ORGANIC

People sometimes assume that fair trade and organic standards are the same. This is not the case, though there is a lot of common ground. While fair trade's first priority is to benefit people in terms of income, working conditions and control over their lives, organic farming begins with production methods that help rather than harm the environment. And while organic standards can apply to farming in the industrialised North, fair trade is focused only on the South. Fair trade also recognises that not all Southern producers have the income or capacity to go fully organic, at least in the short term.

That said, the benefits almost always work both ways. Fair trade is committed to protecting farm workers from harmful agrochemicals (Reason 25), for example, while the international organic farming movement – of which the UK's Soil Association is part – has guidelines that require workers to have decent minimum employment conditions.

If the environment thrives, it's better for the people working in it. And if farmers and workers are fairly paid and have more say in decisions, they are far more likely to choose to work with, rather than against, nature.

SUSTAINABLE PRODUCTION AND LIVING

As many of the examples in this book show, fair trade almost always leads to environmental improvements. Fairtrade certification requires traders to "pay a price to producers that covers the costs of sustainable production and living". Sustainable production and living are only possible if there is care for the environment.

Fair trade producer co-operatives worldwide invest their social premium in environmental improvements and training on their farms and estates. Examples include soil and water conservation, tree planting, agroforestry (growing crops and trees together), organic production, terracing, composting and environmentally friendly post-harvest processing techniques. There are benefits for people's immediate living environment too: improved drinking water and sanitation, electric lighting, better-quality and healthier housing, cleaner and more pleasant surroundings.

Interviews with banana farmers and workers from the Juliana-Jaramillo group in the Dominican Republic show the kind of progress possible after only two years of fair trade sales to the UK – although as farmer-agronomist Felipe Rivas put it, "You need to educate people so that they understand the issues."

Felipe was leading a clean-up of the old plastic bags used to protect growing bananas. Fair trade's environmental standards ban farmers from leaving plastic lying around the countryside, a common problem in banana-growing districts. The bags are an environmental hazard, and the chemicals sometimes used in them can contaminate drinking water. The Juliana-Jaramillo banana farmers collect the plastic bags for transportation to a central site and employ a team of workers to clear away other farmers' bags from nearby roads and rivers.

Felipe, who is one of four agronomists employed by the group, also helped the farmers set up an organic compost system so that they could reduce their chemical fertiliser use. "Organic fertiliser gives to the soil what the chemical fertiliser takes away," he said.

Environmental benefits can be far-reaching. Empowered by the economic stability provided by fair trade, members of the COSURCA coffee co-operative in Colombia successfully prevented the cultivation of more than 1,600 acres of coca and poppy, used for the production of illicit drugs.

"Buying Fairtrade-certified products encourages environmentally friendly cultivation, which protects land, wildlife, and human communities," sums up TransFair USA.

28. End child exploitation

Millions of children worldwide are exploited, trafficked and enslaved by adults for money, and some are injured or die as a result. It's hard to know whether children have been exploited in producing your food, drink and other purchases – unless you buy fair trade.

Work is not always bad for children, as long as it is light, undertaken willingly, and does not interfere with their health, safety or education. Such work is allowed under international law for children aged twelve and over. But the International Labour Organization (ILO) estimates that 126 million children aged 5–14 work in hazardous and illegal conditions worldwide – 73 million of them younger than ten. Many are trapped in forced and slave labour, debt bondage and prostitution.

Poverty is the overriding reason why children are exploited. With adult wages often not enough to feed, clothe and house a family, children are sent out to work. Coffee, cocoa (chocolate), bananas, oranges and sugar are among the food industry supply chains that exploit child labour most badly. Other sectors include cotton and textiles (see Reason 10), carpets and rugs (Reason 20), jewellery and sportsballs (Reason 24).

PLANTATION SLAVERY

Cocoa is one of the worst cases. A few years ago evidence emerged about the trafficking of boys and youths as forced labourers on cocoa farms in West Africa. In Côte d'Ivoire, which produces almost half the cocoa for the world's chocolate industry, more than 200,000 children were estimated as working in dangerous conditions on cocoa plantations, many of them trafficked from Burkina Faso and Mali. There were reports of boys as young as nine working. Many were never paid. Beatings were common. Boys who tried to escape were sometimes killed. Drissa from Mali, who was enslaved as a teenager, said:

> I traveled over 300 miles from home. ... I worked on a cocoa plantation in Côte d'Ivoire ... from dawn till dusk tending and collecting the cocoa pods. I was weak from hunger. If I slowed in my work, I was beaten. When I tried to run away, I was savagely beaten.

When these stories broke, the large US and UK chocolate manufacturers denied responsibility. They could not be expected to know what happened on hundreds of thousands of cocoa farms in Côte d'Ivoire, they said.

In 2002 US chocolate companies, the World Cocoa Foundation, the ILO and campaigners agreed they would eliminate child slave labour from the cocoa plantations. Some progress has been made, but the extent of improvements is not fully known, and the agreed phase-out by July 2005 was not achieved. In 2005 the International Labor Rights Fund filed a US lawsuit against chocolate companies Nestlé, ADM and Cargill, claiming they shared responsibility in the trafficking, torture and forced labour of Côte d'Ivoire child cocoa workers. In 2006 US courts were still considering whether the case should be tried.

Children and young adults have traditionally worked on plantations in West Africa, going from poorer neighbouring countries to Côte d'Ivoire to learn farming skills and earn money for their families. But the situation deteriorated sharply as world cocoa prices plummeted from $4.89 per pound in 1977 to as low as 51 cents per pound by the early 2000s. Transnational companies drove down prices as more and more developing countries grew cocoa for export.

A fair trade activist commented, "The trade issue is exactly what is exacerbating the slavery problem."

FANCY A BANANA?

Ecuador is the world's largest banana exporter. As in many developing countries, child labour is technically illegal there. But thousands of children still work on the country's banana plantations. Human Rights Watch (HRW) found in 2002 that child banana workers as young as ten worked twelve hours a day or more, often suffering pesticide exposure and sexual harassment. HRW reported that some boys:

> had attached harnesses to themselves, hooked themselves to pulleys on cables from which banana stalks were hung and used this pulley system to drag approximately 20 banana-laden stalks, weighing between 50 and 100 pounds each, over one mile from the fields to the packing plants five or six times a day.

The ultra-modern Los Álamos plantation, Ecuador's leading exporter of Bonita brand bananas, is owned by the country's richest man and ex-presidential candidate, Álvaro Noboa. Though claiming to "love his workers", Noboa was revealed in 2002 to be employing young children.

Several of Ecuador's plantations stopped employing child workers after HRW published its report, but worker families suffered as their incomes dropped. "With my husband's salary, we did not have enough for school, not enough for food," said Patricia Céspedes, explaining why she had sent her eleven-year-old nephew to work full time.

In the unfair banana trade, wholesalers and retailers take most of the profits. Plantations get little more than 10 per cent of the retail price, and their workers just a fraction.

THE BEST GUARANTEE

The problem of child labour needs large-scale political and economic solutions. Campaigning groups such as Anti-Slavery International and Save the Children are working for change. But individual action is important too. By switching to, and staying with, fair trade produce we can help low-income households earn a decent living, so they don't have to send their children to work. We can ensure that no child has been exploited or trafficked to produce what we buy. And we put pressure on the unfair traders by showing that as consumers we are committed to, and expect, seriously ethical purchasing.

All Fairtrade-certified food, drink and other produce is guaranteed not to involve exploitative child labour. The Fairtrade Mark means that children aged under 15 are not employed at all, except in helping out on the small family farm. Older children (15–18) may only work if this does not harm their education or their social, moral or physical development, and if they are given non-hazardous tasks. International Fair Trade Association (IFAT) member organisations (Reason 3) commit to ensuring that:

> the participation of children in production processes of fairly traded articles ... does not adversely affect their well-being, security, educational requirements and need for play. Organisations working directly with informally organised producers disclose the involvement of children in production.

The Network of European Worldshops (NEWS!) permits children's work in producing goods sold as long as it is temporary, part-time, healthy and non-exploitative. NEWS! reflects the views of many who believe that an immediate and total ban on child work could force the issue underground and make child protection more difficult.

All Fairtrade-certified produce has to meet rigorous standards applied through independent inspection and monitoring of producers (Reason 3). This contrasts with claims made by big chocolate manufacturers who said it was too difficult to monitor the origins of cocoa used in their chocolate.

Buying fair trade is the best and only assurance that you are not involved – however indirectly – in exploiting children.

29. Lift the debt burden

Small-scale farmers and craftspeople are often burdened by heavy debts to moneylenders. With fair trade, they can borrow what they need at lower cost.

Small farmers and craftspeople in developing countries are often burdened by heavy debts to moneylenders. The slump in prices for their produce in the mainstream trading system, both internationally and locally, has had a catastrophic impact on the lives of millions. It has forced many small-scale producers into crippling debt, and countless others to lose their land, their homes and even their lives. For among small farmers, suicides are all too common (see Reason 10).

MOUNTING DEBTS

Thirty-two-year-old Lachi Reddy had been worried for months about the mounting debts on his three acres of potatoes in the Indian state of Andhra Pradesh. Even using all the latest pesticides and chemicals to try to increase output, Lachi struggled to make a living. Over the years, sales had not come close to covering costs.

He borrowed money, first from the banks and when they said no, from the private lenders. There were plenty of those and they rarely said no. Their yes came at a cost: 36 per cent interest on the repayments. But the situation deteriorated when the last of the surface water evaporated in the storage tanks around his village, victim of a severe drought. Without water there was no hope. So Lachi did what all his neighbours had done, and borrowed even more money – 80,000 rupees (£970) – to dig a bore well in the hope of finding water. It was a gamble but it seemed to pay off. There was water.

Only now his troubles lay elsewhere. The price of potatoes fell too low even to repay the interest on the loan for the well, let alone all his other debts which now amounted to some 170,000 rupees (£2,060).

So Lachi decided to change to another crop. Sugar cane was the answer, he thought. It seemed a more reliable cash crop than potatoes.

And he couldn't go back to traditional farming. Given his debts, just growing the crops he needed for his own family was no longer an option.

The trouble was that by then he did not have enough money to buy the sugar cane or the labour to plant the crop. The banks continued to refuse any more loans, and even the private lenders were saying no. The only option left open to this proud man was to go round to his friends and neighbours pleading with them to lend him some money. It is hard to imagine what it took for Lachi to ask this. Finally, in utter desperation, he swallowed a bottle of Endo Sulfan pesticide. He collapsed, never regained consciousness and died later that day in the local hospital.

Lachi Reddy's case has been tragically repeated thousands of times in developing countries. More than 4,000 farmers in Andhra Pradesh alone have taken their lives since 1997 "as liberalised trade policies cause havoc with the region's agriculture", says Christian Aid.

Fair trade provides farmers and others in the fair trade system with a return that enables them to pay off loans more easily. Like master craftsman Mohd Usman who specialises in making gifts:

> We were not prosperous and did not get money on time. We were in debt. It was a very hard time. When we came into contact with Tara [Trade Alternative Reform Action] Projects our lives changed. We have already paid off our debt and have saved some money for our daughters' marriages.

Tara Projects is a non-profit organisation based in Delhi, serving some 25 community-based groups of artisans from regions in North India. Tara's objective is to help craft workers to achieve self-sufficiency by providing income-generating opportunities and developing marketing skills; it is one of Traidcraft's biggest supplier of crafts.

BORROWING AT LOWER COST

If people in the fair trade system need to borrow, they can often borrow at lower cost. The Kuapa Kokoo Union cocoa farmers co-operative in Ghana, for example (Reason 44) has a credit union from which members can borrow.

The Eksteenskuill Farmers Association in South Africa produces raisins and sultanas which Traidcraft use in their muesli, cakes and snack bars. With the premium the farmers receive, they have bought equipment which the farmers can borrow, again keeping them clear of moneylenders. But many more indebted farmers remain to be covered by fair trade.

"One always lives with uncertainty, always in debt," says Vitelio Manza, a Colombian coffee farmer, expressing the insecurity which comes from relying on world market coffee prices. "It's always borrow here, borrow there; we live dependent on credit. There is no peace living with such uncertainty. It would be very good if the fair trade initiative reached as far as here."

The good news for Vitelio Manza and others in his position is that people are buying more fair trade products and helping to lift a burden that can take a heavy toll.

30. Say no to GMOs

Besides posing health and environmental risks that are poorly understood, farming based on genetically modified crops threatens the livelihoods of small-scale farmers in poor countries. Fair trade helps farmers stay independent of the biotech giants.

Commercial cultivation of genetically modified (GM) crops began in the mid 1990s with insecticide-resistant cotton and maize and weed-killer-resistant soybeans. A decade later, the debate for and against rages on.

About 8.5 million farmers in 21 countries grow GM crops. Soybean, maize, canola (rapeseed) and cotton are the main ones. Others include GM rice (in Iran) and squash and papaya (in the USA). GM coffee, tomatoes, potatoes and other foodstuffs are under development. The world's leading GM-growing country by far is the USA, followed by Argentina, Brazil, Canada and China. Other notable growers include Mexico, South Africa, India, the Philippines, Colombia, Iran and Honduras, and in the EU France, Germany, Portugal and Spain.

The main claims for GM crops are that they will help "feed the world" by increasing farmers' yields and, in future, providing foods higher in vitamins and minerals. GM crops are said to help reduce problems with pests, diseases and weed control, reduce the need for chemical applications, save fuel, help prevent soil erosion and enable crops to grow in salty or arid conditions. But the benefits claimed are largely unproven, and serious questions have been asked about the health effects of consuming GM crops and the environmental risks of growing them. Plus there's a strong political and economic dimension to the debate.

POTENTIAL TO DEVASTATE

Among small-scale farmers in developing countries – the people the biotech companies say they are trying to help – as well as development charities and the general public, there's widespread suspicion of GMOs and often strong opposition. A key objection for many is that GM farming strengthens the power of the agribusiness transnationals that develop and sell modified seeds, and weakens the ability of low-income rural communities to control their lives.

An investigation by Christian Aid concluded that GM crops offer "false promises" to farmers while giving "a handful of GM corporations ... increasing control over the global food system". The charity noted that "Too little is yet known about the possible environmental or ecological and health effects. Commercial and other interests are in danger of overriding public concern, democratic decision making and local control."

Another development charity, ActionAid, has campaigned against the development and cultivation of GM coffee on the basis that it threatens to put "millions of smallholder growers out of business" by replacing traditional, small-scale production of good quality beans on family farms with industrial-type plantations.

GM coffee, developed by a Hawaii-based company, makes all the coffee berries ripen at the same time, but only when chemically sprayed. If this coffee became commercially cultivated, farmers would need to buy the seeds and chemical sprays every year. Less manual work would be needed, suiting larger-scale mechanised coffee growing rather than small family farms. "Small farmers will be squeezed out of the market with GM coffee," says Dr Tewolde Egziabler, Ethiopia's delegate to the UN Food and Agriculture Organization. ActionAid, adds "This technology has the potential to devastate the lives of millions of growers throughout the developing world."

GM cotton is another focus of concern. According to the Fairtrade Foundation, "Research to date indicates that the benefits are negligible. Indian farmers who planted [GM] cotton reported decreased average yields compared to conventional varieties." The Foundation goes on:

> There is also no evidence that GM cotton has resulted in the promised reduction in herbicide usage. GM seeds can cost up to ten times more that conventional cotton seeds and farmers are often compelled by biotechnology companies to purchase the associated farming inputs as a package. ... This can lead them into long-term financial commitments which increase their indebtedness.

Some Indian farmers' groups have taken to pulling up and burning trial plots of GM cotton to defend their livelihoods.

As for rice – which 2.5 billion people depend on as a staple food – leading Indian journalist and food activist Devinder Sharma has joined forces with Western campaigners in warning that control over rice through genetic manipulation and patents is passing into the hands of European and US transnationals. Sharma speaks of the danger of "daylight robbery" of the genetic wealth of developing countries by Western agribusiness.

Evidence of the potential health risks associated with GM crops has at times been suppressed. One well-known case is the work of leading researcher Dr Arpad Pusztai, who was hounded out of his post at the prestigious Rowett Research Institute in Scotland by the UK's political and medical establishment after he found that rats were seriously harmed by a diet of GM potato.

In 2006 the London-based Institute of Science in Society (I-SIS) reported a trail of "dead sheep, ill workers and dead villagers" associated with severe toxicity poisoning from GM cotton grown in Andhra Pradesh, India. Similar illnesses and deaths have been found among cotton growers in Madhya Pradesh and villagers exposed to GM maize in the Philippines. According to I-SIS, local shepherds said that their sheep became "dull" and "depressed" after grazing on GM cotton crop residues, started coughing with nasal discharges, developed red lesions in the mouth, became bloated, suffered blackish diarrhoea and sometimes passed red urine. Death occurred within five to seven days of grazing. At least 1,820 sheep deaths were recorded in four villages.

There are also real risks of cross-contamination. Wind-blown pollen can transmit genetic characteristics. GM and non-GM crops cannot coexist, and there are no safe distances between them.

A DIFFERENT MODEL

There is widespread public resistance to GM crops in Europe. But the biotech giants and their supporters are unlikely to be satisfied without pushing for more control over world agriculture.

Fair trade offers a very different model. In place of high-cost, high-tech agricultural inputs developed by university scientists funded by transnationals, which then must be paid for by poor farmers with little income to spare, fair trade helps local people produce crops they know, in ways they – and we – understand. Currently all Fairtrade-certified food, drinks and cotton products are GM-free. Some fair trade organisations have committed never to buy or sell GMOs, and a few have campaigned actively against GM agriculture.

31. Do something funky with your furniture

From coffee tables to dining room suites, more and more distinctive fair trade furniture ranges are now available.

Furniture ads – you can scarcely turn on a television without seeing them. One thing you will not see advertised is fair trade furniture. But from tables to chairs, sideboards to desks, loungers to beds, sales of fair trade furniture are growing fast – without being advertised. More and more fair trade furniture ranges are becoming available. And it's making a big difference to people's lives.

"Fair trade gives us great development opportunities and can bring changes to our lives," says Dr Sharma of Tara Projects in India, which supplies fair trade crafts and furniture to Traidcraft. A non-profit organisation based in Delhi, Tara Projects serves some 25 community-based groups of artisans from all regions in North India. Several thousand people are involved (see Reason 29). Tara's objective is to help workers to achieve self-sufficiency. They have brought about major changes in groups and their communities due to fair trade sales. One of the products they make, and which Traidcraft sells, is the magnificent hand-carved "Sheesham Table", with a removable top and hinged base.

"Our fair trade furniture bring you examples of master-craftsmanship from all over the world," says Traidcraft. Also in Traidcraft's range is a handmade natural cane and wood table from Development Trading Ltd of Malawi, which works with "disadvantaged and vulnerable groups".

Based near Marlborough in Wiltshire, a small family business, New Overseas Traders (The India Shop), stocks a wide range of furniture made in India. It trades with family firms and co-operatives, aiming at long-term working relationships and continuous employment for craftspeople. Through fair trade, their aim is:

to provide much needed employment particularly in rural areas and also to keep alive traditional craft skills. ... All workers involved in making and packing our products are treated with respect in reasonable working conditions and are paid fair wages. No child is exploited. Our goods and production techniques are environmentally friendly. We support ideas for improving social, medical and education conditions for worker families involved in the production of our goods.

Included in its range are:

- hand-made slatted wooden sun loungers
- painted wooden bedside tables with twist legs and drawer
- white painted wooden benches
- elegant painted iron benches
- carved chairs with jute seat
- wooden tables
- coffee tables
- *bajot* tables with drawer
- occasional tables
- low tables
- Indian teak day beds
- wooden benches with ceramic tiles
- *jali* dining chair in sheesham wood and iron
- old shutter doors set into tables with glass
- traditional Takhat dining tables with hand carved side panels
- Takhat coffee tables
- grain wheel coffee tables
- *bajots* – a multi purpose piece of furniture that can be used as a footstool, plant stand or as an individual table for an oriental meal
- low long tables with carved legs
- south Indian desks
- cupboard and wardrobes
- shutter cupboards
- Himachal Pradesh chests

- old apothecary-type chests
- storage units
- lime-washed cupboards.

The India Shop is a member of the British Association of Fair Trade Shops (BAFTS).

Every toddler loves a chair of its own. Urchin specialises in fair trade products for kids. Included in its range are iron beds with raised sides that help to prevent bedding ending up on the floor. It also sells fair trade rattan chairs and stool sets, as well as Victorian-style wrought iron benches.

When you sit on your fair trade furniture to relax you can light up the room with hand-crafted candle lanterns, hanging lights and table lamps offered in the fair trade handicraft range of Bali Spirit.

Anjuna is a fair trade retail company based in County Armagh that specialises in providing furniture, gifts and handicrafts from India, Kashmir, Tibet, Nepal and Thailand. It is the first BAFTS-approved fair trade outlet in Northern Ireland. Nearly all its suppliers are BAFTS-approved importers.

For many items of fair trade furniture it's worth taking a good look in your nearest One World Shop. The One World Shop in Edinburgh, for example, stocks a wide range of fair trade furniture, including stylish Indian rosewood furniture, contemporary kitchen glassware from Bolivia, bamboo trays and vessels in citrus colours, vibrant basket ware from Ghana.

Project Feelgood Fair Trade Furniture is the name of a project mounted by students in the department of art, media and design at the London Metropolitan University. The project is using fair trade principles to design furniture such as rocking chairs, loungers, footstools/leg-rests, and drinks/reading tables. The aim is that most of the manufacturing will be done in Africa.

And why not spread fair trade furniture to the garden? Jute Works of Bangladesh supplies a hand-braided hammock, providing work that helps rural women in Bangladesh to improve their standing in society. The hammock, which is sold by Traidcraft, comes in a drawstring jute bag for storage.

Every item of fair trade furniture is unique and not mass produced. It is above all unique in the opportunities it gives the women and men who produce it. And when you invite guests to your home, your fair trade furniture makes a great talking point!

32. Rebuild lives and livelihoods

Fair trade has helped communities in the South recover from disasters like the 2004 tsunami and hurricanes Mitch and Stan. It's not just the money. Long-term relationships prove their worth in times of trouble.

Natural disasters often have a far more lasting impact in developing than in developed countries. And some human-made disasters hit the global South that would never be allowed to happen in the North. Either way, fair trade has offered a helping hand for over 30 years.

As early as the 1970s, People Tree's partner Action Bag, based in Saidpur, Bangladesh, was set up after the war of independence with Pakistan in 1971 to help Bangladesh's Urdu-speaking Bihari refugee community at a time of famine. The project initially trained 50 women, and their first orders came from Gepa, the leading German fair trade company. People Tree has worked with Action Bag for a decade.

Fair trade has played a part in Bhopal's recovery too. One night in December 1984, a maintenance error at the Union Carbide pesticide factory in the central Indian city released 40 tons of deadly gas. Half a million people were affected immediately, and 20,000 have since died. The toll continues, with blindness, breathing problems, gynae-cological disorders, cancer and birth defects. Affected communities still seek justice. In 1985 the Bhopal Rehabilitation Centre was set up to support victims of the tragedy with training in crafts production,

[114]

self-employment and marketing. Leather wash bags made there are now marketed by Traidcraft.

Twenty years on, and Robert Mugabe inflicted Operation Murambatsvina ("Drive out rubbish") on Zimbabwe's urban poor, destroying the homes and businesses of 250,000 citizens. Most of the workers at Dezign Inc – a screen-printing company supplying Traidcraft – were evicted. Traidcraft quickly developed a new item for Dezign to make, providing much-needed work, and asked supporters for donations. By early 2006 sales and donations were enough to pay for land preparation, installation of water, drainage and electricity, and building foundations for new homes for 95 families.

AFTER THE TSUNAMI

When the tsunami hit South and Southeast Asia on Boxing Day 2004, an estimated 130,000 people died; 37,000 more are still missing. Half a million lost their homes. The fair trade movement was quick to respond. Traidcraft had links with producer groups in six affected countries, and some of these groups immediately helped with emergency relief.

In Sri Lanka, one of the worst affected countries, Traidcraft partner Gospel House helped deliver fresh water, food and clothing to badly hit communities and set up a medical centre. Other partners in Thailand, Indonesia and India assisted people who had lost their livelihoods, and Traidcraft made a donation towards rebuilding affected communities.

ForesTrade – importers of fair trade organic spices, vanilla beans, essential oils and coffee into the UK, USA and EU from small-scale farmers in Indonesia, India and Sri Lanka – set up a tsunami relief fund. It sent money to a partner, the Gayo Organic Coffee Farmers Association, in Aceh province, Indonesia, where the death toll was high and conditions were desperate. Gayo used its coffee warehouse as an emergency shelter and distributed blankets, clothing and food. "We're well rehearsed in disaster relief," said ForesTrade co-founder Thomas Fricke. "We were primed for immediate response. ... We have warehouses and trucks and a lot of people working, we were able to ... channel the resources where they're most urgently needed."

Many Asian members of the International Fair Trade Association (IFAT) provided post-tsunami aid and longer-term community support. In Sri Lanka the national Fair Trade Forum provided food, shelter, clothing and cooking utensils. Two Indonesian organisations, Pekerti and Yayasan Puspa Indah, set up rehabilitation programmes involving handicraft trading, home-based industry, start-up loans and business development.

India's Fair Trade Forum launched an emergency fund, while fair trade organisations provided relief and longer-term support to tsunami-affected coastal communities in southern India. Asha Handicrafts of Mumbai and the Indian Association for Fair Trade ran a rehabilitation programme for tsunami-devastated fishing communities in Tamil Nadu. Organising households into self-help groups, they distributed fishing nets, sewing machines, utensils, clothes, cooking oil and a telephone booth. Overseas support came from Tonbridge Baptist Church in the UK.

Help for Asian tsunami victims came from fair traders as far away as Peru. Café Femenino Foundation, founded by women coffee growers, sent relief funds to tsunami-affected growers in Sumatra, Indonesia.

MITCH AND STAN

Hurricane Mitch, one of the strongest, deadliest Atlantic hurricanes ever, battered Central America in October 1998. Close to 11,000 people died, mainly from flooding and mudslides. Thousands of people have never been accounted for. Honduras, Nicaragua and Guatemala were the worst-hit countries.

Fair trade importers responded wholeheartedly. Cafédirect donated £67,500 to the regional relief effort. In Nicaragua, Cafédirect partner PRODECOOP became a channel for outside aid, rebuilding homes and roads, and repairing coffee processing equipment. In Guatemala, the Fedecocagua co-operative, which supplies Fairtrade coffee to the UK Co-op, used international donations to rebuild damaged farms, processing plants, roads, bridges and a school.

Hurricane Stan, following seven years to the month after Mitch, was less severe and caused fewer deaths but still left a trail of destruction across southern Mexico and Central America. Coffee harvest losses in Guatemala were estimated at between 30 and 80 per cent.

Cafédirect took action again, setting up an online shop to assist grower communities in Chiapas, southern Mexico, and making an extra donation for every pack of Palenque-brand Fairtrade coffee sold. In February 2006 the president of the Cesmach coffee co-op, growers of Palenque, visited the UK and thanked people who had bought the coffee to help the relief effort.

Many US fair trade coffee importers raised donations and sent money to hurricane-affected farmer co-ops in southern Mexico and Guatemala too. In-country, the funds were used to reach out to remote communities where aid was most urgently needed, providing food, medicines and other essentials, and undertaking reconstruction efforts like repairing processing plants and reconditioning damaged coffee fields.

Several fair trade websites carried updates about the relief effort. "Practically all the roadways between the main cities and the communities are cut off," reported one. "Our biggest concern is for the communities that are further away and are in even steeper areas which tend to suffer landslides; these are the poorest communities."

"The major problem at the moment is disease and the associated risk of epidemics," said another. "Many people are suffering from intestinal infections, the flu, pneumonia and dermatologic diseases." A third explained:

> The harvest is about to begin, which means we will have to attend to many different situations: first, of course is providing relief where needed and then assisting with the reconstruction of the infrastructure of the production areas, and finally, the work of the harvest and export, to generate income for the producer families.

In raising funds for relief and reconstruction, US fair traders Equal Exchange said:

> Fair trade means having direct and long-term relationships with our trading partners. In addition to buying the farmers'

[117]

products at fair prices, we also try to accompany the co-operatives through whatever successes and challenges they face. ... Right now accompaniment means supporting those co-operatives whose members have been devastated by Hurricane Stan.

Others agreed: "Our commitment does not end with the purchase of the fair trade coffee bean. The families ... need our help now more then ever."

33. Make transnationals trade more fairly

Fair trade is a model of how international trade can and should be. There are signs that it's starting to put pressure on the big corporations to clean up their act.

Revolution is not too strong a word to explain the change in Britain's supermarkets when shoppers started buying fair trade goods.

At the end of the 1990s, shoppers would have found it difficult to buy a single Fairtrade-certified product from the supermarkets. Fair trade goods were largely purchased in specialist shops or by mail-order. But fair trade has proved too good for large companies to pass by. Supermarkets know that not to stock Fairtrade-certified goods would be to lose sales. They hope that the success enjoyed by these products will come to them. Sainsbury's, the Co-op, Waitrose, Tesco, Asda, Budgens, Spar, Somerfield, Booths and Morrisons – all the UK's major supermarkets – stock a growing range of Fairtrade-certified products. And it is not just food. In March 2006, Marks & Spencer became the first high-street retailer to offer a range of own-brand items made with Fairtrade-certified cotton, including T-shirts and socks.

The revolution has spread beyond the high street. Train travellers are increasingly enjoying Fairtrade-certified goods. Virgin Trains has switched all the tea, coffee, hot chocolate, sugar and chocolate sprinkles on board its trains to Fairtrade. And it has introduced Fairtrade into its executive lounges in several rail stations. The AMT Coffee takeaway coffee company – which has coffee kiosks in around 100 UK railway stations – serves only Fairtrade-certified coffee in its kiosks. Customer feedback had shown that their coffee drinkers wanted Fairtrade. Starbucks, Costa Coffee and Pret a Manger have responded to the demand.

The legal obligation of limited liability corporations is to make a profit for the people who own them – their shareholders. And selling more fair trade products helps them to fulfil that obligation. Not to respond to consumer demand would be fail shareholders. The opportunity for fair trade to scale up and influence large companies is therefore considerable.

But not all is sweetness and light. Limited liability companies can abuse their power and pursue profits in a unconstrained manner, regarding people and environment as resources to exploit. The big supermarkets have been accused of using their power to drive down prices to producers in developing countries. And while they embrace fair trade, supermarkets also engage in "price wars" that hit producers. In March 2006, for example, Asda started "a potentially savage price war" over bananas. It cut its banana prices by a quarter from an already low price "in a desperate bid to wean customers away from its rivals", say campaigners at Banana Link. They point out that:

> This is a war which spells major collateral damage for people and the environment in banana exporting communities in West Africa and Latin America. Serious damage. It could mean that banana workers will be forced to stop sending their children to school.

By insisting on fair trade bananas, shoppers are making their views known to the supermarkets and can help to discourage such ruinous price wars.

THE NESTLÉ CONTROVERSY

Controversies can arise when major transnational corporations get involved with fair trade. This was brought into sharp focus when in 2005 a Nestlé product, Partners Blend, received certification from the Fairtrade Foundation.

Nestlé is Britain's most boycotted company. Campaigners have pointed to its "aggressive marketing of baby foods", "trade union busting activities, involvement in child labour, environmental destruction of its water bottling business, use of GM technology ..."

The coffee in Partners Blend comes from co-operatives of small farmers in El Salvador and Ethiopia and meets Fairtrade certification standards. "This is a turning point for us and for the coffee growers," said Harriet Lamb, director of the Fairtrade Foundation. "It's also a turning point for the many people who support Fairtrade and have been pressing the major companies to offer Fairtrade coffees. This just shows what we, the public, can achieve. Here is a major multinational listening to people and giving them what they want – a Fairtrade product."

Nestlé is the world's largest food company, with 8,500 products. Apart from Partners Blend, these continue to be traded as before. It had previously criticised fair trade but now said that market forces had changed its mind. "We found that there are consumers out there who are very interested in development issues that are probably not currently buying a Fairtrade product, and they would be attracted into this market by the strength of the Nescafe brand," said Hilary Parsons, head of Partners Blend.

Fairtrade Foundation member organisations Oxfam, the Women's Institute (WI) and People and Planet welcomed the move but with caution. Oxfam said Partners Blend was a "small first step" and that it was "pleased to see Nestlé responding to pressure from campaigners", although Nestlé and other major coffee roasters still had "a long way to go to address the coffee crisis".

The WI was "pleased that the Fairtrade certification granted to Nestlé will bring benefits to ... disadvantaged producers in Ethiopia and El Salvador. We hope the product is successful and that it will introduce the Fairtrade concept to a new audience." But it also said that it remained "seriously concerned about Nestlé's wider practices".

The student group People and Planet commented: "Whilst recognising that the introduction of a Fairtrade product is a step forward, we see no reason to review our support for the boycott of Nestlé"

Many campaigners, however, are strongly critical of this certification of a Nestlé product. According to a researcher with the Colombian Food Workers' Union, 150,000 coffee-farming families have lost their livelihoods due to Nestlé's policies. He labelled the Fairtrade product "a big joke".

According to Benedict Southworth, director of the World Development Movement, (a founder member of the Fairtrade Foundation):

> The launch of Nestlé Partner's Blend coffee is more likely to be an attempt to cash in a growing market or a cynical marketing exercise than represent the beginning of a fundamental shift in Nestlé's business model. If Nestlé really believes in Fairtrade coffee it will ... radically overhaul its business to ensure that all coffee farmers get a fair return for their efforts. Until then Nestlé will remain part of the problem not the solution.

"Anything that leads to companies such as Nestlé having a fairer relationship with suppliers is good," says Julian Oram of ActionAid. "But the FT mark could be used as a fig leaf to deflect attention away from some of the other issues that it has not resolved."

KRAFT

Problems may also arise when large companies launch products that appear to be fair trade but in reality fall short. Kraft, for example – the world's second largest food company, owning Kenco and Maxwell House – has launched a coffee brand called Kenco Sustainable Development.

Kraft says the coffee is made entirely from beans from certified sustainable farming sources and is independently certified by the

Rainforest Alliance, a not-for-profit organisation. It claims that on farms certified by the Alliance, forests and wildlife are preserved, and farm workers are treated with respect and have access to clean water, medical care and education for their children.

Kraft pays farmers who adhere to its ethical criteria a 20 per cent premium on the price of green coffee beans on the open market. When the world price is below 100 cents a pound – as it normally was between 2000 and August 2006 – farmers receive less than the 126 cents paid to them under the Fairtrade system.

The Fairtrade Foundation believes a proliferation of rival certifications "is bound to confuse people". "When people suggest these initiatives are 'like Fairtrade'," says deputy director Ian Bretman, "we have to point out they are, in fact, not Fairtrade."

Buying fair trade could help to establish improved practice among large companies. But entry into the fair trade system needs to be earned.

Paul Chandler, chief executive of Traidcraft, foresees the involvement of "mainstream" commercial companies accounting for "much of the growth in fair trade products". But more dedicated fair trade consumers will, he believes, "continue to give preference to buying from those organisations which are committed to the full fair trade vision".

Transnational companies talk much about "corporate responsibility", but need to turn the rhetoric into reality. By buying fair trade products, consumers are pressing transnational companies to trade more ethically and helping to raise standards.

The need for socially responsible behaviour by corporations is described by Paul Chandler as "more compelling than ever". Awareness of this is, he says, "in part attributable to the increased consumer support for fairer ways of doing trade".

34. Put paid to sweatshops

Worker exploitation is still all too common in the world's textile and clothing industries. Buying fair trade supports a genuine alternative that guarantees decent working conditions for all.

The world spends hundreds of billions of dollars a year on clothes. Western Europe accounts for about a third of the market. Most clothes we buy are imported from developing countries, where labour costs are lowest, and often from poorly regulated "free trade zones". In 2004 more than half the European Union's garment imports came from China, Turkey, Romania, Bangladesh and Tunisia.

Clothes are a labour-intensive, low-technology product. Labour costs are often less than 5 per cent – sometimes under 1 per cent – of the retail price. The industry is notorious for "sweatshops", defined by the US Labor Department as manufacturing workplaces that violate at least two basic labour laws such as apply to minimum wages, child labour and fire safety. Poverty pay, forced overtime, unsafe and unhealthy conditions, and lack of maternity and union rights are behind many of the high-street brand-name clothes we buy and wear. "Workers work in sweatshops because the alternatives are even worse," say UK campaigners No Sweat. "Indonesia's sweatshop workers take $60 per month ... the alternative is to join the tens of millions with no work at all in a country where there is not even a basic welfare state."

The vast majority of workers in this industry are women, often young unmarried rural migrants. Women comprise 85 per cent of garment workers in Bangladesh, 90 per cent in Cambodia. Unskilled female labour is seen as low cost and disposable. According to Oxfam's estimates, fewer than half the women in Bangladesh's textile and garment export industries have a contract; most have no maternity or health cover; they work on average 80 hours' overtime a month and receive on average only 60–80 per cent of earnings due. Sexual harassment is common. Those who complain are dismissed.

Women workers also often have to live in overcrowded, unsanitary dormitories. Severe ill health is common. Few last more than a few years in the industry.

Factory accidents happen frequently. In April 2005 the nine-floor Spectrum Sweater factory in Bangladesh – built without planning permission – collapsed at night, killing 64 shift workers. Survivors said their concerns about dangerous conditions were ignored by management.

Those who defend their rights are intimidated. After garment workers on an industrial estate near Dhaka, Bangladesh, demanded overdue wages in November 2003, a battle with police left one dead, five missing presumed dead, and 200 injured. A pay strike in May 2006 led to another clash in which one person was killed and 80 were injured as police opened fire.

Problems are not confined to developing countries. The US Labor Department found 67 per cent of garment factories in Los Angeles and 63 per cent in New York violating minimum wage and overtime laws.

Exploitation in this industry results from fierce competition between suppliers for orders. Big buyers, brands and retailers play off contractors against each other. "Reverse auctions" drive down prices. Orders are unpredictable, with short lead times. Factories cannot plan or maintain steady workloads. Workers have to stay overnight to meet deadlines. Cost-cutting suppliers use subcontractors and temporary and home workers, which means more insecurity and fewer rights.

Research since the 1990s has found oppressive and abusive working conditions behind many of the best-known brands. The UK's Arcadia Group (Topshop, Dorothy Perkins, Burton, Miss Selfridge), supermarket chain Tesco and global sportswear brands like Nike and Adidas have all been heavily criticised for worker exploitation in their supply chains.

In response, many leading brands and retailers have adopted codes of conduct, claiming this improves wages and working conditions. The UK government-backed Ethical Trading Initiative has strongly supported such schemes. Yet despite improvements little has changed for millions of the world's textile and garment workers. Codes of conduct are often poorly audited. Clothing supply chains for supermarkets, discount stores, mail order companies and sportswear are thought to perform particularly badly.

Oxfam's 2006 report *Offside! Labour rights and sportswear production in Asia* exposed the exploitation and sometimes violent oppression of Asian workers in the production of football boots and sports kits for global brands. Fila was found to be one of the worst offenders. During the 2006 World Cup, Oxfam criticised Adidas for failing to have an Indonesian supplier reinstate 33 workers whose sacking for a one-day strike was ruled illegal by the Indonesian Human Rights Commission.

SO WHAT'S THE ALTERNATIVE?

Buying clothes made from Fairtrade-certified cotton helps, because this ensures cotton growers earn a fair wage and that excessive agro-chemicals use is avoided (see Reason 10). But cotton production is only the first stage in the supply chain. While major UK clothes retailers like Marks & Spencer have begun to sell some Fairtrade-certified cotton garments, the Fairtrade minimum price and social premium do not apply to other groups in the supply chain such as spinners or weavers.

This is why the fair trade movement is working on new industry-wide standards so that it can guarantee a better deal to other garment workers, but these have yet to be agreed. In the meantime, the best bet is to buy from smaller, dedicated fair trade and alternative trading companies that have signed up to the International Fair Trade Association (IFAT) code of practice (Reason 3). UK suppliers of 100 per cent fair trade clothing include Bishopston Trading, Chandni Chowk, Epona, Ethical Threads, Ganesha, Gossypium, Howies, Hug, Natural Collection, Pachacuti, People Tree and Traidcraft. These companies know which workshop produces what they sell and take a much closer interest in wage levels, working conditions and local communities' welfare than the big companies usually do.

People Tree, for example, aims to "set an example ... of Fair Trade as a form of business ... based on mutual respect between producer, trader and consumer". Its policies commit it to paying a fair price to producers; prompt payment; equal pay for women and men; safe and healthy working conditions; no exploitative child labour; giving opportunities to disadvantaged people; preserving traditional skills; environmentally careful production, packaging and transportation; and working with movements like the Clean Clothes Campaign for industry-wide change. People Tree's suppliers include small-scale producers and co-ops in Bangladesh, India, Kenya, Nepal and Peru that employ people with disabilities (Reason 49), low-income women, members of rural communities, and traditional craftspeople.

Ganesha, another leading UK ethical clothes company, works with geographically isolated and socially marginalised low-caste groups and religious minorities in India. Most dedicated fair trade clothing suppliers have a similar approach.

For people seeking sports kits, Fair Deal Trading currently seems to be the only UK supplier.

Though still tiny compared with the mainly exploitative global garment industry, the fair trade clothing business is growing steadily as a genuine alternative, offering an ever-widening range of "sweatshop-free" clothes to choose from.

35. Buy into a longer–term relationship

Fair trade importers sign long-term agreements with suppliers, sharing knowledge and commitment to help farmers succeed.

Mainstream international trade is a cut and thrust business, where loyalty counts for little. A company may think it has a good outlet for its product, customers it can rely on. But a competitor comes along, shaves a little off the price – and it's all change. Its business may collapse. There is no stability, no guarantee of a long-term business relationship.

Poorer producers especially need stability if they are to venture into exporting their goods. Fair trade encourages importers to place long-term contracts with co-operatives, and to place orders well in advance so that producers can plan their business with some security. Fair trade importers sign long-term agreements with suppliers. This enables even the poorest producers to have access to markets in developed countries for their products.

The trading standards of the "International Fairtrade Labelling Organisations" stipulate that traders must "sign contracts that allow for long-term planning and sustainable production practices", and "make partial advance payments when requested by producers".

The YMCA (Y Development Co-operative Co Ltd) in Chiang Mai, northern Thailand, has been exporting crafts to fair trade organisations since 1982, as well as selling locally. It works with more than 50 producer groups in northern, north-eastern and southern Thailand.

Many of the producers are women, who earn supplementary income through craftwork. It is also keen to encourage traditional skills, which are in danger of dying out, and to promote environmental awareness. Fair trade provides a significant market for some of the producers linked to the YMCA – ceramic and jewellery makers for example. Benefits include advance payments and design advice.

Some small-scale producers find it difficult to obtain finance to make their products available for export and often have to pay very high interest rates. Under the fair trade system, producers may request part-payment of orders in advance of delivery, for which a fair commercial cost should be passed on by the importer.

"The long-term relationship with fair trade organisations is important," says Nalinee Pussateva, the YMCA's export manager. Traidcraft point out that the stability that comes from a long-term trading relationship can encourage producers to "find wider groups of customers in a range of markets". One of Traidcraft's five key aims is to "build up long-term relationships, rather than looking for short-term commercial advantage".

The value of long-term trading relationships is stressed by all fair trade enterprises, and with different emphases. Gossypium, which specialises in fair trade and organic cotton products, highlights trust and understanding:

> We aim to work respectfully with our suppliers through a process of mutual respect and review. We believe in building up long-term trading relationships with our suppliers which enables all parties to develop the highest level of understanding about each others needs and constraints ... to foster trust and enable the development of quality products and the continuous assessment of ethical and environmental techniques ... leading to the development of reasonable and positive working conditions.

A long-term relationship allows more scope for buyers to share information with producers that will help them succeed in the marketplace. And the knowledge that funds are assured for a certain period makes producers more willing and able to invest in their enterprise. According to a report on the development of Max Havelaar coffee:

> Insecurity about income makes farmers and their organisations become hesitant to invest in, for instance, soil conservation or the best maintenance for their coffee plants. For this reason, the importers are asked to enter into contracts for longer periods, wherever the market development allows.

And it's not all one-way. "Direct, long-term relations with suppliers allow [coffee] roasters to maintain the continuity that they need for their blends," says the report.

HOW LONG IS LONG-TERM?

How long is long-term in the fair trade system? Fairtrade Labelling Organisations International (FLO) does not define "long-term" precisely. Its standards for banana growers do make a suggestion. They state that importers should sign a contract of purchase for Fairtrade bananas with every producer/exporter, "for a period of at least one year and preferably for longer". Fairtrade-certified banana producers like Regina Joseph (see Reason 23) have only a twelve-month contract with Tesco.

On cocoa and coffee, no period is mentioned in FLO's standards. On cocoa they state that buyers and sellers will "establish a long-term and stable relationship in which the rights and interests of both are mutually respected". For small-farmer coffee growers, the standards state that buyer and seller "will sign contractual agreements for the first part of the season and a letter of intent for the rest of the season, to be confirmed by purchase contracts as the harvest progresses".

Some companies have maintained a relationship with growers over a long period. Green & Black's, for example, have bought cocoa beans from Mayan farmers since 1994 for their Maya Gold chocolate (Reason 44). "We now have a long-term contract with them, guaranteeing to buy all the cocoa they can produce. This security has helped them to improve the quality of life and provide a better education for their families," says Green & Black's.

Some "long-term" contracts could usefully be longer and more specific. At present they may not be long enough for producers to plan ahead and have stability. What the retailer may regard as "long-term" may be seen differently by producers.

But shoppers too can buy into a longer-term relationship with fair trade products – and we can make our own choice about how long is long-term. Buying a product consistently over a long period – of course providing that it satisfies on quality – encourages retailers to keep on stocking it. They will soon take fair trade products off the shelves if they don't sell.

The Max Havelaar report, mentioned above, stresses that fair trade "is embedded in the entire operation of the organisations and their empowerment process, which develops gradually. The effect of fair trade is a long-term effect and cannot be isolated from other factors and influences."

Fair trade is long-term trade. When we buy fair trade we know that buying a product consistently over a long period of time gives the producer stability, and assurance of income and livelihood.

36. Show solidarity with Palestinian farmers

Both Palestinians and Israelis have suffered immensely from conflict in the Middle East. Palestinian farming communities have been among the worst-hit economically. Now there's a way to enjoy flavoursome food while acting in solidarity.

Cultivation of olive trees began thousands of years ago in the eastern Mediterranean, and some of the world's oldest olive groves are in Palestine. Their age, the local climate, fertile soils and traditional organic farming are said to give Palestinian olive oil a special quality.

With two-thirds of Palestinian families living in the countryside, farming is central to the local economy. Olive production provides essential income for more than 70,000 Palestinian farming households. But production has suffered drastically as a result of Israel's occupation of the West Bank, the Israeli settlements, the Palestinian *intifada* (uprising) and, most recently, construction of Israel's "security fence" or "separation wall".

Many farmers have had their lands confiscated, their groves destroyed, are refused access or have to seek authorisation from the Israeli military to tend their trees. Irrigation water has been shut off. Farmers have sometimes been attacked by settlers while picking their fruit. According to Jerusalem's Applied Research Institute, more than half a million olive trees have been uprooted, bulldozed and burned by Israeli soldiers and settlers since 2000.

To produce high-quality oil, olives need pressing within hours of being picked. With movement of people and goods so restricted, Palestinian farmers have found it increasingly hard to process and sell their oil. Local markets have shrunk as economic hardship has taken hold in the West Bank and Gaza, and prices have slumped. It's said that over half the West Bank's olive oil is currently thrown away for lack of markets. Yet Palestinians must harvest their crops, because the Israeli state confiscates unfarmed land.

Olive grower Nazeeh Hassan Shalabi, a 37-year-old father of seven, can no longer access the 400 trees his family has owned for generations. Lacking the right transit permit, Nazeeh farms 240 trees on rented land near his home instead. "We use olive oil for so many things," he says. "Cooking, soap, as medicine on the skin, wood from the olive trees for heating – everything. Olive oil is at the soul of this community."

Inam, Nazeeh's wife, adds, "There are so many things that I would like to buy for the children but cannot, like clothes. My dream is just to have a normal life." For Palestinian student Reem Ihmaid:

> It is obvious that poverty is all over the place – now more than ever before. People here are so desperate. Palestinian farmers are willing to sell olive oil, or whatever they have, for just about any price they can, so they can put food on the table.

WORKING TOWARDS FAIR TRADE

Solidarity organisations and groups in Israel, Europe and North America market Palestinian olive oil under fair trade terms, while formal Fairtrade certification is pending. Among these groups are the Palestinian Fair Trade Association and Palestinian Agricultural Relief Committees, Green Action Israel, Olive Co-operative (UK), Oxfam International, Zatoun Canada, Zaytoun UK, Jews for Justice for Palestinians, and Alter-Eco France.

Tel-Aviv-based and Oxfam-backed Green Action sells Palestinian olive oil in Israel. The oil is bottled in the West Bank to maximise the value retained locally. Green Action's director Avi Levi says, "We want to bring both Palestinians and Israelis together by making the most of this economic opportunity and gradually we will start to see the development of a closer understanding between the two sides."

Zaytoun is the leading UK supplier, set up in 2003 by Heather Gardener and Cathi Davis, with support from Edinburgh fair trade co-op Equal Exchange and the Triodos Bank. Working on a non-profit basis, Zaytoun (Arabic for "olives") buys olive oil at fair trade prices from 80 West Bank co-operatives representing thousands of family farms, and from women-led Israeli fair trade suppliers Sindyanna, who work with Arab Israeli growers. Proceeds are channelled back to the producer communities.

"One of the guiding principles of fair trade is early payment to producers. The finance from Triodos allowed us to pay Palestinian farmers for enough oil to meet fast-growing demand in the UK," says Zaytoun's Cathi Davis.

There have been setbacks, such as in 2004 when a shipment of oil intended for the UK Christmas market was diverted to Italy and arrived three months late. But in 2005 Zaytoun sold three times as much as the year before. Sales channels include fair trade shops and worldshops, churches and other faith groups, solidarity groups and distribution partners such as Olive Co-op, which promotes responsible travel (see Reason 26) during the olive harvest season as well as educational and solidarity links in Palestine and Israel.

Together, Zaytoun and Olive Co-op have launched an olive tree replanting and sponsorship programme under the title Trees for Life – Planting Peace in Palestine. The Palestine Fair Trade Association distributes the trees to farmers who follow fair trade guidelines, bringing the promise of better livelihoods.

"Our ancestors planted the trees so that we could eat. We protect the trees so that we may live. It's how we remember our past and how we safeguard our future," says Jehad Abdo, chair of the West Bank Al-Zaytouna farmers' co-operative, set up with support from Zaytoun, War on Want and others.

Zaytoun also supports producer communities in improving their processes and infrastructure. It hopes soon to get the olive oil into the Co-op and other UK supermarkets, and is starting to import other agricultural produce from Palestine such as dates, almonds and couscous.

Another way to support Palestinian olive farming families is to buy traditional natural olive oil soap made by women in the West Bank and Gaza, supplied in the UK by Ganesha.

37. Reach for the goals

The world has set itself the enormous challenge of halving poverty by 2015. Fair trade, our purchasing power, can help get us there.

A bold and historic commitment. At the United Nations Millennium Summit in September 2000, leaders of 189 countries unanimously agreed on goals that were bold, historic and visionary. Goals that were a fitting way to mark the start of a new millennium.

Leaders committed to eight Millennium Development Goals (MDGs), designed to rescue people from poverty and bring hope of a better life for all. Comprising 18 targets and 48 indicators, the goals provide a clear, unambiguous plan to reduce poverty, hunger and disease.

- Goal number 1 is to eradicate extreme poverty and hunger. "Reduce by half the proportion of people living on less than a dollar a day. Reduce by half the proportion of people who suffer from hunger."
- Goal 2 is to achieve universal primary education. "Ensure that all boys and girls complete a full course of primary schooling."
- Goal 3 is to promote gender equality and empower women. "Eliminate gender disparity in primary and secondary education preferably by 2005, and at all levels by 2015."
- Goal 4 is to reduce child mortality. "Reduce by two-thirds the mortality rate among children under five."
- Goal 5 is about improving maternal health. "Reduce by three-quarters the maternal mortality ratio."
- Goal 6 concerns the need to combat HIV/AIDS, malaria and other diseases. "Halt and begin to reverse the spread of HIV/AIDS. Halt and begin to reverse the incidence of malaria and other major diseases."
- Goal 7 aims to reverse the "loss of environmental resources. Reduce by half the proportion of people without sustainable access to safe drinking water. Achieve significant improvement in lives of at least 100 million slum dwellers, by 2020."
- And finally, Goal 8 is to "develop a global partnership for development".

[133]

But almost half way to 2015, progress in achieving the goals is painfully slow. They are not being given either enough priority or resources. At the present rate of progress, most developing countries are likely to miss most of the goals.

There has been little improvement in the number of people living in poverty. "Progress towards reducing the number of hungry people in developing countries by half by 2015 has been very slow and the international community is far from reaching its hunger reduction targets and commitments set by the MDGs," said Dr Jacques Diouf, director-general of the UN Food and Agriculture Organization, in 2005. The number of hungry people remains obstinately high at over 800 million.

According to a World Bank report, undernourishment increased in sub-Saharan Africa between 1992 and 2002. Over a billion people continue to scrape by on less than a dollar a day. At the present rate of progress it could take some countries over 100 years rather than ten years to meet the poverty goal.

On reducing child mortality by two-thirds, some regions have made substantial progress, says the World Bank – East Asia, Latin America, the Middle East and North Africa, for example.

On primary education, 51 countries have achieved the goal of complete enrolment of eligible children but progress is slow in parts of Africa and Asia. Worldwide, over 100 million children of primary-school age remain out of school, almost 60 per cent of them girls.

The goals will not be met unless there is action in a number of ways. More resources are needed.

"A substantial increase in official development assistance is required in order to achieve the MDGs by 2015," said G8 leaders at the end of their summit in July 2005. Yet they are not providing those resources. The Organisation for Economic Co-operation and Development predicts an increase in development aid of $50 billion a year by 2010 – from $79 billion in 2004 to around $130 billion in 2010. Oxfam points to United Nations estimates that $180 billion a year is needed by 2010 if the goals are to be reached. An additional $100 billion a year, rather than $50 billion, is therefore called for.

"If rich countries reach the internationally agreed target of 0.7 per cent of gross national income," estimates Jo Leadbeater of Oxfam, "this would mean $250 billion in aid each year by 2010."

Aid will have to increase substantially by 2010 if the MDGs are to be met, rising from the envisaged $130 billion a year to $180 billion a year. This would still be short of the 0.7 per cent aid target. But a world summit of leaders at the United Nations in September 2005 did little to advance the goals. No additional commitments were made.

An increase in aid would be an important advance, but not enough to achieve the MDGs. The goals will not be reached unless there is action on trade justice (see Reason 43), debt relief (Reason 29), good governance and climate change.

On governance there is progress. Democracies are increasing. The 2005 Africa Commission report spoke of improvements in governance in Africa. But on climate change the situation is literally deadly. "A staggering 182 million people in sub-Saharan Africa alone could die of disease directly attributable to climate change by the end of the century," said a Christian Aid report in May 2006. Climate-induced floods and drought are becoming more common. Climate change is reducing the area of land available for farming.

FAIR TRADE AND THE GOALS

The world's poor deserve better. We need to press governments – but not wait for them. Action is needed by consumers. An expansion in sales of fair trade products could help millions of people to overcome poverty and bring the Millennium Development Goals within reach for more countries and people.

Fair trade gives producers a fair deal, paying a proper and stable price for their products, thus raising their income and opportunities to escape from poverty. It helps more children to go to school and to get a better deal from society (Reason 14). The fair trade movement has been instrumental, for example, in building up consumer pressure on coffee and banana companies to stop using forced and child labour and to examine their business practices.

Again fair trade helps to promote gender equality and to empower women (Reason 8). It helps to improve people's health and to ensure environmental sustainability. And it does a great deal to "develop a global partnership for development".

Among organisations linking fair trade with the MDGs is Women of Reform Judaism. Its executive committee declared in 2006, "Fair trade rules are necessary to meet the development goals."

So in addition to aid, debt relief, trade justice, action on climate change and other measures, fair trade is needed to rescue the MDGs. Says Harriet Lamb, executive director of the Fairtrade Foundation:

> If we are to reverse the catastrophic trends on poverty and reach the Millennium Development Goals, a whole new global economics needs to take centre stage, focusing on increased aid flows and further debt cancellation but also, and most critically, a more just global trade regime which puts at its core and has as a declared aim, not liberalisation but sustainable development.

The Millennium Development Goals are too crucial to be missed.

38. Be a progressive coffee drinker

Our high streets are full of coffee shops. Most of the coffee chains will sell you a cup of fair trade. But only one of them is co-owned by the coffee growers. That's Progreso.

The world slump in coffee prices has seen incomes of most of the world's 25 million coffee growers fall to a quarter of their 1960 purchasing power. Farm-gate prices often don't even cover production costs (see Reasons 2 and 9). The lost income means less to eat for the family, poorer healthcare, children out of school (especially girls), some farmers turning to grow illegal crops like coca in Colombia, migration to the cities (Reason 48) and a host of other problems.

Yet it's obvious that the price crash has not hurt the transnational coffee brands and retailers. Quite the opposite. Their profits have increased year on year as their market dominance has grown. Coffee drinking has undergone a sea change in the global North with the spread of chains of coffee shops like Starbucks, Coffee Republic and Costa. Yet coffee farmers usually earn 1p or less when you buy an unfair-trade cup of coffee in one of these chains.

At least we can now buy fair trade coffee almost everywhere. And in some places, like Marks & Spencer's cafés, all the coffee is fair trade. It's an improvement, bringing a slightly better share to the growers. Let's not knock it.

But Starbucks, the world's leading coffee chain, sells only a small proportion of its coffee as Fairtrade certified – less than 4 per cent in 2005. Starbucks does have its own schemes supporting producers, and it buys and sells more fair trade coffee each year. Even so, as Harriet Lamb, Fairtrade Foundation director, puts it, "The effort to which Starbucks has gone in comparison with the potential difference it could make is very small."

MAKING PROGRESS

Progreso Cafés Ltd is a different sort of coffee chain. There are still just two cafés so far – in London's Portobello Road and, the first to open, in late 2004, Covent Garden. But it's a chain run for the coffee growers, not to make fat cats fatter.

Naturally, Progreso sells 100-per-cent high-quality Fairtrade-certified coffee, tea and drinking chocolate, along with Fairtrade banana smoothies and a range of tasty cakes, savouries, soups, salads and sandwiches, fair trade and organic wherever possible.

The biggest difference, though, is that the growers also own a share of the business and will profit from its success. The idea was thought up by Oxfam and La Central coffee producers' co-operative in Honduras. The concept is simple. Twenty-five per cent of the shares in Progreso belong to the producer co-ops that supply the coffee. Another 25 per cent of company shares are held in a trust fund to support development projects in poor coffee-producer communities. And Oxfam, which has worked with small-scale coffee farmers since the 1960s, holds the other half of the shares.

For now, profits are ploughed back into the business. The aim is to have 20 Progreso branches running as soon as possible. "Bohemian urban villages" in London, south-east England and central Scotland are targeted for expansion. With growth, shareholders will begin to receive dividend payments.

Currently Progreso's coffee comes from three main suppliers, two of which co-own the company: La Central in Honduras, a nationwide network of more than 10,000 farmers organised in 80 co-operatives, and Oromia Coffee Farmers Co-operative Union in Ethiopia, which represents 35 co-ops, about 23,000 members and 100,000 families. The third main supplier, the Gayo Organic Coffee Farmers' Association in Aceh, Indonesia, is not yet a shareholding member of the company. They're working on it.

Another key partner is Glasgow-based Matthew Algie & Co., the UK's largest independent coffee-roasting company.

Actor Colin Firth is on Progreso's board and has worked hard to support and promote the chain. During 2005 he learned about every stage of coffee production, visiting the Oromia co-op in Ethiopia, going to Glasgow to see the beans being roasted, and serving behind the counter in Portobello Road. Firth was impressed by the people he met in Ethiopia. "They are incredibly articulate, they have first-hand experience of everything," he said. "They're the people that should be speaking, but they don't get heard."

Progreso is also supporting another great idea: One water. When you buy a bottle of One water in a Progreso café, all the profit is used to fund a South African-based charity called Roundabout. Roundabout install "roundabout play-pumps" in African villages – fun roundabouts that harness children's energy when they play to drive a water pump, bringing clean water up from underground into storage tanks. Each roundabout – more than 650 installed so far – is sited near a school or crèche to ensure there are plenty of willing young workers available to keep the water flowing.

Progreso is establishing itself in a very competitive sector. "Our café at Covent Garden used to be a Starbucks. Anecdotally we're doing more business than they used to and the Portobello site is getting busier," board member David Williamson said in 2005. "The stores have to be successful because of the quality of the coffee, the staff and the atmosphere. And they are."

39. Send hope to a hungry country

How Fairtrade-certified mangos are making a huge difference to people's lives in West Africa.

Burkina Faso is one of sub-Saharan Africa's poorest and most malnourished countries. In the southwest of the country, Issaka Sommande grows mangos on five hectares of land. He is a member of a co-operative known as Association Ton, which is situated in Niangoloko, near the border of Cote d'Ivoire, and was set up in 1991. It's a large co-operative of 2,000 members, all living in the villages of the area.

Both women and men work on mango production. Men look after the pruning and harvesting of trees and planting of new stock, while women are responsible for cutting and drying the fruit. Farmers in the area intercrop food crops such as millet, maize, sorghum and beans with their mangos. The dried mangos can provide their only cash income.

Each week a different village supplies fresh organic mangoes to Ton's central drying station, which is operated by a team of 100 women from the villages – all of whom are also members of the co-operative. The women then slice and dry them ready for export.

In 2003 Association Ton came across Fairtrade Labelling Organisations International. There was already a spirit of democratic and good governance in the co-operative and this helped them to gain certification from FLO. "Fairtrade certification has enabled us to lift ourselves up. It has given us a higher price, about 30 per cent higher – around £3.50 per kilo – and a much bigger market," says Issaka. And it truly is a much bigger market – "double what it was before they gained certification". So he is selling twice as much – and getting 30 per cent more!

Before Fairtrade certification, there was a lot of waste, he says, as not all the producers could find markets. Some of his mangos were just left on the trees.

In addition to growing mangos, Issaka is also employed by the co-operative, working as a project manager. He trains people in literacy training, HIV/AIDS prevention, and helping people to combat malaria. Ton runs literacy campaigns for its members and promotes reafforestation and good agricultural practice among members. Trees are viewed as important in keeping the nearby desert at bay.

As Ton's members are completely organic, everything has to be mulched and composted. The higher returns that members now receive for their mangos enables them to plant new trees more often. And new trees are more productive than older trees.

ASSOCIATION WOUOL

Arsene Sourabie grows mangos on his seven hectares for another co-operative in Burkina Faso, Association Wouol. Set up in 1975, Association Wouol has 1,300 members, with landholdings averaging around five hectares in size.

Not all the members grow mangos. Some work for the co-operative at its mango cutting and drying station, which employs 170 women. About 70 per cent of Wouol's members are women. Arsene also works for his co-operative as quality control manager in the drying stations.

"Fair trade has given me the hope of a market and I've extended the area under mangos," he says.

Wouol promotes good agricultural practice amongst its members, actively training them in organic farming. Members are also encouraged to diversify into new activities such as hibiscus, cashew nut and sesame farming. Antoine Sombie, chairman of Wouol, describes the co-operative's mission as being "to work with the producers and elevate their condition".

Issaka and Arsene say that selling through the fair trade system has made a big difference to them personally and to their community as a whole. More children are now able to go to school and the rate of malnutrition has declined to very low levels.

The two co-operatives have only just begun to receive the Fairtrade premium. In both cases, the way the premium will be used is to be decided democratically by an assembly of the co-operative, elected by members.

The recent war and continuing unrest in Cote d'Ivoire has stifled traffic through the area where the co-operatives operate, meaning that all the restaurants and shops have lost their customary trade from passing lorries and cars. To add to this squeeze on resources, many refugees from Cote d'Ivoire have travelled into the area, looking for help from relatives living on the Burkina Faso side of the border. Especially in this difficult context, Fairtrade-certified mangos have been a lifeline for many people.

All the mangoes from Ton and Wouol are Fairtrade and organic (Soil Association) certified, and 100 per cent free from preservatives. The two co-operatives sell their dried mangos to a UK-based company Tropical Wholefoods which imports tropical foods. The company became involved in fair trade about 15 years ago. "We heard about Burkina Faso's mango producers through TwinTrading, one of the UK's first fair trade organisations," says Kate Sebag, a director of Tropical Wholefoods. "Fair trade gives people the confidence to believe there is a market for their goods."

Tropical Wholefoods sells through health food shops, fair trade shops and Oxfam shops throughout the UK, and through mail order. It also has a bakery which uses dried fruits to make Tropical Wholefoods Fairtrade-certified cereal bars.

Fairtrade certification is enabling Issaka and Arsene and the 3,000 plus members of their co-operatives to enjoy the fruits of their labours.

Most of Burkina Faso's mangos are not however sold under the fair trade system. Many producers are vulnerable to exploitation by traders who come to their villages to buy fruit. In the country as a whole, hunger and malnutrition are rife. This is in stark contrast to the area where Association Ton and Wouol operate.

An expansion in sales of Fairtrade-certified mangos could give more producers the chance to enter the system and the opportunity of a better life.

40. Co-operate with co-operatives

Co-operatives and fair trade belong together.

Today's international co-operative movement began when the Rochdale Pioneers – low-paid Lancashire cotton weavers – set up a co-op shop to sell household groceries to working families in 1844. The Pioneers meant their business to be different from other local shops that exploited them. Each customer would be a voting member, with a say in how the shop was run. When there was a profit, every member would get a share. The Rochdale co-op was not the first but became a model that many other groups of working people followed.

Of course, co-operative working was not "invented" in the nineteenth century or in the UK. Throughout the global South, traditional societies have managed natural resources and met their needs collectively since time immemorial.

Today millions of co-ops large and small around the world have an estimated 800 million members and 100 million employees. One in three Canadians, one in four Singaporeans, one in five Kenyans and one in ten Colombians is said to belong to a co-op. Co-ops are active in every sector, from agriculture and fisheries to housing and financial services, from manufacturing and crafts to child care and health, from education and sport to water supply and public transport.

CO-OPS AND FAIR TRADE

The principles behind co-operatives are close to those of fair trade. Co-ops are set up to meet shared needs, belong to their members, are democratically run, distribute profits fairly and aim to provide quality goods and services for a fair price. "Co-operatives ... foster economic fairness by ensuring equal access to markets and services for their members, with membership being free and open," says the International Labour Organization. It's no surprise that co-ops have been associated with fair trade since it began. Or that many – if not most – fair trade producers are co-operatives.

. In the UK, the Co-operative Group helped pioneer fair trade. "The Fairtrade stance ... has the potential to combine all the elements of being a successful co-operative business," the Co-op says. "Fairtrade is obviously about business (not charity), but doing business in a co-operative spirit reflecting the values and principles of the co-operative movement."

The Co-op got into fair trade because "Many of our members and customers are concerned about the effects of world trading systems and about the people producing goods in developing countries." The Co-op has led Fairtrade-certified food and drink retailing in the UK. It was the first major chain to sell Cafédirect coffee, brought the first fair trade bananas and pineapples to the UK and launched the country's first supermarket fair trade wine.

In 2003 the Co-op's fair trade own-label coffee became the first sold at a lower price than the commercial brands. This was hugely significant. Until then, fair trade coffee had usually cost more than mainstream. The Co-op's move meant that customers who bought solely on price could now buy fair trade – it came within reach of a lot more people.

STRENGTH IN NUMBERS

Among fair trade producers, the link with co-operative working is equally strong. The first ever fair trade coffee was imported into the Netherlands in 1973 from Guatemalan farmer co-ops. Today nearly 200 coffee co-ops worldwide, representing 675,000 farmers, produce Fairtrade coffee.

In many producer countries co-operative principles have found fertile ground in traditional culture. Low-income coffee producers of indigenous Mayan descent in the Chiapas region of Mexico, for example, formed the Kulaktik co-op in 1991 and sell to the fair trade market. Being a co-op is important to them: "We have been unified by the organisation. ... The group helps us to be independent of some of the problems in the area."

Working with other co-ops is a key strategy. "We have been able to connect with six other indigenous coffee co-operatives," says Kulaktik's president Juan Girón Lopez. "A smaller group would be unable to apply for credit. With credit, we are paid throughout the harvest."

Many producer co-operatives working in fair trade are umbrella organisations representing smaller co-ops. The Organisation of Northern Coffee Cooperatives (Cecocafen) in Nicaragua, for example, is made up of eleven such members. And Coocafé in Costa Rica, one of the first Fairtrade coffee producer co-ops, represents nine others.

Well-organised co-ops can be a powerful force for change. Peruvian coffee growers' co-ops set up a national association that has lobbied their government for support for the coffee sector and led in the development of regional policy on coffee among Andean countries.

A co-op with a high profile in the fair trade sector is Kuapa Kokoo of Ghana. Established in 1993, Kuapa Kokoo (the name means "Good Cocoa Farmers Company") comprises a farmers' union run by elected representatives of regional groupings of village societies, a trading company, a trust that allocates the Fairtrade social premium to community projects, and a farmers' credit union and banking service.

By 2005 Kuapa had 45,000 cocoa farmer members – almost a third of them women – grouped in over 1,000 village societies. The organisation maintains a strong level of women's representation on its councils and committees. Kuapa Kokoo member Mary, aged 53, a widow with seven children, says:

> Life before the farmer co-operative was set up was extremely difficult. ... Now, people look at me and they cannot believe that I have money. ... Before I joined Kuapa I never had a voice. Now I am treasurer of my society and I can speak.

Kuapa's output represents about 8 per cent of total world cocoa sales. It's unique in Ghana as the only licensed cocoa buying company owned and run by farmers.

It has another claim to fame too. Kuapa owns 47 per cent of the Day Chocolate Company, the UK company it set up in 1998 with Twin Trading, supported by the Body Shop, Christian Aid, Comic Relief, the UK's Department for International Development and NatWest Bank, to launch Divine brand Fairtrade chocolate (see Reason 44). Two elected Kuapa representatives sit on the company's board.

Day Chocolate makes Dubble, the Fairtrade chocolate bar for children. Not surprisingly, it also supplies all the chocolate for the Co-op's own-label range.

YOUNG CO-OPERATIVES

An imaginative link between the co-operative and fair trade movements in the UK is Young Co-operatives. Run with support from Traidcraft and the Co-operative Group, the programme enables 14–17-year-olds to manage their own democratic co-operative, gain business skills and learn about fair trade.

Young Co-operatives groups range in size from 2 to 30 youngsters. Under adult supervision, they make a business plan, select and price stock, research markets, design promotions, sell fair trade products from stalls in schools, churches, shopping centres and at events, manage the money and take part in a range of other activities.

Young Co-operatives also provides nationally recognised training credits, with successful participants gaining a Certificate in Co-operative and Fair Trade Enterprise accredited by the Open College Network – probably the UK's first fair trade qualification for young people.

There are more than 200 registered Young Co-operatives groups in the country. "These Young Co-operatives may not recognise them-selves as leading a worldwide social revolution, but in a small way they are," says *Guardian* journalist John Vidal.

41. Prove the free trade eggheads wrong

Some free trade economists disagree with fair trade. They say it distorts world markets, making everybody worse off in the long run. Here's why they are wrong.

Fair trade is one of the great successes of our time. In 2002 around 100 Fairtrade-certified products were available in the UK. By 2006 there were 2,000. Thousands of low income farmers and other producers in developing counties have worked their way out of poverty because of fair trade.

Yet a small number of people don't like fair trade – chiefly econ-omists who believe in the dogma of the free play of market forces. They dislike anything that distorts an eighteenth-century theory of economists such as Adam Smith and David Ricardo that we would all be better off if nothing stands in the way of market forces.

It was Ricardo who developed a theory known as "comparative advantage". This maintains that everyone will gain when countries specialise in producing those goods and services in which they have an advantage – that they can produce at lower cost than other countries. They then exchange those goods with goods produced by other countries on the same principle – in other words, trade them freely, without restrictions or distortions.

The theory sounds good – in theory. There are at least three big problems with it.

First, "free" trade fails the poor.
The theory may work if trade takes place between countries at equal stages of economic development. When it takes place between rich countries selling industrial goods and much poorer countries selling primary products, like coffee and tea, the theory collapses. The stronger gain, the poorer lose. This happened throughout the twentieth century when the theory was given every chance to work – but failed. It failed especially the poor and the hungry.

"Free" trade has a price tag. And the price is paid by the poor. "Free" trade has plunged millions into destitution and bankruptcy. As trade has been liberalised, especially since the 1980s, so cheap, often subsidised, goods have surged into developing countries, costing millions of their farmers and industrial workers their livelihoods.

"Free" trade advocates believe that countries should increase trade in foodstuffs and that the money earned from the exports would enable people to buy more food than they could have produced themselves. This is not supported by the facts. Says environmentalist and international women's rights campaigner Vandana Shiva of India:

> We were told we would be able to buy more food by selling flowers than we grew for ourselves. But selling flowers destroys your food security – you can only buy a quarter of the food that you stopped producing. For every dollar earned by shrimp exports, more than ten dollars in local food security is being destroyed.

Second, "free" trade theory does not deal with power.
Transnational corporations (TNCs) have effectively captured the

international trading system. It is TNCs that distort the system, not fair trade. They have moulded the system in their image, to suit their purposes. They argue for "free" trade when it suits them and for protection when that suits them. It is the subsidies that TNCs demand and get from Western governments that distort the system. They exercise undue influence in the World Trade Organization to secure the rules they want, and are subject to no international regulation (see Reason 35).

Long-time fair trade campaigner Pauline Tiffen describes "free" trade as:

> a myth, an exercise in self-deception, a lie. The history of trade is the history of organised commercial groups conniving and lobbying for protection and preferential treatment for themselves. ... Regulating and controlling trade has generally been the prerogative of the rich and privileged.

Says NGO campaigner Peggy Antrobus:

> "Free" trade to uphold unfair practices between powerful and powerless countries is anything but free. It speaks of a "rules-based" trading system while leaving unregulated the largest corporations and financial flows of the wealthy. It claims to reduce poverty while exacerbating the impoverishment of increasing numbers of people. It claims to create a "level playing field" while denying the major structural imbalances – political, economic and technological – between countries.

Third, it's damaging the environment.
"Free" trade philosophy encourages quite similar products (apples, for example) to be flown thousands of miles across the world, causing carbon emissions and adding to global warming. "Free" trade is not consistent with sustainable development.

Some of the trade has led to severe local environmental damage. Take the case of intensive prawn farming in coastal areas of Asian countries, for example. Because it is capable of earning additional foreign exchange, this type of farming has been encouraged by the IMF and the World Bank. In Asia it has led to mangrove forests being destroyed, to make way for shrimp farms. Mangroves serve to protect coastlines. When the tsunami struck Asian coastlines in December 2004 it caused more damage in areas where the mangroves and natural protection had gone.

THE CHARGE

The charge against fair trade (specifically in coffee) was put in an Adam Smith Institute report in 2004. This claimed:

> Well intentioned, interventionist schemes to lift prices above market levels ignore ... market realities. Accordingly, they are doomed to end in failure – or to offer cures that are worse than the disease. There are constructive measures that can help to ease the plight of struggling coffee farmers, but they consist of efforts to improve the market's performance – not block it or demonize it. ... Symbolic victories are the only kind that the fair trade movement is likely to achieve.

It is not easy to imagine how a system that guarantees poor farmers a fair return for their crop could make the situation for coffee growers any worse.

The charge against fair trade was developed in a report by Nestlé – before one of its products was given the Fairtrade Mark (Reason 33):

> If coffee farmers were paid fair trade prices exceeding the market price the result would be to encourage those farmers to increase coffee production, further distorting the imbalance between supply and demand and, therefore, depressing prices for green coffee.

It is certainly the case that too much coffee has been produced around the world. But if the situation ever came about where all coffee was fair traded, many millions of producers would be far better off than they are today.

According to *Guardian* journalist John Vidal, the Adam Smith Institute's paper:

> recommends that the public does nothing to help the poorest, that developing countries open up more to world trade and that peasant farmers diversify. Considering that the [UK] Government ... the World Bank and UN accept that unfettered trade can have a dreadful human toll, this seems a particularly stupid piece of work.

"Free" trade economists claim that free trade will contribute to people's welfare in the long term. But this overlooks the kind of the world that free trade is leading to – a world of disposessed small farmers, where TNCs own the means of production and have economic control of the lives of the poor. In this situation, poverty is hardly likely to be alleviated. The poor cannot rely on the long term to solve problems the international trading system has created for them in the short term.

Western countries did not develop by "free" trade alone but with a combination of open markets and protectionism. In the nineteenth and twentieth centuries, Britain opened its markets for some products while protecting sectors of the economy that could not face competition. A two-track approach was pursued.

Fair trade is a viable economic option for the third millennium. It is a proven approach to trade that is helping the poor to develop. Says the Fairtrade Foundation:

> Free trade puts farmers and social and environmental concerns last, pushes prices down and monopolies up. Fairtrade works in and through the market but with new techniques: it puts farmers, their communities and environment first, prices are guaranteed, the disadvantaged are given access, and more control is put into the hands of producers.

Fair trade does not distort markets. It makes markets work for the poor (Reason 46). In today's international economy, what passes for "free" trade is unfair trade. By their attacks on fair trade, "free trade" economists push a dogma which is an insult to the many thousands whose lives have been transformed by fair trade.

But in the words of the Biblical book of Proverbs – "a wise person overlooks an insult".

42. Make tomorrow's business happen today

Tomorrow's best companies will make many of today's ruthless, short-sighted businesses look like dinosaurs. Fair trade is one of the best models we have for taking capitalism on to a new, higher level.

There's a struggle going on at the heart of business. Between yesterday and tomorrow. Yesterday's men – like those who ran Enron – have been top dogs for too long. Tomorrow's women and men are on the rise. Many of them work in fair trade.

What's wrong with yesterday's view of business is neatly summarised in an article by socially responsible business guru Terry Mollner. "Capitalism is not the end of history," he writes. "There are higher layers of maturity of thinking ... [that] will eventually result in more mature economic agreements."

Mollner criticises the *Economist* magazine, which preaches the cause of global free-market capitalism, for saying that managers of publicly owned companies have only one duty, which is to maximise the value of business owners' assets. "At one time it was assumed to be ethical to use slaves," Mollner comments. "At another time it was assumed to be ethical to discriminate against women and minorities when it came to promotions ... [or] to allow people downstream to die from pollution."

Times change, and so does awareness of what's important in business. "Co-operation, not competition, is fundamental in nature," argues Mollner. "This means that the true highest self-interest is the good of all as one." Yet much of the business world is still trapped in the past:

> many of the most powerful organizations on the planet are not being run by people but by contracts that are not giving highest priority to the good of all as one. We would not support our children to run a lemonade stand in this way and it is frightening to think that we are running the planet in this way.

Mollner's view that "the time of allowing a single child to be born into poverty is over" is shared by many of the most progressive business thinkers today. The UK's Institute of Business Ethics, for example, says:

> People expect companies to look after their staff and tell customers the truth. They also increasingly expect companies to address their environmental impacts and make sure that the people who make their products are treated fairly, wherever the company operates.

And ethics pays in the longer term. Research shows that companies with a code of ethics generally outperform those without.

The Co-operative Bank says it turned away potential business worth £10 million on ethical grounds in 2005. But this was easily outweighed by the 34 per cent of its £96.5 million pre-tax profit that it claims resulted from being known for its ethical and sustainability policies.

THE SHAPE OF BUSINESS TO COME?

As tomorrow's business model emerges, a lot of it looks like fair trade. A Costa Rican delegate at an international conference on social development in 2000 put it this way:

The fair trade movement has become a tool in the search for a new international economic order in that it expresses the desire to reach a greater balance and social equality in trade relations between industrialized and developing countries ... helping reduce the unfair exchange that is detrimental to and increasingly impoverishing developing countries.

He went on:

The fair trade movement is a clear example of a social initiative to reduce poverty that offsets the powerful exclusionary forces that are created by the current globalization process. The movement shows ... how private investment strategies can be changed to better meet the needs of the poor. ... Through fair trade, the poor have more opportunities to play more meaningful roles in political and economic processes, creating a safer environment, strengthening human rights and stimulating cultural diversity.

Corporate responsibility commentator Alice Owen is another advocate of tomorrow's kind of business who sees fair trade as a model. She writes that "links between business activity and poverty may seem obvious, but they are not obvious in how businesses currently make decisions. ... The model that underpins these business decisions is wrong." In Owen's view:

there is a role for each individual ... in making personal decisions that reflect the complexity of the world. We all need to get beyond the fragmented view of the world and consider ourselves connected in a myriad of ways to other people and to the rest of the world. ... Acting as a connected consumer is the basis of the fair trade movement.

Owen imagines fair trade expanding into new areas such as the renewable energy market:

> Even your choice of energy supply has an effect far beyond your energy bill or the climate change effects. ... There is an important connection between third-world poverty and the amount of money that developed countries spend on fossil fuels. ... Your choice to buy renewable energy makes a difference. The growth of small-scale renewable energy generation could enable developing countries to determine their own energy policies, rather than becoming dependent on the system that the developed world has established.

"Thinking in a connected way actually enables you to make better decisions," Owen concludes.

New approaches to business developed by fair trade entrepreneurs are gaining increasing recognition. In 2006 Traidcraft, one of the UK's leading fair trade companies, won a Queen's Award for Enterprise. Traidcraft's mission is to fight poverty through trade and to change the way business works.

"For more than a quarter of a century Traidcraft has pioneered an approach to business which challenges the mainstream to adopt ways of doing business that are both equitable and sustainable," said Traidcraft managing director Paul Chandler on receiving the award. "If a small organisation like Traidcraft can do it – and benefit from it – then so can everyone."

The idea that a business's environmental and social impacts are just as important as its financial results is the basis of Triple Bottom Line (TBL) accounting. Instead of just one bottom line – money – forward-thinking companies recognise two more: impacts on people and on the environment.

Many companies talk about TBL, but few take it as seriously as Traidcraft, which has published annual "social accounts" since the early 1990s. It was one of the UK's first plcs – if not the first – to do so. Traidcraft's social accounts describe how the company's actions have contributed to reducing poverty and to "mobilising public opinion behind fair trade" and "influencing the ways that private sector companies and governmental bodies think about trade and its impact on the developing world". The accounts also report on how Traidcraft has contributed to "more sustainable livelihoods for our producers" and on efforts to meet environmental targets and improve environmental monitoring.

Traidcraft's future plans include opening regional offices in Africa and Asia to scale up its impact on poverty. And its development charity, Traidcraft Exchange, has been voted one of the UK's most innovative (see Reason 46).

43. Vote for trade justice

The movement for trade justice is growing all around the world. Fair trade is part of the solution.

People all over the world are buying and enjoying fair trade goods and services – and showing that they want fairness in the international trading system. They want producers to get a fair return. The growth is particularly apparent in the worlds richest countries, the G7 – Canada, France, Germany, Italy, Japan, the UK and the USA. Says Fairtrade Foundation executive director Harriet Lamb:

> The public across the G7 countries seem to have an insatiable appetite for Fairtrade. The Fairtrade Foundation and other organisations in FLO are rushing to keep up with the demand for a greater volume and range of products. Ordinary people, in this way, are showing that they do care about trade, it is important to them and they want trade justice. They buy Fairtrade products as a practical demonstration of their demand for trade justice. The governments of the G8 countries should follow their lead and put trade justice at the heart of trade.

When we buy fair trade, we vote for trade justice. Because fair trade points the way to trade justice. The rules of fair trade could be a model for the mainstream trading system.

"We have begun to engage trade negotiators in a dialogue over what fair trade can offer as a model for good trade rules – ones that truly contribute to sustainable development and the elimination of poverty," says Mark Ritchie of the US-based Institute for Agriculture and Trade Policy.

But are the governments of the G8 countries (the G7 + Russia) putting trade justice at the heart of trade? Hardly. They continue to push trade liberalisation, "free" trade, apparently having difficulty with the idea of "justice". Slow to listen, they are even slower to act.

Campaigners are pressing for trade justice in a number of ways, not least through the Trade Justice Movement (TJM). Formed in 2000, TJM is a UK initiative supported by more than 70 organisations with over 9 million members, and "new organisations are joining every month," it says. The movement includes trade unions, aid agencies, environment and human rights campaigns, fair trade organisations, faith and consumer groups. The TJM wants radical changes in the rules of international trade, rules:

> weighted to benefit poor people and the environment. We believe that everyone has the right to feed their families, make a decent living and protect their environment. But the rich and powerful are pursuing trade policies that put profits before the needs of people and the planet. To end poverty and protect the environment we need trade justice not free trade.

In particular, the movement is urging Western country governments to:

- Ensure that poor countries can choose the best solutions to end poverty and protect the environment.
- End export dumping that damages the livelihoods of poor communities around the world.
- Make laws that stop big business profiting at the expense of people and the environment.

Let's consider these points one by one.

Allowing developing countries to choose their own solutions is a matter of the most basic justice. At the G8 summit in 2005, governments of leading Western countries recognised that right. "We agreed that poor countries must decide and lead their own development strategies and economic policies," they said.

Especially through the World Bank and the International Monetary Fund, however, the West continues to make aid and debt relief conditional on developing countries liberalising their trade system. It's all part of the myth that "free" trade is the answer to poverty. Poor countries everywhere are being forced to open their markets to foreign companies and cheap – often subsidised – imports, to stop helping vulnerable producers and to privatise essential services. The results are devastating, the cost heavy.

According to a Christian Aid report, the countries of sub-Saharan Africa are a massive US$272 billion worse off because of "free" trade policies forced on them as a condition of receiving aid and debt relief. The figure represents the income that poor countries there have lost over the past 20 years as a result of being forced to open their markets to imports. "In human terms it represents tens of thousands of destroyed lives and years of lost opportunity. Two decades of liberalisation have cost sub-Saharan Africa roughly what it has received in aid over the same period," the report says.

The European Union wants to impose free-trade Economic Partnership Agreements (EPAs) on African, Caribbean and Pacific (ACP) countries. It proposes the elimination of all barriers on 90 per cent of trade between the two blocs. This would mean that nearly all the tariffs and other barriers on European agricultural and industrial goods to ACP countries would be scrapped. It's survival of the fittest – the richest. EU countries have the funds to exploit the new market opportunities. They stand to benefit far more than the poorer countries. This is the very opposite of helping the poor out of poverty, the opposite of trade justice.

Dumping of agricultural produce damages the livelihoods of poor communities and should be stopped. Dumping – selling goods below the cost of producing them – happens because of the large subsidies the Western governments hand to their farmers. These encourage overproduction. Much of the surplus is then dumped in developing countries, often putting local farmers out of business.

Yet governments have moved at a snail's pace to reform their farm subsidy regimes in a way that would stop dumping. At the WTO's ministerial meeting in Hong Kong in December 2005, agreement was reached to end farm export subsidies by 2013. Western governments made much of this. But export subsidies are only one type of farm support – they account for less than 5 per cent of overall farm supports. Ending export subsidies is unlikely to stop most of the dumping. Other forms of support will continue. The injustice goes on.

The focus for the TJM in the first half of 2006 was a campaign for laws to stop business profiting at the expense of people and the environment. A Company Law Reform Bill passing through the UK Parliament in 2006 sought to modernise company law and included measures to give company directors new duties to act in the interests of workers and the environment. But it appeared to have too many loopholes that could allow directors to wriggle out of their obligations. Campaigners believed the Bill would deny justice to people in other countries whose livelihoods and environments are being harmed by companies that behave irresponsibly. So they pressed for it to be amended to include a new clause which states that company directors should be held accountable for the social and environmental impact of their company's activities (see Reason 5).

A growing number of people support fair trade and trade justice. They are challenging a system which is failing the poor. "The success of the Fairtrade model challenges the neo-liberal paradigm of free trade which has unequivocally failed the poorest communities in Africa," says Harriet Lamb.

Trade justice is about making trade work for everybody. And fair trade is a key part of the effort to secure trade justice.

44. Enjoy that sweeter taste

Whether you're an occasional nibbler or an out-and-out chocoholic, buying fair trade chocolate leaves a sweeter taste in the mouth.

The cocoa (or cacao) tree *Theobroma cacao* originated in South America. The Maya and Aztecs fermented its beans and consumed it as a bitter, spicy drink. For the Aztecs it was an aphrodisiac. Montezuma is said to have drunk it 50 times a day.

The Spanish conquistador Hernan Cortés brought chocolate – so called from the Mayan word *xocoatl* – to Europe, where with added sugar and vanilla it became a popular drink. European colonisers set up cocoa plantations in the Caribbean and South America using slave labour. Later, in the nineteenth century, large-scale production began in West Africa.

In the UK we eat and drink half a million tonnes of chocolate a year, spending close to £4 billion annually, an average of £1.20 per person each week. Europe and North America account for more than half of global consumption.

Once the cocoa pods are harvested, a process of extracting and fermenting the beans, drying, roasting, grinding and blending turns the raw cocoa into chocolate.

West Africa produces more than two-thirds of the world's cocoa. Côte d'Ivoire is the leading producer country, followed by Ghana. An estimated 14 million people work in cocoa production worldwide, mainly on small family farms.

Nestlé, Mars, Cadbury-Schweppes and a few other transnationals dominate the world chocolate business, making a great deal of money from it. So do players on the international futures market, whose speculations result in sudden price movements that can hit small-scale cocoa growers hard.

Producers' incomes have fallen sharply since the mid-1980s to a level of only about 6 per cent of the value of retail sales. In Ghana this means average earnings below £200 a year. Cocoa farming in Côte d'Ivoire has been linked to the use of illegal child labour (see Reason 28).

Luckily there's plenty of fair trade chocolate on the market, including Green & Black's, Divine, Dubble, Co-op own brand, Traid-craft and Chocaid. Cocoa is a fair trade crop for farmer co-operatives in Belize, Bolivia, Cameroon, Costa Rica, Dominican Republic, Ecuador, Ghana and Nicaragua.

Problem solved? Not quite. Fair trade demand, through growing pretty fast, still represents only a fraction of the total chocolate market. So producers still have to sell most of their cocoa on the open market, at unpredictable and often damagingly low prices.

THE FIRST FAIR TRADE PRODUCT

In 1994 Green & Black's Maya Gold organic chocolate became the first UK Fairtrade-certified product. It began when Craig Sams, founder of Whole Earth Foods, visited Belize's poor Toledo district and enjoyed the local cocoa- and spice-flavoured brew made by indigenous Mayan farmers. The community had a lot of cocoa to sell but little hope of a decent price. Sams offered to buy direct from the local growers' association, committing to a fair, stable price for the next five years.

Farmers supplying Green & Black's cultivate their cocoa trees organically under native shade trees and alongside other crops (Reason 27). Green & Black's buys all the cocoa produced by the Toledo growers' association, paying a good minimum price plus the Fairtrade social premium and the cost of organic certification. It helps train local extension officers in agronomy, IT and administration. Secondary school enrolment of local children has risen seven-fold since Green & Black's got involved, and families have upgraded their homes to solid-floored wooden bungalows. When Hurricane Iris hit southern Belize in 2001, Green & Black's and the UK government helped foot the bill for replacing damaged and destroyed cocoa trees.

The community are setting up a local-language radio station, and working in a producer co-op helped the Maya become strong enough politically to prevent 250,000 acres of rainforest being logged for timber.

Not everybody was pleased when Sams sold Green & Black's to transnational Cadbury-Schweppes in 2005. Tim Lang, professor of food policy at City University, saw "a tension and contradiction" between a small ethical company like Green & Black's and its transnational owner. But Cadbury's said it was committed to the fair trade arrangements with Belizean cocoa farmers, and to Green & Black's moving forward as a separate business within the company.

For Sams, although not all Green & Black's brands are Fairtrade-certified brand, "All our trading practices have been fair and ethical from the beginning." The tie-up with Cadbury's, he says, "has facilitated the planting of nearly one million new organic cacao trees ... to help smallholder farmers keep up with escalating demand".

BEST OF THE BEST

For another fair trade chocolate success story, look no further than Kuapa Kokoo. "Just a lovely idea. But it cannot be done," a Ghanaian government representative told fair traders Twin Trading in 1993. Their aim was to help small cocoa farmers in Ghana set up their own company and sell their cocoa to the fair trade market.

Kuapa Kokoo – "The Good Cocoa Farmers Company" – was born when Twin gave start-up loans to 22 founding villages to buy weighing scales and other essentials. Kuapa adopted the motto "Pa Pa Pa" ("best of the best"). Most of the farmers who joined produced less than 20 bags of cocoa a year each at the time.

Kuapa is now a democratic co-operative comprising 1,000 village societies and tens of thousands of farmers. Organised on three levels – village, regional and national – it runs a trading company, a credit union, a social development fund and mobile health clinics. It has financed water and sanitation projects, income generation schemes, schools, corn mills and more.

Kuapa sells about 650 tonnes of cocoa annually to the fair trade market – supplying cocoa to Traidcraft, which uses it in many of its chocolate products, such as the chocolate Geobar and gift-wrapped Belgian chocolates.

Uniquely, Kuapa's members also own 47 per cent of the Day

Chocolate Company in the UK. Day makes Divine Chocolate (launched in 1998) and Dubble (launched with Comic Relief in 2000). With fast-rising sales, Divine and Dubble now offer a popular Fairtrade alternative to the big brands.

Dubble – a mixture of chocolate and puffed rice – is named after the double benefits of purchasing the product: the buyer gets good chocolate, and the cocoa growers get a better price. "Cocoa farmers feel really proud," says Kwabena Ohemeng-Tinyase, managing director of Kuapa Kokoo Limited and Day Chocolate board member. Day's managing director Sophi Tranchell believes Fairtrade chocolate can help raise standards industry-wide:

> It makes other companies look at their supply chains. ... We never expected everyone to turn into fair trade companies, but we hoped that they would ... do business better. It's worked in environmental terms – people have put pressure on companies and companies have had to change.

In mid 2006 Dubble, Comic Relief and educational charity Trading Visions held a series of "cocoa summits" for young people across the UK, to "bring alive the connection between the chocolate we all love and the not-so-sweet issues facing cocoa farmers in the developing world". The outcome was a "Chocolate Challenge Manifesto" presented by a Ghanaian–British youth delegation to UK International Development Secretary Hilary Benn, calling for a better deal for all cocoa farmers everywhere. Thirteen-year-old Isaac Owusu told Hilary Benn:

> We want the UK government to continue to support Fairtrade. ... My grandfather is a cocoa farmer and has been for a long time. Before, our lives were hard. Then my uncle read a book about Fairtrade and now my grandfather sends his cocoa beans to Fairtrade companies such as the Kuapa Kokoo and he gets a fair price for his products.

Accepting the manifesto, Mr Benn said:

[162]

Buying Fairtrade products is a way for everyone to make a difference in the lives of people living in poor countries. But we can all do more. We need to keep reminding people about Fairtrade, to keep talking about it.

45. Celebrate in March – and again in May

On the first two weeks in March and the second Saturday of May each year, fair trade organisations, campaigners and shoppers celebrate a better way of doing business.

And in March 2006 it was some celebration! Fairtrade Fortnight, traditionally held each year in the UK in first two weeks of March, was celebrated in 9,000 to 10,000 activities around the country. In workplaces, clubs, universities, cafes and restaurants, shops and supermarkets, churches and other venues, people gathered to taste the food and the fashions, drink the wine and the fruit juice – and do all sorts of different things. Fair trade parades, concerts and debates, to tea dances, fiestas and family days were among them. Activists were able to explain how a small change in shopping habits brings big changes for farmers and their communities in developing countries.

Fairtrade Fortnight is the brainchild of the Fairtrade Foundation but the events are organised locally. Every year has a different theme. The theme in 2006 was "Make Fairtrade Your Habit". The aim was to encourage people to become part of the "quiet revolution" which has seen such great Fairtrade success in the UK. And to persuade consumers who have purchased products carrying the Fairtrade Mark to buy a more varied selection from the wide range of products.

"So many people in the UK are won over by the idea of Fairtrade and want to shop with respect. Our challenge now is to make it easy to get the Fairtrade habit and switch to buying Fairtrade-certified goods," says the Fairtrade Foundation.

The biggest concentration of activities was in the 150 Fairtrade Towns, where Fairtrade is bringing together networks of supporters from local councillors to schoolchildren, retailers to faith groups (see Reason 16). More than 20 more cities, boroughs and towns achieved and announced Fairtrade Town status by the end of Fairtrade Fortnight (see Appendix 2).

A small number of fair trade growers are invited to the UK in the fortnight, and travel around the UK, taking in as many events as they can. Says Harriet Lamb of the Fairtrade Foundation:

> The thousands of Fairtrade Fortnight events bring Fairtrade alive because people can hear from the growers and workers themselves about the benefits of Fairtrade and taste-test products they have not tried before. Our experience is that when people understand the difference Fairtrade can make they are all too willing to choose the products, especially when they realise how good they are.

In 2007 the theme of Fairtrade Fortnight will be Change Today Choose Fairtrade.

WORLD FAIR TRADE DAY

World Fair Trade Day is an international celebration of fair trade, held each year on the second Saturday in May. Events take place worldwide and some of them continue throughout the whole of May.

World Fair Trade Day started as a European movement of over 2,000 world shops and fair trade shops, working together through NEWS! Movements to celebrate the same day and to campaign for fair trade in Japan and the USA joined them. "World Fair Trade Day" was initiated by Safia Minney, founder of People Tree, and adopted by IFAT members at a meeting in 2001.

The annual day has been raising the profile of fair trade ever since. IFAT member organisations in 70 countries, together with fair trade shops and networks, host events such as fair trade breakfasts, talks, music concerts, fashion shows and (again) a range of activities to promote fair trade and campaign for justice in trade. Fair trade products from marginalised communities, including coffee and tea, clothes, jewellery and handicrafts, are traditionally showcased on this day.

Fair trade shops and organisations have been crucial to the development of internationally agreed fair trade standards. With their knowledge and supply chain relationships, they have often led the way in launching new products.

Like Fairtrade Fortnight, World Fair Trade Day takes a different theme each year. In 2006 the theme was: Fair Trade Organisations NOW!

The day focused on the unique role of fair trade organisations, ranging from producer groups and fair trade companies, to retailers, and also the fair trade network. This is now huge, consisting of producer and consumer co-operatives, shops, collectives, advocacy groups, unions, producer groups, family workshops, fair trade shops, Internet stores, catalogue companies, religious institutions, NGOs, regional networks, national networks and many more.

Celebrating the day is again an opportunity to encourage conventional companies to sell more fair trade products. Said IFAT of the 2006 day:

> We call on 65 nations to push fair trade to the front of the political agenda. This year's World Fair Trade Day will showcase IFAT's dynamic network of FTOs around the world, proving what excellent role models for Business Sustainability they are, and highlighting their pioneering work in alleviating poverty through trade.

As developing countries face falling prices, subsidies and dumping, increased poverty and income disparities, and globalisation rules that are written by the rich countries, said IFAT, "there is a need for poverty alleviation through trade, and through campaigning to level the playing field. Fair Trade Organisations pioneer this international movement."

One of the messages for World Fair Trade Day 2006, received from Norma Velasquez Traverso, director of Peruvian producer group Minka Fair Trade, read:

We, as all southern poor producers, need more than better prices for our production. We need fair trade terms, we need equal partners, we need friends who can trust in us. We want to participate, with better roles, in changes of our unfair situation. We know that all together through joined actions can be built a better world. We know the way but we need that you are on our side.

By raising the profile of fair trade, the activities in March and May each year give a boost to poorer producers throughout the developing world.

46. Make markets really work for the poor

Fair trade organisations know more than most about the impacts markets have on poor people. And they have a pretty good record of delivering support and assistance where they're most needed.

It's official: MMW4P.

That's jargon for "Making Markets Work for the Poor", and at last governments are recognising the need to do this. Government aid agencies like the UK's Department for International Development and Sweden's International Development Cooperation Agency now recognise that globalised markets all too often work *against* poor people and the environment. So they're adopting the MMW4P approach. That means looking at ways to achieve "pro-poor growth" by reforming "market imperfections".

This would be fine if the same governments – and intergovernmental organisations like the European Union, World Bank, International Monetary Fund and World Trade Organization – were not also pushing international trade policies that keep making markets work *against* the poor and in favour of big business.

Western governments talk about the globalised market as if it's basically sound, with just a few "imperfections" that need fine-tuning. But with poverty killing 30,000-plus people a day, global income and wealth inequality growing year on year, and many environmental problems getting worse not better, the problems clearly go deeper.

To quote Nobel Prize-winning economist Joseph Stiglitz: "Critics of globalization accuse Western countries of hypocrisy, and the critics are right."

ANTIDOTE

The antidote to hypocrisy is putting your money where your mouth is. The fair trade movement does this in more ways than one. Traidcraft, for example, well known as the UK's largest fair trade organisation, also runs a successful international development programme, working through its charity Traidcraft Exchange – "the UK's only development charity specialising in making trade work for the poor".

The two sides of Traidcraft's work are complementary but independently financed. Traidcraft Plc ploughs back most of its surplus into growing the business, whereas Traidcraft Exchange runs mainly on grants and donations. Traidcraft Exchange promotes pro-poor trade approaches, fairer terms of trade and market access. It links fair trade buyers with suppliers and helps local organisations working with low-income people in some of the world's poorest countries build practical business skills and capacity.

DEVELOPMENT MODEL

Drawing on 25 years' experience, Traidcraft Exchange's "development model" concentrates on working with small and medium-sized enterprises in four regions where poverty and hardship are rife: East Africa, Southern Africa, South Asia and South-east Asia.

Take Kenya, where an estimated 80,000 people rely on wood-carving for a livelihood. As a result of markets not working for the poor, Kenyan woodcarvers have lost most of their international sales due to changing consumer trends, poor-quality finishing, lack of new designs and tough international competition. Traidcraft Exchange has been running a programme of product development support, helping Kenyan craftspeople develop products that are more suitable for export markets.

In neighbouring Tanzania, beekeeping and organic honey production have supported many low-income and landless households in the forested mid-west Tabora region. But again, market forces have had negative impacts. Responding to the collapse of the regionwide beekeepers' co-operative, Traidcraft Exchange has joined Tanzanian non-profit organisations in providing business support and employment opportunities to 900 beekeepers.

In Orissa, one of India's poorest states, many people struggle to earn a living through traditional crafts production but are often badly exploited by local traders. Traidcraft Exchange and its partners are running a capacity-building programme here for local business support organisations, with training workshops, mentoring and other forms of help.

Orissa's large indigenous population includes many communities that depend for their livelihood on production of non-timber forest products such as cashew nuts, tamarind, and medicinal and herbal extracts. Unregulated private traders rule the market. Traidcraft Exchange's Trade Justice for Tribal Communities project helps producers find alternative markets, improve terms of trade and have a say in decision making that affects their lives.

Traidcraft Exchange is also active in Bangladesh, helping develop income-generation projects among low-income villagers who live on the *chars* – temporary sandbanks in the river Brahmaputra. And in South-east Asia it has programmes in Cambodia, Laos, the Philippines and Viet Nam.

SHOELESS TECHNICIANS

Traidcraft is not the only fair trade organisation that runs and supports development programmes. Oxfam, Tearfund and other non-governmental organisations that played a key role in the early years of fair trade have been doing it for decades.

Training is often the key, with far-reaching impacts for individuals and communities. Elvia Marroquin Corea received training in organic coffee production as a member of the COMUCAP coffee co-op in an Oxfam-supported programme in Honduras:

> We received one year of training, then follow-up training. ... We were given the title *tecnicas descalzas* [shoeless technicians]. Shoeless because we were going to work very hard, so hard that we would have no shoes at the end of it! They chose me and two other women.
>
> The first year they sent us to the fields with the different groups, and we taught the other women what we had learned about organic coffee production – how to survey the land, prepare the earth, dig the holes, and apply the fertilizer. We started to put our learning into practice – and to learn by doing, because that's how you learn. With the little salary that we are starting to receive, I have been able to buy a little plot of land, and last year I grew five *quintales* [500 lb] of cherry coffee. This year I still haven't cut my coffee, so we will see how much I will get.

Fairtrade Labelling Organisations International (FLO), the umbrella certification body based in Germany, has set up in partnership with Netherlands-based international development organisation SNV to work with disadvantaged workers and producers in developing countries and support them in gaining access to international markets under fair conditions.

AgroFair, the Netherlands-based fair trade tropical fruit importer with sales across Western Europe including the UK, has its own development arm. AgroFair Assistance and Development works with local partners to help topical fruit producers with conversion to fair trade and organic production, certification and export promotion.

Buying fair trade – especially from dedicated fair trade suppliers – helps strengthen the movement. And the stronger the movement, the more it can do to ensure that markets really do benefit poor people.

47. Invest in fair trade

You can invest in the future by investing in fair trade

Buying fair trade goods is one thing – but there's more, much more. You can buy into fair trade by putting your money into enterprises that help fund the trade – Shared interest, the Co-operative Bank, and Triodos Bank, for example. Shared Interest is "the world's leading fair trade finance organisation". A co-operative, it aims to reduce poverty in the world by providing fair and just financial services. It started in 1990 and now has around 8,300 members who have invested more than £20 million. Owned and controlled by its members, it pools their savings to facilitate fair trade.

Shared Interest finances fair trade by:

• lending to and working with producer and buyer organisations who are committed to using fair trade principles
• promoting a North–South partnership
• enabling investors in the UK to share risk and take positive action to direct funds to borrowers working in poorer parts of the world
• listening to and promoting Southern voices and views
• strengthening the fair trade movement so that it continues to present a more just model of trade.

Shared Interest works with fair trade businesses all over the world, both producers and buyers, providing credit to enable producers to be paid in advance and to help fair trade develop. In 2005 it provided credit to 43 fair trade producers' organisations in 25 countries, and to 38 fair trade buyer organisations in 16 countries.

Shared Interest is a member of the International Fair Trade Association (IFAT), the Trade Justice Movement and the Fairtrade Foundation. It provides credit to fair trade organisations through its Clearing House. Like for example to Yayasan Mitra Bali (Mitra Bali Foundation) in Indonesia.

BALI

Yayasan Mitra Bali was established in 1993 with the support of local Oxfam representatives. Adhering to fair trade principles, it acts as a market and export facilitator for small craft producers who are missing out to large, well-established, businesses in the Bali tourism bonanza.

Without direct access to the tourist centres, it was difficult for those producers to access orders or even local trade. Yet, the contribution of these artisans to the development of the island is substantial. Their artistic output represents the visible face of Balinese Culture, which, ironically, helps to draw tourists and buyers to Bali.

A member of IFAT, Yayasan Mitra Bali works with around 100 producer groups employing over 1,000 men and women. To counter the marginalisation of these producers, it markets their products both locally and internationally, and exports internationally to both alternative and commercial buyers. Shared Interest and Yayasan Mitra Bali began working together in 2001. Shared Interest provides trade finance for their orders from several large buyer organisations.

Due to the terrorist bomb in October 2002, Bali has suffered a dramatic downturn in tourism and this has affected the livelihoods of many craftspeople on the island. But because of the relationships that Yayasan Mitra Bali has established with international fair trade buyers, the small producers they work with have been able to survive this difficult period and are now looking forward as the tourist trade picks up slowly.

Membership of Shared Interest's Clearing House is open to both buyer and producer members of IFAT, and to producers certified by FLO who have satisfied the credit criteria.

In addition to putting money into Shared Interest, investors are also offered the chance of becoming an "ambassador", speaking at local events and generating media interest, for example.

The Co-operative Bank advocates support for International Labour Organization Conventions, supporting businesses which take a responsible position with "regard to fair trade [and] labour rights in their own operations and through their supply chains in developing countries".

Triodos Bank lends only to charities, community groups, social businesses and environmental initiatives, from welfare to wind farms, health to housing, and organic food to fair trade organisations such as Cafédirect. The bank runs partnership accounts which connect people's money with "the causes closest to their hearts". It works, for example, with the Fairtrade Foundation, Friends of the Earth, the Soil Association, Amnesty International and the World Development Movement. Triodos offers a Fairtrade Saver Account and an ethical Individual Savings Account (ISA).

Jupiter Asset Management favours companies that ensure that the materials they use are "from organic or fair trade sources".

You can also invest in fair trade companies when they make a share issue. Cafédirect and Traidcraft have both done this. Investing in fair trade co-operatives, banks and companies may yield savers a lower interest rate but a high rate of satisfaction, knowing that you are helping to spread the benefits of fair trade to more people.

It is also worth looking at your mortgage and your pension. "Ask your provider whether they support Fairtrade companies. Let them know that you want returns but not at the cost of people's livelihoods," suggests *New Consumer* magazine.

Governments could be encouraged to invest in fair trade. The Commission for Africa, which reported in March 2005, said that increased funding from developed countries:

would help increase the participation of producer groups in

"fairtrade". The demand for products carrying the "fair-trade" mark is growing but investment is needed in building the capacity of producer groups in Africa to meet the rigorous demands of developed country markets.

Encourage governments yes, but also take a good look at your savings and ask – how can my money help to change the world?

48. Keep families and communities together

Family farms and rural communities are under threat everywhere from global economic forces. Fair trade helps them survive and thrive.

"To leave our land is to suffer," says Eduardo Verdugo, a coffee producer from Chiapas, southern Mexico.

For some, migration may be an act of choice, the pursuit of opportunity. But for many, little choice is left when earning a decent living at home becomes impossible. Within countries, says the UN, 180,000 rural people migrate to towns and cities daily. Internationally, 86 million workers are migrants. Some take family with them. Millions migrate alone.

Causes are complex, but the global economy plays a central role. "Actions of transnational corporations, international development and financial institutions ... heighten inequality among and within states, increas[ing] pressure to migrate," delegates at the World Conference Against Racism in 2000 concluded.

Because rural communities are often tied to a single commodity, migration can be seasonal. Haitian coffee producer Mercius Aristil told Oxfam:

When the coffee season is over, men tend to cross the border and leave the women at home with all the responsibilities of the house and the children. The money the men send home doesn't make up for this absence.

Worse happens when cash crop prices fall. When coffee prices collapsed in the late 1990s, millions of coffee farmers in Haiti, Mexico, Tanzania and other Southern countries were badly hit, and many were forced to migrate in search of work.

Interviews by Oxfam with Caribbean banana and coffee producers in 2002–04 told the same story:

- "Now farmers are leaving the industry. ... People are migrating or growing drugs," said St Vincent banana grower Nioka Abbott. Most of the farmers left locally were women.
- "We're not seeing young people coming into farming now," Amos Wiltshire, a Dominica banana farmer, told Oxfam. "Kids leave school and they don't want to work on the family farm. They're not interested in farming. ... Family life starts to disintegrate."
- "Young women are not so interested in staying in the countryside. There isn't much for them here," said Soutene Jean Baptise, a Haitian coffee producer.

Quality of life for migrants is notoriously bad. Millions who seek a new life in the cities of the global South cannot find decent work and get trapped in the shantytowns. "People [who] leave the countryside and migrate to the city," says Bernardo Jaén, a pineapple farmer in Costa Rica, "come into contact with serious problems such as unemployment, drug addiction and prostitution. They have no jobs to go to and no training to help them."

Much of world commodity production centres on large estates and plantations using migrant labour.

Whether rural-to-urban or international, migration disrupts families and communities, separating spouses and generations, often forever.

RIGHT TO REMAIN

The scale of the problem is huge, but fair trade makes a difference for individuals, families and communities.

Rural people in developing countries have a right to remain in their community if they choose. Fair trade offers decent livelihoods in place of poverty, dignity and hope in the face of humiliation and despair, staying put as an alternative to migration.

An important strategy is help for small-scale producers to diversify sources of income and reduce their dependency on a single market or crop. More labour-intensive organic and environmentally sensitive production (see Reason 27) helps create jobs, and farmers who receive a better price can in turn create better jobs for even poorer people who have no land of their own but survive as harvest labourers. Besides, fair trade's support for democratic structures (Reason 5) and community development projects promotes solidarity, collective decision making and hands-on solutions.

Many fair trade producers see it that way too.

Comments Nicaraguan coffee farmer Vincent Hernandez:

> The Fairtrade premium is absolutely critical to our survival as a community. Without it, we would be with the 21,000 unemployed coffee workers and their families camped out in the streets having lost their livelihoods and their homes.

Merling Preza, another Nicaraguan coffee grower, agrees: "Thanks to fair trade, the 2,400 families in our co-operative are staying on the land. ... They are eating fairly well at a time when hunger is a reality for many of their neighbours." Jorge Reina Aguilar of the ISMAM coffee co-op in Mexico says the same: "The more Fairtrade coffee we sell, the more stability we have in our community, and the less we have to migrate." And for St Vincent banana grower Denise Sutherland, "As long as I am selling in Fairtrade, I can earn enough to support my family. It is a vicious circle when you are not selling the Fairtrade bananas."

A small family farm in a developing country may support between six and eight people – working adults, children and grandparents. Fair trade offers hope to future generations too, as Haitian coffee farmer Luckson Bastien points out:

> There are some younger people joining the co-op. ... By involving them in the training we motivated them to take part. ... I think that the co-op will continue into the next generation.

Reporting on its fair trade organic cotton initiative in India, Traidcraft found that, besides farmer incomes rising, "There is evidence that young people in the area are making a choice to get into agriculture rather than migrate to cities in search of employment. Migration to urban areas from the project area has decreased."

Going further, the Fairtrade Foundation reports a study in India that links fair trade cotton production to the first signs of migration *back to* the villages from urban centres. Alternative clothing company Bishopston Trading puts it well in the context of Bangladesh:

> Fair trade clothing has provided thousands of jobs for handweavers, hand embroiderers, block printers and tailors in the rural areas ... Fair trade provides an alternative to urban migration, enabling families to stay together, avoid the appalling living conditions of life in Dhaka slums.

Fair trade's recognition of the social importance of women is another important element in keeping families and communities together (Reason 8).

And let's not forget the multiplier effect. US faith-based NGO Lutheran World Relief provides this persuasive scenario:

> Someone, somewhere in North America buys a fair trade product. Because it's fair trade, more of the purchase price reaches the family who produced it. The extra income helps that family buy a hen it could never afford before. The family sells some eggs for income, supplements its meager diet with the remainder and raises some of the chicks to sell, generating more income.

Repeating the process, the family uses part of the income to pay school fees that they were unable to pay before. Because she returns to school instead of leaving the family to look for work in the city, the eldest daughter isn't lured into a lifestyle that puts her at risk of contracting HIV/AIDS. The math and literacy skills she gains in school come in handy when she starts her own small handcrafts business, generating further income and employing her brother.

Because this family is part of a fair trade co-operative, success stories like this are repeated dozens of times within this small community. Using profits re-invested by the co-op, the community makes quality-of-life improvements such as digging wells, upgrading sanitation systems and building schools and churches. Gradually, the economic, educational and healthcare systems of several communities improve, which begin to be felt at regional and even national levels.

It's a story too good to ignore.

49. Defend diversity

Everybody's in favour of diversity these days. Fair trade's commitment runs deeper than most.

Margaret Thatcher's 1980s catchphrase "There is no alternative" was supposed to justify rising inequality and social dislocation caused by hard-line neo-liberal policies. The "Iron Lady" even applied the phrase to Africa. Was the world's poorest continent meant to embrace full economic globalisation or fall off the map?

When it comes to trade and development, one size does not fit all, and there are alternatives, as this book shows. In 2001 "Another world is possible" became the motto of the World Social Forum's annual gatherings of social movements and networks opposed to corporate globalisation and committed to justice and sustainability.

Fair trade shares this alternative vision, one that celebrates human diversity and embraces partnerships with people the mainstream economy often rejects, such as indigenous peoples and people affected by disabilities. It's a vision of one world with space for many different worlds.

PEOPLE WITH DISABILITIES

One in five of the world's poorest people has a disability. Poverty will never be history until such people have a place in the economic system.

Ganesha and People Tree are among the UK's most successful suppliers of fair trade clothes, accessories and gifts, and both have active partnerships with disabled producers' organisations. Among People's Tree's suppliers are Assisi Garments in India and the Bombolulu Workshop in Kenya. Assisi employs deaf and mute women in Tamil Nadu in the manufacture and supply of cotton clothing. Bombolulu, one of Kenya's largest jewellery workshops, employs blind and visually impaired people, as well as people affected by other disabilities, in making famously beautiful jewellery.

Ganesha sells items made by disabled people's organisations in India, and its leather and felt bags and handicrafts are supplied by the Nepal Leprosy Trust, where sheltered workshops train and employ people affected by leprosy and other disabling conditions.

Other notable fair trade suppliers whose work by people with disabilities is sold in fair trade and worldshops in the UK include Jacaranda of Kenya and Reaching Out Handicrafts of Viet Nam. Jacaranda employs ex-students of a Nairobi school for children with learning difficulties. Its workshop produces fashion jewellery for export and local sale, using mainly local clay, ceramic beads and brass. Pay is costed to ensure a living wage.

Reaching Out Handicrafts works with disabled artisans across Viet Nam and hires them at its workshop in Hoi An. Currently supplying Silkwood Traders in the UK and Global Village in Canada, it provides training, advice and support programmes for its disabled workforce. Reaching Out takes pride in the fact that unlike other handicraft businesses in the country it retained all its workers during the 2003 SARS-induced slump in tourism.

INDIGENOUS PEOPLES

Three to four hundred million people worldwide belong to indigenous peoples (sometimes known as Aboriginal, First Nations, Native or Tribal peoples). With unique ancestral land-based cultures, they rely more directly than the rest of us on natural resources. Throughout the global South they are among the poorest of the poor.

Fair trade's fine record of working with indigenous peoples has earned it praise from the European Parliament: "Fair Trade has proven to be an effective tool to support indigenous people by giving them the opportunity to sell their goods directly to European markets while pursuing traditional ways of life and production."

The first growers to sell organic fair trade coffee were indigenous farmers in Oaxaca, Mexico. After a visit in 1985 from Dutch and German agronomists and fair traders, their organisation Union of Indigenous Communities in the Isthmus Region (UCIRI) switched to organic production and began selling to Gepa in Germany and Max Havelaar in the Netherlands.

Income among UCIRI's 2,000-plus member families is said to have doubled since then, and the farmers have set up the region's first public bus line. UCIRI's impressive website states: "We try to maintain our culture and wisdom ... and to value the good things given to us by our ancestors. We encourage our compatriots to speak their own languages, because it is our culture."

In Honduras, COMUCAP, an indigenous women's organisation, has developed from next to nothing to become another producer group exporting fair trade coffee to Europe. Dulce Marlen Contreras, COMUCAP's co-ordinator, tells the story:

> In this region the majority of people are Lenca. The Lenca people have lost their language. It is believed that when the Spanish arrived and found the 'Indians', as they called us,

there were many more of us. It is thought that a great fight
began. The only Indians left alive were those who emigrated
to the mountains, and that is where we are found today. ...

We have a very special, deep respect for nature and for the
land. ... Our ancestors were forced to exchange their land ...
because they were very poor. After many years, the peasant
groups got organised to recover their land, and that created
conflict. During the 1980s many indigenous leaders were killed.

COMUCAP was formed in 1993, initially to promote women's
rights, later moving into income generation:

Coffee is the main product grown in this area. Women used
to go to work on other people's *fincas* [estates], and we
realised that they already knew a lot about coffee. So we
decided to start training them in organic coffee production –
that was in 1999. ...

We trained the women in surveying, terracing, soil
protection, making organic fertiliser, drilling the holes, and
organic seedbed maintenance. Then we gave training on
managing a tree nursery, planting trees, looking after the
coffee. ... When Oxfam saw what we had done with the
manzana [1.7 hectare plot] they had funded, they gave us
the money to buy another 40. ...

Last year we sold our coffee for the first time. ... This
year will be our first real harvest, and we hope to produce
400 *quintales* [1 *quintale* = 100 lb].

For the Advisais (indigenous peoples) of India, fair trade tea may
prove equally important. Tea plantation workers and small producers
include many Adivasi people.

Just Change is one of the most original approaches to working
with Adivasi tea growers. Describing itself as "Fair Trade Plus", it
was set up by activists and social entrepreneurs Mari and Stan
Thekaekara with the idea of "taking fair trade further" by linking
poor communities and encouraging them to trade among themselves.

Just Change India Producer Company is a co-operative founded by four Adivasi, women's and community groups. It has trading links with consumer groups in the UK and Germany. While currently trading internationally only in tea – grown by Adivasis in the Gudalur valley of the Nilgiri Hills, southern India – community groups involved in India also trade in rice, coconut oil, honey, soaps and umbrellas among themselves.

UK trading partners of Just Change include Unicorn and Eighth Day Co-op in Manchester, Out of This World in Newcastle, Soundbites in Derbyshire, and The Greenhouse in Norwich. Volunteers in London and Manchester are seeking links with like-minded community groups, co-ops, schools and faith groups.

Indigenous peoples also sell traditional crafts through fair trade. Minka Fair Trade in Peru, for example, markets the work of thousands of rural indigenous producers. People Tree, Traidcraft and others sell its hand-knitted woollen garments and other handicrafts. Minka was the first organisation based in the global South to become a member of the International Fair Trade Association (see Reason 3) and now runs ethical tourism projects in partnership with local communities (Reason 26).

50. Change the world!

Step by step ... we can change the world when we shop.

Start with a day in your life. See how far fair trade goods can be part of your life – and then identify the gaps. You can do something about those gaps.

You get out of bed in the morning and get dressed. There is no reason at all why you should not dress yourself from head to toe in fair trade clothes. If you're in doubt, take a good look at the People Tree and Traidcraft catalogues.

You eat breakfast. Wow! Take your pick from a vast range. Fruit juice, muesli, bananas, mangoes, pineapples and other fruits, nuts and raisins, coffee, tea, cocoa, marmalade and much more. Any gaps in the fair trade range? Well it could be the bread, and the wheat that makes it.

You go to work, wearing if it's appropriate your fair trade trainers. If you walk there, fine. But if you use public transport, cycle or drive, the fair trade trail goes cold.

If you work in an office, you may switch on your computer. Problems again (more below). You have a midmorning snack with a delicious Fairtrade Geobar. Lunch – again take your pick from the wide range of fair trade fruits, cook some rice or pasta and maybe spread a little jam or honey on the bread.

If everything stops for tea, you could add a piece of cake made with fairly traded sultanas from South Africa and sugar from Malawi.

Want a gift on your way home for someone? How about a box of Traidcraft's fair trade Belgium chocolates, or the Chocolate Lover's Gift Set?

For dinner, the rice and pasta again looks attractive, also a glass of delicious fair trade wine. For vegetables there are peppers and green beans. There are herbs and spices, chutney and sauces. There are gaps with meat and fish, but you could end with a fair trade yoghurt.

Should you fancy kicking a ball about in the evening, pick up a fair trade football. Maybe you want to read, watch television or listen to the radio – and again there are gaps. If you are planning ahead, consider a fair trade holiday for next year.

And so to bed. You pull on your fair trade pyjamas, take your pick from fair trade cotton sheets or duvet covers, until finally your head hits the fair trade pillow case.

You have a dream. You dream that you would like everything you buy, everything you use, to have been fairly traded. Can the dream be turned into reality? Let's start by asking questions.

Why can't our bread be fair traded? Traidcraft's pasta is made from durum wheat. Bread is of course more perishable, but let's press the case for a way to be found for fair trade bread.

FAIR TRADE MANUFACTURES? EVEN COMPONENTS?

"There is a very powerful message behind fair trade," says Harriet Lamb, executive director of the Fairtrade Foundation. "You can intervene successfully in markets. So logically, then, why not roll it out on a much larger scale?" Lamb expects more manufactured products coming from developing countries to carry the Fairtrade Mark so that more income is earned by the poor.

It's in the mechanical world that the biggest challenges lie. Products such as vehicles or computers – how could they be fairly traded when they are made up of components that probably come from many countries? So there is a need to go beyond finished products – most fair trade goods at present – and take a look at components. And ask – why cannot the components of manufactured goods be fairly traded?

Many manufactured goods are produced in conditions that are a long way from delivering justice to the people who make them. Take computers, for example. More than a third of computers are made in developing countries. The Catholic aid agency CAFOD has uncovered evidence that workers making computers in Thailand, Mexico and China are being exploited.

In China, workers are paid well below the minimum wage of £30 a month. They have to do illegal amounts of overtime to earn enough to live on, alleges CAFOD, and "can be hired and fired easily. They can't get social security benefits like food vouchers, maternity leave, holidays or pension."

The need for improvements is clear. Fair trade manufactured goods and components are worth pursuing. Otherwise too many people will be locked into an unfair system and locked into poverty.

If we ask the difficult questions, raise the unthinkable, then fair trade is ripe for huge expansion.

Sales of fair trade goods and services are already growing every day. The system may still be small compared with the mainstream trading system – an infant among giants, "but the future lies with the infant", says *New Internationalist* journalist David Ransom.

Can the future be fair trade? Could the fair trade system replace the present mainstream trading system as the chief way in which goods are traded? It could, if enough people want it to happen, if enough people insist that they want everything they buy and use to give the producer a fair return. The more fair trade goods we buy, the more we clamour for the range of goods to be increased, the sooner that becomes reality. Says Harriet Lamb:

> I hope that Fairtrade in five years time will be as much a part of British life as fish and chips – enjoyed with a cup of Fairtrade tea! We expect Fairtrade to become the norm – albeit a very special norm – so that products without the Mark are collecting dust on the shops' bottom shelves. And that more and more people in developing countries are getting the chance to build new and exciting Fairtrade businesses – from Colombian small-scale gold miners to rubber tappers in Sri Lanka, small-scale fishermen to silk cultivators.

Paul Chandler, chief executive of Traidcraft, believes that the rapid growth in sales of "fairly traded food and the range of food products will continue". He sees a new emphasis on increasing the proportion of added value generated in the South, "with fair trade producers moving beyond fair trade ingredient supply to supplying a greater range of finished products". Non-food products will be flowing through into the mainstream on a bigger scale "although this will have required new approaches to fair trade production to cope with the quantities, consistency of quality and sufficiently competitive prices required to break through".

Developing countries can be expected to exchange more fair trade goods between them in the coming years. At present, most fair trade is between South and North. But South–South trade in general has been growing rapidly in recent years; fair trade products are well placed to share in this growth.

"We expect that you'll be able to buy products with the Fairtrade Mark when you travel to India, South Africa or Brazil too as the global movement keeps on expanding," says Harriet Lamb, who goes on:

> My hope is that making Fairtrade our habit will become

plain common sense. People who grow our tea, bananas, sugar and cotton deserve the basic dignities of life just as much as we do, and just like us, want their kids to go to school and be treated when they get ill and have clean water to drink and enough food to eat. And they want the chance to sell their great products to us and our children – and show us every day that the future is Fairtrade.

During the next five years we can expect to see "increasing consumer recognition of the differences between Fairtrade-marked products coming from commercial players and those that are from dedicated fair trade organisations ... committed to pioneering new frontiers in fair trade", believes Paul Chandler.

So let's buy and live fair trade. For fair trade is consumer power, our power, in action. When we open our purses, our wallets, when we press for more fair trade, we can change the world for the poor, we can help people out of poverty. What an opportunity!

Notes and sources

The notes below give sources for almost every quotation included in the book, generally in the same order that the quotations appear in each Reason. Some notes give additional information and/or mention a key published or web resource.

INTRODUCTION

Martin Luther King, widely quoted, original source unknown.
Shah Abdus Salam, "Only fair trade can", World Fair Trade Day,
    www.wftday.org/english/messages/sub/articles/index06.htm.
Harriet Lamb, "Better than fair", *Developments*, (25), 2004,
    www.developments.org.uk/data/issue25/behind-fair-trade.htm.
Fairtrade Foundation: www.fairtrade.org.uk.
(Websites accessed 28 July 2006.)

1. BACK A SYSTEM THAT BENEFITS THE POOR

Renato Ruggiero, speech at the Royal Institute of International Affairs, London, 16 January 1998.
Ha-Joon Chang, in John Madeley, *A People's World*, 2003, London, Zed Books, 2003, pp. 40–1.
Make Poverty History: www.makepovertyhistory.com (accessed 4 May 2006).
David Korten, *When Corporations Rule the World*, 1995, London, Earthscan, 1995, p. 12.

2. PAY SMALL-SCALE FARMERS A FAIRER PRICE

Oxfam GB, *Global Partners: Fairtrade and Local Authorities – How to Support Global Sustainable Development in your Locality*, 2001,
    www.fairtrade.org.uk/downloads/pdf/local_authority_guide.pdf.
Fairtrade Foundation, "Fairtrade bananas impact study", 2004,
    www.fairtrade.org.uk/downloads/pdf/dominica_profile.pdf.
Fairtrade Foundation, *Spilling the Beans on the Coffee Trade*, 1997, revised 2002,
    www.fairtrade.org.uk/downloads/pdf/spilling.pdf.
(Websites accessed 14 July 2006.)

[187]

3. BUY PRODUCTS YOU CAN TRUST

FLO: www.fairtrade.net.
IFAT: www.ifat.org/joinifat.shtml.
Traidcraft: www.traidcraft.co.uk.
(Websites accessed 1 August 2006.)

4. HELP PRODUCERS BELIEVE IN TOMORROW

Fairtrade Foundation, *Highlights 2003*,
    www.fairtrade.org.uk/downloads/pdf/Fairtrade_highlights_2003.pdf.
Fairtrade Foundation,
    www.fairtrade.org.uk/suppliers_growers_tea_sivapackiam.htm.
Fairtrade Labelling Organisations International, "Have a nice cup of tea!",
    www.fairtrade.net/sites/impact/story2.html.
Tear Fund, "Fairtrade bananas",
    www.tearfund.org/webdocs/Website/Campaigning/Fairtrade%20bananas
    %20.pdf.
(Websites accessed 14 July 2006.)

5. MAKE TRADE MORE DEMOCRATIC

World Investment Report, 2005, New York and Geneva, UNCTAD.
Institute for Policy Studies: www.ips-dc.org.
FLO: www.fairtrade.net/standards.html
Right Corporate Wrongs: www.tjm.org.uk/action/corporate240106.shtml.
(Websites accessed 1 August 2006.)

6. PUT A HUMAN FACE ON DEVELOPMENT

Interview with Joel Uribe and Luis Villaroel of COASBA (Cooperativa
    Campesina Apícola Santa Bárbara), Santa Bárbara, Chile, 29 December
    2005.

7. ENSURE PLANTATION WORKERS EARN A LIVING WAGE

International Tea Committee: www.intteacomm.co.uk.
UK Tea Council: www.tea.co.uk.
Indian People's Tribunal report: www.oneworld.net/article/view/82821/1/.
Fairtrade Foundation: www.fairtrade.org.
(Websites accessed 1 August 2006.)

8. EMPOWER WOMEN AND GIRLS

Oxfam Make Trade Fair campaign, quoted at www.hattitrading.co.uk/fair_trade.php. Fairtrade Foundation, "Cotton on to Fairtrade", www.fairtrade.org.uk/pr171105.htm.
Fairtrade Foundation, "100 world food producers meet in London as world leaders talk trade in Cancun",
www.fairtrade.org.uk/pr050903.htm.
Traidcraft, "It's a new order – thanks to fair trade",
www.traidcraft.co.uk/template2.asp?pageID=1818.
(Websites accessed 14 July 2006.)

9. BRING HOPE TO COFFEE GROWERS

Interview with Blanca Rosa Molina, Reading International Solidarity Centre, UK, March 2003.

10. SAVE A COTTON FARMER'S LIFE

GM Watch, www.gmwatch.org/archive2.asp?arcid=6055.
India Together, www.indiatogether.org/2005/jan/agr-vidarbha2.htm.
Share the World's Resources, www.stwr.net/content/view/696/37.
Interview with Shailesh Patel during Fairtrade Fortnight, London, March 2006.
Agrocel Industries Ltd: www.agrocel-cotton.com.
(Websites accessed 14 July 2006.)

11. BE PART OF A GROWING GLOBAL MOVEMENT

FLO Annual Reports, 2004 and 2005: www.fairtrade.net.
Global Journey: www.ifat.org/globaljourney.
Fair Trade in Europe 2005: Facts and Figures on Fair Trade in 25 European countries, survey by Marie Krier, Brussels, Fair Trade Advocacy Office, www.ifat.org/downloads/marketing/FairTradeinEurope 2005.pdf.
(Websites accessed 1 August 2006.)

12. SAY "NUTS!" TO UNFAIR TRADE

Twin Trading, "Go nuts for Fairtrade!",
www.fairtradecookbook.org.uk/downloads/060525_twin_fairtrade_nuts.doc.
"Fairtrade nuts reach UK despite Amazon floods",
www.peopleandplanet.net/doc.php?id=2704.
(Websites accessed 14 July 2006.)

13. ENJOY REAL QUALITY, PRODUCED WITH PRIDE

Fairtrade Foundation: www.fairtrade.org.uk/pr190306.htm, www.fairtrade.org.uk/fc-spr00a.htm.
Harrogate Fairtrade campaign: www.harrogatefairtrade.co.uk.
John Vidal, "If you eat chocolate then you can make a difference", *Guardian*, 7 December 1999.
(Websites accessed 1 August 2006.)

14. SEND A CHILD TO SCHOOL

Oxfam Australia, "Coffee farmers' stories", www.oxfam.org.au/campaigns/mtf/coffee/stories/index.html.
Oxfam GB, *Global Partners: Fairtrade and Local Authorities – How to Support Global Sustainable Development in your Locality*, 2001, www.fairtrade.org.uk/downloads/pdf/local_authority_guide.pdf.
Cafédirect, "Day in the life of Cecilia Mwambebule", www.cafedirect.co.uk/news.php/000074.html.
(Websites accessed 14 July 2006.)

15. KEEP ON MAKING POVERTY HISTORY

Caroline Maria de Jesus, *Child of the Dark*, diary of a Brazilian slum dweller, New York, Dutton, 1962, quoted at http://inic.utexas.edu/hemispheres/units/migration/Brazil.pdf.

Make Poverty History report, 28 December 2005: www.makepoverty history.org.

Reading Campaign to Make Poverty History, communication with authors, June 2006.

Harriet Lamb and Raymond Kimaro, www.fairtrade.org.uk/pr300705.htm.

Tony Blair, quoted at www.fairtrade.org.uk/pr080705.htm.

(Websites accessed 6 and 7 June 2006.)

16. MAKE YOUR TOWN A FAIRTRADE TOWN

George Foulkes, Bruce Crowther and Liaquat Ali Amod, quoted at www.fairtrade.org.uk.

Warwick University, quoted at www.peopleandplanet.org.

Information about becoming a Fairtrade town, city, country, borough, village, island, zone, university, college, school or place of worship is available from the Fairtrade Foundation: www.fairtrade.org.uk/get_involved.htm.

By mid-2006 there were 200 Fairtrade towns and other areas in the UK, with well over 200 more working towards Fairtrade status; 2,845 Fairtrade Churches, Cathedrals, Chapels and Quaker Meetings; 13 Fairtrade Synagogues; at least one Fairtrade Mosque; and 34 Fairtrade Colleges and Universities. See Appendix 2.

(Websites accessed 14 July 2006.)

17. BUILD CONFIDENCE, REDUCE RISK

International Coffee Organization, composite indicator price of arabica and robusta coffee, rounded to nearest cent: www.ico.org.

FLO International: www.fairtrade.net.

(Websites accessed 1 August 2006.)

18. GIVE SOMEONE'S HEALTH A BOOST

Fairtrade Foundation, *Unpeeling the Banana Trade*, 2000,
    www.fairtrade.org.uk/downloads/pdf/unpeeling.pdf.
Fairtrade Foundation, "Fairtrade bananas impact study", 2004,
    www.fairtrade.org.uk/downloads/pdf/dominica_profile.pdf.
Tearfund, "Fairtrade coffee",
    www.tearfund.org/webdocs/Website/Campaigning/Fairtrade% 20coffee
    %20.pdf.
(Websites accessed 14 July 2006.)
Nicaragua Solidarity Campaign,
    www.nicaraguasc.org.uk/partners/index.htm (accessed 14 March 2006).

19. PROMOTE HUMAN RIGHTS

United Nations: www.un.org/Overview/rights.html.
Traidcraft: www.traidcraft.co.uk/template2.asp?pageID=1780.
Amnesty International: www.amnesty.org/pages/ec-unnorms_2-eng.
Corporate Europe Observatory: www.corporateeurope.org/norms.html.
Fairtrade Foundation: www.fairtrade.org.uk/fc-spr00a.htm.
(Websites accessed 10 May 2006.)

20. FREE CHILD CARPET WORKERS

Rugmark: www.rugmark.net.
For a list of Rugmark suppliers, see Appendix 1, Where to buy fair trade.
Rugmark Germany, "A tough job on the bike",
    www.rugmark.de/english/navi/frnakg.htm.
Tanya Roberts-Davis "Leaving a 'rug' mark on child labour",
    www.equalitytoday.org/edition5/leaving.html.
(Websites accessed 14 July 2006.)

21. BYPASS THE INTERMEDIARIES

Juan Valverde Sánchez .
    www.fairtrade.org.uk/suppliers_growers_sugar_juan.htm.
Renson, www.fairtrade.org.uk/suppliers_growers_bananas_renson.htm.

Guillermo Vargas Leiton: www.fairtrade.org.uk/suppliers_growers_coffee_
    guillermo.htm.
(Websites accessed 29 March 2006.)

22. DRINK TO A BETTER WORLD

Interview with Sergio Allard, export director, Vinos Los Robles, Santiago,
    Chile, 22 December 2005.
Co-op Fairtrade website: www.co-opfairtrade.co.uk/pages/producers_
    beerwinespirits2.asp (accessed 18 July 2006).
Los Robles and many other fair trade wines are available in the UK from
    Traidcraft, independent stores and supermarkets. See Appendix 1 Where
    to buy fair trade.

23. TRANSFORM LIVES

Interview with Regina Joseph, Oxford, March 2005.
Windward Islands Fairtrade-certified bananas are available at all the big
    supermarket chains.

24. GIVE BAD BALLS THE BOOT

Fair trade sportsballs are available in the UK from Oxfam shops, Save the Chil-
    dren shops and fair trade shops, the Co-op and Fair Deal Trading. See
    Appendix 1, Where to buy fair trade.

25. STAMP OUT PESTICIDE POISONING

FAO press release, "New code on pesticides adopted", 4 November 2002,
    www.fao.org/english/newsroom/news/2002/10525-en.html.
J. Jeyaratnam, "Acute pesticide poisoning: a major global health problem",
    World Health Statistics Quarterly, 1990 43(3), pp. 139–44.
Annual Report of the Pesticide Residues Committee, 2002,
    www.pan-uk.org/poster.htm.
Friends of the Earth, "Do we really know what pesticides are in our food?",
    www.foe.co.uk/pubsinfo/briefings/html/20020111082053.htm.
Nicaraguan producer: www.nicaraguasc.org.uk/campaigns/index.htm.
(Websites accessed 26 and 27 April 2006.)

26. TRAVEL WITH RESPECT

Polly Pattullo with Orely Minelli, *The Ethical Travel Guide: Your Passport To Alternative Holidays*, London, Tourism Concern/Earthscan, 2006.

27. BE A FRIEND OF THE EARTH

Fairtrade Foundation, "Fairtrade standards",
    www.fairtrade.org.uk/about_standards.htm.
Soil Association: www.soilassociation.org.
Fairtrade Foundation, "Benefits of Fairtrade: a cleaner environment",
    www.fairtrade.org.uk/about_benefits_environment.htm.
TransFair USA: "Environmental benefits of fair trade coffee, cocoa & tea",
    www.transfairusa.org/pdfs/env.ben_coffee.cocoa.tea.pdf.
(Websites accessed 4 August 2006.)

28. END CHILD EXPLOITATION

British Association for Fair Trade Shops, "Stand up for their rights",
    campaign leaflet, 2005.
Brooke Shelby Biggs, "Slavery free chocolate?", 2002,
    www.alternet.org/story/12373/.
Human Rights Watch 2002 report, quoted in A. Nicholls and C. Opal, *Fair Trade: Market-Driven Ethical Consumption*, London, Sage, 2005, p. 39.
"Ecuador's banana fields, child labor is key to profits", *New York Times*, 13 July 2002,
    www.organicconsumers.org/Starbucks/0828_fair_trade.cfm.
(Websites accessed 18 July 2006.)

29. LIFT THE DEBT BURDEN

Fairtrade Foundation,
    www.fairtrade.org.uk/suppliers_growers_coffee_isabel.htm, and
    www.fairtrade.org.uk/fc-spr99.htm.
Christian Aid, "The damage done: aid, death and dogma", 2005,
    www.christianaid.org.uk.
Tara Projects: www.taraprojects.com
(Websites accessed 11 May 2006.)

30. SAY NO TO GMOs

Christian Aid, "Genetically modified crops: Christian Aid's concerns",
www.christian-aid.org.uk/indepth/0206gm/gmcrops.htm.

ActionAid, "Robbing coffee's cradle: GM coffee and its threat to poor farmers",
www.risc.org.uk/readingroom/coffee/GMcoffee.pdf.

"GM coffee 'threatens farmers'",
http://news.bbc.co.uk/1/hi/sci/tech/1332477.stm.

Fairtrade Foundation, "Redressing a global imbalance: the case for Fairtrade certified cotton",
www.fairtrade.org.uk/downloads/pdf/cotton_briefing.pdf.

Friends of the Earth, "EU states must reject GM rice",
www.foe.co.uk/resource/press_releases/eu_states_must_reject_gm_r_24032004.html.

Institute of Science in Society, "Mass deaths in sheep grazing on Bt cotton",
www.i-sis.org.uk/MDSGBTC.php.

On Dr Arpad Pusztai, see Andrew Rowell, *Don't Worry (It's Safe to Eat): The True Story of GM Food, BSE and Foot and Mouth*, London, Earthscan, 2003.

(Websites accessed 18 July 2006.)

31. DO SOMETHING FUNKY WITH YOUR FURNITURE

Tara Projects: www.taraprojects.com.

Traidcraft: www.traidcraft.org.

New Overseas Traders: www.theindiashop.co.uk/acatalog/Furniture_ Range.html.

Urchin: www.urchin.co.uk/articles/urchin-fairtrade-kids.html.

Bali Spirit: www.balispirit.com/products/bali_fairtrade_handicraft.html.

Anjuna: www.anjunaonline.com.

London Metropolitan University: www.londonmet.ac.uk/library/k49772_3.pdf.

(Websites accessed 29 and 30 May 2006.)

32. REBUILD LIVES AND LIVELIHOODS

"Thomas Fricke and Sylvia Blanchet: ForesTrade".
www.forestrade.com/images/ForesTade%20Profile%20-%20Fricke%20&%20Blanchet%20(Mar-05).pdf.

Café Campesino, "Hurricane Stan ravages our Guatemalan friends",
www.cafecampesino.com/fairgrounds/0510/hurricane.html.

Sustainable Harvest, "First report in from APOCS leader Raniero Lec",
www.fairtrade.com/coffeefund/guatemala_2.htm.

Equal Exchange, "Hurricane Stan wreaks havoc on Central America and southern Mexico", www.equalexchange.com/hurricane-stan.

TransFair USA, "Three Seattle companies join to aid coffee co-operative destroyed by Hurricane Stan",
www.transfairusa.org/content/Downloads/UDEPOM_Donation_ Release.doc?ndmViewId=news_view&newsId=20051021005051&new sLang=en.

(Websites accessed 18 July 2006.)

33. MAKE TRANSNATIONALS TRADE MORE FAIRLY

Banana Link:
www.bananalink.org.uk/images/walmart_banana_price_cuts_160306.pdf.

Baby Milk Action:
www.babymilkaction.org/press/press6oct05.html.

WDM:
www.wdm.org.uk/news/presrel/current/nestle.htm.

Fairtrade Foundation:
www.fairtrade.org.uk/pr071005.htm.

Nestlé:
www.news.bbc.co.uk/1/hi/business/4788662.stm.

Oxfam:
www.maketradefair.com/en/index.php?file=coffee_pr04.htm.

WI:
www.nfwi.org.uk/newsfile/newsitem.shtml?newsitem=051007-125912.

People and Planet:
www.peopleandplanet.org/news/story540.

Guardian:
www.guardian.co.uk/guardianweekly/outlook/story/0,,1580916,00.html.
www.guardian.co.uk/uk_news/story/0,3604,1356599,00.html.

Paul Chandler, correspondence with authors, July 2006.

34. PUT PAID TO SWEATSHOPS

Oxfam International, *Offside! Labour rights and sportswear production in Asia*, May 2006, www.oxfam.org.uk/what_we_do/issues/trade/offside_sportswear.htm (accessed 18 July 2006).

For fair trade clothes suppliers, see Appendix 1, Where to buy fair trade.

35. BUY INTO A LONGER-TERM RELATIONSHIP

Traidcraft,www.traidcraft.org.uk/template2.asp?pageID=1650&fromID=1276.

Gossypium, www.gossypium.co.uk/x10170.html.

"Making trade work for the producers: 15 years of Fairtrade labelled coffee in the Netherlands", 2003, www.fairtrade.org.uk/resources_reports.htm.

FLO: www.fairtrade.net.

Green & Black's: www.greenandblacks.com/chocolate.php.

(Websites accessed 23 and 26 May 2006.)

36. SHOW SOLIDARITY WITH PALESTINIAN FARMERS

Oxfam GB, "Palestinian olive oil trickles to market", www.oxfam.org.uk/what_we_do/where_we_work/palterr_israel/oliveoil.htm.

Oxfam GB, "Palestinian and Israeli students take action to Make Trade Fair", www.oxfam.org.uk/what_we_do/where_we_work/palterr_israel/mtf_launch.htm.

Triodos Bank, "Slick oil", *Triodosnews*, spring 2006, p. 7, www.triodos.co.uk/uk/whats_new/triodos_news/?lang=.

(Websites accessed 18 July 2006.)

37. REACH FOR THE GOALS

MDGs: www.un.org/millenniumgoals.

FAO, www.fao.org/newsroom/en/news/2005/.

World Development Indicators, 2005: www.worldbank.org.

Oxfam International press release, 8 July 2005, www.oxfam.org/en/news/pressreleases2005.

Christian Aid, "The climate of poverty: facts, fears and hope", www.christian-aid.org.uk.

Women of Reform Judaism: www.wrj.rj.org/reso/ending_poverty.html.
Fairtrade Foundation, July 2005, www.fairtrade.org.uk/pr300705.htm.
(Websites accessed 1 June 06.)

38. BE A PROGRESSIVE COFFEE DRINKER

"Fair dunk'em", *Guardian*, 9 February 2006, http://business.guardian.co.uk/
economicdispatch/story/0,,1706406,00.html.
"Why Mark Darcy is full of beans for the latest fair-trade coffee venture",
Sunday Herald (Scotland), 19 June 2005.
www.sundayherald.com/50367.
(Websites accessed 18 July 2006.)

39. SEND HOPE TO A HUNGRY COUNTRY

Interview with Issaka Sommande, Arsene Sourabie and Kate Sebag, Reading
International Solidarity Centre, UK, March 2006.
Fairtrade mango products from Burkina Faso are sold under the brands Trop-
ical Wholefoods and Traidcraft and also used in the Day Chocolate
Company's Mango Divine Delights.

40. CO-OPERATE WITH CO-OPERATIVES

Working Out of Poverty, Geneva, ILO, 2003, quoted in Commonwealth
Secretariat, *Chains of Fortune: Linking Women Producers and Workers
with Global Markets*, London, 2004,
www.divinechocolate.com/shared_asp_files/uploadedfiles/
F7284775-DFCD-447D-B79F-0CCE784FD654_ChainsofFortune.pdf.
Co-operative Wholesale Society, "Co-op Fairtrade",
www.babymilkaction.org/pdfs/spinpdfs/appendices/Coop_
fairtrade.pdf.
Fairtrade Foundation, *Spilling the Beans on the Coffee Trade*, London, 1997,
revised 2002, www.fairtrade.org.uk/downloads/pdf/spilling.pdf.
Young Co-operatives: www.youngcooperatives.org.uk.
(Websites accessed 8 June 2006.)

41. PROVE THE FREE TRADE EGGHEADS WRONG

Vandana Shiva, speech to a meeting at the Royal Commonwealth Society, London, 14 October 1999.

Pauline Tiffen, speech to Fair Trade Futures Conference, Chicago, October 2005,

www.fairtradefederation.org/2005ftconference/pdf/workshops/Keynote _Pauline.pdf.

Peggy Antrobus, quoted in John Madeley, *A People's World*, London, Zed Books, 2003.

Adam Smith Institute, "Grounds for complaint? 'Fair trade' and the coffee crisis", 2004.

Nestlé report quoted in Oliver Balch, "A bitter pill to swallow", *Guardian*, 22 March 2004,

www.guardian.co.uk/fairtrade/story/0,,1175192,00.html.

John Vidal, "Eco soundings", *Guardian*, 24 March 2004,

http://society.guardian.co.uk/environment/story/0,,1176046,00.html.

Fairtrade Foundation, "Fair comment", autumn 2001,

www.fairtrade.org.uk/fc-aut01a.htm.

Proverbs 12-16b.

(Websites accessed 24 and 25 May 2006.)

42. MAKE TOMORROW'S BUSINESS HAPPEN TODAY

Terry Mollner, "The *Economist*'s thinking is yesterday, CSR thinking is today",www.via3.net/pooled/articles/BF_DOCART/view.asp?Q=BF_D OCART_131655.

Institute of Business Ethics, www.ibe.org.uk/faq.htm#diff.

Hernando Monje Granados, "Fair Trade: a social innovation for reducing poverty", www.icsw.org/copenhagen_implementation/copenhagen_ papers/paper10/granados.htm.

Anne Owen, "Poverty, governance and individual action: how can the smallest of cogs turn the biggest of wheels?", www.article13.com/A13_ ContentList.asp?strAction=GetPublication&PNID=1038.

International Fair Trade Association, "Alternative approach gains royal accolade", www.ifat.org/current/traidcraftqa.shtml.

Traidcraft, "Traidcraft's 2005 social accounts",

www.traidcraft.co.uk/socialaccounts.

(Websites accessed 18 July 2006.)

43. VOTE FOR TRADE JUSTICE

Fairtrade Foundation, July 2005, www.fairtrade.org.uk/pr300705.htm.

Mark Ritchie, "Fair trade and the WTO ministerial at Cancun", *Landmark*, January/February 2004.

Trade Justice Movement: www.tjm.org.uk.

Christian Aid, "The economics of failure: the real cost of 'free' trade for poor countries", June 2005,
www.christianaid.org.uk/indepth/506liberalisation/index.htm.

G8 Gleanagles 2005, Chair's summary, 8 July.

(Websites accessed 5 and 6 May 2006.)

44. ENJOY THAT SWEETER TASTE

"When big business bites", *Guardian*, 8 June 2006,
http://business.guardian.co.uk/story/0,,1792511,00.html.

"How a £1.50 chocolate bar saved a Mayan community from destruction", *Observer*, 28 May 2006,
http://observer.guardian.co.uk/foodmonthly/story/0,,1781908,00.html.

Divine Chocolate: www.divinechocolate.com.

"Raising the bar", *Developments* (25), 2004,
www.developments.org.uk/data/issue25/chocolate-save-world.htm.

Divine Chocolate, "Young Fairtraders from UK and Ghana present 'Chocolate Challenge' to International Development Secretary", June 2006,
www.divinechocolate.com/Templates/Internal.asp?NodeID=90736&strAreaColor=.

Craig Sams, *Guardian* letters page, 12 June 2006.

(Websites accessed 18 July 2006.)

45. CELEBRATE IN MARCH – AND AGAIN IN MAY

Fairtrade Foundation, www.fairtrade.org.uk/pr060306.htm.

World Fair Trade Day: www.wftday.org/english/about_wftday/this_yrs_theme/index.htm.

Norma Velasquez Traverso, quoted at www.wftday.org/english/messages/sub/articles/index04.htm.

(Websites accessed 3 July and 1 August 2006.)

46. MAKE MARKETS REALLY WORK FOR THE POOR

Joseph Stiglitz, *Globalization and Its Discontents*, London, Penguin 2004.
Interview with Elvia Marroquin Corea, Honduras, 2003, kindly provided by Oxfam GB.

47. INVEST IN FAIR TRADE

Shared Interest: www.shared-interest.com/files/soc_ac_sum.pdf.
Co-operative Bank: www.co-operativebank.co.uk/s ... CoopBank/Page/tplPageStandard&c=Page.
Triodos Bank: www.triodos.co.uk/uk/personal_banking/savings/140289/?version=1&lang=en.
Jupiter Asset Management: www.jupiteronline.co.uk.
New Consumer: www.newconsumer.org/index2.php?pageId=267.
Commission for Africa, qoted at www.fairtrade.org.uk/pr300705.htm.
(Websites accessed 3, 4 and 31 July 2006.)

48. KEEP FAMILIES AND COMMUNITIES TOGETHER

Oxfam interviews kindly provided by Oxfam GB.
Columban Fathers, www.columban.org/jpic/Migration/BorderIssues/July%2016%20-%20economic%20factors.PDF.
Dallas Peace Center, "The debate you're not hearing: immigration and trade", http://dallaspeacecenter.org/?q=node/847.
Fairtrade Foundation, "The world's first Fairtrade pineapples arrive in the UK", *Fair Comment*, spring 2003,
www.fairtrade.org.uk/fc-spr03.htm.
Tearfund, "Uncovered: the lowdown – fairtrade", http://youth.tearfund.org/webdocs/Website/Youth/Bible%20study%20Fairtrade.pdf.
Claire Stoscheck, "The growing fair trade movement", Committee on US–Latin America Relations *Newsletter*, spring 2003,
www.rso.cornell.edu/cuslar/newsletter/spring03/fairtrade.htm.
TransFair USA, www.transfairusa.org/content/about/global_reach.php#.
Wales Fair Trade Forum, *Newsletter*, spring 2003,
www.walesfairtradeforum.org.uk/Newsletter4.html.
Traidcraft, Social Accounts 2004/5,
www.traidcraft.co.uk/socialaccounts/sa_a6.html.

[201]

Bishopston Trading Company, www.bishopstontrading.co.uk/fair.htm.
Lutheran World Relief, "Fair trade and human rights: the perfect combination", www.lwr.org/toto/FT_HR.pdf.
(Websites accessed 18 July 2006.)

49. DEFEND DIVERSITY

Interview with Dulce Marlen Contreras, Honduras, kindly provided by Oxfam GB.
European Parliament, *Report on Fair Trade and Development*, rapporteur Frithjof Schmidt, 2006,
www.europarl.europa.eu/omk/sipade3?PUBREF=-//EP//NONGML+ REPORT+A6-2006-0207+0+DOC+PDF+V0//EN&L=EN&LEVEL= 0& NAV=S&LSTDOC=Y (accessed 18 July 2006).

50. CHANGE THE WORLD!

CAFOD, "Clean up your computer" campaign, www.cafod.org.uk/get_ involved/campaigning/clean_up_your_computer/what_s_wrong_ with_my_computer.
David Ransom, *The No-Nonsense Guide to Fair Trade*, Oxford, New Internationalist, 2001.
"Better than fair", *Developments* (25), first quarter 2004,
www.developments.org.uk/data/issue25/behind-fair-trade.htm.
Fairtrade Foundation press release, July 2005,
www.fairtrade.org.uk/pr080705 .htm.
Paul Chandler and Harriet Lamb, correspondence with authors, July 2006.
(Websites accessed 12 July 2006.)

Appendix 1:
Where to buy fair trade

CONTENTS

Hundreds of Oxfam shops sell fair trade products. Find your nearest shop at: www.oxfam.org.uk/shop/online/index.htm.

All major supermarkets and most coffee-shop chains now sell Fairtrade-certified food and drink. For details of these and other retailers see the lists on the Fairtrade Foundation website at www.fairtrade.org.uk/suppliers_retailers.htm.

For the full range of Fairtrade-certified products, visit www.fairtrade.org.uk/products.htm.

1. FAIR TRADE AND WORLD SHOPS (BRITISH ASSOCIATION FOR FAIR TRADE SHOPS – BAFTS)

Channel Isles
mondomundi
Unit 4
St Martin's Court
St Martin's
Guernsey GY4 6AA
Tel: 07781 132686
phil.soulsby@fairtradeci.com
www.mondomundi.com

East Anglia
Art Gecko
15 Rose Crescent
Cambridge
Cambridgeshire CB2 3LL
Tel: 01223 367483
artgecko6@hotmail.com
www.Artgecko.co.uk

Just Sharing
The Free Church (URC)
Market Hill
St Ives, Huntingdon
Cambs PE27 5AL
Tel: 01480 496570
jsharing@fish.co.uk
www.stivesfreechurch.org

The Fair Trade Shop
15 Orwell Place
Ipswich IP4 1BD
Tel: 01473 288225
mlfish@fish.co.uk

Traders Fair World Shop
12 Museum Street
Colchester
Essex CO1 1TN
Tel: 01206 763380
tradersfair@fish.co.uk

The World Shop, Norwich
NEAD, 38 Exchange Street
Norwich
Norfolk NR2 1AX
Tel: 01603 610993
teresa@nead.org.uk
www.worldshop.org.uk

Midlands
Ethos
Little Tarrington Farm
Little Tarrington
Herefordshire HR1 4JA
Tel: 01432 890423
annie@hopline.farmcom.net
fairtrade@stmichaels

The Fair Trading Place
28 Market Place
Melbourne
Derbyshire DE73 8DS
Tel: 0845 458 5078
leesderby@aol.com

The Fairtrading Post
8a Burton Street
Melton Mowbray
Leicestershire LE13 1AE
Tel: 01664 503027
dolores.harvey@ntlworld.com

Just Fair Trade
10 Bishop Street
Town Hall Square
Leicester
Leicestershire LE1 6AF
Tel: 0116 2559123
sarah@justfairtrade.com
www.justfairtrade.com

St Michael at the Northgate
Cornmarket Street
Oxford
Oxfordshire OX1 3EY
Tel: 01865 722505
claretegla@hotmail.com

Shared Earth
87 New Street
Birmingham B2 4BA
Tel: 0121 633 0151
jp@sharedearth.co.uk
www.sharedearth.co.uk

Traid Links
20 Market Place

Wirksworth
Derbyshire DE4 4ET
Tel: 01629 824393
info@traid-links.co.uk
www.traid-links.co.uk

Wikijum
61 High Street
Stone
Staffs ST15 8AD
Tel: 01785 819508
wikijum@aol.com

World of Difference
20 High St
Rugby
Warks CV21 3BG
Tel: 01788 579191
info@worldofdifference.org.uk

North East
3W Trading
St Mary's Court Shopping Arca
North Bar Within
Beverley
Yorkshire HU17 8DG
Tel: 01482-888020
info@3wtrading.com
www.3wtrading.com

Elemental
8 Main Street
Ingleton
Via Carnforth
N Yorks LA6 3EB
Tel: 015242 42626
heather@elementallife.co.uk
www.elementallife.co.uk

Fair Trade Parties
13 Farnley Lane, Otley
West Yorkshire LS21 2AB
Tel: 01943 850645
sima@fairtradeparties.co.uk
www.fairtradeparties.co.uk

Fairer World
84 Gillygate
York YO31 7EQ
Tel: 01904 655116
fairerwrld@aol.com

Gateway World Shop
Market Place
Durham DH1 3NJ
Tel: 0191 384 7173
info@gatewayworldshop.co.uk

Hull One World Shop
c/o Methodist Central Hall
Waltham St, King Edward Street
Hull HU1 3SQ
Tel: 01482 327727
info@oneworldhull.co.uk
www.oneworldhull.co.uk

Just Bazaar
Unit 20, The Colonnade
Piece Hall
Halifax
West Yorkshire HX1 1RE
Tel: 01422 832248
philippateal@ukonline.co.uk
www.justbazaar.co.uk

Radish
128 Harrogate Road
Chapel Allerton

Leeds
Yorks LS7 4NZ
Tel: 0113 2694241
info@radishweb.co.uk
www.radishweb.co.uk

Shared Earth
86 The Merrion Centre
Leeds
Yorkshire LS2 8PJ
Tel: 0113 2426424
jp@sharedearth.co.uk
www.sharedearth.co.uk

Shared Earth
1 Minster Gates
York
Yorkshire YO1 7HL
Tel: 01904 655314
jp@sharedearth.co.uk
www.sharedearth.co.uk

Sonia's Smile
85 Main street
Haworth, West Yorks BD22 8DA
Tel: 01535 647776
rita@soniassmile.com
www.soniassmile.com

Traidcraft shop
(different location each Christmas)
Middlesbrough
Teesside TS21 1DR
Tel: 01740 630475
medhurst@clara.co.uk

North West
  Carlisle World Shop
  1 Lowthian's Lane, English Street

Carlisle CA3 8JR
Tel: 01228 550385
l.strong@rattenrow.co.uk

Chester Fair Trading
Wesley Methodist Church
St.John's Street
Chester CH1 1DA
Tel: 01829 770847
info@bafts.org.uk

Fair 4 All
Stall 38/39, Retail Market
Academy Way
Warrington WA1 2EN
Tel: 01925 415121
afthomson@ntlworld.com

Fairground
Wesley Hall Methodist Church
Paradise Lane
Blackburn BB2 1LQ
Tel: 01254 682210
info@bafts.org.uk

Fairly Goods
4 Woodfield Road
Chorley
Lancashire PR7 1QT
Tel: 01257 271216
info@fairlygoods.co.uk
www.fairlygoods.co.uk

Justicia
81 Knowsley Street
Bolton
Lancs BL1 2BJ
Tel: 01204 363308
shop@justicia.greenisp.org

Shakti Man
68 Parliament Street
Ramsey
Isle of Man IM8 1AJ
Tel: 01624 815060
shaktinepal@hotmail.com

Shared Earth
51 Piccadilly
Manchester M1 2AP
Tel: 0161 236 1014
jp@sharedearth.co.uk
www.sharedearth.co.uk

Tierra Canela
60 Dickens Lane
Poynton
Cheshire SK12 1NT
Tel: 01625 850160
info@tierracanela.com
www.tierracanela.com

World Museum Liverpool Shop
World Museum Liverpool
William Brown Street
Liverpool L3 8EN
Tel: 0151 478 4025
karen.grant@liverpoolmuseums.
org.uk
worldmuseumliverpool.org.uk

Northern Ireland
Anjuna
79 Union Street
Lurgan
Craigavon
County Armagh BT66 8EB
Tel: 02838 344299

info@anjunaonline.com
www.anjunaonline.com

Scotland
Earth Matters
67 High Street
North Berwick EH39 4 HG
Tel: 01620 895401
earthmattersltd@fsmail.co.uk
www.earthmatters.co.uk

Fair Shares
128 High Street
Burntisland
Fife KY3 9AP
Tel: 01592 870071/07952/161305
info@fairshares-shop.co.uk
www.fairshares-shop.co.uk

Fayre Trade Limited
7 Newton Street
Greenock PA16 8UH
Tel: 01475 787876
eve@fayretrade.co.uk
www.fayretrade.co.uk

Hadeel
St George's West Church
58 Shandwick Place
Edinburgh EH2 4RT
Tel: 0131 225 1922
palcrafts@fish.co.uk
www.hadeel.org

One World Shop (Edinburgh)
St.John's Church
Princes Street
Edinburgh EH2 4BJ
Tel: 0131 229 4541

rfarey@oneworldshop.co.uk
www.oneworldshop.co.uk

Rainbow Turtle
28 The Vennel, Linlithgow
West Lothian EH49 7EX
Tel: 01506 840348
info@rainbowturtle.org.uk
www.rainbowturtle.org.uk

Rainbow Turtle
7 Gauze Street
Paisley PA1 1EP
Tel: 0141 887 1881
info@rainbowturtle.org.uk
www.rainbowturtle.org.uk

The Coach House
Balmore
Torrance
Glasgow G64 4AE
Tel: 01360 620742
info@bafts.org.uk

Third World Centre
St Mary's Chapel, Church of St
Correction Wynd
Aberdeen
Aberdeenshire AB10 1JZ
Tel: 01224 645650
sue.good101@btopenworld.com
http://beehive.thisisnorthscot

Trenabies
16 Albert Street
Kirkwall
Orkney KW15 1HP
Tel: 01856 874336
leannerendall@hotmail.com

Wrap Around
84 Queensbury Street
Dumfries DG1 1BH
Tel: 01387 250053
nettie@alternativedumfries.co.uk
www.dumfries-gifts.co.uk

South East and London
Bread of Life Fair Trade Centre
Christchurch URC and Methodist
263 Barry Road
East Dulwich
London SE22 0JT
Tel: 020 8693 4170
breadoflifecentre@hotmail.co.uk
www.cced.org.uk

Chandni Chowk
13 Marmion Road
Southsea
Hants PO5 2AT
Tel: 02392 751576
mail@chandnichowk.co.uk
www.chandnichowk.co.uk

Fair Enough
136 Church Street
Croydon
Surrey CR0 1RF
Tel: 020 8688 9213
Nigel.Eltringham@ntlworld.com

Fair Share
102 Berwick Street
London W1F 0QP
Tel: 020 7287 8827
fairshare@tiscali.co.uk
www.fairshare-soho.org

Fair Trade Fairies
2 Runnalow
Letchworth
Hertfordshire SG6 4DT
Tel: 07951 758294
info@fairtradefairies.com
www.fairtradefairies.com

Fairwind
47 Park Road
Crouch End
London N8 8TE
Tel: 020 8374 6254
info@fairwindonline.com
www.fairwindonline.com

Ganesha
3 Gabriel's Wharf
56 Upper Ground
London SE1 9PP
Tel: 020 7928 3444
shop@ganesha.co.uk
www.ganesha.co.uk

Lovethatstuff
29 Coleman Street
Brighton
East Sussex BN2 9SQ
Tel: 01273 675778
kipp.wilson@virgin.net
www.lovethatstuff.co.uk

Natural Flow Direct
Unit 11, Mews Business Centre
Clifford Road
Bexhill-on-Sea
East Sussex TN40 3QA
Tel: 01424 220688

enquiries@naturalflowdirect.
com
www.NaturalFlowDirect.com

One Village
(On A44 Woodstock-Oxford)
Charlbury
OX7 3SQ
Tel: 01608 811811
progress@onevillage.org
www.onevillage.com

One World Shop (Waterloo)
St John's Church
Waterloo Road
London SE1 8TY
Tel: 020 7450 4601
ehamilton9@hotmail.com

Paper High
Flat 4, 30 Elmbourne Road
Balham, London SW17 8JR
Tel: 020 8675 2794
mark@paperhigh.com
www.paperhigh.com

Siesta
1 Palace Street
Canterbury
Kent CT1 2DY
Tel: 01227 464614
siesta@btconnect.com
www.siestacrafts.co.uk

Sust!
Food Centre
Secklow Gate
Milton Keynes MK9 3NE
Tel: 01908 232255

sust@phonecoop.coop
www.sustmk.co.uk

Ta-lmari
High Street
Ventnor
Isle of Wight PO38 1RZ
Tel: 01983 857707
enigmisle@onetel.com

The Fair Trade Shop Southampton
106 Shirley High Street
Shirley
Southampton
Hampshire SO16 4FB
Tel: 02380513344
clem.elaine@tesco.net

The World Shop, Reading
RISC, 35–39 London Street
Reading
Berks RG1 4PS
Tel: 0118 9586692
catherine@risc.org.uk
www.risc.org.uk

South West
Bishopston Trading Company
8A High Street
Glastonbury
Somerset BA6 9DU
Tel: 0145 883 5386
mail@bishopstontrading.fsnet.
co.uk

Bishopston Trading Company
79 High Street
Totnes
Devon TQ9 5PB

Tel: 0180 386 8488
mail@bishopstontrading.fsnet.
co.uk

Bishopston Trading Company
33 Silver St
Bradford-on-Avon
Wilts BA15 1JX
Tel: 01225 867485
mail@bishopstontrading.fsnet.
co.uk

Bishopston Trading Company
33 High Street, Stroud
Glos GL5 1AJ
Tel: 0145 3766355
mail@bishopstontrading.fsnet.
co.uk

Bishopston Trading Company
193 Gloucester Rd
Bishopston, Bristol
Avon & Bristol BS7 8BG
Tel: 0117 9245598
mail@bishopstontrading.co.uk
www.bishopstontrading.co.uk

Chandni Chowk
102 Boutport St
Barnstaple
Devon EX31 1SY
Tel: 01271 374714
mail@chandnichowk.co.uk
www.chandnichowk.co.uk

Chandni Chowk
6 New Bond St
Bath
Bath and Bristol BA1 1BH

Tel: 01225 484700
mail@chandnichowk.co.uk
www.chandnichowk.co.uk

Chandni Chowk
66 Park St
Bristol
Bath and Bristol BS1 5JN
Tel: 0117 9300059
mail@chandnichowk.co.uk
www.chandnichowk.co.uk

Chandni Chowk
1 Harlequins
Paul Street
Exeter
Devon EX4 3TT
Tel: 01392 410201
mail@chandnichowk.co.uk
www.chandnichowk.co.uk

Chandni Chowk
14a The Bridge
Riverside Place
Taunton
Somerset TA1 1UG
Tel: 01823 327377
mail@chandnichowk.co.uk
www.chandnichowk.co.uk

fair's fair
17 Bear Street
Barnstaple
North Devon EX32 7BX
Tel: 01271 370877
herad@fish.co.uk

Moon Dragon
Fraziers Yard, East Wharf

Mevagissey
Cornwall PL26 6QQ
Tel: 01726 844555
moon_dragon@madasafish.com

Quipu
Brewers Quay, Hope Square
Weymouth
Dorset DT4 8TP
Tel: 01305 788474
quipu@tiscali.co.uk
www.quipucrafts.co.uk

The India Shop
35 Duke Street
Henley-on-Thames
Oxon RG9 1VR
Tel: 01491 579315
info@theindiashop.co.uk
www.theindiashop.co.uk

The India Shop
5 Hilliers Yard
Marlborough
Wilts SN8 1BE
Tel: 01672 515585
info@theindiashop.co.uk
www.theindiashop.co.uk

The India Shop
35 High Street
Salisbury
Wilts SP1 2JD
Tel: 01722 321421
info@theindiashop.co.uk
www.theindiashop.co.uk

The India Shop
39 Market Place

Wantage
Oxon OX12 8AW
Tel: 01235 771040
info@theindiashop.co.uk
www.theindiashop.co.uk

Tumi
8/9 New Bond St Place
Bath BA1 1BH
Tel: 01225 446025
info@tumi.co.uk
www.tumi.co.uk

Tumi
1/2 Little Clarendon St
Oxford
Oxfordshire OX1 2HP
Tel: 01865 512307
info@tumi.co.uk
www.tumi.co.uk

Uneeka
Lemon Street Market
Lemon Street
Truro
Cornwall TR1 2PN
Tel: 01872 242276
jodi@uneeka.com
www.uneeka.com

Utani-UK
6 Richmond Gate
160 Charminster Road
Bournemouth
Dorset BH8 8UX
Tel: 01202 528262
joy@utani-uk.com
www.utani-uk.com

Wales

Fair Do's/Siopa Teg
10 Llandaff Road
Canton
Cardiff
Glamorgan CF11 9NJ
Tel: 029 2022 2066
jtucker@fairdos.com
www.fairdos.com

Jo Pott, Mercer
127 High Street, Bangor
Gwynedd LL57 1NT
Tel: 01248 362434
jo.pott@virgin.net
www.jopott.com

Just Shopping/Cynnyrch Cyfiawn
13 Bangor Road
Conwy LL32 8NG
Tel: 01492 593500
lis@fish.co.uk
www.justshopping.co.uk

Oyster
28 Castle Arcade
Cardiff
S. Wales CF10 1BW
Tel: 02920 644107
info@oysterclothing.co.uk
www.oysterclothing.co.uk

Shared Earth
14–16 Royal Arcade
Cardiff CF10 1AE
Tel: 02920 396900
jp@sharedearth.co.uk
www.sharedearth.co.uk

Siop Clare
Ty Ebrill
Y Sgwar
Crymych
Pembrokeshire SA41 3RJ

Tel: 01239 831666
clarebutler@crymych.fsworld.
co.uk

2. OTHER DEDICATED FAIR TRADE RETAILERS, MAIL ORDER AND INTERNET SUPPLIERS

Art Gecko
15 Rose Crescent
Cambridge
Cambridgeshire CB2 3LL
Tel: 01223 367483
artgecko6@hotmail.com
www.Artgecko.co.uk

Clean Slate
19 Dig Street, Ashbourne
Derbyshire DE6 1GF
Tel: 0845 3372963
enquiries@cleanslateclothing.co.uk
www.cleanslateclothing.co.uk

Concepts of Peru
87 Genesta Road
London SE18 3EX
Tel: 020 8855 3282
concepts.peru@virgin.net
www.conceptsofperu.co.uk

Epona
Unit 5, Lilford Business Centre
61 Lilford Road
London SE5 9HR
Tel: 020 7095 1222
info@eponasport.com
www.eponasport.com

Equal Exchange Trading Ltd
Suite 1, 2 Commercial Street
Edinburgh EH6 6JA
Tel. 031 554 5912
info@equalexchange.co.uk
www.equalexchange.co.uk

Ethical Junction
info@ethicaljunction.org.uk
www.ethical-
junction.org/contact.html

Ethical Shopper
4 Windsor Terrace
City Road, Islington
London N1 7TF
Tel: 020 7490 7952
ian@ethicalshopper.co.uk
www.ethicalshopper.co.uk

Ethical Threads
Tel: 020 7241 1717 / 07939 250108
info@ethicalthreads.co.uk
www.ethicalthreads.co.uk

Fair Deal Trading
m.kunz@fairdealtrading.co.uk
www.fairdealtrading.com

Fair Trade Design
440 Lichfeld Road
Sutton Coldfield
West Midlands B74 4BL
Tel: 0121 308 0387
sales@fairtradedesign.co.uk
www.fairtradedesign.co.uk

Fairs Fayre
Workshop 8, Fairground Craft
Weyhill
Andover
Hants SP11 0QN
Tel: 01264 771112
fairsfayre@tiscali.co.uk

Fair Trade Media
Tel: 0191 211 1934.
info@fairtrademedia.co.uk
www.fairtrademedia.co.uk

Get Ethical
Unit 3n, Leroy House
436 Essex Road
London N1 3QP
sales@getethical.com
www.getethical.com

Go Fair
Pump Works (AUTOOL)
Padiham Road, Sabden
Clitheroe
Lancashire BB7 9EW
Tel: 01200 440300
info@gofair.co.uk
www.gofair.co.uk

Gossypium
210 High Street

Lewes BN7 2NH
Tel: 0800 085 65 49
info@gossypium.co.uk
www.gossypium.co.uk

Hire Education Ltd
Unit 8, Navigation Way
Ripon Business Park, Ripon
N. Yorks HG4 1AB
Tel: 01765 607 815
peter@starbeck.com
www.starbeck.com

Hug
Unit 5, Lilford Business Centre
61 Lilford Rd
London SE5 9HR
Tel: 0845 130 15 25
info@hug.co.uk
www.hug.co.uk

Jungle Berry Trading
19 Lethaby House
Rubens Place
London SW4 7RB
Tel: 020 7274 4800
info@jungleberry.co.uk
www.jungleberry.co.uk

Just Change
john@justchangeuk.org
manchester@justchangeuk.org
justchangelondon@yahoo.co.uk
www.justchangeuk.org
www.justchangeindia.com

Manumit Fair Trade Limited
PO Box 6097
Newbury

Berkshire RG14 9BL
Tel: 01635 231211
info@manumituk.com
www.manumituk.com

New Consumer Shop
6–8 Charlotte Square
Newcastle-upon-Tyne
Tyne and Wear NE1 4XF
Tel: 0191 211 1934
shop@newconsumershop.org
www.newconsumershop.org/shop

Nomads Clothing
Priory Yard
Launceston
Cornwall PL15 8HU
Tel: 0845 1306633
enquiresaw05@nomadsclothing.com
www.nomadsclothing.com

Olive Co-operative
Bridge 5 Mill
22a Beswick Street
Manchester M4 7HR
Tel: 0161 273 1970
info@olivecoop.com
www.olivecoop.com

One World Is Enough
18 Ronald Rolph Court
Wadloes Road
Cambridge CB5 9PX
Tel: 0845 1661212
mail@one-world-is-enough.net
www.one-world-is-enough.net

Orchid Trading
131 Alstone Lane

Cheltenham
Gloucestershire GL51 8HX
Tel: 01242 282191
info@orchid-trading.co.uk
www.orchid-trading.co.uk

Oxfam
www.oxfam.org.uk/shop/online/
index.htm
Search for your nearest Oxfam shop at
www.multimap.com/clients/places.c
gi?client=oxfam3&searchtype=shop
&SUBMIT=Search

Pachacuti
19 Dig Street
Ashbourne,
Derbyshire DE6 1GF.
Tel: 01335 300003
hats@panamas.co.uk
www.pachacuti.co.uk

People Tree
Unit 7
8–13 New Inn Street
London EC2A 3PY
Tel: 020 7739 0660
support@ptree.co.uk
www.peopletree.co.uk

PointOV
6-8 Charlotte Square
Newcastle NE1 4XF
Tel: 0191 2111934
andy@pointov.com
www.newconsumershop.org

Progreso coffee bars
156 Portobello Road

London W11 2EB
Tel: 020 7985 0304
portobello@progreso.org.uk
and
Downstairs, Tomas Neal's Centre
35 Earlham Street,
London WC2H 9LD
Tel: 020 7379 3608
neals@progreso.org.uk
www.progreso.org.uk

Ralper
64 Rosamond Road
Bedford MK40 3UQ
Tel: 0845 226 1040
enquiries@ralper.co.uk
www.ralper.co.uk

Rugmark
www.rugmark.net
For a list of Rugmark suppliers in the
UK see http://rugmarkuk.mysite.wan
adoo-members.co.uk/page4.html

Sacred Lotus
54 Hamilton Square
Birkenhead
Wirral CH41 5AS
Tel: 0151 6508757
ayesha@sacredlotus.co.uk
www.sacredlotus.co.uk

Schmidt Natural Clothing
Tel: 0845 345 0498
catalogue@naturalclothing.co.uk
www.naturalclothing.co.uk

Silkwood Traders
The Old Main Post Office

Ship Street, Brighton
Tel: 01273 884587
info@silkwoodtraders.com
www.silkwoodtraders.com

Silverchilli.com
Tel: 0208 342 8883
directors@silverchilli.com
www.silverchilli.com

Simply Fair
Tel: 0191 491 5400
helpdesk@simplyfair.co.uk
www.simplyfair.co.uk

Sunlover
Leigh Farm Buildings
Standerwick, Frome
Somerset BA11 2PR
Tel: 01373 831153
sales@sunlover-gifts.co.uk
www.sunlover-gifts.co.uk

SuSuMaMa World Wear
2 Brambletyne Avenue
Saltdean, Brighton BN2 8EJ
Tel: 01273 300606
carli@susumama.co.uk
www.susumama.co.uk

Tearcraft
PO Box 5050
Annesley
Nottingham NG15 0DL
Tel: 0870 2404896
tearcraft@prolog.uk.com
www.tearcraft.org/cgi-bin/tcraft

The Fair Trade Stand
164 Hardy Mill Road
Bolton
Lancs BL2 3PW
Tel: 01204 528409
sales@fartradestand.net
www.fairtradestand.net

The Pink Planet Company
107 Hollywood Lane
Wainscott
Rochester
Kent ME3 8AT
Tel: 01634 313112
claire.greenway@pink-planet.co.uk
www.pink-planet.co.uk

Think Clothing
2nd Floor, 145–157 St John Street

London EC1V 4PY
info@thinkfairtrade.com
www.thinkfairtrade.com

Traidcraft
Kingsway, Gateshead
Tyne & Wear NE11 0NE
Tel: 0191 491 0591
comms@traidcraft.co.uk
www.traidcraft.co.uk
Search for the nearest retailers selling
products from the Traidcraft range at
www.traidcraft.co.uk/template2.asp?
pageID=1895

Zaytoun
Tel: 0845 345 4887
order@zaytoun.org
http://zaytoun.org

3. CATERING DISTRIBUTORS AND WHOLESALERS OF FAIRTRADE-CERTIFIED PRODUCE

Links to lists of catering distributors and wholesalers of Fairtrade-certified produce on the Fairtrade Foundation website:
    Catering distributors: www.fairtrade.org.uk/suppliers_caterers.htm
    Wholesalers: www.fairtrade.org.uk/suppliers_wholesalers.htm

4. ETHICAL TRAVEL

www.responsibletravel.com

Tourism Concern
Stapleton House
277-281 Holloway Road
London N7 8HN
Tel: 020 7133 3330
info@tourismconcern.org.uk
www.tourismconcern.org.uk

Ethical tourism links:
www.tourismconcern.org.uk/links/
ethical-links.html

A wide range of ethical holidays are
listed in Tourism Concern's book:
Polly Pattullo with Orely Minelli,
*The Ethical Travel Guide: Your
Passport To Alternative Holidays,*

London, Tourism Concern/Earth-
scan, 2006

Traidcraft Meet the People Tours
www.traidcraftinteractive.co.uk/
calendar.php?9701

5. FAIR TRADE FINANCE

Shared Interest
No.2 Cathedral Square
The Groat Market
Newcastle upon Tyne NE1 1EH
Tel: 0191 233 9100
enquirer@shared-interest.com
www.shared-interest.com

Triodos Fairtrade Saver Account
Triodos Bank
Brunel House
11 The Promenade
Bristol
BS8 3NN
Tel: 0117 973 9339
mail@triodos.co.uk
www.triodos.co.uk/uk/personal_
banking/savings/our_accounts/
fairtrade_saver/

Appendix 2: Fairtrade Towns and other areas in the UK

By mid 2006 there were 200 declared Fairtrade Towns, Cities, Boroughs etc., with well over 200 more working towards Fairtrade status – all listed below. There were also 2,845 Fairtrade Churches, Cathedrals, Chapels and Quaker Meetings; 13 Fairtrade Synagogues; at least one Fairtrade Mosque; and 34 Fairtrade Colleges and Universities. According to the Fairtrade Foundation, new applications come in every week.

Information kindly provided by the Fairtrade Foundation (and see www.fairtrade.org.uk/get_involved_ fairtrade_towns.htm).

FAIRTRADE TOWNS, CITIES, BOROUGHS, VILLAGES, ZONES, ISLANDS, COUNTIES AND DISTRICTS

Key: T = Town, C = City, B = Borough, V = Village, Z = Zone, I = Island, Co = County, D = District

1. Aberdeen (C)
2. Aberfeldy (T)
3. Aberystwyth (T)
4. Altrincham (T)
5. Ammanford (T)
6. Arundel (T)
7. Ashbourne (T)
8. Baildon (T)
9. Banbury (T)
10. Barnstaple (T)
11. Bath & NE Somerset (Z)
12. Belfast (C)
13. Bewdley (T)
14. Bideford (T)
15. Bingley (T)
16. Birmingham (C)
17. Bolton (T)
18. Bradford (Z)
19. Bradford-on-Avon (V)
20. Brampton (T)
21. Brecon (T)
22. Bridgnorth (T)
23. Brighton & Hove (C)
24. Bristol (C)
25. Burgess Hill (T)
26. Burntisland (T)
27. Cam & Dursley (T)
28. Cambridge (C)
29. Canterbury (C)
30. Cardiff (C)
31. Carlisle (C)
32. Castle Cary (T)
33. Charnwood (B)
34. Chelmsford (T)
35. Cherry Burton (V)
36. Chesham (T)

37. Chester (C)
38. Chorlton-cum-Hardy (Z)
39. Colchester (C)
40. Conwy (Co)
41. Coventry (C)
42. Criccieth, N. Wales (V)
43. Cumbria (Co)
44. Denbighshire (Co)
45. Derby (C)
46. Doncaster (T)
47. Dorchester (T)
48. Dorking (T)
49. Dornoch (T)
50. Dundee (C)
51. Dunoon (T)
52. Dyfi Valley (Z)
53. East Grinstead (T)
54. Edenbridge (T)
55. Eden Valley (Z)
56. Edinburgh (C)
57. Exeter (C)
58. Fairlie (V)
59. Fair Isle (I)
60. Falkirk (T)
61. Falmouth (T)
62. Faringdon (T)
63. Faversham (C)
64. Flintshire (Co)
65. Frome (T)
66. Garstang (T)
67. Glasgow (C)
68. Glastonbury (T)
69. Guernsey (I)
70. Guildford (C)
71. Guisborough (T)
72. Hamilton (T)
73. Hartlepool (T)
74. Harrogate (B)
75. Haworth (V)

76. Hebden Bridge (Z)
77. Hereford (C)
78. Herefordshire (C)
79. Hitchin (T)
80. Holme Valley (T)
81. Horsham (T)
82. Hornsea (T)
83. Horwich (T)
84. Hull (C)
85. Isle of Wight (I)
86. Ilkley (T)
87. Jersey (I)
88. Kendal (T)
89. Keswick (T)
90. Keynsham (T)
91. Kilmacolm & Quarriers (V)
92. Kinross-shire (Co)
93. Knighton (T)
94. Lakes Parish (Z)
95. Lampeter (T)
96. Lancaster (C)
97. Largs (T)
98. Ledbury (T)
99. Leeds (C)
100. Leicester (C)
101. Leighton Linslade (T)
102. Leominster (T)
103. Lewes (T)
104. Lingfield & Dormansland (Z)
105. Linlithgow (T)
106. Liverpool (C)
107. Livingston (T)
108. Llanidloes (T)
109. Lochgelly (T)
110. London, Camden (B)
111. London, Croydon (B)
112. London, Greenwich (B)
113. London, Hammersmith & Fulham (B)

114. London, Islington (B)
115. London, Kingston (B)
116. London, Lambeth (B)
117. London, Lewisham (B)
118. London, Richmond (B)
119. Lowestoft (T)
120. Ludlow (T)
121. Macclesfield (T)
122. Malvern (T)
123. Manchester (C)
124. Market Harborough (T)
125. Matlock & District (T)
126. Milford Haven (T)
127. Millom (T)
128. Milton Keynes (B)
129. Minehead (T)
130. Mirfield (T)
131. Monmouth (T)
132. Morpeth (T)
133. Nailsworth (T)
134. Newbury (T)
135. Newcastle-upon-Tyne (C)
136. Newton Abbot (T)
137. Northallerton (T)
138. Norwich (C)
139. Nottingham (C)
140. Oswestry (T)
141. Oxford (C)
142. Paisley (T)
143. Peebles & Tweeddale (Z)
144. Penarth (T)
145. Pendle (B)
146. Perth (C)
147. Plymouth (C)
148. Porthcawl (T)
149. Portsmouth (C)
150. Preston (C)
151. Purbeck (D)
152. Reading (T)

153. Rochdale (B)
154. Romsey (T)
155. Rotherham (T)
156. Royal Leamington Spa (T)
157. Salford (C)
158. Sevenoaks (T)
159. Sheffield (C)
160. Shetland Islands (I)
161. Shipley (T)
162. Somerset (Co)
163. Southampton (C)
164. Southwell (T)
165. St Albans (C)
166. St Andrews (T)
167. St Neots (T)
168. Stafford (T)
169. Stirling (C)
170. Stockport (B)
171. Stoke-on-Trent (C)
172. Stourport-on-Severn (T)
173. Strathaven (T)
174. Stroud (T)
175. Swanage (T)
176. Swansea (C & Co)
177. Swindon (B)
178. Taunton (T)
179. Tavistock (T)
180. Teignmouth (T)
181. Thornbury (T)
182. Uckfield (T)
183. Vale Royal Borough (B)
184. Wareham (T)
185. Warrington (B)
186. Wells (C)
187. Weymouth and Portland (Z)
188. Wimborne Minster (T)
189. Wiveliscombe (T)
190. Windermere and Bowness (T)
191. Windsor and Maidenhead (B)

192. Wirral (B)
193. Worcester (T)
194. Woking (B)
195. Wolverhampton (C)
196. Worthing (T)

197. Wotton-under-Edge (T)
198. Wrexham (Z)
199. York (C)
200. Yatton & Claverham (Z)

TOWNS AND OTHER AREAS WORKING TOWARDS FAIRTRADE STATUS

1. Abingdon, Oxfordshire
2. Addlestone, Surrey
3. Adlington
4. Allerdale
5. Andover
6. Anglesey
7. Arbroath
8. Ashburton
9. Ashford
10. Aylesbury
11. Ayr
12. Balfron
13. Ballymoney
14. Bangor
15. Barrow-in-Furness
16. Basingstoke
17. Bathrone
18. Batley and Spen
19. Beaconsfield
20. Beccles
21. Bedford
22. Berwick
23. Beverley
24. Bexhill-on-Sea
25. Billericay
26. Bishopton
27. Blackpool
28. Bognor
29. Bournemouth
30. Braintree District
31. Bridgend
32. Broseley
33. Broxtowe
34. Burscough
35. Burton upon Trent
36. Bury St Edmunds
37. Buxton
38. Caernarfon
39. Caerphilly
40. Caradon District
41. Castle Douglas
42. Castle Point
43. Chapel Allerton
44. Chesterfield
45. Chester-le-Street
46. Chew Magna
47. Chorley
48. Chichester
49. Cleckheaton
50. Clitheroe
51. Cockermouth
52. Coleraine
53. Congleton
54. Coniston & Torver
55. Coupar
56. Crawley
57. Dacorum
58. Darlington
59. Dawlish
60. Devizes

61. Dinas Powys
62. Deal
63. Droitwich Spa
64. Dundonald
65. Durham
66. East Dunbartonshire
67. East Renfrewshire
68. East Staffordshire
69. East Sussex
70. Eastbourne
71. Eastleigh
72. Eden Valley
73. Egremont
74. Ellesmere Port and Neston
75. Ellon
76. Elmbridge
77. Epsom
78. Evesham & District
79. Fareham
80. Farnham
81. Ferndown
82. Fylde
83. Gateshead
84. Glossop
85. Gloucester
86. Grange-over-Sands
87. Grove, Oxfordshire
88. Gwynedd
89. Hadleigh
90. Harlow
91. Hastings and St Leonards
92. Havant
93. Heathfield
94. Heswall, Wirral
95. Hinckley & Bosworth
96. Honiton & Sidmouth
97. Hope Valley, Derbyshire
98. Hornchurch
99. Huntingdon
100. Hyndburn
101. Inverclyde
102. Inverness
103. Ipswich
104. Isle of Man
105. Isle of Arran
106. Kent
107. Kidderminster
108. Kilwinning
109. Knaresborough and Harrogate
110. Knutsford
111. Lancashire
112. Larkhall
113. Lavenham
114. Leek
115. Letchworth
116. Lichfield
117. Limpsfield
118. Llandrindod and Builth Wells
119. London, Barking and Dagenham
120. London, Barnet
121. London, Bexley
122. London, Brent
123. London, Bromley
124. London, Ealing
125. London, Enfield
126. London, Haringey
127. London, Harrow
128. London, Havering
129. London, Hounslow
130. London, Merton
131. London, Newham
132. London, Redbridge
133. London, Southwark
134. London, Sutton
135. London, Tower Hamlets
136. London, Waltham Forest
137. Longniddry, Scotland

138. Louth
139. Lydney
140. Lymington
141. Lyndhurst
142. Malton
143. Mansfield
144. Marlborough
145. Medway
146. Melton Mowbray
147. Middlesbrough
148. Milnthorpe
149. Moreton-in-Marsh
150. Newcastle-under-Lyme
151. Newmarket
152. Norfolk
153. North Ayrshire
154. North Yorkshire
155. Northampton
156. Nottinghamshire
157. Oban and District
158. Ormskirk
159. Orpington
160. Otley
161. Ottershaw
162. Oundle
163. Oxted
164. Painswick
165. Penistone
166. Penwortham
167. Penzance
168. Polesworth
169. Pontypridd
170. Poole
171. Powys
172. Redditch
173. Retford
174. Richmond, Yorkshire
175. Rutland
176. Salisbury

177. Sandhurst, Berkshire
178. Seaford
179. Scarborough
180. Sefton
181. Shaftesbury
182. Sherbourne
183. Shrewsbury
184. Shropshire
185. Skipton
186. Slough
187. Southend-on-Sea
188. South Holland
189. South Tyneside
190. Southwell, Nottinghamshire
191. St Bees
192. St Helens
193. St Leonards on Sea
194. Stamford
195. Stevenage
196. Stockton
197. Stourbridge
198. Strathblane and Blanefield
199. Sunderland
200. Tarporley
201. Tenby
202. Thanet
203. Three Rivers
204. Todmorden
205. Torbay
206. Trafford
207. Tring
208. Ullapool
209. Wakefield
210. Ware
211. Warminster
212. Waterside Area
213. Watford
214. Welwyn Garden City
215. West Lothian

Appendix 3:
Where to find out more

CONTENTS

1. LEADING UK FAIR TRADE ORGANISATIONS AND INFORMATION SOURCES

British Association for Fair Trade
Shops (BAFTS)
Unit 7, 8–13 New Inn Street
London EC2A 3PY
Tel: 07796 050045
info@bafts.org.uk
www.bafts.org.uk

Ethical Consumer magazine and
research services
Unit 21, 41 Old Birtley Street
Manchester M15 5RF
Tel: 0161 226 2929
mail@ethicalconsumer.org
www.ethicalconsumer.org

Fairtrade Foundation
Room 204
16 Baldwin's Gardens
London EC1N 7RJ
Tel: 020 7405 5942
mail@fairtrade.org.uk

www.fairtrade.org.uk

New Consumer magazine
51 Timberbush
Edinburgh EH6 6QH
Tel: 0131 561 1780
editorial@newconsumer.org
www.newconsumer.org

Trading Visions
4 Gainsford Street
London SE1 2NE
www.tradingvisions.org

Traidcraft
Kingsway
Gateshead
Tyne & Wear NE11 0NE
Tel: 0191 491 0591
comms@traidcraft.co.uk
www.traidcraft.org

Twin Trading
1 Curtain Road
London EC2A 3LT
Tel: 020 7375 1221
info@twin.org.uk
www.twin.org.uk

2. TRADE-RELATED CAMPAIGNS

Banana Link
www.bananalink.org.uk

Clean Clothes Campaign
www.cleanclothes.org

CORE, the Corporate Responsibility
Coalition
www.corporate-responsibility.org

Labour Behind the Label
www.labourbehindthelabel.org

Make Trade Fair
www.maketradefair.com

No Sweat
www.nosweat.org.uk

People & Planet fair trade campaign
www.peopleandplanet.org/fairtrade

Trade Justice Movement
www.tjm.org.uk

3. INTERNATIONAL FAIR TRADE ORGANISATIONS

European Fair Trade Association
(EFTA)
Kerkewegje 1
6305 BC Schin op Geul
The Netherlands
Tel: +31 43 325 69 17
efta@antenna.nl
www.european-fair-trade-
association.org

Fairtrade Labelling Organisations
International (FLO)
FLO International
Bonner Talweg 177

53129 Bonn
Germany
Tel: +49 228 949230
info@fairtrade.net
www.fairtrade.net

Fair Trade Advocacy Office (FINE)
43 Rue de la Charite
1210 Brussels
Belgium
Tel: +32 02 217 36 17
osterhaus@fairtrade-advocacy.org

International Fair Trade Association
(IFAT)
Prijssestraat 24
4101 CR Culemborg
The Netherlands
Tel: +31 0345 53 59 14
info@ifat.org
www.ifat.org

Network of European Worldshops
(NEWS)
Christofsstrasse 13
55116 Mainz
Germany
Tel: +49 6131 9066 410
office@worldshops.org
www.worldshops.org

4. FAIR TRADE AROUND THE WORLD

Full members of Fairtrade Labelling
Organisations International (FLO):

Fairtrade Labelling Australia &
New Zealand
PO Box 306
Flinders Lane PO
8009 Victoria
Australia
Tel: +61 3966 22919
admin@fta.org.au
www.fta.org.au
www.fta.org.nz

Fairtrade Austria
Wohllebengasse 12–14
1040 Wien
Austria
Tel: +43 1 533 0956
office@fairtrade.at
www.fairtrade.at

Max Havelaar Belgium
Troonstraat 173
Rue du Trone
B 1050, Bruxelles
Belgium
Tel: +32 2 500 1060

info@maxhavelaar.be
www.maxhavelaar.be

Transfair Canada
302-251 Bank Street
Ottawa, ON K2P 1X3
Canada
Tel: +1 613 563 3351
fairtrade@transfair.ca
www.transfair.ca

Max Havelaar Denmark
c/o WWF, Ryesgade 3F
2200 København N
Denmark
Tel: +45 70231345
info@maxhavelaar.dk
www.maxhavelaar.dk

Reilun kaupan edistämisyhdistys ry
Finland
Kolmes Linja 4
00530 Helsinki
Finland
Tel: +358 9 5658680
reilukauppa@reilukauppa.fi
www.reilukauppa.fi

Max Havelaar France
Immeuble le Méliès
261 rue de Paris
93100 Montreuil
France
Tel: +33 1 42877021
info@maxhavelaarfrance.org
www.maxhavelaarfrance.org

TransFair Germany
Remigiusstrasse 21
50937 Köln
Germany
Tel: +49 221 942 040 0
info@transfair.org
www.transfair.org

Fairtrade Mark Ireland
Carmichael Centre
North Brunswick Street
Dublin 7
Ireland
Tel: +353 1 475 3515
info@fairtrade.ie
www.fairtrade.ie

Fairtrade TransFair Italy
Passagio De Gasperi 3
35131 Padova
Italy
Tel: +39 049 8750 823
info@fairtradeitalia.it
www.fairtradeitalia.it

Fairtrade Label Japan
c/o St. Paul Lutheran Church of the
JELC
5-3-1-Koutoubashi, Sumida-ku
Tokyo 130

Japan
Tel: +81 3 3634 7867
info@fairtrade-jp.org
www.fairtrade-jp.org

TransFair Minka Luxemburg
2a Rue de la Gare
6910 Roodt sur Syre
Luxemburg
Tel: +352 35 07 62
info@transfair.lu
www.transfair.lu

Stichting Max Havelaar
Netherlands
Lucasbolwerk 7
3512 EG Utrecht
the Netherlands
Tel: +31 30 2337070
vanderijke@maxhavelaar.nl
www.maxhavelaar.nl

Max Havelaar Norge
Storgata 11
0155 Oslo
Norway
Tel: +47 23010330
maxhavelaar@maxhavelaar.no
www.maxhavelaar.no

Asociación para el Sello de
Comercio Justo España
Gaztambide 50
28015 Madrid
Spain
Tel: +34 91 543 33 99
info@sellocomerciojusto.org
www.sellocomerciojusto.org

Rättvisemärkt Sweden
Pustegränd 1-3
11820 Stockholm
Sweden
Tel: +46 8 505 756 90
info@rattvisemarkt.se
www.rattvisemarkt.se

Max Havelaar Stiftung Schweiz
Malzgasse 25
4052 Basel
Switzerland
Tel: +41 61 2717500
postmaster@maxhavelaar.ch
www.maxhavelaar.ch

TransFair USA
1611 Telegraph Ave, Suite 900

Oakland
CA 94612
USA
Tel: +1 510 663 5260
info@transfairusa.org
www.transfairusa.org

Associate FLO member:

Comercio Justo México
Guanajuato 131, Desp. 302
Colonia Roma Norte
Delegación Cuauhtémoc
06700 México DF
Mexico
Tel: +52 55 55 74 71 16
info@comerciojusto.com.mx
www.comerciojusto.com.mx

Acronyms

ACP	African, Caribbean and Pacific
AFTF	Asia Fair Trade Forum
BAFTS	British Association of Fair Trade Shops
CAFOD	Catholic Agency for Overseas Development
CECOCAFEN	Organisation of Northern Coffee Cooperatives, Nicaragua
COASBA	Cooperativa Campesina Apícola Santa Bárbara (beekeepers' co-operative, Santa Bárbara, Chile)
COFTA	Cooperation for Fair Trade in Africa
COMUCAP	indigenous women's coffee co-op, Honduras
Coocafé	Fairtrade coffee producer co-op, Costa Rica
COSURCA	coffee co-operative, Colombia
EFTA	European Fair Trade Association
EPA	Economic Partnership Agreement
FIFA	Fédération Internationale de Football Association
FINE	collaboration between FLO International, IFAT, NEWS! and EFTA
FLO	Fairtrade Labelling Organisations International
FTO	Fair Trade Organisation
GM/GMO	genetically modified/genetically modified organism
HIV/AIDS	Human Immuno-Deficiency Virus/Acquired Immuno-Deficiency Syndrome
HRW	Human Rights Watch
IFAT	International Fair Trade Association
ILO	International Labour Organization
ISA	individual savings account
I-SIS	Institute of Science in Society, London
ISMAM	coffee co-op, Mexico
KNCU	coffee co-operative, Tanzania
MDGs	Millennium Development Goals
NEWS!	Network of European World Shops
NGO	non-governmental organisation
PRODECOOP	Cafédirect partner, Nicaragua
SARS	Severe Acute Respiratory Syndrome
SCIAF	Scottish Catholic International Aid Fund
SNV	Netherlands-based international development organisation
SOPPEXCCA	fair trade coffee co-operative in Nicaragua

[231]

Tara	Trade Alternative Reform Action
TJM	Trade Justice Movement
TNC	transnational corporation
Ton	mango growers co-operative, Burkina Faso
TBL	Triple Bottom Line
TRIM	trade-related investment measure
TRIP	trade-related intellectual property right
UCIRI	Union of Indigenous Communities in the Isthmus Region, Mexico
UNCTAD	United Nations Conference on Trade and Development
UNICEF	United Nations Children's Fund
WTO	World Trade Organization
WWF	Worldwide Fund for Nature
YMCA	Y Development Co-operative Co Ltd

Green Economics Institute   *Economics as if people mattered*

The Green Economics Institute exists to promote change, through both academic and non-academic channels. At the centre of Green Economics are connections – between cultures and between generations, between natural and social sciences and between people and the planet.

Traditional economic models ignore the value and real wealth created by a large segment of the Earth's population – those engaged in "women's work", subsistence farming and small rural crafts production – and in fact ignore all activities and existing values that are not measurable in direct monetary terms. Like our natural resources, the people at the bottom of the poverty pyramid are regarded as expendable inputs to the system – without intrinsic value and of interest only as a target market.

Green economics seeks to change the way we look at the world. The new models it proposes listen to what natural scientists tell us, emphasising climate change over business cycles, long-term responsibility over short-term profit. It favours local goals in decision making, and attention to cultural difference, against the interests of globalisation, defined as rolling out one limited concept everywhere in the world.

Green economics is about connectedness. It recognises overall well-being and happiness as key values by which economic development should be assessed – while acknowledging that these cannot be achieved without addressing claims of justice, global poverty, and the biosphere.

The Green Economics Institute brings people together through events, conferences and publications, with the aim of developing an ethical and just view of the world we can change.

Green Economics Institute
6 Strachey Close
Tidmarsh
Reading RG8 8EP
UK
www.greeneconomics.org.uk
greeneconomicsinstitute@yahoo.com

Index